PROVERBS

Eric Lane

Eric Lane trained to be a minister in the Church of England where he remained for 7 years. He was then called to be the minister of an Independent Evangelical Church where he pastored for 30 further years. Now retired Eric's special interest is in the 'Wisdom' books of the Old Testament. He has also written Focus on the Bible commentaries on the book of Psalms:- *Psalms 1–89: The Lord Saves* (ISBN 978-1-184550-180-8) and *Psalms 90-150: The Lord Reigns* (ISBN 978-1-84550-202-7)

PROVERBS

Everyday Wisdom for Everyone

Eric Lane

CHRISTIAN FOCUS

ISBN 1-84550-267-1
ISBN 978-1-84550267-6
© Eric Lane

10 9 8 7 6 5 4 3 2 1

First edition published in 2000
(ISBN 978-1-85792-451-0)
Reprinted in 2007
in the
Focus on the Bible Commentary series
by
Christian Focus Publications, Ltd.,
Geanies House, Fearn, Ross-shire,
IV20 1TW, Great Britain.

www.christianfocus.com

Cover design by Danie Van Straaten
Printed by CPD Wales

Contents

Introduction

Before coming to grips with the text of the book there are certain things it would be helpful to know.

A. WHAT PROVERBS IS ALL ABOUT

Most of the books of the Old Testament are either *narrative* (the story of Israel in 17 books) or *prophecy* (in 16 books). But there are also 6 books of *poetry*: **Job, Psalms, Proverbs, Ecclesiastes, Song of Songs** and **Lamentations**. Of these, three are books of *Wisdom*: **Job, Proverbs and Ecclesiastes**. So we first need some idea of what the Hebrews meant by *Wisdom*.

The concept of *Wisdom* is about how best to find our way through the maze of this world. 'Basically wisdom is the art of being successful, of forming the correct plan to gain the desired results' (*New Bible Dictionary*). This does not make it selfish calculation or put it on a par with, 'How to make friends and influence people'. That is the wisdom Satan offered through the fruit of the tree of the knowledge of good and evil (Gen. 3:6). The *Wisdom* of the Bible is the fruit of 'the tree of life' (3:18), since it is born of 'the fear of the LORD' (1:7). It is the *Wisdom* found in God himself and stamped on his creation (3:19, Ps. 104:24). The wisdom that made the world will help us understand why it is as it is and how we can make the best of our lives in it. It is therefore supremely expressed in the great plan of redemption by which we are delivered from the world's evil (Eph. 3:10f) and is personified in the redeemer, the Lord Jesus Christ (1 Cor. 1:30).

However, to possess wisdom involves more than believing the Creator and trusting the Redeemer. It is a study in its own right, for which God has given us these three great books. But they are not all alike. JOB and ECCLESIASTES are speculative wisdom, for they investigate **why** things are as they are and **how** we can make sense of them. PROVERBS is **practical** wisdom, showing us **what** we can do to get on in this puzzling world without losing our way and ending in disaster. Whether or not we ever come to solve the problems aired in the other two books, we can still come to terms with this world. We don't have to opt out and spend the whole of our lives **thinking**. We can get on with **living** in the real world, conquer our limitations and get along with other people. No book gives us more help in this than PROVERBS.

To put it another way, PROVERBS gives us a **window on the world**. It is truth in street clothes. It provides some keys as to how things work and how people behave. It gives 'understanding' and 'insight' (1:2). Even if it doesn't answer the deep questions raised in JOB and ECCLESIASTES it does give us stepping stones across the raging torrent that perplexed the writers of those books, by showing what to expect from people and how to react to them. The Christian needs this more even than the Israelite, who lived in a society sympathetic to godliness, whereas the Christian faces a hostile one. This was what moved JAMES to do for the Christian what PROVERBS did for the Israelite. PROVERBS, however, is far more extensive and therefore still needed, provided we view it through the eyes of Jesus and the new covenant.

B. Who Wrote It

PROVERBS is a composite work, bringing together the writings and sayings of a number of 'the wise'. It appears to have been compiled in the reign of Hezekiah (25:1), although some think the final complete edition did not appear until after the Exile and may be the work of Ezra. The body of it comes from the mouth of **Solomon**: chs. 10 – 22:16 and 25 – 29. Yet this is only a selection from his complete works, which number 3000 sayings, of which only about 800 appear in PROVERBS (see 1 Kings 4:29-34).

Solomon is prominent because he attained his wisdom as a gift of God in answer to prayer (1 Kings 3:5-15). It is hard not to feel that someone who is offered a *carte blanche* by God and chooses wisdom must already be wise! He probably was to some extent through his father David's instruction (Prov. 4:1-4). But he asked God for a particular kind of wisdom – the ability to adjudicate and to govern his people. JAMES turns us **all** into Solomons, telling us we too can ask God for the wisdom we need (James 1:5).

Although he overshadowed all others Solomon was not the only wise man in Israel. In his own time there were Ethan and the sons of Mahol: Heman, Calcol and Darda (1 Kings 4:31). Previously under David there had been Ahithophel (2 Sam. 15:12), Jonadab the friend of Amnon, 'a very shrewd man' (2 Sam. 13:3), and 'the wise woman of Tekoa' (2 Sam. 14). Since David quoted 'a proverb of the ancients' (1 Sam. 24:13), wisdom was even older than this. It is possible that some of the above are represented in a section called 'Sayings of the wise' (22:17–24:34).

Nor was wisdom confined to the covenant people. Ch. 30 gives us 'Sayings of Agur' and 31:1-9 has 'Sayings of King Lemuel', both thought to be from northern Arabia. The anonymous Epilogue may have been the work of the final editor, as may the Prologue (1:1-7) or even the extended Prologue (chs. 1–9).

C. THE TIMES IN WHICH IT WAS WRITTEN

Knowing the background to the book's composition will help explain how this other material came to be included, especially that of foreign sages. Solomon's reign was one of expanding horizons for Israel as it traded with other nations (1 Kings 10:22, 28f). For this Solomon built a large navy (1 Kings 9:26-28). Trading was not only in goods but culture and ideas. Solomon had many foreign women in his harem, which involved visits to their countries and families. Here he learned something of 'the wisdom of the men of the east', especially Egypt (1 Kings 4:30). Because of his special gift he soon outshone them all, so that they began to come and visit him and learn from him (1 Kings 4:29-34, 10:1-13). Could it have been at this period that the story of Job was brought from Arabia to Israel and his book written and published? As F. D. Kidner has written, 'shared ground existed between the truly wise of any nation' (*Wisdom to Live By, p.15*).

D. THE WAY IT WAS WRITTEN

PROVERBS is not a book which a man sat down and wrote according to a fixed plan. Even those parts attributed to Solomon were not written down at one time. They are sayings uttered at different times and put together without much regard for an overall plan. The book is more like Luther's *Table Talk* or Pascal's *Pensees* than Locke's *Essay on Human Understanding* or Marx's *Das Kapital*. There is no necessary connection between one saying and the next and the chapters are not given to one particular theme. Sayings on a particular topic recur throughout the book and some are repeated verbatim more than once.

Apart from the Prologue (1–9) and Epilogue (31:10-31) the body of the book consists of these separate sayings, to which the term 'proverb' (Hebrew MASHAL) is applied. Literally the word means a 'comparison', which might be a brief simile (11:22, 12:4) or a whole allegory (Ezek. 17:2ff, Judg. 9:8ff). Later it came to be used of any wise pronouncement, from a maxim to a sermon (ch. 5), or from a wisecrack (Ezek. 18:2) to a revelation (Ps. 49:4).

For the purposes of this book we may say that a proverb is:

(a) *terse.* It is complete in itself, not requiring development or qualification. Much is contained in little. This can at times produce a paradox, as when we are told in one verse not to 'answer a fool according to his folly' and in the next to do just that (26:4-5)! But we have a similar problem with secular proverbs, as in: 'Many hands make light work' but 'Too many cooks spoil the broth'; 'Absence makes the heart grow fonder' but 'Out of sight out of mind'. This is bound to happen where generalizations are drastically condensed. Usually the development of a statement will clarify the apparent confusion, as in the passage referred to above.

(b) *poetic.* Although it may not be obvious to us, the proverbs are in verse. Hebrew poetry is unlike English, lacking both rhyme and precise rhythmic forms. It consists mainly in parallelism, in which the second member of the sentence balances or contrasts with the first, as in 1:7, 10:1. This helps explain the book's 'black and white' view of life, in which people are either 'wise' or 'foolish', 'righteous' or 'wicked'.

(c) *popular.* The wisdom of PROVERBS is overtly practical. There is no abstract discussion of theories of the universe, as in some Wisdom literature. There is little of what can be called 'Theology'. The subjects are all everyday ones: honesty, money, children, the tongue, sloth, pride, anger. We see ourselves and each other as nowhere else in Scripture. We see the man who is bright and cheerful first thing in the morning and expects everyone else to be the same (27:14); the woman who is always popping next door for a cup of tea and a chat (25:17); the shopper in the market who tricks the stall-holder into a bargain (20:14), and even the practical joker (26:19)! It penetrates our own mind and exposes our self-images and delusions (13:7). A true 'window on the world'. To use a different illustration, it puts us under the microscope and magnifies those little blemishes which can spoil both our character and relationships, the flies in the ointment which turn its odour bad (Eccles. 10:1). It is James' 'mirror', showing how we appear to others (James 1:23-25).

E. WHY IT WAS WRITTEN

Clearly it was written for the purpose of education (1:8). Since in ancient Israel education was in the hands of parents, its method had to be very simple. Terse, poetic sayings on common themes are easily taught, grasped and remembered. The role of education in old covenant Israel was very different from that in a modern secular state. Its purpose was simply to ensure that each new generation knew what God's covenant with his people was and how to keep it. This information was essential if the people were to remain in their land and enjoy God's presence and blessing (see the 5th Commandment). So 'obedience' as well as 'knowledge' was part of their education.

To us 'education' means a whole range of specialized subjects, unlike education as PROVERBS saw it. But this doesn't make PROVERBS out of date, since the matters it covers are not those taught in our schools. PROVERBS is education for the whole of life, designed to produce mature people, free from the naivety which sucks them into the clutches of thieves and harlots on one hand or on the other makes them vulnerable to exploitation by the rich and powerful. This does not make PROVERBS mere worldly wisdom, since its spiritual basis and aim is declared at the outset (1:7). But spiritual people are not to be soft touches; they should have the wisdom of the serpent without his deadly bite (Matt. 10:16).

This wisdom is depicted as a beautiful lady, to be wooed and won like a lover (4:5-9, 8–9:6). This personification is often seen as a foreshadowing of Jesus, 'in whom are hidden all the treasures of wisdom and knowledge' (Col. 2:3) and who is 'greater than Solomon' (Matt. 12:42). He who embraces this wisdom shares the beauty of Jesus, who did not despise the kind of details to which PROVERBS draws attention, but in fact taught us to begin by learning trustworthiness in small things (Luke 16:10) and that we will be judged by our idle words (Matt. 12:36). 'If the Psalms bring a glow upon the heart, the Proverbs make the face shine' (Bridges).

F. How It Is To Be Interpreted
Now that we know something about the book we are in a position to decide how to interpret it. The following are the main principles:

1. *Each verse is an entity in itself.* With other books of the Bible the meaning of a verse is determined largely by the context. Not so here. Each saying is self-contained and bears no necessary connection with what precedes or follows. Whereas 'other parts of Scripture are like a rich mine where the precious ore runs along in one continuous vein, this is like a heap of pearls, which though unstrung are not therefore less valuable' (Ezekiel Hopkins). This of course applies to the body of the book rather than to the more continuous passages which begin and end it.

2. *Most of it is in the spirit of the old covenant (the Law).* While there are sayings that still apply literally, most are addressed to the people to whom the promises of the old covenant were given. These said that those who obeyed the Law were assured of plenty of the good things of life, whereas those who disobeyed would be deprived of them (Deut. 11:26-28). This teaching colours PROVERBS, for example when it promises peace and prosperity to the righteous (8:21, 35) and trouble to the wicked (8:36).

Under the new covenant life is not so simple. Christians are like grown-up children, weaned from the carrot-and-stick approach. We are promised suffering and deprivation **as part of God's blessing** (Phil. 1:29) and his way of fellowship with us (Phil. 3:10). Yet many of the sayings are universal in their application. Even those which are 'dispensational' in the above sense have a principle on which we may build some profitable New Testament teaching.

3. *Allegorizing, typologizing and spiritualizing are inappropriate.* These do not accord with the purpose of the book. We must face the fact that there is little 'gospel' in PROVERBS and to read it in will make us miss God's message to us. It is a book to be taken at its face value. This is not to say that the points made are incapable of application to Christ, the gospel and the Christian life. But these must be derived from an understanding of the plain meaning.

G. What Its Value Is For Christians

This unique book is, as it claims, worth its weight in gold (2:4, 4:9, 8:10f, 17-19), for it fills a gap in our knowledge. The Bible is mainly about how we come from sin to salvation and are born into the family and kingdom of God. But how do we go on and grow? How do we live in this corrupt world? There is a tendency for believers to be naive, unsophisticated, gullible and credulous in the things of the world (Luke 16:8). Jesus told us to be 'wise as serpents' without copying their deceit and malignity, and to learn from the people of the world. In fact 'prudence' in 1:4 is the word used of the serpent in Gen. 3:1 (KJV 'subtle', NIV 'crafty'). This quality is capable of either good or bad use. PROVERBS encourages the cultivation of this quality and shows how to direct it to holy ends, which it does in a number of ways, for example:

1. *It teaches us shrewdness in the common things of life*, showing us how to discern the motives and methods of the people we deal with. Even in God's Israel there were gangs on the lookout for recruits, prostitutes on the lookout for punters, and swindlers on the lookout for the gullible.

2. *It teaches us tact in handling our relationships*, such as with our *friends* (25:17, 27:14, 17), with the *bad-tempered* (26:17), with

the *foolish* (23:9) and the *powerful* (23:1-3, 25:15). The very first instance of Solomon's wisdom the Bible gives us is one in which he discerned character, and on the basis of that exposed the truth (1 Kings 3:16-28).

3. *It teaches us to be aware of the dangers which surround us* and the kind of people it is best to avoid altogether, lest we come off worse. Don't try to take a mad dog by the ears (26:17).

Because it is rooted in the old covenant much of this can only work in a godly society (e.g. 10:2f, 6f, 9-11). This is why it is good to study it along with JAMES, which is a book of wisdom for Christians in an ungodly society. These books are not so much about how to be saved as about how to equip yourself for everyday life in the real world and become a street-wise Christian.

H. How It Is Structured
Because of its composite authorship and the various editions it passed through, PROVERBS has a literary structure like this:

Chs. 1–9:	The Prologue.
Ch. 10–22:16:	The main collection of Solomon's sayings.
Ch. 22:17–24:34:	The sayings of other sages of Israel.
Chs. 25–29:	A further collection of Solomon's sayings.
Ch. 30:	The sayings of Agur.
Ch. 31:1–9:	The sayings of Lemuel.
Ch. 31:10–31:	The Epilogue.

We do not need to take much notice of this in studying the book, but can give our attention rather to the themes which emerge as we proceed. In spite of the lack of a logical structure it is possible to highlight themes that dominate particular chapters and concentrate our thoughts on these. This will involve some rearrangement of the order of verses but this should make more sense to the ordinary reader than a painstaking verse-by-verse approach more appropriate to the scholar. Since the same themes crop up repeatedly throughout the book, a certain amount of cross-referencing is necessary. This will avoid tedious repetition and reduce the size of the book to manageable proportions.

The Prologue: Wisdom and its Benefits
Proverbs 1–9

As mentioned in the Introduction, these opening chapters are not strictly speaking proverbs. They introduce the Proverbs proper by explaining what Wisdom is, why it is so desirable and how to acquire it. They are therefore written in continuous style and do not require the reclassification described in the Introduction. We shall simply follow the paragraphs as they stand.

1

Definitions
(Proverbs 1)

Verse 1 is the *title* of the whole book, which is attributed to Solomon, although not all of it came from his mouth or pen. However, the greater part is Solomon's and the remainder closely related to his thinking. No doubt the title was attached when the sayings were edited and published in the reign of Hezekiah (25:1). The same editor composed this little introduction to commend his collection of Proverbs to the public. It is possible he (or another) wrote the remainder of the Prologue up to the end of chapter 9, although it could have come from Solomon or a sage of any period, since it is an example of the way a parent instructs his children or a teacher his pupils.

He begins by defining his subject (*wisdom*) and his readers.

A. WHAT WISDOM IS (vv. 2-3).
Wisdom is the overall term, which he defines by using three others.

1. Discipline. This is what we would call 'training' – not so much in skills as in character. The child or pupil is taught from an early age how to behave. As he regularly practises these lessons, so they begin to mould his character.

2. *Understanding.* This shows that the discipline is not blind obedience but teaching the child to discern for himself between right and wrong, the best and the less good (cf. Phil. 1:10), so that he will want to behave rightly.

3. *Prudence*. The fruit of the discipline and understanding is to produce a mature person able to relate to others. He is trained to treat them in a way that is right, just and fair. He learns how to get on with people, exemplified in Abigail (1 Sam. 25:3) and perfectly in Jesus (Isa. 52:13).

Questions
1. Consider the importance for the Christian of good relationships by referring to Ephesians 5:21-6:9.
2. What does the Christian use to cultivate the discipline and understanding that produces this sociability? (See Col. 3:15f).

B. WHO NEEDS WISDOM (vv. 4-6).
As we saw in the Introduction (E) PROVERBS is educational. We are now told at whom this education is aimed.

1. *The simple* (**v. 4**). These are not the weak-minded but the untaught and immature. Basically they are the young, who have not yet had the opportunity to become wise. But it can apply to others, such as Israelites whose parents had neglected their education, or Gentile slaves and prisoners totally ignorant of God's law. Such needed knowledge of the right way to live, in order to acquire the discretion and prudence necessary for mixing in society and becoming good citizens. (See Introduction [G]).

2. *The wise* (**v. 5**). These have already been trained and are leading righteous lives. But they do not know everything and are not perfect. 'For,' says Charles Bridges, 'a truly wise man is one, not who has attained, but who knows that he has not attained and is pressing on to perfection.' Matthew Henry comments: 'This book not only makes the foolish wise but the wise better.' Such can *add to their learning*, receive *guidance* in more difficult areas and become skilful in handling more complex people. Perhaps it was for such that the writings of men other than Solomon were included in later parts of the book, described by the terms in verse 6 as 'enigmas and hard questions' (*parables and riddles*).

Questions
1. As well as young children, to whom does the term *simple* apply in the gospel age? See 1 Peter 2:2 and 1 Corinthians 3:1.

2. Do you think verses 5-6 encourage the mature Christian to explore non-Christian systems of thought and life? Consider this in relation to evangelism among, say, Muslims and Marxists.

C. HOW TO BEGIN (v. 7).
The wisdom the Bible is interested in cannot be acquired merely from books, parents and teachers, even if those teachings are rigorously practised. Ultimately wisdom is what God is and we can only attain to it through personal knowledge of him. This is what the Old Testament calls *fear*, meaning trust, love and obedience. This is why *the fool* has no interest in things like character and relationships. He does not know God (Ps. 14:1). To him *wisdom* is boredom, and *discipline* irksome.

This is the first true 'proverb', and governs all the rest. It has that balance and contrast that make it ideal for memorization. It is not original but is found in David's writings (Ps. 111:10), and he may have learned it from the earliest book of wisdom – Job (28:28). It will recur in 9:10 and 15:33.

Learn this verse by heart and **think** how readily it can be adapted to personal faith in Christ as the only path to a life of righteousness (1 Cor. 1:30).

Chapter 1:8–9:19: Wisdom's Benefits
Having been told what wisdom is and whom it is for, we now have its glories displayed before us, so that we see what it can do for us. But before we can go to the heart of it we need our interest aroused and our appetite whetted. We Christians will see more in it than did the people of Israel for whom it was originally composed. To us wisdom is the whole word of God, indeed it is Christ himself 'who has become for us wisdom from God – that is, our righteousness, holiness and redemption' (1 Cor. 1:30).

1:8–2:22. First Benefit: Protection.
PROVERBS is written primarily for the young – in years or godliness. The chief characteristic of youth is vulnerability; the young are ignorant of the ways of the world and lack the power of self-control. They need first to be protected from

falling into disaster before they have hardly begun. So our book begins with warnings against those who are most likely to harm the young, and with advice on how to avoid falling into their net.

Chapter 1:8-33: Protection from Evil Companions

The first lesson is put into the mouth of the parents (v. 8). After all, as was said in the Introduction (E), *Proverbs* was basically an educational manual. This task was entrusted to the father and mother in whose hands was the *instruction* and *teaching* of their children. Refresh your mind on the purpose of education in old covenant Israel by re-reading the section 'Why it was written' on page 11.

Since this *instruction* is to begin with some rather harsh lessons, the first thing is to get the child to *listen* (**v. 8**). What is the best way of doing this? Not so much with the stick as the carrot, the offer of a reward rather than the threat of punishment, as God himself did in the Fifth Commandment with the promise of 'long life in the land' (Exod. 20:12). Here, however, the promise is of victory and power, for a *garland* was placed on the head of a general returning victorious from battle and a *chain* or necklace hung round the neck of a king on his coronation. So the *son* or child of God who heeds his heavenly Father's word will have victory and power in his personal life (Rev. 12:11).

Now we come to the actual lesson on protection from evil company (**vv. 10-19**). There are *sinners* out there – a strong word describing those for whom sin has become a way of life. Either these were not *instructed* by their parents or if they were they have '*forsaken*' it (v. 8). They live not by honest labour but on the proceeds of crime. They form gangs and are on the look-out for new recruits (v. 10). Two things the youth needs to know about them.

1. *The methods they use to entice him* (**vv. 11-14**).
They make it sound easy (v. 11) and look tough (v. 12); they offer lucrative rewards (v. 13), not least a place in the gang (v. 14). The youth who has been finding parental control constricting 'pictures himself a person to be reckoned with

instead of patronized and kept in his place, and above all accepted as one of the gang' (Kidner). An offer he can't refuse! How up-to-date it all is! There is nothing new about gangs of youths graduating into vice-rings and incorporated crime. Here is how it all begins – with a macho appeal and tempting offer to one who has been kept down and kept short. The task of today's parents is not so dissimilar to that facing parents in ancient Israel.

2. *The ends to which they come* (**vv. 15-19**). The criminals didn't include this in their advert! But the truth is that while there may be short-term gains the end result is disaster, which provides the parent with good arguments for his warning (v. 15):

(a) a course of crime, once embarked on, is unstoppable – it starts with mugging but may end with murder (v. 16);

(b) the idea of keeping it secret is a myth (v. 17) – when birds see trappers laying snares they fly off, which is to say people soon get to know who the criminals are and take evasive action;

(c) once their identity is known they are soon caught and what they did to others is done to them (v. 18).

The conclusion (v. 19) is that, instead of the riches he was originally offered (v. 13), he loses everything, perhaps even his life. The only way to avoid this is to avoid their company (v. 15).

Question
What dangers lie before the young Christian and how may he learn to protect himself from them? See Ephesians 6:10-18.

In **verses 20-23** the lesson is taken from the parent and placed in the mouth of *Wisdom* herself and she is now the *enticer*. This is the first time *Wisdom* is presented as a person – God speaking his word, possibly foreshadowing Jesus. The word is plural – *wisdoms* – for this is God in whom all wisdom perfectly dwells (Col. 2:3). So instead of the teaching being given in the home or classroom it is proclaimed *aloud in the street ... in the public squares ... the noisy streets ... and the gateways of the city* (where public notices were read out) (vv. 20-21). This shows that the warning of verses 8-19 is not the fussing of an over-protective parent but the very word of God for all. What authority and confidence parents may feel who know that what they teach their children is simply an exposition and application of God's word!

There is a sense of desperation in this appeal which we don't find in the parents' words. It suggests the youth has not followed their advice and become involved with bad company. How long, she pleads, is this to go on? (v. 22). When will the young (*simple*) grow up, the conceited cynics (*mockers*) who think crime is clever wake up, and those who have turned their backs on knowledge (*fools*) give up?

She almost makes it sound too late in verse 23 by speaking of what might have been if the parents' teaching had been heeded earlier. There would have been abundant help – of a spiritual and divine nature, it appears – for *heart* is literally 'spirit' and *thoughts* are 'words'. A simple, 'Yes, I will' to the call of God opens the door to the fullness of his grace.

In this case that was not to be and so we get the first *but* of the book (v. 24). The initial response to God's word is a pivot on which the rest of life turns. Make the wrong decision at a motorway junction and there is no turning back. See how God has done all he can to encourage us to make the right decision: *called, stretched out his hand* (v. 24), given his *advice*, and because of our slowness even issued his *rebuke* (v. 25). But each move is refused – *rejected, unheeded, ignored*, not *accepted*.

So from what *would have* been we are shown what *will* be (vv. 26-27). A wrong course of life may be temporarily successful, but eventually *disaster* and *calamity* will come and hit you like a tropical storm. Then you will seek an experienced counsellor, the God who is *Wisdom*. But now his strict justice comes into operation. You laughed at his warnings about keeping bad company (v. 22). Now the laugh is on you. You did not take his warnings seriously and he will appear not to take your woes seriously. This does not mean God is callous, but simply shows the absurdity of choosing folly when wisdom is on offer.

This is why the Scriptures of Old and New Testaments alike impress on us that childhood and youth are the best time to learn God's way and choose it. It is the time of the uncluttered mind and the avid quest for knowledge; the time when trust comes readily and what is learned is retained and moulds character for life (22:6, Eccles. 12:1-7, Matt. 18:1-4, 19:13-14). But if the pliable mind and heart of the young hardens at this point, it is a rare thing for it to soften later – rare yet not impossible, since none is too hard for the Lord. God's mercy is greater than ours and 'endures for ever', and his power can break the hardest heart (Jer. 23:29). No one is past praying for or speaking to. But God is not to be trifled with, by young or old.

So we see now that verse 26 does not mean that God finds the calamities of those who refuse him funny. To him it is an awful tragedy that he who loves to be asked and to answer prayer has to shut his ears and mouth (v. 28). To him it is the tragedy of the foolish girls who did not listen to those who told them to take oil as well as lamps to the wedding, and ended up hammering on a door that would never be opened (Matt. 25:1-12). It is the tragedy of the people of Jerusalem, over whom Jesus shed salt tears because by refusing him they lost everything (Luke 19:41-44). God does not enjoy this but his justice demands it, as the logical construction of verses 29-31 brings out, with its *since they ... since they ... they will*. We reap what we sow and eat the fruit of what we grow (Gal. 6:7-8).

How beautifully **verses 32-33** sum up this first chapter! Here is the genius of the proverbial style. A long discourse of teaching and application can be poured into an egg cup and drunk in a mouthful. A clear, simple and pointed message. Would that all our sermons were thus! Here are summed up the two ways which the whole passage sets forth.

1. *The way of those who won't be taught* (**v. 32**). No one is blamed for being *simple*. This is how we all start. But we are responsible for what we do with the teaching designed to make us wise (v. 4). If we won't be taught because of *waywardness*, we become fools, a stage worse than *simple*, for we are guilty of *complacency* about remaining ignorant. This is nothing less than suicide. We may drift into a life of vice or crime and suffer

the consequences, or be refused help when disaster strikes. We shall certainly live in a state of spiritual death and end up in one of eternal death.

2. *The way of those who listen* (**v. 33**). We've not heard too much about these lately, since the word has concentrated on warning the refusers. But we recall this is how the lesson began – with the carrot not the stick (v. 9). Then the public appeal took this up (v. 23). As indicated in the Introduction (F2) the Old Testament carrot is a material one: peace, prosperity and happiness in this life. Not that it always worked like this, as Psalm 73 shows. But the exception proves the rule.

Question
What safety and ease are offered to believers in the gospel age? See Romans 8:35-39, Philippians 4:4-7, Hebrews 13:5-6.

2

Protection from Wayward Women
(Proverbs 2)

In part 2 of the lesson on *Protection* (see v. 11), we are taken from the open air and the loud, public impassioned appealing of 'Wisdom' herself, back into the parlour or classroom where we hear the quieter more personal tones of the parent or teacher as he addresses himself to *my son* (v. 1). It is almost as if the previous passage was a bad dream about what might be, from which we now awake and return to our lesson.

However, *Wisdom*'s eloquence has left its mark on the teacher, for he seems to speak with greater authority here. We who are parents or teachers can learn from this: if we ourselves listen to the voice of *Wisdom*, that is, God in Christ, we shall come to our children with greater authority, and nothing is more infectious than the language of conviction (see 1 Thess. 1:5f).

A. BASIS OF THE LESSON (vv. 1-11).
We can see this authority in the way the speaker imitates the style employed by 'Wisdom'. He constructs his lesson around *ifs* (vv. 1-4) and *thens* (vv. 5,9). The *ifs* stand for the **means** by which wisdom is attained, and the *thens* for the **ends** or fruits it produces. This is a great enlargement on the lesson taught in ch.1, for the youth is here shown the five ways in which he should be reacting to the teaching. This we apply to our own response to God's word.

1. Means.

(a) **Receive it** (*accept*) **(v. 1a)**, that is, believe it, consent to it, like those of 1:33 not those of 1:22-25.

(b) **Retain it (v. 1b)** – *store* it in the mind where it is safe; memorize it if possible, but always remember the message.

(c) **Attend to it (v. 2)**, that is, don't just hear it once, but be continually *turning your ear* to it, and dwelling on it by *applying your heart* and feeling it deeply.

(d) **Pray over it (v. 3)**, ask to *understand* what it requires of you and do so sincerely as one *calling out* for help and *crying aloud* for food.

(e) **Value it (v. 4)**, as you do your hard-earned cash (*silver*), or if you are really rich, the *treasure* you have *hidden* in a secret place out of the reach of crooks and cadgers.

If the teaching is received in this way, *then* it will yield up its fruits.

2. Fruits.

First, verses 5-8: *it will bring you into a personal relationship with God*, based on trust (*fear*) and love (*knowledge*). This is always the primary purpose for which God approaches us in his word – to make himself known to us and bring us to himself, from whom we became estranged through sin. It was the main task he set his Son in sending him among us to die for sins – it was 'to bring us to God' (1 Pet. 3:18). This *knowledge* of him or *wisdom* (v. 6) comes entirely from his grace – *the Lord gives* it. The steps in verses 1-4 are means not qualifications, ways of receiving the grace enshrined in his word.

This is the basis of that particular benefit that this first lesson is all about – the **protection** of his own (vv. 7-8). For this comes not so much from accepting instruction and advice as from the personal help of the one who is the author of that instruction. This is why it is referred to here in such glowing terms, as *victory ... a shield ... guards ... protects*.

Second, verses 9-11: *it will set you on the right course of living*. We and our children will only live rightly if we are clear about the difference between right and wrong. While there is an innate moral sense in all who are made in God's image (Rom. 2:14f), only the wisdom or word of God spells out precisely *what is right, just and fair* (v. 9) and shows us **every good path**.

This is because, unlike the moral teachings of humans, the word of God penetrates the very centre of our personality (*heart*, v. 10a). As James put it, the word is 'planted in you' (James 1:21). By nature the core of our being is rotten and cannot be relied on to respond to moral teaching. But the word not only informs us, it also regenerates (James 1:18). The result is that righteousness becomes *pleasant* (v. 10b) to us and no longer has to be enforced. From then on the word will take us safely across all the pitfalls of this dangerous world (v. 11).

B. THE LESSON ITSELF (vv. 12-27).

1. Repeat of warning against evil companions (vv. 12-15).
This passage is composed in such a way as to bring out the unstoppable progress of sin. It begins with an individual (*wicked men* in verse 12 is in fact singular) who soon forms a gang (*men*, cf. 1:10ff). The gang is even recruited from those brought up in righteousness (v. 13). At first they find these new habits strange and *dark*, but soon they begin to *delight in* doing them and *rejoice in* seeing them done (v. 14). So they gradually come to feel at home with this life-style, no longer out of their element. But the word of wisdom sees it for what it is: *crooked and ... devious* (v. 15). Those who listen to the word will therefore be forewarned about these men, and thus forearmed and less likely to be taken in.

2. Warning against wayward women (vv. 16-19).
Whereas male company can open up a variety of sins (none is specified in verses 12-15), that of a bad woman usually means one thing. Literally verse 16 speaks of the *alien woman ... foreigner*, possibly because prostitution was condoned by Israel's neighbours and tended to be practised by foreign women living in Israel. Alternatively, it can mean that this sin is 'foreign' to a true Israelite woman, since verse 17 refers to her as having made a covenant before God (cf. Mal. 2:14), that is she has undergone a religious marriage ceremony in which

vows were made to her young companion, of whom she has now wearied.

Her method is to begin by 'chatting up' the innocent youth *with her seductive words* (v. 16). Then she gets him into *her house* (v. 18) and soon leads him to walk along *her paths*. What this means in practice is left to our imagination, since the Bible rarely becomes sexually explicit. In fact the teacher here is less interested in describing present pleasure than in painting a picture of future pain. *Death* may be meant literally since it was the penalty for adultery and prostitution (Lev. 20:10); or it may be used metaphorically to give a sense of the finality of this way of life. Like death it is a way of no return. This applies not only to the prostitute herself but to those who associate with her (v. 19).

C. Summing up (vv. 20-22).

With such men and women around 'how can a young man keep his way pure?' (Ps. 119:9). The psalmist's answer is the same as the sage's: 'By living according to your word', or *wisdom will save you* (vv. 12,16). It *saves* you from falling into bad company and keeps you in the company of *good men*, so that you follow their example (v. 20). This is eminently worthwhile because it is the way of true happiness, as verse 21 tells us. It talks in terms of *the land* (Israel) because it was written for those under the old covenant, in which the supreme blessing was to live with God and his people in the land of promise (Exod. 20:12).

Similarly the judgment on the wicked (v. 22) is to be *cut off from the land*, that is, to die an early death, or to become a prisoner of war and live in slavery in a foreign country, as happened to almost the entire nation in the sixth century BC.

Questions
Are (1) the blessings of obedience to the gospel, or (2) the curses of unbelief, less or greater than they were under the law? For (1) see Matthew 5:5, Ephesians 1:3; for (2) see Matthew 22:13.

3

Second Benefit: Promises
(Proverbs 3)

In this section the parent or teacher turns from warning to encouraging. This is one of the high points of the whole book and contains some of its best-known sayings. It catalogues the advantages of pursuing the way of wisdom. These are couched in Old Covenant language and need some adaptation to the Gospel age, which does not hold out quite the same assurance of earthly health and happiness. However, this does not mean it is totally other-worldly, 'holding promise for both the present life and the life to come' (1 Tim. 4:8; see also 6:6).

Each of these benefits is prefixed by a call to obey the word of wisdom, for God's promises are conditional. The way the call is expressed is in keeping with the particular benefit under review.

A. LONG LIFE (vv. 1-2).
The first benefit derived from wisdom concerns the whole of life, both its quantity (2a) and quality (2b). *Prosperity* (NIV) is literally 'peace' (SHALOM), a package word which certainly includes material prosperity, but is combined with mental serenity and spiritual joy. It is far from the prosperity of the business person with his work-alcoholism and perpetual worrying, driving him to an early grave, for the life of the wise is prolonged by many years. This is because it is based on the word of God (v. 1). Its *teaching* (the doctrine and promises) keeps him mentally at peace, and its *commands* (the behaviour

pattern) teach him to be disciplined in his life-style as well as ethical in his methods. If he *keeps* the word throughout his life, the word will keep him in peace to a ripe old age.

This was an excellent prescription for those under the Old Covenant, being based on a promise at the heart of the Ten Commandments – Exodus 20:12: 'that you may **live long** in the land the Lord your God is giving you'. It was something the godly Israelite prized highly (Ps. 91:16) and which encouraged a life of obedience to the Law.

Question
Since believers are just as susceptible to disease and accident as unbelievers (and some die young as martyrs for Christ), how does this promise apply in the gospel age? Do you think it means 'everlasting life'? Or is it the 'life to the full' of John 10:10? If so, what is 'life to the full'?

B. GOOD REPUTATION (vv. 3-4).
Whereas the first benefit of wisdom concerned a person's own life the second has to do with his relationships. Others see from his long prosperous life that God favours him and they respect him (v. 4), for example Job before tragedy overtook him (Job 29).

To achieve this involves more than remembering the *teaching* and practising the *commands* (v. 1). These responses must bear fruit in character, especially *love and faithfulness* (v. 3). These are two of God's most glorious perfections, at the very heart of his covenant with Israel. Where he sees them in one of his people he sees one 'after his own heart' and delights in him. Other godly people will respect and admire him. But he must be consistent: he must *bind them around* his *neck* in the way a lover wears a locket with his beloved's picture on it next to his heart, or engrave them on his mind like words written on a wax *tablet*.

Question
Does this mean that the Christian who bears the fruit of the Spirit can expect not only blessing but popularity? On the positive side consider Matthew 5:16, Acts 2:43, 47; on the negative Matthew 24:9, Luke 6:26, John 15:18-25.

C. Clear Guidance (vv. 5-6).

In this case the conditions occupy three sentences (vv. 5-6a) and the promise only one (v. 6b). But what a promise! *He will make your paths straight.* Most people would give a lot to be sure of this. For us creatures of time the future is at once a reality and an uncertainty. We know there is a future but we don't know what it holds. God offers us a future in which we can see our way ahead clearly, like a straight road with no obstacles to hinder us (cf. v. 23, 4:11f).

This may sound too good to be true – like an offer of infallible foresight combined with a cosmic bulldozer to cut out all the corners and flatten all the bumps. This is not what it means or even says, for it is *he* (God) who makes our path straight. A path is only a way to a destination. Our destination is sure – final glory, to which we are 'predestined' (Rom. 8:29). It is what happens on the way that is uncertain. The bus to London has its destination on the front, but what sort of journey will it be?

The way which not only gets us to our destination but is *straight* is the subject of the first three sentences.

1. It is the way of *trust* (v. 5a) – trust of *the heart*, that is, trust in one we know loves us. It is not important that **we** don't know the future, only that we know **he** knows.

2. It is the way of humility (v. 5b), in the sense of renouncing our self-confidence. *Understanding* is good, it is one of PROVERBS' key words and we need as much as we can get, but we mustn't rely on it. It is not important that **we** don't understand what happens to us, only that we know **he** does.

3. It is the way of submission (v. 6a). *Acknowledge him* means follow where he leads, don't try to manipulate your life the way **you** think it should go. Remember he is the God of providence who is behind all that happens and will work it together 'for the good of those who love him' (Rom. 8:28). It is not important that **we** can't control events, only that we know **he** does and submit.

Compare these verses with 2 Corinthians 5:7 and consider how they throw light on each other and on your own life.

D. Bodily Health (vv. 7-8).

Here we have a connection drawn between spirituality (v. 7) and bodily health (v. 8). The way it describes health is interesting: it speaks, as far as it can in the days before the art of medicine, of our innermost being, suggesting that spirituality reaches the parts that human means can't! Body is literally 'navel', the place where the vital umbilical cord originally gave us our only means of sustenance, and when cut proved we could survive on our own. The *bones* make up our entire structure, enabling us to remain upright and mobile. These need inward *nourishment* to keep them supple, as branches need sap – an old-fashioned but not inaccurate description of a healthy body. Many books, old and new, tell us how to attain this desirable state of health: diet, exercise, regular habits, avoiding harmful substances, etc. Few come up with the prescription given here:

1. Humility in your attitude to yourself (similar to v. 5b) – not thinking you know it all, but continuing to listen and learn from others (Rom. 12:3, Phil. 2:3);

2. Trust in (*fear* of) God, which goes with humbleminded-ness, for if we know our own inadequacy we will be more inclined to look up to him;

3. Hatred of evil, which goes with 'fear of God' (Ps. 97:10): 'where God is honoured, sin is hated, loathed and resisted' (Bridges).

Questions
1. What connection is there under the new covenant between spirituality and health? Can you accept the position of Christian Science or the more recent 'prosperity and health' gospel? If not, why not?
2. Do faith and prayer prevent sickness and guarantee healing? (Ref. to 2 Cor. 12:7-10, James 5:13-16).
3. Does the offer of healing or health come into the offer of the gospel? If not, why not? If so, prove.

E. Material Prosperity (vv. 9-10).

As verses 7-8 connect spirituality with health, so these verses connect it with prosperity. The form of words reflects an agrarian society, where wealth was measured in crops and cattle rather than cash and credit. The godly Israelite *honoured the Lord* in this area by returning to him *the first-fruits* of what he believed God gave him. This was a thanksgiving to God not only as Creator and Provider but also as Redeemer, for it was a memorial of his release from Egypt (Exod. 13:11-16, Deut. 26:1-11).

In addition he gave tithes or tenths of everything else that came his way. All this produce was used to supply the Temple, sustain the priests and Levites who had no land of their own to work, and to help the poor. Those who did this faithfully were promised they would gain rather than lose. It was those who withheld their dues who lost out (Hag. 1:3-11, Mal. 3:8-12).

Whether this worked invariably under the old covenant is something we can't know, but there is no reason to doubt that it did. The 'church' was in its infancy and we teach infants good ways by rewarding them until they learn the value of goodness in itself apart from any consequences. We have to re-assess the position now that the church of Christ is in the full light of truth and its members have attained the status of grown-up sons (Gal. 4:1-7).

Questions
1. How do Christians honour the Lord in the use of material possessions? Refer to 1 Timothy 4:3f, 2 Corinthians 9:6-11, Galatians 6:6, 10.
2. Does piety still bring plenty? Refer to Matthew 6:25-34, Philippians 4:10-13, 1 Timothy 6:6,10.

F. FATHERLY DISCIPLINE (vv. 11-12).
These verses told the Israelite what to expect when he wasn't observing the conditions for health (vv. 7-8) or prosperity (vv. 9-10). *The Lord's discipline* would come into operation and he would not enjoy health and prosperity. Job experienced loss both of health and prosperity and was told by Eliphaz that this was 'the discipline of the Almighty' (Job 5:17). Sometimes the whole nation was under discipline, for example Hag. 1:5-11.

Since it is a youth who is being addressed (*my son*), the father–son analogy is particularly apt. He is told two things.

1. How not to react to it.

(a) By under-reacting, failing to take it seriously and thus to *despise* it. This might be done by attributing it only to prevailing conditions and not seeing the hand of God in it, or by stoically brushing it aside with, 'It's nothing I can't handle'.

(b) By over-reacting, taking it too seriously and so to resent it. The introvert who inclines to paranoia easily jumps to the conclusion that God has turned against him, like Jacob in Genesis 42:36. Even a more balanced person, suffering under a particularly harsh or long-lasting affliction may become embittered, or 'weary', as the KJV has it.

2. How to react to it.

The right way is to trust that the God who is disciplining you is acting not as judge but *father*; he is not punishing you in anger but correcting you because *he loves* and *delights* in you. Solomon here goes beyond Eliphaz, who spoke of God nursing the wound (Job 5:18), but not of showing love. Those who look on their afflictions in this positive way know what James meant by saying '**consider** it pure joy when you face trials' (1:2), that is, react not with the emotions but the mind. It means that when troubles come to us we stop and ask, 'What is God saying to me? How is he trying to improve me?'

Questions
1. In what ways does the use of this passage in Hebrews 12:4-11 go beyond both Job and Proverbs?
2. Is it right to conclude that whereas under the old covenant an afflicted believer was the exception, under the new covenant he is the norm? See for example Philippians 1:29f and 1 Peter 4:12-16. Does this help explain why the greatest thinkers of his day had no answer to Job's problem?

G. PARADISE RESTORED (VV. 13-18).

Lest the previous passage on the discipline of adversity should discourage the child or pupil, he hastens to re-assure him that the blessings of learning wisdom more than compensate for any necessary chastisement.

In fact, *wisdom*, the way of trust in and submission to God, is the way of true happiness, for such are *blessed* (v. 13). This verse hints that the state of wisdom is the gift not of nature but grace. You have to *find* it, which involves setting out to look for it like buried treasure. For this you need a map indicating its location, that is, the word of God. Then, as with treasure, you have to *draw it* out (the literal meaning of *gains*), that is, you ask God to help you apply it to your heart and life.

If you succeed, then, like the treasure-seeker you will find something more *profitable* than the best *returns* yielded by trading (v. 14). In fact the wisdom you have come to possess is of more value to you than are the precious stones which the treasure seeker has unearthed (v. 15). The word for *rubies* is 'corals', which would be unknown in Palestine and so of the highest value.

But so far he has only **enthused** about the blessings of wisdom, he hasn't spelt them out. This is because he is working up to the climax of verse 18. First he repeats some he has already mentioned. **Long life** (v. 16) has first place and so is in her right hand, since you won't achieve much *riches and honour* if you die young. Then **peace** (v. 17) which really combines points already made, such as **good reputation** (v. 4), **clear guidance** (v. 6), **bodily health** (v. 8) and **material prosperity** (v. 10).

'All this and heaven too', as the old song puts it. For wisdom gives, not just the gifts of God but God himself (v. 18). The *tree of life* symbolizes the happy relationship with God which Adam and Eve enjoyed in the paradise garden, Eden (Gen. 2:9), but which through failing to trust and obey him they lost (Gen. 3:24). Even this can be restored by possessing *wisdom*, which under the old covenant meant living in *the fear of God* (1:7), that is, acknowledging and worshipping him as the only God, taking his commandments to heart, and believing his promise of forgiveness for those who not only use the existing sacrificial system but believe the promise of a Messiah who would 'restore all things' by making of himself a perfect sacrifice.

Questions
1. What is the way to wisdom under the new covenant? See 2 Timothy 3:15.
2. What is the 'paradise' enjoyed by the Christian – here (John 10:10) and hereafter (Rev. 22:1-5)? Who is admitted to this paradise? See Luke 23:39-43.

H. UNSHAKEABLE ASSURANCE (vv. 19-20).

The benefit referred to here is implicit rather than explicit, but follows logically from verse 18. If *Wisdom* brings us to God himself, it makes us one with him who created us and all things.

The writer here takes the basic words of his treatise: *wisdom ... understanding ... knowledge*, and makes them the building blocks of which the universe is constructed. **Verse 19** speaks of the material creation, the solid matter from which *the earth* and *the* (cosmic) *heavens* were built, so that they are immovable except by the one who made them. **Verse 20** speaks of the other element – water, essential to maintaining life on the earth, without which it would be as barren as the moon or planets. This has two sources: underground (*the deeps*), emerging in springs and wells, and over-head, *the clouds* in the sky (cf. Gen. 1:6, 7:11f). *Wisdom* is as basic as the solids and liquids that constitute the material universe. It is both God's nature and his means of creating and preserving the world, and **we** are offered it by his Word!

Therefore the benefits offered here are not uncertain and elusive but as real and solid as the earth itself.

Question
How does all this encourage us who come to *Wisdom* through Christ? See Hebrews 1:1-2.

I. SAFE KEEPING (vv. 21-26).

There is a link between verse 21 and verses 19f which NIV doesn't bring out because it reverses the order of the Hebrew words, which read: *do not let them* (the *wisdom, understanding and knowledge* by which he created the earth) *out of your sight, preserve sound judgment.* It is because these qualities are God's own attributes that this particular benefit can be yours. They give you a quality of life (v. 22) which is as evident to others as a sparking necklace. The grace of God will shine out from you.

Moreover, you will have nothing to fear, for he who is your life is the great Creator. By day (v. 23) *you will not stumble*, which is probably meant in a moral or spiritual sense, since the word tends to refer to falling into sin (Ps. 37:24; 73:2). By night you can relax and go to sleep (v. 24). *Sudden disaster* (v. 25) is something that *overtakes the wicked* (Ps. 73:18f.; 1 Thess. 5:3), from which God preserves the righteous. It's all a matter of confidence, not in self, weapons and security systems, but in *the Lord who laid the earth's foundations*.

Question
What added danger does the New Testament believer face and how does this passage help in this respect? See 1 Peter 5:8f.

J. HAPPY RELATIONSHIPS (vv. 27-35).
Wisdom is not only about our relationship with God, our personal holiness and the enjoyment of his favours, but also about our human relationships. We come up against various types of people and need to know how to conduct ourselves. Here are the attitudes we should cultivate if we are to keep on good terms with other people – similar to those we find in the New Testament.

1. Honesty and generosity (vv. 27-28). This states negatively what Paul puts positively in Rom. 13:7: 'Give everyone what you owe him'. For the literal translation of *those who deserve it* (v. 27) is 'the owners', which may apply to personal debts, to the payment of wages, fees and bills, taxes and dues, as in Rom. 13:7. We must not say, 'Can't pay' when we have the means. What we owe actually belongs to our creditor, and to withhold is stealing. Nor should we play for time (v. 28), for our creditor may be in dire need of what we owe, and we may cause him hardship by our delay. It is not only a matter of honesty but also of consideration. 'He gives twice who gives promptly'.

Undoubtedly giving to the needy also comes under this heading. We **owe** help to those in need and we should neither refuse them outright nor put them off with vague promises. James (2:15f) makes this a proof of true saving faith. We disprove our claim to faith by ungenerosity as much as by dishonesty.

Question
What does every Christian owe everyone? See Romans 1:14.

2. Peaceableness (vv. 29-30). Paul again comes to mind: 'As far as it depends on you, live at peace with everyone' (Rom. 12:18). If we would achieve this we must avoid two things.

(a) **Treachery (v. 29)**. Here is someone who is on good terms with you, he *lives trustfully near you*. Yet all unsuspected by him you are trying to harm him. Maybe you are craftily taking away his business, or undermining his reputation, or surreptitiously turning his friends or even his wife and children against him. Sooner or later your happy relationship with him will explode.

(b) **Quarrelsomeness (v. 30)**. This may, as NIV seems to think, refer to litigation (*accuse* in the sense of 'sue'), but is probably of broader application, meaning 'pick a quarrel', out of sheer peevishness and cantankerousness, without any grounds.

Question
In what way should the Christian go beyond avoiding treachery and quarrelsomeness in living peaceably (Rom. 12:17-21)?

3. Contentment (vv. 31-35). Contentment with what we are and have is the way to avoid the sin of *envy*. While we may feel repugnance against a *violent man* (v. 31), remember that violence is not only physical, it can be verbal. It includes the domineering person who insists on his own way, whether governor, boss, husband, father or even pastor! Beware of envying the power that such have over others, especially if you are the one being domineered.

The best antidote is to remember that as an upright person you have something far better than power over others; you have an intimate relationship with the ruler of the universe, who *takes you into his confidence* (v. 32). You are an Abraham from whom he won't 'hide what he is about to do' (Gen. 18:17); you are a prophet, of whom it is said, 'The Sovereign LORD does nothing without revealing his plan to his servants the prophets' (Amos 3:7). Indeed you are more, for you have been admitted to 'the mysteries of the kingdom' (Matt. 13:11), the gospel of universal saving grace (Eph. 3:2-6). You may not have power over others, but your God does. Look at the way **he** uses it: **for** his own and **against** the violent (vv. 33-35). The latter he calls *wicked* for the way they abuse their power; *proud mockers* for the way they despise his chosen; and *fools* for the way they reject him (Ps. 14:1). They are not to be envied, for they are under his *curse*; that is, in the present they are objects of his scorn, and in the future their destiny is not glory but *shame*. Rather should **they** *envy* **you** for he calls you *righteous ... humble ... wise*; and for you there is *blessing – grace* in the present and *honour* at the end.

Question
How far do you think the New Testament goes along with the 'black-and-white' world view evident both in this passage and in PROVERBS generally? Refer, for example, to Romans 2:7-11.

4

Third Benefit: Excellency
(Proverbs 4)

There is little fresh material in this chapter. After the riches of chapter 3 is there any more to say about *wisdom*? But what it lacks in content it makes up for in fervour. The father or teacher is desperate to gain the attention of his hearers and to elicit a response. So he goes out of his way to share with us the surpassing **excellence** of wisdom.

We can take this in two ways: (1) as the Lord calling on us to give our best attention to the wisdom of his Word as we read it ourselves or hear it proclaimed; (2) as an example of how we should teach our children or pupils: with a fervent desire they should hear and respond, and with the enthusiasm that what we teach them towers above anything they hear from anyone in the world. It is not all repetition and the appeal is three-fold.

A. HE APPEALS TO HIS OWN UPBRINGING (vv. 1-9).
We all come into the world in a state of ignorance (*simple* or untaught, 1:4). The only way to acquire *knowledge, learning, understanding and wisdom* is to listen to those who already have it and are willing to give it to us in their *instruction* (v. 1) or *teaching* (v. 2), that is, our parents or teachers.

Here is Solomon with his family around him (*my sons*) recalling a time when he sat where they sit and David stood where he stands (vv. 3-4). Solomon was not literally the *only child* of David and Bathsheba who had four sons (1 Chron. 3:5), so the meaning is probably 'favourite', because special to God (2 Sam. 12:24f). He is making the point that the teaching he received from his father and mother was not of the formal, academic, classroom style, but was personal, warm and loving. There is no doubt this is the best kind of teaching. 'The best things are transmitted mainly by personal influence along the channels of affection' (Kidner).

Solomon wants his sons to have what he had in his childhood. Happy are those parents who can appeal to their own upbringing when teaching their children, as Timothy could (2 Tim. 1:5). Those who were denied this blessing can appeal to the contrast: 'I want you to have what I didn't.' It is always good for children to realize their parents were once young, ignorant and foolish themselves. They cannot visualize us as other than we are – middle-aged – and any photos we can show or anecdotes we can recount will help them realize we were once like them. Then they will more readily listen to what we have to say, for there will be more sympathy and patience on both sides. Solomon even remembers the words his father spoke to him. Most expositors think verses 4-9, not just verse 4, are, if not verbatim, at least a summary of David's teaching, as Solomon remembered it.

1. He remembers the **earnestness** with which his father encouraged him to see wisdom as the highest good and make it his aim. There are twelve verbs in the imperative in these six verses. It is a stirring passage. We need this in listening to God's Word, as do our children – not just to be told blandly, 'This is right and that's wrong', but to be urged with all the passion that can be commanded. Our children need to feel it is important to us that they embrace the faith. This applies to all we say in his name, whether preaching or personal testimony. If it comes direct from the heart it is more likely to reach the heart.

2. He remembers the **arguments** with which his father sought to persuade him to embrace his teaching. We are creatures of reason and need to know not only what we should do but why we should do it. If God is prepared to 'reason together' with his children (Isa. 1:18), how much more should we with ours. Here he recalls how David had displayed before him the benefits which make wisdom excellent.

First and foremost is *life* (**v. 4**). We have talked about this under 3:16,18, and how it particularly refers to quality of life: security, happiness, usefulness. To Christians it is the 'life to the full' which Jesus brought – sharing the life of God, experiencing him and the sanctifying power of his presence.

Second is *protection* (**vv. 5-6**). On this we have had nearly two chapters, for, as already said, this chapter does not break new ground, but seeks to persuade us to embrace the teaching already given. We need reminding that we live in an evil and dangerous world. Nature can harm us, as can our fellow human beings. Most of all, there is a supernatural, evil being out to get us (1 Pet. 5:8). The knowledge of God which breeds faith will save us from much of this evil. Who knows how often God may have intervened to prevent physical disasters falling on us? How many potential muggers or intruders he may have restrained? How often he has stood in the way of the devil? We who commit ourselves daily to him, as Jesus taught us (Matt. 6:13) can walk the world without that craven fear which grips many.

Third is *honour* (**vv. 7-9**, cf. 3:4,16), a lovely picture of the reputation gained by those who become wise. In a theocracy like Israel it was usually the most godly who were most honoured by society. Christians live in the real world, among God's enemies, who may hate godliness (see on 3:3f). But our fellow-Christians will esteem us now, and hereafter we will 'receive a rich welcome into the eternal kingdom of our Lord and Saviour Jesus Christ' (2 Pet. 1:11). Whether we are loved or hated for it, a reputation for godliness is the highest prize, above fame and popularity.

Consider: since in the gospel age wisdom is the person of Christ himself (1 Cor. 1:30, Col. 2:3), go through this passage again, substituting 'Christ' for wisdom, to enhance him in your eyes.

B. HE APPEALS TO THE CONTRAST BETWEEN WISDOM AND WICKEDNESS (vv. 10-19).

Contrast is a powerful teaching weapon. We can best appreciate the value of something good by looking at its opposite. So in this section he not only describes the excellencies of the way of wisdom but shows the grim alternative.

1. The Way of Wisdom (vv. 10-13).

Verse 10 shows he is still feeling hot under the collar, anxious to keep his family's attention. There is no particular significance in his reverting from the plural *sons* (v. 1) to the singular *son* (v. 10). What is addressed to all is addressed to each. All this effort was not lavished only on the reprobate Rehoboam, or it would have been wasted! Again he backs up his appeal by specifying the excellencies of wisdom:

(a) *verse 10, long life,* a promise already discussed under 3:1-2.

(b) *verse 11, a sense of purpose.* Paths which are *straight* enable us to keep our sense of direction. The *wise* know where they are going in life. This too was discussed fully under 3:5-6.

(c) *verse 12, consistent living.* This does not mean the *wise* are faultless, but that God saves them from the pitfalls that lie before us all, into which the *wicked* try to lure us (v. 16).

(d) *verse 13, quality of life,* derived from the *tree of life,* discussed in 3:18.

All this is contrasted with:

2. The Way of Wickedness (vv. 14-17).

Again we see the earnestness of his appeal, with six imperatives in the first two verses. He is warning his hearers in every possible way, depicting wickedness as a journey, a path on which we should not even begin to set foot (v. 14).

Again too, not content with emotion, he gives us a good reason – look at those who practise wickedness. They become totally addicted. They can't sleep unless they have committed a crime or corrupted someone (v. 16). If they don't rob someone, sleep will rob them! They are like an alcoholic or drug addict needing a daily fix. Indeed wickedness is their bread and butter (v. 17) – as commonplace and regular as their daily food. Who wants to become like that? Yet just a little experimenting with it and you may be hooked for ever. Hold to the way of wisdom and you won't go down that road (v. 15).

But in case he hasn't got his point over he makes an even more powerful contrast in verses 18-19: the difference between the two ways is no less than the difference between light and darkness.

1. The Way of Wisdom (v. 18) is the Way of Light.

Light stands for *knowledge* of truth, happiness and holiness. He refers to it as *the first gleam of dawn*, to indicate that we are not naturally righteous but come to it from a long night, like the dawn of a new day. In gospel language we are 'made righteous by faith', by coming 'out of darkness into his wonderful light' (1 Pet. 2:9). That first light is enough to illuminate our way so that we do not fall, for it is Christ himself (John 1:9). It is also enough for others to notice (Phil. 2:15f). But it isn't perfect any more than is the first light of day. As the sun ascends the heavens so the strength of its light increases. In the same way the light of righteous living is a gradual growing thing which will only reach perfection when we arrive at the goal and receive the prize. Paul expounds this idea at length and in depth in Philippians 3:7-14. In Christ we have a true righteousness (v. 9) but have not yet 'obtained all or been made perfect'. But we will be if we are 'in the light' and 'walk in the light' (1 John 1:5-7).

2. The Way of Wickedness (v. 19) is the Way of Darkness.

The word used, translated *deep darkness* is that of Exodus 10:22, the plague of darkness, so intense it could be 'felt', so 'total' the eyes could not adjust to it. Darkness stands for ignorance and error, misery and sin (Eph. 4:18-19). Those who walk that way *stumble*; they are always in some kind of trouble, and ultimately come to ruin, consigned to 'outer darkness', a state which the light of God never penetrates.

Question
This passage raises the subject of *separation*. Consider what this does **not** mean from 1 Corinthians 5:9f and what it **does** mean from John 17:15.

C. He appeals to the basic principles of wisdom (vv. 20-27).
As he begins a new section he again calls for close *attention* (v. 20). This must not lapse when the lesson ends, but be kept in mind afterwards (v. 21). We think of James' apt illustration of the Word as a mirror (James 1:22-25). Someone who sees his image keeps it in his mind and goes away to correct the blemish or improve his appearance. Listening to the Word is not just

a way of passing an hour. It is to be taken away and worked out. Those who don't are 'deceiving themselves' – hypocrites.

How can he impress this on us? Only by once again referring to the words of wisdom as *life* (**v. 22**), since nothing is more basic. But he doesn't feel this is saying enough. There is a life which is mere existence. *Wisdom* is life as it is meant to be – *health*. To live in a state of ill health is to live with no enjoyment and possibly no usefulness. So is it to try to live without wisdom.

But he still cannot leave the subject. He must persuade us of its importance. So he describes in detail what he means by a healthy life. It begins in *the heart* (**v. 23**). Just as the physical organ to which we give this name is vital to the existence of life, so is that for which it stands vital to the quality of life. *Heart* refers to the core of our being: mind, emotions and will. This is our *well-spring*; everything about us 'issues' (kjv) or 'flows' from this inner being. Jesus brought this out astutely in Mark 7:15-23, Luke 6:45 and John 7:38.

The proof of this lies in **verses 24-27** where other bodily organs are mentioned: *mouth* (24), *eyes* (25) and *feet* (26-27). Only the continual beating of the heart enables these organs to function. Only a mind under the control of the Word of the wise God enables:

1. our *lips* to speak purely and profitably (**v. 24**, Eph. 4:29, Col. 4:6);

2. the *eyes* of our mind as well as those in our head to be directed towards the way of righteousness (**v. 25**, Eph. 1:18);

3. our *feet*, **verse 26f,** that is, our behaviour, life-style, general course, to be consistent with the teaching we profess to have received (Ps. 119:9).

What powerful arguments are these to persuade us to follow God's word of wisdom! What heartfelt pleas to prove he really wants us to! Let them move us to adopt this way ourselves, then let us use them to persuade our children or anyone, young or older, to whom God gives us the opportunity to speak of his Word.

Question
What is the gospel believer's more excellent way of achieving this proper use of the parts of his body (Rom. 6:11-23)?

5

Fourth Benefit: Warning
(Proverbs 5–7)

So far he has dealt with the positive benefits of wisdom: protection, promises and excellence. Now he turns to the negative, the warnings. These make less pleasant reading but are just as necessary and therefore just as wise. All good things have their flip side. Each mechanical device we buy for our convenience, from a mixer to a motor car, contains a warning against the dangers of its wrong use. It is wise to heed these warnings lest our purchase prove more of a curse than a blessing. The young person on the brink of discovering the pleasures of life needs to be warned of their dangers. The principal one to which Solomon draws attention here is that of promiscuous sex, although others have a briefer mention in 6:1-19.

A. CHAPTER 5: FIRST WARNING AGAINST SEXUAL TEMPTATION. This subject has had an airing in the context of the protection from bad company that wisdom affords (2:10-19). Now it is given full treatment.

1. His appeal (vv. 1-2).
Although addressed *my son* the warning is needed as much by daughters, if not more, as we shall see. He begins with his usual call for attention. To secure this he makes a twofold appeal.

(a) **To the excellence of his teaching** in itself **(v. 1)**: it is a combination of God's revealed truth (*wisdom*) and his own observation (*insight*). Some would say it arises from Solomon's own personal experience as one who 'loved many foreign women' (1 Kings 11:1 cf. Eccles. 7:26).

(b) **To its practical value (v. 2):**

(i) it enables one to act with discretion, that is, to live a carefully disciplined life based on good moral standards;

(ii) it inspires wholesome conversation – the *lips* will talk of the *knowledge* that has been received from the father or teacher. Both are vital in facing the temptress, for she uses both speech and action in luring the unwary, as will now be seen.

2. The psychology of sexual temptation (vv. 3-5).

The adulteress is anyone who is not the wife of the one under consideration here. So it applies to all sinful relationships and casual sex.

Verse 3 describes her initial approach, enlarging on 2:16's *seductive words*. Her words are sweet as the honey actually dripping from the *honeycomb*, when it is at its sweetest. Her voice is smooth and feels like *oil* on the skin. She flatters, comforts, offers, promises, all in a soft voice as alluring as the sirens. It takes one trained in godly conversation (v. 2) to see through it and resist it. Those not brought up in the word of God are more than likely to be seduced by her, for self-discipline alone is not strong enough in this area.

As usual the Bible passes over the act of adultery which presumably follows this and proceeds immediately to the after-effects. The pleasure is over so quickly (**v. 4**) and *the end* so different from the beginning. Not *sweet as honey* but bitter as poison, an apt description of the pangs of conscience: 'The horrid memories, self-remorse, ruined health and reputation, blasted hopes' (David Thomas). Not *smooth as oil* but piercing as a *double-edged sword*, describing the sense of divine anger and impending judgment that torments the bad conscience. Nor is this fear exaggerated (**v. 5**), for this is sin, and 'the wages of sin is death', that is, death in a state of sin, which leads on to SHEOL (*the grave*). The Old Testament view of the after-life is unclear, hovering somewhere between the non-existence of pagan religion and the everlasting torment of Christ's teaching. SHEOL is neither oblivion on the one hand nor the place of punishment (for which Jesus used the term GEHENNA) on the other, but an unknown shadowy though conscious existence. The speaker stresses the direct route from the bed of sin to this doom: *Her feet go down ... her steps lead straight...*

This does not make sexual sin worse than any other form, nor does it mean that there is no way of repentance and restoration. All sins of the flesh are the fruit of an unregenerate nature, a **state** of sin, alienation from God. It is for this that hell exists, this that God judges. Sins of the flesh bring right home to the individual that he is away from God and without grace. They thus preach judgment to him. But while he is in process of committing them he is in no condition to get right with God.

The reason lies in **verse 6**: this particular sin can only be practised in a most intimate relationship with one who is already a confirmed sinner him/herself. Paul in fact goes so far as to say that 'he who unites himself with a prostitute is one with her in body' (1 Cor. 6:6). Such a one *gives no thought to the way of life*, and is not going to show his or her companion that way! The KJV may be nearer the original at this point: *Lest thou shouldst ponder the path of life, her ways are moveable that thou canst not know them*; that is, she deliberately distracts him from considering *the path of life* by constantly adapting to the changing moods and circumstances or the different characters and outlooks of her clients. If she were to let them start thinking about God she would be acting against her own interests.

Consider how James 1:14-15 brings out in a similar way the sequence of events that follows the will's consent to a particular temptation.

3. The consequences of sexual promiscuity (vv. 7-14).
He does not feel he has said enough about *the end* (**v. 4**) of yielding to this temptation and must go into more detail. So he asks his hearers to sustain their attention (**v. 7a**) while he continues, and more – to make it their practice for the whole of their life (**v. 7b**).

He begins with a simple rule (**v. 8**): to avoid this sin avoid the place where the temptation arises, such as the house of the one by whom you are tempted. Take a different route lest you weaken when you pass her door or see her in the window. This may be applied to temptation generally. It is no good asking God to 'lead us not into temptation' if we deliberately go to those places or do those things likely to arouse it (see 4:14f). 'Those that would be kept from harm must keep out of harm's way' (Henry). It was this kind of self-discipline Jesus was referring to in Matthew 5:28-30, which he said in the context of adultery. This plain speaking is more than justified by the awful picture he now gives of the consequences of becoming enslaved to sexual sin.

(a) *verse 9. It takes away the bloom of youth* and the best years of life. There are some sinister undertones here: *others* suggests being caught in a whole network of evil-minded people, and *one who is cruel* may hint at the possibility of blackmail.

(b) *verse 10. It costs a great deal of money.* Sexual sin is expensive – not only are there the prostitute's high fees or the mistress's expenses, but possible protection money, plus providing for the wife and children who may have been driven from home because this behaviour had become intolerable.

(c) *verse 11. It undermines health.* The physical dangers of promiscuity are well known. Venereal diseases existed in Solomon's time besides which we today face AIDS. Those who manage to avoid these cannot claim to live a healthy life, since such things as excessive drinking, over-eating, smoking and drugs, are usually connected with this life-style.

(d) *verses 12f. It breeds remorse and self condemnation.* Here is the prodigal 'coming to his senses' (Luke 15:17) in later life, remembering what he had been taught in youth but turned his back on. Now he suffers the pangs of remorse and self-reproach. Jesus was probably referring to remorse when he described hell as the state in which 'their worm does not die and the fire is not quenched' (Mark 9:48).

(e) *verse 14. It leads to the brink of utter ruin.* A life of sexual promiscuity is not the end of the world but it is fairly near it. Literally this reads, 'It wanted but a little and I would have fallen into all kinds of evil'. For sexual sin breeds many other sins: lying; debt, theft and fraud (to finance it); neglect or ill-treatment of family; violence and even murder. This was the point reached by the Lost Son of Luke 15.

Question
What do the words *in the midst of the whole assembly* (v. 14) suggest about the effect of such behaviour on the offender's position in the godly community? Look up 1 Corinthians 5 to see the similarity of the situation in the New Testament church.

4. The way of sexual purity (vv. 15-20).
There is no need to get entangled in the way just described, with all its dire consequences. There is an alternative – not abstinence or celibacy. This is nowhere required in Scripture: see 1 Timothy 4:3, where Paul condemns compulsory celibacy along with other forms of asceticism as 'taught by demons'. Where a particular calling involves singleness grace is given (Matt. 19:10-12; 1 Cor. 7:7). The alternative is marriage, which God has given not only to satisfy those desires for the opposite sex which he built into us, but much more, which can never be enjoyed from casual sex. These are: life-long companionship, the increase of the human race and the upbringing of the next generation (Gen. 2:24, 3:16b, 20). Now let us look at this in more detail.

(a) *Verses 15-17: His advice.*
Briefly, this is to enjoy the full delights of conjugal love. To liken the marriage relationship to drinking water (**v. 15**) may not seem much of a compliment to us, but in ancient Israel water was a precious commodity. The rain when it came was stored in a *cistern* by those who could afford one. Even happier were those who had access to a *well* from which they could draw fresh (*running*) water. In a hot and thirsty land this was one of the greatest pleasures imaginable. Let your married love be like that, says Solomon; satisfy your thirst for physical satisfaction by taking a partner.

Verse 16 develops this by comparing a wife to a private domestic water supply, whereas a prostitute is like a village pump, available to all! 'Since you have your own water supply,' he is saying, 'you don't need to obtain it *in the streets* or *public squares*.' **Verse 17** adds that in a similar way your *water* (partner) is not *shared with strangers*. This telling illustration vividly shows the advantages of marriage above promiscuity.

(b) *Verses 18-19: His Blessing.*
Solomon is not giving the cold detached advice of a marriage guidance counsellor, but is personally and passionately concerned for his sons. Speaking in God's name he shows how greatly God desires our happiness in marriage as well as our faithfulness. The love of one partner need not be dull but enjoyable (*rejoice*, v. 18), *satisfying* (v. 19), even *captivating*. The language becomes highly erotic, unusual in Scripture but found also in Song of Songs. But he is after all trying to direct us from a relationship which is solely that of short-lived but sinful erotic pleasure to one which is sanctioned by God and long-lasting. He is saying that this does not need to lessen the physical pleasure. The illustration of the doe and the deer backs this up, for they are pictures of female beauty and erotic love. Indeed the word for *love* in verse 19 is the eros term.

(c) *Verse 20: His Challenge.*
He puts the logical conclusion from all this in the form of a question. Since everything you find in the unlawful partner you can enjoy in marriage, and much more, what possible reason can there be for going down the road of promiscuity? It is a rhetorical but unanswerable question.

5. The sinfulness of sexual promiscuity (vv. 21-23).
The little particle *for* indicates he is now laying down the theology on which his warnings are founded. He has argued from the natural. Now he turns to the supernatural. It is not just that monogamous marriage is more obviously happy than promiscuity but that the latter is sinful in the sight of God who will judge it, whereas married love fulfils his will and pleases him. There are three considerations to bring into the equation.

(a) *Verse 21. All sin is known to God.*
The adulterer is only concerned not to be seen by another person (Job 24:15). He fails to take account of God. Two factors about the nature of God are relevant here.

(i) **His omniscience.** Literally, 'a man's ways are before the eyes of the Lord.' Unlike a human inspector who can make only occasional visits, our every thought and act are known to God. This should not alarm but encourage, as it did David in Psalm 139. Because God knew all about him (vv. 1-4) he would 'lead him in the way everlasting' (vv. 23f). It is the same for us: the Spirit who 'searches' us (1 Cor. 2:10) also 'leads' us (Rom. 8:14).

(ii) **His righteousness.** The last remark does not mean that God passes over what he discovers amiss. For he *weighs* us (which RVmg and AMP prefer to *examines*) against the standard of his righteousness. This applies to *all his paths*, literally 'wagon-tracks', those ruts which develop with continual use and therefore refer to what has become habitual. It is not the single lapse that is in view so much as its developing into a life-style.

(b) *Verse 22. Sin brings bondage.*
Whereas verse 21 is a general statement applying to the actions and thoughts of us all, this is addressed to one who has actually fallen into this sin (*the wicked man*). Those who commit it think they are indulging their freedom and will listen to no warnings against it (vv. 12f). After a while they find they have got into a web from which they cannot disentangle themselves. Whether a man uses a prostitute or takes a mistress he loses his freedom. He may have an uncontrollable craving for her which he has to feed; he may have to yield to her demands; he may be compromised because the matter has come to the attention of others. Many get to the point of wishing they had never set off down that road, and find themselves unable to turn back. They are *ensnared* and *held fast*. They may lay the blame elsewhere, but the truth is that it is their own sins that are responsible. That freedom they thought they were enjoying has proved a pipe-dream.

(c) *Verse 23. Sin is punished.*
That enslavement which turns pleasure into misery in this life
is not sin's punishment, it is simply the working of the law of
cause and effect. Neither is it the punishment which in the Old
Testament Israel inflicted on sex offenders, which could be the
death penalty (Lev. 20:10-20) and which is changed under the
New Testament to excommunication – the 'death' of church
fellowship and access to the means of grace (1 Cor. 5:1-5). It
is the judgment to come at the last day (1 Cor. 6:9f, Heb. 13:4,
Rev. 21:8).

Solomon points out the justice of this. The one who has
come to this state has failed to heed the *instruction* he was
offered and to submit to the *discipline* of practising that
instruction. Now he only has himself to blame. He is *led astray
by his own great folly*. It is ironical that the term *led astray* is
the same as that for *captivated* in both verse 19 and verse 20.
To be captivated by any other than your own partner is to be
captivated by your own folly.

Question
What hope does the gospel give the sexual sinner that the law
could not? See 1 Corinthians 6:11, Romans 6:14, 17f.

B. Chapter 6:1-19. Warnings Against Other Common Pitfalls
In this section Solomon addresses a number of pitfalls into
which the young and inexperienced can easily fall and against
which they therefore need warning.

1. Putting up security (vv. 1-5).
Literally the opening verses read, 'If you are a surety'.
A 'surety' is someone 'who undertakes responsibility for
a debt' (New Bible Dictionary). Since the Law code does not
cover this practice we may take Solomon's words as advisory
rather than mandatory. In fact, if the Law were strictly followed
the situation need not arise. For Israelites were to lend to the
needy freely without interest (Exod. 22:25). If the loan was
secured the pledge was not to be something essential to a man's
livelihood, such as his millstones (Deut. 24:6) or his coat, since
it was also his bed-covering (Exod. 22:26). The idea of another

person putting up security never came into the matter. This practice may only just have been developing during Solomon's time with the growth of international trade. What Israelites did not do among themselves might be done with foreigners. One merchant asks a fellow-merchant to guarantee his debt to a foreign trader and a financial transaction is born.

The situation here however appears to be more informal. There are no witnesses or documents, just a verbal agreement (**v. 2**) sealed with a handshake (**v. 1**). This may have taken place among friends, but not necessarily, since the word *neighbour* applied to anyone (Exod. 20:17), as its parallel *for another* indicates. Solomon strongly advises his *son* against this practice, comparing it to an animal or bird caught in a trap (vv. 2, 5). You are at your neighbour's mercy as much as a beast or bird trapped in a snare. If he fails to pay his debt the creditor will come to you for it.

Solomon does not say it is immoral, only that it is highly risky. He advises anyone who has entered into such an undertaking to disentangle himself with as much expedition as an animal caught in a trap, who will try to get himself free before the hunter or fowler gets to him and he is lost for ever.

But didn't the Israelite and doesn't the Christian have an obligation to come to the aid of a brother in financial need (Ps. 37:26, Matt. 5:42)? Indeed, but not in this way. If he is nearing destitution then give him what he needs and save him from the debt trap. If he has got into debt pay it off before it accumulates in the hands of an unmerciful money-lender. Even then you need to ask: can I afford to give this amount (2 Cor. 8:12f)? Am I happy to give it (2 Cor. 8:10-12, 9:7)? Is it really necessary (2 Cor. 8:14) or am I financing some wasteful or even sinful practice, such as gambling, drinking or whoring?

In fact, in our modern society we might be even less advised to take on the role of surety. In view of the exorbitant and ever-changing interest rates now attached to loans, to underwrite another's debt is to take on something open-ended. Repaying the principal is the smallest part of the matter. While we are to be generous to the needy we are not expected to commit ourselves beyond our capacity to an unknown future. We live in a society

run on credit and debt, and most of us for a large part of our
lives have commitments such as mortgages and hire-purchase
agreements. We find it hard enough to meet these without taking
on someone else's debt. We should only do so if we are quite sure
of our ability to meet it should the need arise. Let us conduct our
financial transactions with great care. Debt is a terrible thing.
(For Suretyship see also 11:15, 17:18 and 22:26-27.)

Question
What has Jesus done for us in this connection that we are not
required to do for another? See Hebrews 7:22.

2. Laziness (vv. 6-11).
Although the transition from verses 1-5 seems abrupt, there
may be a connection of thought: 'I've warned you of one route
to poverty; here is another'. But why does Solomon suddenly
become so direct and personal – **you** *sluggard*? Maybe he had
one in his family or the class he was teaching. In any case this
is how the Word of God comes to us – not with abstractions
addressed to no one in particular, but with a message to me
about myself. I must look at myself, ask if I am a sluggard and
listen to what God has to say about such.

(a) He must be *willing to be taught a lesson (vv. 6-8).*
What makes someone a sluggard is not the mind but the flesh.
He lives as he feels, does what his body craves. So he must first
consider (**v. 6**), get his thinking right and follow it; the youth
must grow out of the childish state of doing what pleases him
physically, use his mind and act on considered principles.
    Now Solomon has another shock for us. To learn this lesson
we must go, not to the classroom but the ant-hill! Our teacher
must be, not a learned, wise, adult human to whom we look
up, but a tiny ant whom we tread on! Of course, he is seeking
to shame the lazy one. Sloth is a condition you cannot sit
down and theorize about. It is a habit which has to be kicked –
literally! Solomon's kick is to tell us to follow the ant's example.
We, the crown of creation, made in God's image, created to
rule, have to learn from the ant how to function! But we have
already made ourselves like an insect – the slug, from whom

this condition gets its name (or is it the other way round?). We are to stop behaving like slugs and start behaving like ants.

Nor is this all. We are told the ant works without the kicking the sluggard needs. He has no *commander* ... (**v. 7**). His society is not structured like ours, where each has someone above him to whom he is responsible. Neither does the ant have calendars and clocks or knowledge of the seasons. Yet he is found busy gathering his stores at the right time (**v. 8**). Surely if an ant can work for itself, an intelligent human can?

Here ends the fable of the ant, but not the whole matter. *Consideration* is not enough, there must be action.

(b) Secondly, the sluggard must be *stirred to act (vv. 9-11).*
Verse 9 depicts him still lying there *considering* the lesson, or more likely dropping off to sleep again. This is his basic trouble – he loves his bed too much. Solomon is not asking him to fix a time for getting out of bed. Rather he is saying, 'You've already overslept – get up **now**.' But the sluggard does not take him literally and replies (**v. 10**), 'Just five more minutes.' But he is deceiving himself. In five minutes' time he will say, 'Just another five minutes'. His words give him away, for to *fold the hands* is symbolic of idleness (Eccles. 4:5); it means he has no intention of using them. For this is not the sleep that comes from tiredness of body but from sedation of the brain. It is the sleep of one under a drug, only this drug is laziness.

The NIV (**v. 10**) indicates that the sluggard's reply is cut short and interrupted by the speaker. The *and* (**v. 11**) has the sense of 'so', that is, 'if you give in to laziness the result will be *poverty and scarcity*.' He tries to get him to see himself lying half-asleep and suddenly set upon by an armed robber. But the robber is called Poverty, who creeps up unseen and strikes. The result of laziness is as irresistible as being set upon.

Question
How would you apply this principle to the matter of our response to God's Word:

1. As regards his invitation to come to him for salvation? See Luke 13:24.

2. As regards 'working out our salvation'? See Matthew 25:14-30, James 2:14-26.

3. The Deceiver (vv. 12-15).

Here is another good reason for combating our natural sloth and keeping awake. There are some bad people about who live to cause trouble. Those in view here are not mindless louts but smart Alecs. They are called (literally) 'men of worthlessness and evil' (**v. 12**). No creature of God is 'worthless' in the absolute sense, but if he devotes his life to causing trouble, the world is better off without him; he does nothing of any worth. Such is the one we call the 'con-man' (who is in reality just a liar), of whom there was never a better description than this.

The NIV may be incorrect in making **verse 14b** the predicate or main clause, and it may be better to follow most other translators who make **verse 12b** the predicate. For example, AMP reads, 'A worthless person, a wicked man, is **he** who goes about with a perverse mouth. He winks ...' So the passage works out as follows.

(a) *The Wickedness of the Liar exposed* (**v. 12**).

This is not the person who has at some time told a lie to gain an advantage or get out of a scrape. It is the habitual liar, who 'walks with a crooked mouth' (lit.), every word that comes from his mouth is twisted, he makes a practice of lying, in fact he makes his living from it, he is a professional deceiver. The Bible faces the fact that such people exist, and so must we and our children. If they existed in the 'holy nation' how much more will they in our secular society!

(b) *The Subtlety of the Liar exposed* (**v. 13**).

Even his body language demonstrates his deceitfulness. His slightest movement is deceptive. He is such a practised deceiver that he can't move a muscle without it confirming the lies he speaks. Winking the eye, shuffling or tapping the feet, motioning with the fingers, it all has a meaning. These are signals to his accomplices, or even to neutral members of the company, that he is 'conning' his unfortunate victim. Some think him clever and even amusing, a practical joker who means no harm. That he is not clowning but in dead earnest is shown in the next verse.

(c) *The Intention of the Liar exposed* (**v. 14**).
The three phrases here form a crescendo:

(i) 'Frowardness (perversity) is in his heart' (KJV). Whatever the spectators think of his words and actions, what is going on in his heart is only bad. What is this?

(ii) 'He is plotting evil all the time' (lit.). These are the lines on which his thoughts run – plotting and scheming are second nature. But what is he plotting? Here is the crux.

(iii) 'He lets loose discord' (AMP). While he keeps out of trouble by his cleverness, he gets his victims into trouble. His lies encourage them to courses of action which make others angry, even violent. While he melts into the crowd, they are getting beaten up.

(d) *The Fate of the Liar exposed* (**v. 15**).
He won't escape for ever. One day he'll make a mistake and implicate himself. Someone will get wise to him and seek vengeance. Or the authorities will catch him in the act. That this is more than human justice catching up on a miscreant is shown in the next section.

4. Seven Deadly Sins (vv. 16-19).
Although not part of the previous passage, it is closely connected (cf. verse 14b with **verse 19b**). The basic reason why deceivers come to grief (**v. 15**) is because *the Lord hates* their practices. He may not personally and directly destroy them, for, as we have seen, they bring about their own destruction by the anger they provoke and the crimes they commit. God simply leaves them to the vengeance of their enemies or to justice. Human hatred and punishment thus become the instrument of God's justice.

But this passage is aimed not just at the con-man. Perhaps Solomon's family or class, perhaps ours, perhaps we ourselves have been listening to all this smugly, thinking, 'I'll never become anyone's surety. I'm not a sluggard. I'm no con-man. So I've nothing to fear from God's displeasure.'

But these aren't the only things that displease the Lord. There are more general sins – and plenty of them. For his *six or seven* indicates this is not a complete list. There is no mention of sexual sin or stealing here. The meaning is 'there is a number of things the Lord hates; for example ...' All these are sins that harm others. So the con-man is not the only enemy of humanity. Any of us can hurt others. It is noticeable that the various organs with which the deceiver sins (vv. 12-14) are all present here: eyes, tongue, hands, feet and heart. Because we aren't inveterate liars doesn't mean we don't abuse these faculties. This particular pitfall then is one that lies within each one of us. It is a passage to be used for self-examination.

Are my eyes *haughty* (**v. 17a**)? Do I have bloated views of my own abilities and importance, and look with contempt on those who I think don't reach my standard?

Have I a lying tongue (**v. 17b**)? Do I falsify facts in order to maintain my reputation as a talented and important person, or to blacken another's character?

Do I have a cruel and vicious streak (**v. 17c**)? Even if I don't literally *shed innocent blood*, do I hurt people? If I am guilty of either or both of the first two sins, the likelihood is that I have caused someone pain. Pride, lying and murder go together, for they originate from Satan (John 8:44), into whose power our father Adam delivered us.

What goes on in my mind (*heart*)? How do I use my imagination (**v. 18a**)? Does my brain teem with endless schemes as to how I can get one-up on everyone else?

What makes *my* feet move quickly or press the accelerator to the floor? Where can I not wait to be (**v. 18b**)? The deceiver uses his feet to tap out a message (**v. 13b**). But feet can do worse things than that. They can take you to places and situations where you can do yourself and others immense harm. He has already warned us against patronizing the haunts of criminals (1:10-19) and the houses of prostitutes (5:1-14). Time would fail us to list all the possible opportunities for evil.

What sort of things do I say about other people (**v. 19a**)? This refers to a somewhat different form of lying from v. 17b, for the word means 'fictions, stories', rather than the falsification of facts. It refers not only to outright slander but malicious gossip. It asks us how much of our conversation is about other people, for if this is our chief subject we are almost sure to sin in this way. Our tales nearly always have a sting in them!

Finally, have I or do I ever set people against each other (**v. 19b**)? This is probably the climax of the passage, corresponding to what he has said about the ultimate outcome of the ways of the deceiver (**v. 14b**). But it is possible for any of us to do this. Christian people are particularly prone to it. Why are there so many sects, schisms and divisions among us? Did most not originate when someone sought a following for himself and separated others from their previous loyalty? This is certainly the view of James (4:1-3) and Paul (1 Cor. 3:1-4). If the gospel and our allegiance to it causes division, that is one thing (Luke 12:49-53), but if it is self-assertion, then it is sin. The first meaning of 'heretic' is 'one who divides' rather than 'one who is unorthodox'. It is possible to fall into unorthodoxy without causing division. It is equally possible, but far more common, to remain orthodox and foment a party spirit.

Questions
1. Where does lying originate and why is it universal? See Jeremiah 17:9, John 8:44.
2. What cure is there for this condition? See Ephesians 4:20-24.

C. CHAPTER 6:20-35. SECOND WARNING AGAINST SEXUAL TEMPTATION.

1. A Call to Attention (vv. 20-23).
Before launching into his further warning against sexual sin Solomon calls for **a renewed commitment to his teaching**. This takes us back to the beginning, to his opening appeal in 1:8-9, with which 6:20-21 is almost identical. Since then his appeals have tended to be simply 'listen ... pay attention'. Here he calls upon his hearers to make every effort to retain and practise their parental instruction, so that it will remain with them wherever they are, like a pendant *around the neck*.

In order to encourage this he goes far beyond 1:8-9 by making astonishing claims for his teaching (**vv. 22-23**). The promises made here clearly show he is equating his teaching with the very words of God. In fact the actual terms used are the Old Testament ones for the Word of God: *commands* – the MITZVOTH referring to God's 'commandments'; and *teaching* – the TORAH which represents the entire body of God's instruction of his covenant people through Moses. This explains his daring language, for *binding and fastening* are what Moses called on Israel to do with the Law code God dictated to him on Sinai (Deut. 6:6-9). That passage includes the injunction, 'Impress them on your children'. This is what Solomon is doing, and encouraging all godly parents to do.

So what Solomon claims to be doing here is teaching his children the Word of God, not expressing his own views on education. This is why he can speak with such authority, not only in commanding obedience but in making promises (**vv. 22-23**). He says of his words what God elsewhere said of his: they are a *lamp* and a *light* (Ps. 119:105), that is, they *correct* what is wrong and train (*discipline*) in the way that is right, so that a child walks in that *way* which alone can be called *life*, the way which God blesses with longevity and prosperity.

The total care the Word affords is shown in the promises of **verse 22**. *Walk* (or 'go') ... *sleep* ... *awake* cover our day-by-day living. Life is made up of *going* here and there by day, *sleeping* by night, and the *waking up* which is something between the two. At all times his words are a guide and protector, in fact a companion, who is always speaking to you, pointing you in the right direction, warning you off false trails and constantly encouraging and teaching you. Even in your unconscious moments the words are at work, for they are the words of the God who never sleeps, but ever remains near, alert and active (Ps. 121, 1 Thess. 5:10).

In the light of such promises, who can refuse the commitment Solomon calls for here? Yet all this is a prelude to a further lesson on the dangers of sinful sex. For it is in this area that we are all at our weakest. This instinct is as old and basic as hunger and thirst. It was inbuilt to induce us to fulfil the mandate to increase the human race. But like every other instinct it suffered in the Fall. So it is just as open to abuse, but with consequences more disastrous than most other basic instincts, hence Solomon's somewhat lengthy treatment of the subject.

The passage on sexual sin and the Word of God begins with a promise and a command (**vv. 24-25**). **Verse 24**, the promise, is a continuation of the sentence which set forth the Word as a guide to the long and good life. The same Word will enable you to avoid this dread pitfall: *keeping you from the immoral woman* (and) *the wayward wife*. There are two types of promiscuous woman in view here (see **v. 26**): *the prostitute*, who is only interested in obtaining money for her favours; and the *adulteress*, who is married (**vv. 29, 34**) but is bored and unsatisfied in her marriage.

2. How the Word keeps the Youth or Man from this Sin (vv. 24-35).

(a) *It identifies this type of woman (vv. 24-25)* so that the inexperienced know when they are in her company and thus in danger. She can be identified in the following ways.

(i) *by the way she speaks* – in a sweet voice and with flattering words (**v. 24**, cf.5:3). The youth who is being scolded by his mother (or perhaps the married man who is nagged by his wife!) is vulnerable here and needs this discernment.

(ii) *by the way she flaunts her sexuality*, making you admire her *beauty* (**v. 25a**), with clothes, cosmetics and suggestive movements of the body, all designed to arouse *lust*. Jesus was to speak of lust as equivalent to adultery (Matt. 5:28), but in the Old Testament it was simply the step which led to the actual deed.

(iii) *by the way she makes eyes at the one she seeks to capture* (**v. 25b**). The picture of the con-man showed us how much can be said without speaking (v. 13), true too of the prostitute's body language.

So powerful is the attraction that Solomon has to change quickly from the language of promise to that of command: *do not*. This is no time for polite speech. When someone is within an ace of death you don't stand on ceremony.

(b) *It points out the dire consequences of falling prey to such a person (vv. 26-35)*.

(i) *Poverty (v. 26a)*. The financial cost of sexual sin has already been mentioned in 5:10. This goes further, for it is not just that riches are exhausted but that nothing is left for bare necessities. The NIV may be too generous in leaving him with a loaf of bread, for the word is 'round', which may be a small roll or just a slice of bread! We feed this lust at the cost of starving our stomach.

(ii) *Misery (v. 26b)*. This gives a picture of one who is reduced to the status of victim, preyed upon by an evil woman. This sad state has already been mentioned in connection with one who puts up security (vv. 2, 5). Immorality too can deprive someone of their freedom.

At this point Solomon seems to anticipate objections from his hearers: 'Isn't this over-reacting to what is normal and natural? Everyone must sow his wild oats'. For he suddenly rounds on us and fires two questions (**vv. 27-28**). In fact he is rhetorically answering our objections by telling us we are playing with fire. Sexual lust is like fire and if you indulge it every time it is aroused you are just fuelling the flames. If you take fire in your arms it will burn your clothes (**v. 27**). If you embrace a promiscuous woman she will set your lust aflame and you won't be able to quench it.

His second question (**v. 28**) takes us a stage further. Walking barefoot on burning coals will do more than set light to your clothes, it will burn your flesh and leave a permanent mark like a brand. This *walking* indicates that resorting to the prostitute or adulteress has now become a habit. So you become 'branded' as a womanizer, you have let yourself become her prey. This is probably what *punishment* (**v. 29**) refers to, rather than the death penalty for adultery prescribed under the Law (Deut. 22:22).

(iii) *Shame and disgrace (vv. 30-32)*. The scorch marks or branding of the womanizer are there for all to see – and despise. Such a one is lower than a thief who steals not out of greed but desperate need (**v. 30**). It is true he has broken the law and must pay his debt to it, even if he has to sell all his possessions to do so (**v. 31**). But this only makes him more the object of pity to society. The adulterer, however, is in a different category. As Matthew Henry says, he is driven 'not by want but wantonness'. Since the same pleasure is available in lawful marriage, resorting to prostitutes is unnecessary (5:15-20). His problem is 'not lack of bread but of understanding' (Bridges). He has rejected the arguments of his parents and teachers. He is therefore the victim, not of adverse circumstances, but of his own utter folly and depravity. He *destroys himself* (**v. 32**) – not only his substance and independence but his reputation.

(iv) *Vengeance (vv. 33-35).* This section applies to adultery rather than prostitution, for the woman's husband now comes on to the scene. The Law of Moses was severe on adultery and inflicted the death penalty by stoning (Deut. 22:22). No doubt this passage depicts the guilty woman's husband insisting that the full weight of the Law be visited on the couple. Possibly he is a witness and 'casts the first stone' (Deut. 17:7). What Solomon brings out is the implacable jealousy of the wronged husband, who shows no mercy and accepts no compensation.

The Gospel has done away with such punishments for adultery, but even that cannot guarantee that the offender won't feel the full effect of jealousy in some other way. Jealousy leads people to take the law into their own hands and sometimes do unspeakable things, which is probably why the Mosaic law brought it under control by means of the ceremony of Numbers 5. As Solomon himself wrote, 'Love is strong as death and jealousy cruel as the grave' (Song 8:6). At the very least the offender is going to make an enemy of the woman's husband, adding to the other problems he has already brought on himself.

Question
While we cannot expect the state to punish sexual sin as Israel did, do you think our society takes it seriously enough in comparison with such things as robbery and violence? Why do you think this is?

D. Chapter 7: Third Warning Against Sexual Temptation.

Almost one third of the first nine chapters of PROVERBS is devoted to the subject of sex. In a time when alcohol and drugs were not in plentiful supply and currency was still a thing of the future, promiscuity was perhaps the greatest danger confronting the growing youth. Solomon did not write about it because he secretly enjoyed doing so. He had one aim in view, as he repeatedly tells us: 'to save (his sons) from the adulteress' (2:16), 'to keep (them) from the immoral woman' (6:24). The best way to do this was to teach and apply the Word of God.

Three thousand years later there are many other and arguably worse dangers facing young people. Yet they still need to be taught and warned about this one. Possibly they need it even more since the seriousness of immorality in general has been demoted. It is now chastity that is despised. Nor can sexual sin be isolated from other dangers lying before the rising generation. Drugs, drink, easy money and promiscuity are all part of a great sin syndrome. So that while its pleasures seem unrivalled and innocuous, the miserable consequences are probably even worse than those against which Solomon warned his sons. The greater part of this chapter recounts an actual incident of seduction, but is preceded by an introductory call to heed these words as those of God, and a closing exhortation to take them to heart.

1. Introductory Call (vv. 1-5).

Solomon's remedy for promiscuity is to know and obey the Word of God. However out-dated and simplistic this may seem, the same is true in our age, where those being advocated – sex education, contraception, free love, etc. – have all failed. As in the previous warning (6:20-23), he equates his instructions with those of God himself. He uses the same terms for the instructions themselves: *words ... commands ... teachings* (**vv. 1-2**); he uses the same metaphors for our response (**v. 3**, cf. Deut. 6:6); and he gives them the same authority: *keep ... store ... bind ... guard*. If you keep them, they will keep you from the arms of the immoral woman (**v. 5**). All this he presses on us in a series of vivid comparisons.

(a) *Keep* them as you would treasure (**v. 1** – *store*).

(b) *Keep* them as you would your life (**v. 2a**). Obedience to God's Word is a matter of life, both its length and quality (4:20-23).

(c) *Keep* them as you would the tenderest part of your anatomy (**v. 2b**), such as the pupil of the eye, which is sensitive to the slightest speck. We are to God as *the apple of his eye* (Deut. 32:10, Ps. 17:8, Zech. 2:8), so let his words be thus to us.

(d) *Keep* them as you would something precious to you personally, **v. 3a**, such as the ring on your finger, which may have monetary value, and will certainly have sentimental value.

(e) *Keep* them as you would those whom you are most fond of, like the friends whose names you cherish in *your heart* (**v. 3b**).

(f) *Keep* them as you would the affection of a close relative (**v. 4**). This means cultivating familiarity and intimacy with the Word, as if it were speaking personally to you (cf. 1:20f, 3:13-18). Keep his words like this and they will keep you from dangerous liaisons. Lest that seem abstract and theoretical he makes it real and dramatic by relating a personal observation.

2. The Story of a Seduction (vv. 6-23).

To prove what he has just been saying Solomon now recounts a real life situation to show what may happen to those who do not *keep his words*. To do this he is as explicit as possible short of pornography. This is characteristic of Scripture – it shows the reality of sin in such a way as to alarm rather than attract us. Although he describes it as if he personally witnessed it (**v. 6**), we can't be certain that Solomon's palace overlooked the main street, and he may therefore be describing a typical rather than actual case. It is interesting to compare this with what his father David saw from his house-top and subsequently did about it (2 Sam. 11)! It is possible to observe or consider acts of sin as a teacher not a voyeur. Those who are responsible for others, especially for the young, need to know what goes on among them so that they can teach them what they need to know. They will not be defiled but rather moved to compassion and indignation, as Solomon was. Jesus socialized with 'sinners' (Matt. 9:10f, Luke 15:2, 19:7) and became known as their 'friend' (Matt. 11:19).

Scene 1: The Youth (vv. 6-9).

His looking *through the lattice* of his window suggests the blind was down and he was peering through the slats in order to see without being seen. There he notices (**v. 7**) a group of untaught

(*simple*, see 1:4, 22) youths in the main street or square chatting
and going nowhere in particular, just as we would find in any
town centre today. Perhaps they are talking about the woman
who features in the story, or women like her. He notices one
of them, perhaps a new member of the gang, who had either
never been warned against such things or if he had been taught
them he had not kept them, for he *lacked understanding*. This
one seems to detach himself from the others (**v. 8**) and start
walking up and down the street passing the corner where her
house was situated. It was *twilight* (v. 9) and since that is a
very brief period in the orient it quickly grew quite dark.

So here are most of the things against which Solomon had
been warning his *sons* in these first seven chapters: the wrong
company (1:10ff), idleness (6:6-10), places where temptation
lurks (5:8), and above all not heeding the teaching of parents
(4:1, 10; 5:1, 7; 6:20-22 cf. vv. 1-5). This scenario has all the
ingredients of a major moral disaster: the wrong person among
the wrong company in the wrong place at the wrong time.

Scene 2: The Woman (vv. 10-12).

Verse 10 begins in the Hebrew with 'look', for Solomon is
trying to get us to visualize the incident. Here he wants us to
form a picture of the type of woman who spells danger. She
may not be a prostitute but a married woman perhaps tired
of her husband or just plain promiscuous ('wayward', 6:24).
But you would think she was a prostitute from the way she
was 'dressed to kill'. The key to this whole incident lies in
the phrase *crafty intent* (lit. 'guarded heart'). It means she is
quite insincere in all she is going to do with this youth. She
does not feel for him what she appears to with her flattering
words and her kisses. The foolish youth is led to believe she is
in love with him, which makes him fall in love with her. But
it's all an act.

What she is really like is now revealed. She is all mouth
– plenty to say and in a *loud* voice for everyone to hear
(**v. 11**). She is quite unashamed of her (presumably) lewd
conversation. For she is self-willed (*defiant*), governed not by
principles but lusts. She is restless and finds no pleasure in
domesticity. She is always on show (**v. 12**), either out in her

front garden, walking the *streets* or standing at the *corners*. It is probably here she encounters the youth as he parades up and down (v. 8).

Scene 3: The Invitation (vv. 13-20).

Now that he has introduced the characters in his little play, Solomon comes to the drama itself. And how dramatically it begins (**v. 13**)! Before saying a word she *grabs hold of him* ('seizes' in the Hebrew) and *kisses* him as if they were acknowledged lovers. Although this takes place in the public street she is not in the least embarrassed. In fact she becomes even bolder as she outlines her plan to the youth.

First comes the invitation to supper, **verse 14**. There may be no more significance than this in the *fellowship* (or peace) *offerings*. These were made as a special thanksgiving usually for a personal reason (Lev. 3). She had made a *vow* to offer these for some unknown cause and had now performed it (or so she says). With the *fellowship offering* a substantial portion of the meat could be brought home but must be consumed the same day. She was thus offering him a share in her celebratory and substantial feast. Some think she says this to give an appearance of piety and this may be so. Certainly it indicates that she was unlikely to be a prostitute and was thought to be a respectable married woman.

Her claim (**v. 15**) is that she had *come out* purposely to *look for* him and invite him to join her. By now he must have been feeling he was someone really special, at least to her. Normally what was to follow the supper would be left unspoken, as in, 'Will you come in for a coffee?' This one is so brazen-faced she spells it all out, perhaps because this is the youth's first experience and he doesn't realize the full nature of the invitation. So from the dining room she proceeds to describe the bed-room (**v. 16**). Her 'bed-stead' (as the word means) is well upholstered with soft cushions, a delightful prospect in itself if he were from an ordinary house where 'bed' meant a few rushes on the floor and a cloak for a covering.

But her *coverings* are of the finest linen from Egypt, expensive and beautiful, for her *husband* appears to be a prosperous merchant, away at the moment on a business trip (**vv. 19-20**).

With these their two bodies will be covered as they lie together. Nor is this all – the sense of smell will be gratified with exotic perfumes from eastern lands like Persia and India (**v. 17**) in which her husband possibly traded. These would help arouse the senses and prepare for what is to follow.

Only one more sensual pleasure remained and this would be the climax of the evening – the *love*-making (**v. 18**). Even this she describes metaphorically as *drinking our fill of love*, getting drunk on *love*. But when she says, 'We've got all night to enjoy it' the youth is a little alarmed. Won't her husband return and find them together? She hastily reassures him (**vv. 19-20**). He is far away, probably on business, hence the reference to his full purse, and won't be back for a fortnight. In any case she cares little for him; the NIV is generous in representing her as saying *my husband*, for the word is just 'the man'. She recognizes no bond between them of law or love. So what remains to be said? If anyone had 'an offer he can't refuse' this was it!

Scene 4: The Consent (vv. 21-23).

Verse 21 suggests the youth's fears and scruples have not been assuaged by the plausible case she has just put forward. If this was his first offer of these delights he is probably being held back by conscience, especially if he has been taught on the lines on which Solomon was teaching his sons. It takes time to counteract this, but she is patient. We see him 'gradually yielding' (as the word for *led astray* suggests) and finally 'conquered' (*seduced*, NIV). Now that the mind has consented the rest follows quickly: *all at once he followed her* (**v. 22**). Avoiding the lurid details Solomon resorts to illustrations, very similar to those he used of the destiny of one who agrees to become a surety (6:1-5). For consent to adultery is falling into a trap unwittingly *like an ox* led not to the pasture he expects but the *slaughter*-house.

We are told that the text of **verse 22c** is corrupt, so that many modern translations emend it to fit the hunting similes in this and the next verse, and to lead on to the *arrow piercing the liver* which certainly sounds like stag hunting. If the Hebrew is taken as it stands it reads literally 'as one chained to the chastisement of a fool'. It depicts the youth following the woman as a fool being led in chains to his punishment, oblivious of what lies ahead of him *until* (**v. 23**) death strikes. This creates a problem with *an arrow pierces his liver*, which would not be the way of inflicting capital punishment even on a fool! So if we take this reading it seems Solomon was mixing his metaphors!

The point is that when the pleasure is over it has to be paid for, 'the wages of sin'. Under the Mosaic law this could be death. But bearing in mind 6:32-35 there is the death of self-respect and reputation apart from any physical or financial consequences. His final simile (**v. 23b**) is apt: the bird swoops on the bait ahead of his competitors, but instead of food death awaits him there. So the youth, having consented, wastes no time, but hurries into the house, hoping he won't be seen (v. 22). The house is the trap which will *cost him his life*. End of story.

3. Concluding Exhortation (vv. 24-27).

Now then (**v. 24**) calls us back from the street to the school-room. This story has not been told for amusement but instruction and warning. So our interest must not flag as the moral is drawn. Solomon tells us to make careful note of the lessons to learn.

(a) *To guard our mind (heart, v. 25a)*, for it is in the imagination and senses that the way into sin begins. We need to avoid whatever tends to awaken sinful fantasies.

(b) *To continue in the ways we have been taught* and not *stray from them* (*v. 25b*). Stray is the word used of the adulterous wife in Numbers 5:12 and so is particularly appropriate here. 'Don't follow her who is astray or you will go astray too.'

(c) *To take note of those who have come to ruin in this way* (*v. 26*). The *victims* of this sin are not only *many* but *mighty*. Perhaps he has in mind Samson with whom a woman succeeded where the armies of the Philistines failed, or even David his father, who refused the offer to go and conquer his enemies, remained at home and was defeated by his own lust (2 Sam. 11). Even Christians are weak and vulnerable here. We who are 'raised with Christ' and whose 'life is hidden with Christ in God' need to be warned to 'put to death whatever belongs to your earthly nature: sexual immorality, impurity, lust, evil desires and greed' (Col. 3:1-5).

(d) *To see sexual sin as it really is (v. 27, see 2:18).* How this verse contrasts with the woman's own picture of her house (vv. 14-17)! What she said was only part of the truth; it stopped before the final outcome. The door to her house leads ultimately to SHEOL, *death* in the sense already described (v. 23). The *chambers* in which the pleasures of the flesh are enjoyed are like tombs, dark and cold to the spirit, far from the warmth of the grace of God. Enjoyable as it was at the time, was it worth it?

We may wonder why Solomon always casts the female as the predator in sexual sin and the male as the victim. Surely experience teaches us that the truth is the reverse and it is more often the man that preys on the woman? Granted it takes two to tango, which usually makes the running? Granted too that prostitution is largely a female occupation and such women are on the look-out for clients, this profession would not exist were there not a demand from the male population for it. So was Solomon some sort of male chauvinist?

The answer lies in the fact that the book represents Solomon instructing his 'sons'. Under the Old Covenant it was the education of sons that was all important. They would take over not only the father's business, but leadership in the family and possibly the town or even the nation. They would be the ones who would retain and pass on the family name, whereas daughters would change theirs by marriage. It was essential for boys to be trained for these tasks and not ruin them by sinful liaisons. No doubt daughters received moral instruction, but they had far less freedom and contact with the world outside the home than sons and were less likely to stray into bad company.

Under the new covenant there is a greater equalizing of the sexes as regards privileges, education, freedom and responsibility. So what has been addressed here to sons may be taken to heart by girls and women, and taught to daughters as well as sons, suitably adapted.

Meditate on the spiritual application of this teaching: the use of married love as a picture of the relationship between God and his people in both Testaments, e.g. Isaiah 62:4f, Ephesians 5:22-32; and conversely unfaithfulness to God as adultery, e.g. Hosea 1:2, 2 Corinthians 11:2f, James 4:4.

6
Fifth Benefit: Glory
(Proverbs 8)

Here Solomon breaks off from speaking wise things to his sons or pupils and makes Wisdom into a person, representing *her* as personally addressing, not just his own family, or even the Jewish nation, but *all mankind* (v. 4). The reason he depicts Wisdom as a woman here is to contrast her with the prostitute or adulteress who has come to take possession of the body and soul of a youth (ch.7). Now we see she has a rival who offers real and lasting pleasure which leads to *life*. We have already heard this lady speak in 1:20-33, a passage which followed the enticement of the bad men of 1:10-19. Here she is competing with a bad woman who later becomes 'the woman Folly' in 9:13-18.

The main point, however, is not who is speaking but what is being said. This is a GLORIFICATION of the wisdom Solomon is teaching and offering, both to his hearers and to us. To encourage us to receive it we need to appreciate something of the greatness and value of Wisdom. Here is a comprehensive summary of the wisdom Solomon is imparting in his book, what we might call a eulogy of Wisdom. It rises from the initial appeal to a glorious climax in verses 22-31, and ends with the call for response (vv. 32-36).

A. WHERE WISDOM IS TO BE FOUND (vv. 1-3).
'Where can wisdom be found?' asks Job in 28:12. The answer of this chapter is **where she can be heard**. She *calls out* and *raises her voice* (**v. 1**); she draws as much attention to herself as possible. God wants the way to goodness and happiness

to be known, not hidden. Whereas the wisdom of man, his philosophy and religion, tends to circulate among scholars and priests, God's wisdom is available to the common people. This is shown here by representing her as speaking from the high places of the city, where she could be seen and heard (**v. 2a**). In Jerusalem this would be the hills on which it was built, especially Zion and Moriah; in Greek cities it would be the acropolis. Failing a city having *heights* she would choose the crossroads (**v. 2b**) because they would be more crowded, as would also the *city gates* (**v. 3**), not only because people entered and left there, but business was conducted and official proclamations were made. If the harlot walks the streets offering herself (7:11-12), Wisdom must do likewise or she will lose souls to her rival. God wants his 'ways to be made known on the earth' (Ps. 67:2).

B. To whom Wisdom speaks (vv. 4-5).

The reason Wisdom makes such a public display of herself is that she wants all to hear: people of all ages and classes, *mankind* generally (**v. 4**); people of all kinds, especially the *simple* (the untaught, unsophisticated) and the *foolish*, who turn their backs on wise teaching through indolence or love of pleasure (**v. 5**). These are the very terms with which the book began (1:4), showing that Solomon is continuing his task of educating the young, albeit in a different way. For he is mindful of the harlot with her universal appeal. But Lady Wisdom has something better to offer.

Compare this passage with Christ's great commission (Matt. 28:19f) and those who chiefly responded to the gospel (1 Cor. 1:26-29).

C. What Wisdom has to say (vv. 6-11).

If Wisdom is to outbid the immoral woman she must have equally good or even better publicity. Here is her shop-window display.

1. Verse 6a: Things that are noble, *worthy* of princes, as the term means. She is like Paul who counsels us to think about 'whatever is noble, etc.' in Phil. 4:8. The reason they are 'noble' is that they are *right* (**v. 6b**), which is explained in what follows.

2. Verse 7: Things that are *true*, by which is meant, not factual truth, for the adulteress speaks this: her description and invitation of 7:14-20 are not a string of lies. This is where the power of sexual sin lies – it does offer people what they crave and enjoy. Rather this means moral truth, which is why its opposite is *wickedness* not falsehood. This is explained in **verse 8**, where *just* is literally 'in righteousness', meaning that she seeks to lead people in the right way, not the *crooked* or *perverse* way, the way which is devious and involves all sorts of tricks and traps. The righteousness is also seen in the way these truths are delivered (**v. 9**) – 'straightforwardly' (*right*). They will not mislead or take you into sin, for they are *faultless* or 'even', so that you won't stumble.

3. Verses 10-11: Things that are enriching. They make you richer even than pure *silver* and solid *gold* do (**v. 10**) or than the most *precious* stones or anything else of high value. Earlier the point was made that following wisdom promotes wealth (3:1, 2, 16). Here it is said she transcends it (cf. 3:15-17), for she gives what is better than wealth. This is not to disparage wealth but to get it into perspective. Let those with wealth value wisdom more highly; let those without it know they can be rich in wisdom (James. 1:9-11).

Compare Lady Wisdom's offer with that of the adulteress (7:14-21).

D. What Wisdom cultivates (vv. 12-13).

As she grows in confidence Wisdom begins to speak more imperiously. She speaks of her companion (**v. 12a**) and her acquisitions (**v. 12b**); those who have her will share in these.

1. Prudence, knowledge and discretion (v. 12). These are all terms from the introduction (1:4) where we noted that *prudence* is the term describing the serpent in Gen. 3:1 (KJV 'subtle', NIV 'crafty'), the quality by which he contrived the fall of Adam and Eve. But the word itself means something good – 'shrewdness', which Jesus said believers need in order to get by in this world of serpents and clever devils: Matt. 10:16,

Luke 16:8. Where it is possessed and used rightly its fruits are *knowledge* (understanding) and *discretion* (the ability to make wise decisions and good plans). If Adam and Eve had used it against the serpent we would not be in the mess we are.

2. Godliness (v. 13) – *to fear the Lord*, which the introduction (1:7) put down as the first and principal fruit of wisdom. This balances verse 12's commendation of 'shrewdness', showing how this can be prevented from degenerating into craftiness by developing faith, love and obedience towards God, which is what *fear* means. The imperious language continues with *I hate* ... which means that those who possess me (Wisdom) also *hate evil*. 'Wisdom dwells with prudence but cannot dwell with evil' (Bridges). The particular form of evil specified here is pride. Christ, the embodiment of wisdom was 'gentle and humble in heart' (Matt. 11:29) and roused to indignation by nothing more than manifestations of pride, whether in his own disciples (Matt. 20:20-28) or the Jewish leaders (Matt. 23). But pride never remains just an attitude of mind; it breeds *evil behaviour and perverse speech*. The proud are always selfish, which makes many of them greedy and cruel, uttering harsh words and performing inconsiderate actions.

Question
Turn to James 3:13-18. Where does James confirm the points made in these verses (12-13) and where does he go further?

E. How mighty Wisdom is (vv. 14-16).
Because wisdom encourages humility and opposes pride doesn't mean that the wise are wimps. In fact they are found in powerful positions. For wisdom possesses the qualities necessary for government: *counsel, sound judgment and understanding* (**v. 14**), not to speak of *power* itself. All who rule justly do so through the heavenly wisdom given them (**vv. 15-16**). This is obvious where there are **godly rulers**. They will be concerned to do the will of God and govern justly. They will recognize their lack of wisdom, and pray to God for it (as Solomon himself did, 1 Kings 3:7-9). They may make mistakes but will try to follow those policies which promote peace and prosperity. While they will not legislate for one particular creed, their style of government will

produce the climate in which the gospel can spread. It is on such lines that Paul exhorts us to pray for rulers (1 Tim. 2:1-6).

But what of **ungodly rulers** or those who take power for their own ends or those of a particular party or class? Since God has placed them in office to maintain law and order (Rom. 13:1-4) they will through his 'common grace' have a sense of responsibility to the whole nation. Whatever kind of people they are by nature or whatever their political philosophy or religion, they will find their best policy is justice and the promotion of good. However, this will not always happen. Love of power for its own sake can produce megalomaniacs who inflict great suffering on their people. God may give a nation up to such monsters for a period of time, possibly as a judgment (e.g. Hosea. 13:11). But he who placed them there can and often does remove them (Ps. 75:7).

Question
Does this help you to understand better the overthrow of many tyrannical governments in recent years? Does it guide and encourage you to pray for those tyrants that are still in power?

F. What rewards Wisdom bestows (vv. 17-21).
Wisdom's rivalry with the immoral woman has not been lost sight of in considering government. Many an otherwise good ruler has been corrupted by an evil consort. Wisdom is the best consort for a ruler to have. But now she moves out of the throne room back among the common people and speaks of her personal rewards. This develops 'C' (vv. 6-11), showing the ways in which her noble and true counsels bring *enrichment*, unlike adultery.

1. A loving intimacy which is true and sincere (v. 17), unlike that pretended love of the harlot which is mere blandishments (7:13). This love is available to all and only has to be asked for. Here 'Wisdom' becomes virtually identical with the God who is wisdom. Just as in us wisdom means trust, love and obedience (*the fear of the Lord*), so in God it means personal union and communion with us, supremely realized in Christ (John 14:21).

2. Prosperity (v. 18), or at least sufficiency, for 'enough is as good as a feast'. Wealth that is not needed is like food – it goes bad on us. But Wisdom's wealth never does this – it is *enduring*, a word that looks backwards rather than forwards. Wisdom has been there from eternity (as we are about to see in verses 22-26) and is like wine long stored. Wisdom is not a glamorous girl but a venerable lady. It is she who has a right to give this wealth, for *with me* has the sense of 'it is mine to bestow'. So she can say that those who *find me* have it.

3. Fruitfulness (v. 19). This shows that we are to see Wisdom not just as a store to draw on but as living and growing, venerable but fresh. The wise are like trees which *yield* a crop of fruit. Wisdom regenerates our nature so that we ourselves become like her. This is why she is better than the most solid gold and the purest silver. For these cannot buy us a new nature.

4. A sense of direction (v. 20). Wisdom knows where she is going and keeps on that way, which is the meaning of *walk in the way*. That way is *righteousness*, deliberately chosen and firmly followed. Those who have wisdom have a clear grasp of what is right and do it unwaveringly, cf. 3:5f.

5. A substantial inheritance (v. 21). *Bestow* means 'cause to inherit', for these riches are ours, not as a gift nor as wages, but of right. What could be more secure? This is why it *makes their treasuries full*, for these riches are not subject to the fluctuations of the market, but never lose their value.

Compare these rewards of Lady Wisdom with the consequences of enjoying the harlot's pleasures (7:22-27).

G. What authority Wisdom has (vv. 22-31).

This is the glorious climax of the chapter, showing us why Wisdom is able to speak with such conviction about her rightness and make such high claims and lavish promises. It is tempting to see Wisdom here as Christ in Person. The older commentators don't hesitate and Charles Bridges goes so far as to say, 'It must be a perverted imagination that can suppose an attribute here.'

At the risk of being charged with 'a perverted imagination' I cannot go all the way with this. Of course with hindsight it seems to fit Christ like a glove. But Solomon's use of QANA in verse 22 makes it unlikely he was referring to Christ. NIV translates QANA *brought forth*, the word used by Eve on the birth of Cain (Gen. 4:1), a strong word – 'acquire', breathing a sense of achievement. This is why KJV translates it 'possessed', the idea being that wisdom is something that **belongs** to God and comes to birth in creation. It is best to see it in the same way as we saw 3:19f, rather than refer it to Christ. Arians (the ancestors of Jehovah Witnesses) used it to prove Christ had an origin in time. Solomon is appealing to his sons to heed his teaching because it is identical to the Wisdom that is in God himself and that marks everything God ever did or said. If this is so they and we must take it seriously. Under the Old Covenant it came through the Law and its teachers: parents, priests and prophets. This does not mean Christ has no place here, for under the New Covenant Wisdom is not merely taught by but embodied in Christ, which is why this chapter brings Christ to our minds. But basically it is calling on believers under both covenants to receive the words of Wisdom, because this Wisdom is not human but that of God himself. This is what he now proceeds to prove from three considerations.

1. Wisdom existed in eternity (vv. 22-26).

The first thing he establishes is that there was wisdom before there was anything else (**v. 22**). Wisdom was 'set up' (*appointed*) from eternity (**v. 23**) and is thus the supreme agent in everything that was done subsequently. This is simply a poetic way of describing God as 'the only wise God'. The poetry continues in **verses 24-26** by alluding to the very first works we know of, as recorded in Genesis 1: the seas and rivers, the mountains and hills, the habitable parts of *the earth* and the vast uninhabitable parts (*its fields*), such as deserts, steppes, bush, prairies and islands. **Verse 26b** goes to the extent of referring to the very first speck of matter ever made (*dust*). Before any of this existed God was there, and God is eternally wise. It is from that eternal wisdom that the teaching of PROVERBS comes. What greater incentive to heed it could there be? What more justifiable claim to its authority?

2. Wisdom was supreme in creation (vv. 27-30a).

Since God was wise **before** creation, he was wise **in** creation. This has already been said in 3:19f. These verses also closely follow Gen. 1, but from the standpoint of Wisdom. God was wise on the first day when he made *the heavens* (**v. 27a**); he was wise on the second day when he separated the water on the earth from that above it (**vv. 27b-28**); he was wise on the third day when he separated the water from the dry land (**v. 29**), so that the earth could produce vegetation and be a suitable dwelling-place for his creatures. He could have gone on in this way through the creation week, but he has made his point and cuts it short by calling Wisdom the *craftsman* (or 'architect') *at his side* (**v. 30a**). It is all a poetic way of saying 'God was wise in creation'. Look at the world around, beneath and above you! Does it not breathe wisdom? It is the same wisdom that speaks to you in the pages of PROVERBS. Where will you find better?

3. Wisdom made creation enjoyable (vv. 30b-31).

Here is the wise God delighting in creation, pleased with the results. Here is God on the sixth day standing back to survey his handiwork and saying, 'Very good' (Gen. 1:31) and 'blessing the seventh day' because he had done a good job well. This spirit of delight we get in the psalms, such as 104, which goes through the parts of creation with a great sense of joy, saying, for example, 'How many are your works, O Lord! ... the earth is full of your creatures. There is (this) ... and there is (that) ... look at (these)!' (Ps. 104:24-26). The hymn of creation that God sang to Job is in the same spirit (Job 38, 39). It begins in an ecstasy of wonder with the words, 'the morning stars sang together and all the angels shouted for joy' (38:7).

Question
Does this teaching help you as a Christian to take a positive view of the created world and throw light on such passages as 1 Timothy 4:4f, 6:17?

H. THE RESPONSE WISDOM CALLS FOR (vv. 32-36).

Solomon begins here by reverting to the familiar way of speaking in his own name (**v. 32f**), then goes back to personifying Wisdom (**vv. 34-36**). This shows there is no real difference between what he says and what Wisdom says. The personification is only to make his words more real and personal, as if coming direct from God without the middleman. Arising out of the previous passage is the stress on the happiness that comes to those who listen to the voice of Wisdom (**v. 32b, v. 34a**). Such can share God's own joy (**vv. 30b-31**). This happiness is so superlative he calls it *life*, in other words the enjoyment of the divine *favour* (**v. 35**). To live under the perpetual smile of God, that is life indeed (Ps. 16:11).

To experience this requires more than *listening* (**vv. 32f**). It must be deliberately retained – *keep* it. *Ignore* (**v. 33**) has the sense of 'letting it blow away', like a kite you've let slip from your grasp. It also deserves a serious attitude – *watching daily at my doors* (**v. 34**). Here is the devoted servant waiting for the master to come out with his instructions for the day; or the citizen expecting an important announcement from the King's chamber; or the beggar waiting for the rich man's servant to throw out some scraps for him to feed on. The intensity of concentration on the part of such is what we need in relation to the wise sayings of the Word of God.

But what if we don't do this? This must be mentioned, as it has already been in 1:22-32. The prospect is bleak indeed (**v. 36**). For as finding Wisdom is life, so failing to find it is *death* – a life without the joy of God's favour, ending in the darkness of the grave and the bleakness of an eternity apart from God. For this we have only ourselves to blame. *Fails to find* is literally 'missing the target' by firing in the wrong direction or with the wrong range. It is the word used in Old and New Testaments for 'sin', in the sense of '**falling short** of the glory of God' (Rom. 3:23), not attaining the standard he has set for us. Since the failure is ours we *harm* ourselves and our self-inflicted wound can be fatal (*death*).

Question
In what way is 1 John 5:11f our equivalent to verses 35f?

7

Sixth Benefit: Invitation
(Proverbs 9)

In chapter 8 Wisdom was allowed to speak for herself. How poignantly and powerfully she moved us to seek her! Towards the end she pictured her seekers as people waiting at a house for the doors to open (v. 34). Now she takes us round the house and invites us in. But her rival, the adulteress, has not given up, and in verses 13-18 endeavours to copy-cat Lady Wisdom by displaying her attractions. She too has a house.

A. LADY WISDOM INVITES US TO SHARE HER GLORIES (vv. 1-6).

In doing this she is deliberately competing with the adulteress in bidding for our affections.

1. Does the adulteress have a **nicely-furnished house** (7:16f)? Wisdom has something better, a palace or temple (v. 1), with *pillars*, like Solomon's temple (1 Kings 10:12) and palace (1 Kings 7:2). Pillars give a building strength and beauty. So will the word of the wise God give us **strength**, not sap our energy as adultery does (5:11). Its **beauty** is real and unfading, unlike the prostitute's glamour, dependent on cosmetics and clothes (7:10). *Seven* is no doubt symbolic of completeness and perfection: God's word is sufficient because it comes from the only wise God. It is a home where everything we need is supplied.

2. Does the harlot lay on **a feast** with which to regale her client before the love-making (7:14)? Wisdom provides a meal both nourishing and luxurious (**v. 2**). Indeed, if the

harlot's meat was from the fellowship offering she had made, Wisdom's was better. The words *prepared her meat* are literally 'slaughtered her slaughter'. This suggests not the small animals brought by an individual in payment of a vow (7:14), but the great ox offered for the whole nation (Lev. 4:13f). The *mixed wine* had spices added to it, enriching its substance and sweetening its flavour.

Prophecy spoke of the Messianic kingdom in terms of a feast (Isa. 25:6, cf. Ps. 23:5, Luke 14:15). Jesus used this idea in his parables; indeed the parable of the Wedding Banquet (Matt. 22:1-14) is similar to this passage, and in it Jesus made 'oxen and fat cattle' the main course. This depicts nothing less than our personal intimate fellowship with Jesus through faith (Rev. 3:20). Indeed this is the whole meaning of the house of Wisdom in our passage. A man builds or buys a house in order to live there with his chosen bride and enjoy her company. In giving us his wise Word, God has provided a way by which we can 'enjoy him for ever'. The harlot will give us a night or two; Jesus will marry us and we 'shall dwell in the house of the Lord for ever' (Ps. 23:6), and there we shall feast with him (Rev. 19:9, 21:2f).

3. Does the adulteress **go out** into the street and **accost** the first youth fool enough to go with her (7:10-23)? Wisdom sends her maid-servants to the top of the hill (**v. 3**) so that everyone may hear her invitation, which is addressed to *all* (**v. 4**). For Wisdom has room for as many as want to come, food and drink sufficient for all her guests (**v. 5**). It is here that Jesus's parable comes closest to this passage, for it is mainly about the invitation to the feast and the welcome given even to those at the bottom of the social scale (Matt. 22:3-4, 8-10, cf. Luke 14:15-24).

PROVERBS stresses how wisdom is for *the simple* (v. 6, cf. 1:4), the young and uninitiated. This anticipates the universal preaching of the gospel, which is adapted to the condition of those to whom it comes. *The simple* now are those ignorant of the ways of God who have acquired wrong ideas of him and developed bad habits. The invitation is without strings but says: leave those false trails and *walk in the way of understanding* (**v. 6**).

Compare verse 6 with the master's invitation to the drop-outs of Jesus' parable in Luke 14, especially verses 21 and 23. What does this tell you about the relationship between repentance and faith?

B. The children of Wisdom and folly compared (vv. 7-12).
In spite of the repetition of the quotation marks in NIV it is not certain that this is a continuation of Wisdom's speech which began in v. 4. It doesn't sound like an invitation to dinner! It may be better to see it as an aside by Solomon himself, qualifying the simplicity of the invitation just given. He is saying that those who truly respond to Wisdom's invitation are not those who make a sudden impulsive decision to receive what sounds good, but those who go on to develop the character of the wise, cultivating patience, perseverance and humility. Jesus said, 'Wisdom is proved right by her actions' (Matt. 11:19). Another reading is 'her children' but the meaning is the same. It is like our proverb, 'The proof of the pudding is in the eating'. We have looked at the window-dressing of the adulteress and of Wisdom. Soon we will be introduced to the mother of harlots and their ilk – 'the woman Folly' (v. 13). But first we see what sort of children each produces and how they fare as a result.

1. Verses 7-9. Two contrasting types and how they respond to 'wisdom' (the Word of God) and its speakers.

(a) *First is **the mocker** (vv. 7-8a)*, who not only refuses correction but turns on the speaker, *insults*, *abuses* and *hates* him. Such qualify for our Lord's description of them as 'dogs' or 'pigs' who not only 'trample ... under their feet' these 'pearls' of wisdom, but 'turn' on the one who offers them and 'tear (him) to pieces' (Matt. 7:6).

So it is partly **a note of caution** to those who would seek to help others by speaking the Word of God to them: let them test the waters before they launch into them. Jesus himself was continually confronted *by mockers* in his ministry. Chief among these were the Pharisees who, while not laughing aloud, put trick controversial questions to him with a view to his coming down on one side or the other, thus arousing animosity against him from at least some. Perceiving this, Jesus avoided giving direct answers and often turned the question on them (see Matt. 15:1-3; 22:15-22, 41-46; Mark 10:1-3). This shows how Jesus kept his own precept of not feeding pearls to pigs.

But it is also **a warning** to all who hear to examine themselves to see if this is what they are like. We are all apt to resent criticism. The way we receive it says more about us than all our self-justification in answering it.

(b) *Second is* **the wise** (vv. 8b-9), who realizes he is not perfect, wants to become *wiser still* and *add to his learning*. Such will not only welcome advice but receive *rebukes*. In this way he will both profit himself and create or strengthen a bond with his teacher whom he will *love*.

This can be applied in a similar way to (a): as an **encouragement** to target those who are most receptive, and a **lesson** to us to seek this spirit ourselves. It is one of the hardest parts of wisdom, requiring that 'meekness' Jesus commended in the Sermon on the Mount. 'The meek' are not the hyper-sensitive, who take everything personally and to heart (what today would be called paranoia) which has no place in Christian character. We must be prepared to be told things about ourselves. James spoke of God's Word as a mirror in which we see ourselves (1:22-25). Only a fool, seeing his dirty face in a mirror, smashes the mirror instead of going and getting his face washed!

2. The two contrasting consequences of these responses (vv. 10-12).

The key words are in **verse 12**: *reward* and *suffer*. But we need to see how this conclusion is arrived at. We are told in **verse 10** how this state of wisdom is attained. Verses 7-9 may leave us with the impression that people are wise or foolish by accident of birth, that it's all down to genes. Not so. We all arrive here in a state of foolishness, without a knowledge of God. Wisdom *begins* with *the fear of the Lord* (**v. 10a**), the response of faith to the God who appears to us in his Word. This sentence is of course the motto text of PROVERBS (1:7). It is this response that leads us on to knowing him (**v. 10b**): *the knowledge of the Holy One*, literally *Ones*, probably 'the plural of excellence', as it is with *wisdoms* in verse 1. It is this faith in and knowledge of God which admits a person to the blessings of covenant relationship with God (**v. 11**). In the old covenant this meant long life (Exod. 20:12, Deut. 4:40). Under the new covenant it is 'life to the full' (John 10:10), or 'eternal life' (John 17:3). The length may be long or short in terms of years on earth, but in totality it is for ever.

Verse 12 draws the conclusion and points the contrasts between the wise and the mocker. This long or full life is the *reward* the **wise** receives for his positive response to Wisdom's invitation. In fact the word *reward* is a paraphrase of 'for yourself' – 'if you are wise you are wise for yourself'. This is not to suggest that our wisdom is of no benefit to anyone else, for PROVERBS is always extolling its social benefits (e.g. 10:1). It can also bring glory to God. But it means, 'Whatever the consequences of your faith in God and his Word, good or ill, you will not ultimately be the loser, but in fact the chief gainer'.

The same applies to the **mocker**: you alone *will suffer*. Of course he will probably make others suffer too, and even grieve God's heart. Was not Jesus on the cross heart-broken by the cruel mockery of the bystanders (Ps. 69:7-12, 19-21)? But all this is comparatively short-lived. Our verse is looking to the ultimate, to the end of life (as indeed is verse 11). At the judgment and in eternity no one else will suffer for our foolish rejection of God's offer – only we ourselves.

Question
What does this tell us about what hell is like? Refer to Luke 16:23f and Revelation 22:11 for the New Testament answer.

C. THE WOMAN FOLLY GIVES HER INVITATION (vv. 13-18).

Wisdom has answered the adulteress, who now replies to Wisdom's answer. Most translations have 'the foolish woman' and NIV is daring in going out on its own with *the woman Folly*. However, the Hebrew has 'a woman of foolishness', which would not be the usual way of saying 'a foolish woman'. Delitzsch calls this 'the genitive of apposition', which means 'foolishness' is the name of the woman. If he and NIV are right it balances the personification of Wisdom very neatly and tellingly. It also shows that behind the ways of adulteresses is a whole way of thinking and behaving, which we call temptation and which is almost as old as the human race. All temptation has common features, which are well illustrated by the ways of the harlot. For even when not of a sexual nature temptation is a kind of seduction. James is fond of depicting it thus: 1:14f, 4:4. Perhaps this passage suggested these ideas to that very Jewish brother of Christ. Since temptation draws us from God it is aptly termed Folly. Making it a woman is not being sexist, but in keeping with the long description of the harlot, and with the personification of Wisdom as a lady.

1. Her Character (v. 13). She is *loud* or boisterous; she tries to dominate her clients in order to railroad them into complying with her invitations. But her talk is empty, for she is not just 'simple' but 'simplicity' itself (as *undisciplined* is literally). The word 'simple' in PROVERBS is not a pejorative term, for it refers to the very ones to whom the book is addressed – the young and untaught, the unsophisticated who need instruction to make them 'prudent' (1:4). But her 'simplicity' is endemic and incurable. Temptation will never be anything but foolish. This is why the term is accompanied by a strong expression of her ignorance: *without knowledge*, which reads literally 'and not she knows what'. The negative is not the usual one but very emphatic. We might say, 'she doesn't know what's what.'

2. Her Method (v. 14). She knows Wisdom has a house on the hill, prominent and a good place from which to call (vv. 1, 3), so she emulates her. Temptation is good at advertising itself, a public relations expert, employing the best marketing techniques. The devil sees to it that we all know what sinful pleasures are on offer and that we cannot afford to miss them.

3. Her Target (v. 15). The wording suggests those who are minding their own business, not attending to her, not looking for opportunities for sinful self-indulgence. Perhaps they have been put on the right lines by parents. Yet they are still in danger and she knows how to lure them. Temptation does not only await those who are on the look-out for the pleasures of sin. There is something in all of us to which it can appeal. The devil likes a challenge! He took on Eve in her state of innocence! His 'flaming arrows' strike suddenly and unexpectedly (Eph. 6:16).

4. Her Invitation (v. 16). Her words are an exact replica of those of Wisdom in verse 4. Here is the subtlety of temptation. It was on this quality the serpent relied in approaching Eve (Gen. 3:1). It has ever been his method, especially in seeking to capture the innocent. He knows a blatant appeal to 'come in and sin' won't work with them. So he tries to make it sound true, good and right, an acceptable alternative to the appeal of God's Word. Since he is subtle, we have to learn to be subtler. This is what PROVERBS is trying to teach us: 'prudence' (1:4) or 'shrewdness', the word used of the serpent in Genesis 3:1, a quality Jesus said is needed by believers (Matt. 10:16, Luke 16:8). Paul called it 'discernment' (Phil. 1:9f).

5. Her Attraction (v. 17). She makes no attempt to conceal the unlawfulness of the pleasure she offers. It is stolen – adultery is stealing intimacy from the one to whom it rightly belongs – and therefore has to be indulged in secret. But this only adds to the enjoyment of it! How right she is! We all know that the naughtier something is the nicer it feels. Part of the power of Satan's original temptation lay in the fact that he was daring Eve to take what God had forbidden. We all find a dare hard to refuse. Paul explained the psychology behind this in Romans 7:11. The commandment 'do not covet' acted as a kind of 'agent provocateur' to induce him to do just that. Even in childhood we found an irrepressible urge to do what Mummy said 'don't do'. Unfortunately we never grow out of this.

6. Her End (v. 18). This is saying in the language of the 'house' metaphor what the Bible says elsewhere in plainer language: 'the soul who sins is the one who will die' (Ezek. 18:4); 'the wages of sin is death' (Rom. 6:23). Already PROVERBS has spoken of death as the outcome of adultery (7:26f), and has used the same word as here: REPHAIM, 'the spirits of the dead' (2:18). He is claiming that the house of sinful pleasure is haunted: 'the REPHAIM are there', *the guests* have returned from the *depths of* SHEOL to haunt the newcomer.

This is the reality behind the pleasure offered by Folly. It ends up with all the joy of living in a haunted house! Even worse, for the ghosts are specimens of what all who go there will become. The ghosts are the witnesses to what happens to all who yield to temptation – utter ruin, already described in detail in 5:9-14.

Question
How does this chapter make more vivid the New Testament's teaching on the pull of 'the world' faced by every Christian? See 1 John 2:15-17.

On this solemn note ends, not just this long section on temptation versus wisdom, but the whole INTRODUCTION. It brings out the deep seriousness of the teaching of this book. It is not a manual of decorum and good manners, but the way of life and death. Confrontation with death (and the spirits of the dead) should encourage us to choose life. We shall find much, much more about this way of life as we proceed to the body of the book.

Solomon's Proverbs (first set)
(Proverbs 10–22:16)

The central section of the book contains the first and main selection from Solomon's own sayings, chosen, edited and arranged during the reign of Hezekiah (25:1, see Introduction [H]).

These are different from chapters 1–9 in that there are no extended discussions of particular subjects. However, since the editor himself made an attempt to arrange them, we will group them around particular themes chapter by chapter. Sometimes a proverb will touch on more than one theme and could be classified under another heading than the one chosen. However, in spite of its limitations, this method should prove more meaningful than a strict verse-by-verse approach.

Each proverb presents the individual with a choice: between righteousness and wickedness, wisdom and folly. He is free to choose his course, but the consequences are determined. Choosing righteousness and wisdom leads to prosperity and long life; choosing wickedness and folly brings ruin and death. It is this black-and-white approach to life that raises most questions.

8

Wisdom Put Into practice
(Proverbs 10)

Four themes are touched on in this chapter: **1. Discipline**, particularly in the family. **2. Righteousness** contrasted with wickedness. **3. Work** and the prosperity it brings. **4. Words**, their use and abuse.

A. DISCIPLINE AND THE FAMILY (vv. 1, 17, 26).

Verse 1 is certainly an appropriate saying with which to begin this section, for PROVERBS is basically a book to make the young mature and the *simple wise* (1:2-7). The process **begins** in the family where the parents discipline the child (1:8). There is a sense too in which education and discipline **end** in the family, for the way a child turns out largely determines the happiness or otherwise of the parents. If Solomon's own son Rehoboam showed early signs of that folly that was to mark his reign, then Solomon was writing this from experience (1 Kings 12)! Careful training and loving discipline of our children is in our own interest as well as our children's.

Verse 17 spells out for us the **way to rear** that *wise son* who *brings joy* to his parents, that is by *discipline* and *correction*. These are terms used in the Prologue of the parental training outlined in that section. It thus recalls to our minds those powerful lessons on the benefits of acquiring wisdom that comprise chapters 1-9. Those who heed this are not only *on the way of life* themselves, but are able to *show* it to those who come after them. On the other hand, a well-taught child who chooses to *ignore correction* will both go astray himself and *lead others astray*, especially his own children.

Verse 26 warns us that one who either isn't taught *discipline*, or doesn't *heed it*, will not become self-disciplined and will turn out a *sluggard* (cf. 6:6-11) and become a parasite. Neither his parents nor anyone else can *send* him with a message or on a job. He won't complete it. Employing him is like tasting a glass of wine only to find it sour (*vinegar*), or like lighting a fire only to be blinded by the *smoke*. Parents who fail with their children smart for it (cf. vv. 4-5)!

Question
How do these verses help us understand the disorders in current western society among both the young and adults?

B. RIGHTEOUSNESS AND WICKEDNESS (vv. 2-3, 6-7, 9, 23-25, 27-30). This is one of PROVERBS' main subjects and we must be clear on the meaning of these terms from the outset. Under the old covenant the *righteous* person was the one who kept the Law, to which all Israelites were bound by covenant. *Righteousness*, therefore, was obedience to the Law and *wickedness* the violation of it. Under the new covenant there is something of a change. Jesus in his Sermon on the Mount claimed that his kingdom demanded a higher standard of righteousness (Matt. 5:20). This was why he stressed character and attitude rather than works of law. Paul enlarged on this, saying that the road to righteousness did not lie in the direction of works of the law (Rom. 3:20) but through faith in Jesus Christ (Rom. 3:21f). Jesus is the righteous one, the only perfectly obedient man, who obeyed God not only in the way he lived but the way he died, as an atoning sacrifice for the unrighteous (Rom. 3:25). This active and passive obedience is made a gift to the sinner who believes on him and is consequently 'justified' or 'made righteous' (Rom. 3:24, 26, 28, 4:23-25, 10:4, 2 Cor. 5:21).

So Christians applying PROVERBS to themselves will understand 'the righteous' as equivalent to 'the believer', and 'the wicked' as 'the unbeliever', one who has not received the gospel and therefore is still in his sin. This does not mean that moral obedience is not required under the gospel; in fact a higher standard is expected of Christians even than Israelites, now that 'the hardness of our hearts' has been cured (Matt. 19:8). It means that no amount of morality makes us righteous, that the difference between the righteous and the wicked in our age is seen less in terms of morality than of faith.

1. The Security of *the righteous* in the common things of life. **Verses 2-3** could be considered under 'Work, wealth and poverty' but probably have more to do with righteousness and wickedness. They are in a form fairly common in PROVERBS called 'Chiastic' from the Greek letter CHI written X. It means that the 1st and 4th lines correspond, as do the 2nd and 3rd, thus:

v. 2a   v. 3a

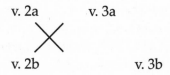

v. 2b   v. 3b

Noticing this can help us take the point being made. Thus here we are told that those who acquire their possessions dishonestly, gain nothing from them (2a) for the reason that God is giving them up to their greed as a judgment on them (3b). On the other hand he treats the righteous well by satisfying their hunger (3a), so that they are in no danger of death (2b, cf.13:25).

The Sermon on the Mount throws more light on this subject. While Jesus taught that God in fact looks after the basic needs of both righteous and wicked without discrimination (Matt. 5:45), the latter gain no benefit, for either they don't know or believe it, or else they are so greedy that the promise of mere food and clothing is contemptible. Their *craving* may lead them to cheat or steal, yet they gain no ultimate benefit from their *ill-gotten treasures*, like Ahab in the Old Testament (1 Kings 21) and Judas in the New (Matt. 27:3-5). On the other hand *the righteous* are thankful for small mercies and therefore content (1 Tim. 4:3-5).

Verse 9 also speaks of security, this time the security of having nothing to hide from God or man. It depicts life as a journey and the righteous man as a traveller who fears nothing because he is honest and not trying to deceive. He is contrasted with the devious person who spends his life trying to avoid discovery, but ultimately is 'found out' (Num. 32:23). The old covenant sees these days of discovery and reckoning, often called 'the day of the Lord', as taking place in history; but under the new covenant we are told not to expect wrongs necessarily to be righted in this age but at the day of judgement when God will call all to account (Rom. 2:12f,16).

2. The Reputation Righteousness gains (vv. 6-7).
As well as material there are social gains for *the righteous*. In this life their friends and neighbours *bless them*, that is, speak well of them, **verse 6**. All good people enjoy hearing the gratitude and praise of their fellows expressed. *The wicked* man however, who has spent his life in cursing and threatening, finds these eventually come back on him. Some stroke from man or God silences him – *overwhelms his mouth*.

Nor does death put an end to this, **verse 7**. The good man is gratefully remembered and his name honoured (Heb. 11). But those who leave a legacy of hatred are soon forgotten, or if remembered, only to their shame, as Jeroboam was always described as the king 'who caused Israel to sin' (1 Kings 15:30, etc.). In the world as we know it things don't always work out quite like this. Jesus warned us that not everybody will speak well of us (Luke 6:26), but we shall be reviled as he was (John 15:18-21). Nevertheless we always have friends and supporters among the godly. Similarly, unbelievers, even the most wicked, can enjoy high popularity, even cult status – Hitler for example. However, subsequent history has a habit of cutting such down to size.

3. The Psychology underlying Righteousness and Wickedness (vv. 23-25).
In these verses we are taken into the very soul of the two kinds.

*First, we see what gives each most **pleasure** (v. 23).* The word for *pleasure* is literally 'laughter', although most translate it 'sport',

in the sense of amusement or 'fun'. The unbeliever (*fool*) lives
for fun and enjoyment. Some even find *evil conduct* fun – fun
to watch in reality or fiction, fun to discuss, and even fun to
perform themselves. This is because they lack *understanding*,
they fail to see the seriousness of sin, the harm it does and the
awful judgment awaiting it.

The believer understands all this and therefore doesn't find
sin at all amusing. But this doesn't make him a kill-joy. He too
loves pleasure, but finds it in *wisdom*, that is, wise as opposed
to *evil conduct*. He looks to things that are 'true ... noble ... right
... pure ... lovely ... admirable ...' (Phil. 4:8). The world is still
full of such things which are there for the enjoyment of us
all (1 Tim. 6:17). Over and above this he has Christ, perfect
wisdom, who gives a pleasure and joy that only the man of
understanding can find.

Second, we see what produces these states of mind (**v. 24**). Why
is the unbeliever such a fun-loving person? It is the only
way he can anaesthetize himself against his deep-seated fear
and dread. He knows that life is uncertain, that he may lose
his health, his money, his job, his family, all that gives him
pleasure. So either he becomes totally absorbed in the present,
to 'eat, drink and be merry' while he can, or he takes a morbid
interest in the future and tries to get it to give up its secrets by
astrology or the occult. He has a great fear of the unknown,
the after-life, the possibility of having to give account and be
repaid for his misdeeds. The psychologist will try to persuade
him these fears are unreal, derived from the primitive past
of the human race or an over-strict upbringing. But the truth
of God is that these fears are justified. Even if he escapes
misfortune in this life, he cannot avoid death 'and after that to
face judgment' (Heb. 2:15, 9:27).

What the righteous desire will be granted is not of course
a blank cheque. What applies here is what applies to Jesus'
promises about prayer: 'anything in his name' or 'according
to his will'. So his desire is the opposite of the unbeliever's
– he wants to see the face of God, and he will, and then all his
desires will be *granted*, all his hopes satisfied.

Verse 25 confirms the reality of these fears and hopes and
spells out what it is that *overtakes the wicked* and is *granted to*

the righteous. For the wicked it is the loss of all he has lived for: pleasure, a good bank balance, a nice home, a happy family, perhaps fame, popularity and promotion. What he has *dreaded* – a natural disaster (*storm*), the loss of health or job, or a family break-up – may remove all this at a stroke and leave him with nothing. But in any case the *storm* of Christ's return will sweep away all that is material, leaving no prospect of recovery, but just a naked soul that 'will not stand in the judgment' (Ps. 1:5).

The *righteous* may suffer the same losses as the other, for Christians are not exempt from accidents, diseases and disasters. But if all goes they still have something left. Their house is built on a rock, on Christ (Matt. 7:24-27) and even if they lose everything else they don't lose heart, for they don't doubt God's continuing love in Christ (Rom. 8:35-38) and *stand firm for ever.*

4. Promises and Warnings to Righteous and Wicked (vv. 27-30). The teaching of the previous verses is now used to bring encouragement to believers and warning to others.

Verse 27 expresses a desire common to all – long life, which is assured to the godly but denied to *the wicked*. Whereas the Old Testament speaks of life in terms of quantity (3:1f), the gospel offers quality, what Jesus called 'life to the full' (John 10:10) found in a life based on love for and trust in God – *the fear of the Lord. The wicked, even* those who are decent and helpful people, don't have this relationship with God. Under the Law they were often cut off in their prime. Under the Gospel, this sudden *cutting short* happens only rarely. The meaning therefore is, that for the unbeliever 'death whene'er he calls must call too soon' (W. S. Gilbert), for he is caught unprepared.

Verse 28 speaks more subjectively of the *prospects* of the two classes. In spite of the future awaiting him the unbeliever is frequently an optimist. But his *hopes* are based on unknown quantities: the interest rate, the stock market, the national economy, his own state of health and so on. When these fail so do his *hopes*. The believer's *hope* 'is fixed on nothing less than Jesus' blood and righteousness' which gives him just cause to feel joy. This will be the same in adversity as in prosperity, for 'hope does not disappoint' (Rom. 5:5).

Verse 29 brings everyone under the same umbrella, called here *the way of the Lord*. Under the old covenant this *way* was the Law, which promised the help and protection of God to those who kept it, but his opposition to those who departed from it (Deut. 27–28). Under the new covenant *the way* is Christ, his life, teaching and salvation (John 14:6), that Gospel which saves those who believe it and condemns those who refuse it (John 3:18) and is thus 'the fragrance of life' to the saved, but 'the smell of death' to 'those who are perishing' (2 Cor. 2:15f).

Verse 30 brings all this to its logical conclusion, as it sets down the final state of *the righteous and the wicked* respectively. Here is a simple word to the believer that since his roots are in Christ they are firm (Eph. 3:17). By contrast the unbeliever is warned he has no security. For an Israelite to be told he won't remain in the land meant to be away from the presence of God and beyond the reach of his blessing, in fact to be among the heathen whom God cursed (Ps. 137). The New Testament speaks not of an earthly land but a spiritual kingdom, which is 'among' or even 'within you' (Luke 17:21), in the present by faith and in its fullness hereafter.

For further study. Go back over these verses and write down in two columns the main differences between *righteous* and *wicked*.

C. WORK, WEALTH AND POVERTY (vv. 4-5, 15-16, 22).

Verses 2-3 show how the topics touched on overlap and also set down the moral and spiritual aspects of working and living. By observing these one can avoid poverty and achieve a measure of prosperity. But there is more to be said on this matter.

1. Our responsibility in the Basics of Life (vv. 4-5).

According to **verse 4** we all have a responsibility to feed ourselves and our dependents. If we starve through laziness we have only ourselves to blame (2 Thess. 3:6-10). Jesus didn't teach 'leave it all to God', but 'don't be anxious' (Matt. 6:25-34). If there is work to be had and we are able to do it then this is how God keeps his promise to us – through the work of our *diligent hands*. If there is no work or we are unable to do it God has other ways of meeting our needs. Rich nations have State benefits, poorer ones are helped through the selfless compassion of those who have enough and to spare (Isa. 58:7, Matt. 25:34-46, 2 Cor. 8:13-15). If people are starving it is because others have failed in their duty, not that God has broken his promise.

According to **verse 5** work must not only be **diligent** but **regular**. We have to work when the work is there, not when the whim takes us. In the agrarian society of ancient Israel, most work was seasonal – intense in the *summer* when *harvest* came, but scarce in the winter, when rest could be enjoyed. In our industrial society we work regular hours in all seasons and have daily and weekly periods for rest and leisure. To earn our living we have to fit in with the pattern of our day as the ancients had to do in theirs. The words *wise ... disgraceful* son show that the discipline of work is best learned in youth from our parents. There is also a spiritual application: wise sons of God spend the summer of their lives labouring in his harvest (John 4:34-37, 9:4). They can rest in the grave.

2. The Realities of the Earth's Economy (vv. 15-16).

Verse 15 tells us that however carefully the above principles are followed, the fact remains that in the world as it is, there will always be rich and poor. Because of this some will have the security that goes with wealth; they will be *fortified* against inflation, adversity, enemies and the temptation to steal. The poor man is like someone living in a *ruin* – vulnerable to inflation, scarcity, creditors and the temptation to steal. He lives in fear and anxiety. These are stark realities. There is nothing glamorous in poverty. Its one compensation is that, having nothing material to trust in, the poor man finds himself more drawn to trust in God, which the rich finds 'hard' (Matt. 19:23). That very trust delivers him from anxiety and makes him more confident than the rich (Matt. 6:25-34).

Verse 16 balances this by drawing attention to the moral element in the **way** possessions are acquired and used (cf. v. 2). This shows whether a person is *righteous* or *wicked*. The *righteous* earns his money by his efforts (*wages*) and uses it for the necessities of *life* – for himself, his family and those poorer than himself (Eph. 4:28). *The wicked* has an *income* which is unearned – acquired at best by inheritance or investment or at worst by stealing or gambling – *ill-gotten treasures* (v. 2). Such will tend to squander it on luxuries or sinful pleasures. We are probably meant to understand the *punishment* as 'death', in contrast to life for *the righteous*. For if he has acquired wealth dishonestly or used it self-indulgently, he will have to answer to God for it – 'the wages of sin is death' (Rom. 6:23).

3. God's Blessing transcends Economic Realities (v. 22).

What we have seen so far are the **secondary** means to prosperity: honesty, diligence, regularity and generosity. Here we have the **primary** cause – the grace of God. The emphasis is well brought out by GNB: 'It is the Lord's blessing that makes you wealthy'. So even one who keeps these godly economic principles can't boast: (i) because it is God who makes him honest, etc. (cf. 1 Cor. 4:7); (ii) because it is God who alone gives the increase, which even hard honest work cannot guarantee. However, the believer comes into his own in that in his case the Lord *adds no trouble to it*. This doesn't mean he is guaranteed prosperity but that, since he lives by faith, even want doesn't depress him (Phil. 4:11-13). Whatever happens he still has Christ (Eph. 1:3).

Question

How does this teaching help your thinking about your job, the problem of unemployment, social security and aid organizations such as TEARFUND?

D. WORDS, SPEECH AND TONGUE (vv. 8, 10-14, 18-21, 31-32).

Here we come to a favourite theme of PROVERBS. No doubt these inspired James (3) to compose his famous statement on the tongue.

1. Good speech comes from good listening (vv. 8 and 10).

The first principle of the right use of the tongue (**v. 8**) is to know when not to use it. We can't talk and listen at the same time!

It is more important to listen to what another has to say to us than to air our own opinions. The world admires the talker but according to the Bible he may just be a *chattering fool*. The one God calls *wise* is the one who is prepared to listen to one of superior knowledge and experience who will point him in the right direction and warn him of the pitfalls. God's wisdom does not consist in quantities of words but is *in heart*, that is, in understanding what we are saying and looking for more instruction. He is 'quick to listen, slow to speak' (James. 1:19), he does not 'presume to be a teacher' (James 3:1). Time shows he is the one who is wise, for he prospers where the other *comes to ruin*.

But not everyone who listens quietly is *wise* in God's book! A fool can keep quiet when it suits him (17:28)! The subject of **verse 10** has his tongue well under control, but for an evil purpose – not to listen but to scheme. He uses *winks* (cf. 6:13) because words would give away his *malicious* intentions. *The chattering fool* doesn't seem so bad alongside this one. He may only be looking for an audience, not seeking to *cause grief*, and if he has evil intentions they are easily detected and quickly suppressed. Unlike the secret plotter he harms himself more than his audience. 'The dog that bites is not always the dog that barks' (Matt. Henry). Eventually *he will be found out*.

2. Good speech comes from a good heart (vv. 11-14).

What a contrast is the way words are used in *the mouth of the righteous* (**v. 11**)! They are like 'living water' (*a fountain of life*) to those who hear. In a land where water is scarce rain has to be collected in cisterns for use in the dry months, and consequently becomes stale. Water from a spring or *fountain* was fresh and therefore more refreshing. This is what the conversation of one who walks with God is like: 'morally strengthening, intellectually elevating and inwardly quickening' (Delitzsch). This is because he is in contact with God who is himself the *fountain of life* (Ps. 36:9, Jer. 2:13, 17:13).

The language of the ungodly on the other hand is harmful: 'He never opens his mouth without pouring out violence' (Bridges). This sounds exaggerated for we have all listened to the conversations and speeches of non-Christians with profit;

otherwise we would never have become educated! However these have been influenced by Christianity, or at least by 'common grace'. There are others so depraved they can only curse, threaten or boast of their savage exploits. Such is the world we live in and we should not be shocked by the way people talk, either in ordinary conversation or in the media.

Verse 12 logically follows verse 11 because it shows that behind the words of the mouth lies the language of the heart: 'Out of the overflow of the heart the mouth speaks' (Matt. 12:34). We speak only what we have thought and felt. One who has hatred in his heart will speak provocative words and draw the one he hates into a fight. On the other hand the one who has *love* in his heart will neither provoke nor be provoked. Even where the other offends him by word or deed he will not retaliate but will excuse, overlook and forgive the offence (1 Cor. 13:4-6). This way often brings the offender to repentance so that he can enjoy God's forgiveness too (James 5:20, 1 Pet. 4:8)

Verse 13 further explains verse 12. The *love* which *covers all wrongs* is not weak sentimentality. It is the fruit of listening to God's teaching and thus receiving *wisdom*. To the world peaceable forgiving words may sound unmanly, but in God's book they represent true *wisdom*. Even though they may be costly in the short term, they pay dividends in the end. This is implied in line 2: he who *lacks judgment*, who has not listened to the wise counsels of God's word, will provoke and retaliate (v. 12a), he will lash his enemies with his tongue. But in fact he is preparing *a rod for* his *own back*, for this will eventually get him into trouble, either from those he has provoked or from the sanctions of the law if he has gone so far as to break it.

Verse 14 is similar, but goes beyond verse 13 in speaking of *the fool* as 'near destruction' (KJV, lit. 'ruin is near'). The *rod for his back* is not something in the future but hanging over him, ready to fall at a moment's notice. It shows how quickly he can blurt something out and provoke a quarrel, invite punishment or even incur God's judgment. How is one to escape this and become *wise*? By *storing up knowledge*. This shows wisdom is not natural to us but acquired, learned piecemeal. The wise man's thoughts are on this acquired knowledge, he is not looking for trouble like the other. So he approaches every situation calmly.

3. How to avoid slips of the tongue (vv. 18-21).

Verse 18 links with verse 12 and shows how difficult a thing to handle is a hating heart. If we try to hide it we will at best but flatter falsely, which is a form of *lying*. On the other hand if we are honest about it we may be guilty of *slander*. The only way to truthful, honest, gracious speech is a heart cleansed of all malice. If you want to know how to get this, read on!

Verse 19 is more than a Biblical version of 'least said soonest mended', which would rule out long discourses and extended conversations and mean that one who speaks at length is bound to sin. It means that those who lack *wisdom* within and harbour malice (vv. 12, 18) may speak truthfully and courteously for a brief time but will give offence (*sin*) sooner or later. But the answer to this is not total silence. No one is more suspicious than the one who says nothing, even when spoken to. Whatever is going on in that mind?! The answer is to have a heart delivered from its malice and filled with grace, which is to say made wise. He who has a gracious heart will speak graciously. This is what the Gospel of grace does for us – it enables our 'conversation (to be) always full of grace, seasoned with salt, so that you may know how to answer everyone' (Col. 4:6).

Verse 20 confirms this. Words can be of great value – *choice silver* is that which has been repeatedly purified by fire, as God's own words are said to be (Ps. 12:6), that is, perfectly pure. This is because God himself is perfectly pure. The only way to cultivate edifying conversation is to undergo a change of heart. So the contrast in part two of the verse is with the *heart of the wicked*, for it is 'out of the overflow of the heart that the mouth speaks' (Matt. 12:34). While in its state of sin the heart has *little value*, for look what comes from it: 'Unwholesome talk ... bitterness, rage and anger, brawling and slander, along with every form of malice' (Eph. 4:29, 31). But when it is made new (Eph. 4:23) then we can begin to speak like God, 'what is helpful for building others up' (Eph. 4:29).

Verse 21 rounds off this little group of verses. It is the climax of the argument, for good words are presented as virtually a matter of life and death, spiritually speaking. *Fools die* because they cannot feed themselves. Their 'heart' (*judgment*) is not the dwelling-place of the pure word of God. *The righteous* are renewed by the word of God which gives them the ability to feed (*nourish*) others too. The word that gave them life can through them save others from death.

4. Words as the reflection of character.

Verses 31-32 can be classified under 'Righteousness' just as fittingly as under 'Words'. Thus they form an appropriate conclusion to the whole chapter in which these have been the two principal themes, occupying 20 of the 32 verses.

These verses are 'Chiastic' (see on verses 2-3), thus

v. 31a   v. 32a

v. 31b   v. 32b.

At the same time there are comparisons and contrasts within the verses themselves. **Verse 31** uses plant imagery. Righteousness in a person 'bears fruit in' or *brings forth wisdom*, well-chosen words which are not only true but sensible and practical. On the contrary the *perverse* or crooked person, whose nature has never been straightened out by regeneration, has nothing to say worth hearing and like a fruitless plant is 'rooted up' (*cut out*).

Verse 32 justifies this strong language. The *righteous* is commended as wise because what he speaks is always *fitting*, appropriate to the subject, the occasion and the audience. He speaks not only with truth but in love (Eph. 4:15) and with grace (Col. 4:6). On the other hand the *perverse* person cannot do this, it is not in his nature. So however he may try, what comes out of his mouth is either false or provocative or both.

It all goes to show that 'righteousness' is ultimately an inward condition. Our words give us away; they are what we are. 'The good man brings good things out of the good things stored up in him' (Matt. 12:35). This is why Jesus went on to say, 'By your words you will be acquitted and by your words you will be condemned' (v. 37). It is not that God is trying to pick us up on everything we say, but that our words are our barometer and record what we truly are.

For further study consider Paul (the apostle) as an example of this teaching. Compare his speech before his encounter with Christ (Acts 9:1) with that after (2 Cor. 10:1, 1 Thess. 2:7, 11f). See how many of the points made here you can illustrate from his preaching, conversation and writing.

9

The Character of a Righteous Man
(Proverbs 11)

This chapter centres around the twin themes of the righteous
and the wicked, their character and behaviour, plus the
consequences of their particular life-style both for themselves
and others. We can follow the order of verses more or less as
they stand.

A. THE MARKS OF THE RIGHTEOUS (vv. 1-6).

First we see what *the righteous* and *the wicked* are **in themselves**,
bearing in mind that under the old covenant *the righteous* were
those who obeyed the law of Moses and *the wicked* those who
flouted it (sometimes the majority). Under the new covenant
righteousness is through faith in Christ. However, this does
not mean the old covenant did not require faith, nor that the
new does not require works. The principles of character and
behaviour underlying this chapter are therefore applicable
under the gospel as well as under the law (see on Chapter 10,
section B).

1. Honest in business (v. 1).

Here is righteousness in the market place or shop, the principle
being that all trading should be performed honestly. Sinai
itself commanded accurate weights and measures: Lev. 19:36,
Deut. 25:13-16, and these commands are themselves based
on the eighth commandment, against stealing. The prophets
denounced this form of fraud along with all other forms of

disobedience: Hosea 12:7, Amos 8:5f, Micah 6:10, and called for accurate measures: Ezek. 45:10-12.

We can take it more broadly: the seller should not overvalue his wares, nor the buyer undervalue them. This is why the proverb mentions God's personal reaction – *delights ... abhorrent* – rather than the abstract *righteousness*. God as perfect justice is offended by any breach of justice because he feels for the victim. Fraud always hurts someone: the seller who sells at a loss or the buyer who overpays are both out of pocket and damage is done to that trust which is essential to all business transactions. Thankfully many unbelievers see things this way and are honest dealers. But because of the unscrupulous, the sanctions of law are necessary to enforce fair trading. The believer practises honesty primarily to *delight the Lord*, not just because it is illegal to do otherwise and he may be caught (See also B.1).

2. Humble in heart (v. 2).
The second principle of righteousness here is humility, the opposite of **pride**, overestimating your importance alongside other people. It includes exaggerating your abilities, achievements and knowledge, and leads to boasting and self-assertion. It covets praise, popularity and even fame and is impatient with criticism. It is illustrated by such as Nebuchadnezzar (Dan. 4:30) and Herod Agrippa (Acts 12:21f) with their delusions of grandeur. There is also religious or spiritual pride – regarding yourself as more holy or nearer to God than others, as the Pharisees did (Luke 18:9-12). The spiritually proud man's prayers are more self-congratulation than supplication. He parades his religiosity in order 'to be seen by men' (Matt. 6:5). But lest we think pride is only to be found in the high and mighty, Jesus also told a little parable about one who took top spot at a wedding reception, thereby showing what he thought of himself and everyone else (Luke 14:7-11). It is such actions – the seats we choose to sit on! – that betray our self-image.

The same parable illustrates **humility**, for Jesus commended the one who took the worst seat at the table. Humility means knowing yourself, having a balanced view of the good and ill in yourself, being modest, not putting yourself forward, but recognizing there may be others with better claims than yourself. This quality is essential to righteousness, for while the proud may be as outwardly moral and respectable as the humble, their attitude to themselves makes righteousness seem an unattractive way of life. We only have to look at Jesus to see that someone can be actually perfect without giving himself airs, putting himself forward and looking down on everyone else. (For comment on *disgrace* and *wisdom* see under B.2.)

3. Faithful to principle (vv. 3, 5f).

These verses either employ the term *righteousness* itself or a closely related one, chosen because it reveals an important aspect of righteousness. For example, *upright* in **vv. 3** and **6** describes the righteous person as one who has not only been taught what is right but remains true to it in his heart. In this way he becomes a person of *integrity*, whose behaviour is consistent and can be relied on. It is in this sense that he is *blameless* (**v. 5**) – he cannot be accused of treachery or *duplicity* (**v. 3**) – of professing one thing and practising another.

Apart from 10:9, *integrity* is used only in JOB, who is a good example of it. For in spite of all Satan could throw at him, he 'maintained his integrity' (Job 2:3, 9). Whatever his friends accused him of, his conscience was clear: 'Till I die I will not deny my integrity. I will maintain my righteousness and not let go of it' (27:5f). Thus the truly righteous person has committed himself to certain God-revealed standards, never ceases to believe in them and consistently practises them.

In the light of all this we see more clearly what *wickedness* is. It is being *unfaithful* (**vv. 3, 6**) to whatever principles are professed. This applies across the board: to Israelites who had learned the Law of Moses; to Gentiles who have an innate sense of right and wrong; and to us who have accepted the ethics of Christianity. The question is whether these have won our hearts and captured our wills. This we show by keeping faith with our principles, or not, as the case may be. *The wicked* is a 'traitor', as the word for *duplicity* may be translated. He is a double-crosser: he appears to accept a code of morality, even if it is only his own, but does not live consistently with it. (For further comment see under B.2 and 3.)

B. The Blessings of the Righteous (vv. 1-8).

To put these principles of righteousness into practice requires personal discipline. But the effort is worthwhile when we see their good results and compare them with the fruits of wickedness.

1. God is pleased (v. 1).

This comes first and shows that although Old Testament righteousness was through obedience to the law it did not have to be legalistic. It was **God's** law and therefore pleased him. It showed those who truly loved God how they could please him. Unfortunately by the time of Christ the law had become a personal achievement rather than a way of pleasing God. Apart from a small remnant of humble God-fearers, the people were living in the disobedience or self-righteousness which God *abhorred*.

Jesus stood out among his contemporaries because he had one aim: 'I always do what pleases him' (John 8:29). To his true disciples he gives the same spirit: 'We obey his commandments and do what pleases him' (1 John 3:22). It is this approach that distinguishes the true Christian on the one hand from those who do righteousness to please themselves and on the other from those who do wickedness to gratify their flesh. But the pleasure they derive from their respective ways is poor compared with that which is enjoyed by those whose 'ways are pleasing to the Lord' (16:7), for to these 'he will give ... the desires of your heart' (Ps. 37:4).

2. Wisdom is acquired (v. 2).

This is the fruit of *humility*. On the face of it self-abasement seems a foolish route to happiness, especially in the modern world where you have to sell yourself with a professionally compiled CV and glowing references. However, in God's book, 'humility comes before honour' (15:33). Those whose concern is *his delight* (v. 1) are happy with his approval even if they don't get far up the ladder of success. This attitude is not natural but only acquired through faith, love and obedience. From these comes the *wisdom* which makes us satisfied with God's approval (15:33).

On the other hand the success of the self-assertive is limited and short-lived. This is expressed in four Hebrew words which, with their rhythm and rhyme, breathe inexorability:

'Comes pride (ZADHON) comes disgrace (QALON)'
akin to the Greek tag HUBRIS NEMESIS, a favourite theme with the tragedians. The Biblical version of this is 'pride goes before a fall' (16:18). It is illustrated by the fate of such as Nebuchadnezzar and Herod Agrippa. Their falls were great because of the heights to which they aspired. But it proves a general truth which will be fulfilled sometime somehow in us all (1 Pet. 5:5).

3. Guidance is given (vv. 3, 5).

Here we see the great advantage of living consistently with the principles of righteousness: it enables us to make right decisions when a choice of courses is open to us. Moral standards form good guidelines. They answer the question, 'What is right and best in this situation?' They *make a straight way*; we can see where we are going and how we will end up. Those without these standards or who don't live consistently with them will make the choice which 'seems' to offer the best reward in the short term (14:12). But failing to look far enough ahead, they are riding for a fall and so are ultimately *brought down* and destroyed.

To those who have some experience of the world, the contrast may appear a little sharply drawn. Moral choices aren't always clear cut, nor does making the right one necessarily keep us out of trouble. In fact those who make what to us is the wrong choice may derive much pleasure and profit from it. The story of Joseph, however, shows us one whose faithfulness to his principles when under temptation brought trouble in the short term but ultimately glory, power and usefulness (Gen. 39–41).

4. Life is saved (vv. 4, 6, 7).

Now we look even further ahead. In this life integrity may never be vindicated or perversity brought to account. But on the final day of reckoning there are only two alternatives – *wrath* bringing about *death* and *deliverance* life. What can save us in that day?

Wealth is worthless, even if honestly gained (cf. v. 1). Jesus spoke of 'the deceitfulness of riches' (Matt. 13:22), because not only do they tend in the present to produce a worldly outlook and a disinterest in spirituality, but they breed 'great expectations' about the future and remove worries about life and death. When the rich man dies he has a grand funeral and an opulent mausoleum; a building, street, hospital ward or scholarship is named after him and his memory is held in honour. But he has been placing his hopes on what continues in this world, disregarding the next. The truth is in **verse 7** line 2 which may read 'the hope of his wealth', that is, the hope he placed in his wealth. After his death the rich man of Jesus' story could not even buy himself a drop of water, let alone his release from hell (Luke 16:19-31).

As for *evil desires* (**v. 6**), they are worse than *worthless,* for they are the very cause of the trouble. They *trapped* you and there you remain. Only *righteousness* avails in the day of death (10:2). The man of integrity could always fall back on this certainty when all else failed him, as Job did in 19:25-27, claiming that although God is not taking his part against his friends' accusations now, he will do so at the last day. We who live in the age of Christ have even greater hope, for we approach that day not in our own righteousness but clothed in Christ's righteousness in which we shall be able to stand bold in that great day. Thank God for a gospel which gives hope to those facing death, which is surely the acid test of any religion.

5. Justice is done (v. 8).

What the righteous need to keep in mind is that the God they trust is himself righteous: 'To the faithful you show yourself faithful, to the blameless you show yourself blameless' (Ps. 18:25). **He** is perfectly honest (v. 1); utterly true and under no illusions (v. 2); faithful to his nature and principles (v. 3); in fact he is all he asks of us and to perfection. So whatever he permits and for however long, he ultimately restores the moral balance. This assurance kept Abraham's faith alive when he heard of the fate of Sodom, where 'righteous Lot' lived: 'Will not the Judge of all the earth do right?' (Gen. 18:25).

No faithful believer ever has any grounds for complaint about God's justice. All may seem awry at present, but God is the great table-turner and what he says here will surely come about.

C. THE GOOD INFLUENCE OF THE RIGHTEOUS (vv. 9-14).
The righteous person benefits not only himself but his society.

1. He keeps the truth alive (v. 9).
The situation here is that some in the community have become 'apostate' (*godless*). They were taught the truth of God and the way of righteousness but have departed from it. Now they are trying to bring others down with them by their hypocritical words which sound sensible but are false. *The righteous*, however, being people of *integrity*, are able to see through this and *escape* contamination. This has a beneficial effect generally, counteracting the apostasy and preserving society from degenerating into error and lawlessness. Jesus spoke of his disciples as 'the salt of the earth' (Matt. 5:13), who hold back the corruption which would otherwise spread uncontrollably. When error and permissiveness creep into churches, the answer is for the faithful Christian to 'hold firmly to the trustworthy message as it has been taught, so that he can encourage others by sound doctrine and refute those who oppose it' (Titus 1:9-11).

2. He promotes happiness in the community (vv. 10-11).
This envisages the possibility of the *wicked* gaining control of a whole community and using their power to *destroy* (**v. 11b**); people are oppressed and reduced to misery. We could exemplify this from tyrannies in the contemporary world, where the rulers' policies persecute some and ruin the economy for all. The only answer is their overthrow and replacement by others who love morality and justice. Then the people enjoy freedom, prosperity is restored and the community can again hold up its head in the world (*exalted*). Thank God this too has happened in our time even if it sometimes takes a revolution to accomplish it. Many nations, small and great, are now

enjoying democracy where for a period there was tyranny with all its misery and destruction.

3. He maintains a spirit of trust (vv. 12-13).
Society can only function properly where there is a spirit of trust between its members. This trust can only exist where people know when, and when not, to speak to or about each other.

Verse 12 is about speaking **to** your neighbour. The time to *hold your tongue* is when he appears to be making a fool of himself. The heartless person (*lacks judgment* is literally 'lacks heart') makes fun of him. Nothing is more infectious than laughter, so he soon becomes the butt of everyone's jokes. This is not only unkind and hurtful but it destroys trust. People come to despise each other, which is wrong (14:21, cf. Matt. 5:22). When the Pharisees tried to make Jesus look foolish he challenged them about the state of their hearts, which God knew (Luke 16:14f).

Verse 13 concerns speaking **about** your neighbour. You may have access to some private information about him. Some can't resist the temptation to pass this on – perhaps for financial gain, perhaps just to look important. Whatever the motive it is foolish. If I tell someone another's confidences, the one I tell won't let me into **his** secrets lest I pass them on to someone else. This will hinder my usefulness as a counsellor and further undermine the spirit of trust on which alone society can happily operate.

4. He gives and takes advice (v. 14).
Here we have a situation of potential danger – a *nation* or 'community' (since the term can apply to smaller groupings) is in danger of *falling*, perhaps in war (see 20:18, 24:6). The decision as to what to do in such a situation should not be left to one person but taken after consultation with experienced people. That failing to take advice brings disaster is exemplified by Rehoboam (1 Kings 12), while the success that follows heeding it (15:22) is proved from Acts 15. When faced with the alternatives of offending weak consciences or undermining the gospel of grace, the early Christians came

together to consult the apostles and elders. Their decision sustained the principle of grace through faith alone, satisfied the scrupulous and kept the church united.

The righteous person is wise, he takes advice when he needs it and gives it when asked. In both ways he benefits his community.

D. Particular Cases which Impinge on Righteousness (vv. 15-17, 22).

1. Suretyship (v. 15).

This subject has been fully examined in 6:1-5 and is mentioned here because it fits the general subject of righteousness. In the light of what has already been said, the naive might think it his duty to stand surety for whoever asks. This is not, however, a necessary part of righteousness. Rather the reverse. The first word in the Hebrew sentence is 'Evil' and the second a verb derived from it, making *surely suffer* a very forcible expression. *Putting up security* makes you the guarantor of another's debt but with no guarantee for yourself. If he fails to keep his promise you have no redress and may suffer bankruptcy and poverty, and bring others down with you (cf. v. 29). God expects that of no one. It deprives us of the ability to do any of the good of which verses 24-30 speak. It makes us a drain on others. We must ensure our own security (*safe*) if possible, and therefore have nothing to do with this practice.

2. Male and Female characteristics (vv. 16f, 22).

NIV may be misleading in making **verse 16** a sharp contrast between female tenderness and male *ruthlessness*. It is better to translate kind-hearted as 'charming' (Moffatt, cf. 31:10) and line 2 'strong (i.e. resolute) men gain riches' (KJV). So here we have two complementary rather than contrasting qualities. Strength of character is necessary in a dog-eat-dog world (e.g. where the feckless are looking for a *surety*, v. 15) and the resolute man will restrain the *kind-hearted woman* from yielding to every request out of softness of heart. At the same time she will tone down the male 'what I have I hold' over-protective attitude.

For the passage indicates that both these qualities are open to abuse. The 'strength' can become *ruthlessness* and lead to *cruelty* (**v. 17**), thus shutting out all *kindness*. Equally 'charm' can be confused with external beauty (**v. 22**, cf. 31:10). A woman pleasing to the eye may be stupid rather than genuinely considerate. NIV softens the Hebrew which says 'a beautiful woman without discretion **is** (not *like* – Hebrew) a nose-ring on a pig'. Her beauty and charm clash with her character. For beauty is a matter of harmony and proportion, not just in form and features but in these harmonizing with character (see also under E).

E. THE CONSEQUENCES OF RIGHTEOUSNESS OR ITS OPPOSITE (vv. 17-21)

Here we see that the courses we choose are not matters of personal preference and equally valid. They have moral significance. A righteous God has established moral laws for his human creatures whom he made in his likeness. If we follow them we live in harmony with his providential order and find good. If we disregard them we get out of step and suffer the consequences. The passage develops this theme, and builds up to a climax.

1. Verses 17-18 simply warn us that **our actions have consequences**. This pair of verses is 'chiastic' (see on 10:2-3):

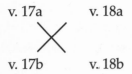

v. 17a   v. 18a

v. 17b   v. 18b

Verse 17a says that the *kindness* he has been commending in verse 16 benefits the giver as well as the recipient. Shakespeare said of 'mercy' that

'it is twice blessed:
It blesses him that gives and him that takes'
('Merchant of Venice' IV.i.186f).

Its opposite *cruelty* bears a corresponding fruit, *trouble*. This states the principle of providence that runs through the whole of Scripture, that God deals with us as we with others (e.g. Ps. 18:25). It was never put better than by Christ himself in the 'Golden Rule': 'Do to others what you would have them do to you, for this sums up the Law and the Prophets' (Matt. 7:12).

Verse 18 takes the thought a little further. 18a expounds 17b: he who acts cruelly hoping for easy gain finds he has been deceived. He may indeed make money but finds it brings grief with it. 18b expounds 17a: the *kind man* helps and gives out of sheer kindness, not expecting any return. But he finds his acts have been seeds from which he eventually *reaps* a harvest of good things (cf. Luke 6:38).

2. Verse 19 spells out **what these *wages* are and this *reward* is** – nothing less than *life* or *death*. These terms are used in a qualitative sense, that is, one has a full rich *life* in harmony with his neighbours, with nature and with God himself; the other is out of step with everything and everyone because his excessive greed prompts him to use any methods to attain his ends, which he never achieves – a kind of living *death*. The words *attains* and *goes to* are not in the Hebrew, suggesting these are not arbitrary awards but latent in these particular life-styles, which are the expression of a person's relationship with God. Thus we have a hint that all this is not just an impersonal law of cause and effect operating, but God is behind it all, spelt out in verse 20.

3. Verse 20 states it is not just natural law that is obeyed or otherwise but God himself. Morality is not just keeping the rules or adopting the best policy, but pleasing or displeasing God. What was said about honesty and dishonesty in verse 1 is here generalized. This is why mention is made not just of *ways* but *heart*. While God does notice our *ways* he also 'looks at the heart' (1 Sam. 16:7). He is interested in motive, particularly in our attitude to himself. It may be 'the best policy' to be honest and even kind, but in that case it is done out of self-love not

love for God or even for the other person (1 Cor. 13:3). I may
gain in the short term but my heart is not right with God and
I shall ultimately face his, 'I never knew you. Away from me,
you evil-doers' (Matt. 7:23).

4. Verse 21 takes up the hint of **the ultimate** we glimpsed when
we brought the personal God into the equation. To speak of
punishment and setting free implies a person. Laws can be
broken but they can't inflict punishment. Only a personal God
can. So ultimately what we are and do we are and do to God.
Here is a court-room picture (cf. 2 Cor. 5:10). Some are *punished*,
others *go free*, depending on our state of heart evidenced by
our behaviour, and whether God has *detested* or *delighted* in
us. Since it is God himself who administers this justice, there
is an inexorability about it, as seen in the literal Hebrew of *Be
sure of this*, which is 'hand in hand'. This describes the handshake that confirms the spoken word. But God's promise to us
in Christ is just as sure (2 Cor. 1:20)! If we have shaken hands
with Christ we can be sure we will be among those who *go free*
on that great day.

**F. PARTICULAR EXAMPLES OF THE CONSEQUENCES OF RIGHTEOUS-
NESS AND WICKEDNESS (VV. 23-29).**
The previous passage established the principle that our actions,
in fact the whole tenor of our lives, have consequences in both
short and long terms. In this passage we have more specific
acts of righteousness and their opposites, plus their results.

1. Desires and hopes (v. 23).
It is not merely what we **do** but what we **desire** and set our
hope on that affects the future. By nature we think that a wish
or hope is like the air – insubstantial and passing. Yet even
these are noted 'in the books' (Rev. 20:12), God's data base.
Terrifying as this thought may be, it is no less than just. For
what we *desire* and *hope* for reflects our outlook and character,
and it is of these that God ultimately takes account. We who
are in Christ have the comfort of knowing that the new birth
changes our very *desires* and *hopes*. Our hearts become 'set on
things above' (Col. 3:1) and our expectations look beyond this

life to the new order (Rom. 8:20f). Such hopes do not *end in wrath*, they 'do not disappoint' (Rom. 5:5) but ensure 'a rich welcome into the eternal kingdom of our Lord and Saviour Jesus Christ' (2 Pet. 1:11).

2. Generosity (vv. 24-25).

Here is a beautiful description of *a generous man*, literally 'a soul of blessing', one who lives to make other people happy. He does this as he *gives freely*. You can't make someone happy without giving something of yourself, even if it's only your time and attention. The truly generous person gives to enrich the other, expecting nothing in return. This is why it is said he *refreshes* them, literally *waters*. Water was a precious commodity in ancient Israel. It could be worth more than money or precious stones which can't save someone dying of thirst (cf. Matt. 10:42). As Jesus said in that verse no giving goes unrewarded by God, even when not recompensed by man. His rewards are *gain, prosperity* and *refreshment*. In God's economy the way to riches is not to hold on to them, which is in fact the way to poverty. This does not mean we must give everything away, for if everyone did that all the time there would be chaos! It is *withholding unduly* that is frowned on, literally 'what is due' or what we owe (see 3:27f).

3. Produce and trade (v. 26).

This verse shows that the previous one was not calling for free hand-outs. It is about selling, which implies the right to own. But there are two kinds of seller and the difference appears in a time of shortage. One man *hoards grain* to force up the price and only sells it when people are desperate. The other sells it at the usual time and the right price. Which is the real gainer? One increases his bank balance but loses people's favour. The other may suffer financially but enjoys the *crown* of popularity. The challenge to us is to put love of others before love of money. For while we can love money, it can't love us.

4. Good and evil (v. 27).

This verse states the principle lying behind the particular cases of verses 24-26. Whoever seeks to do his neighbour *good*, however he does it, will not be the loser, for while he may not be able to measure his profit financially, he will gain *goodwill*, which is far more enjoyable. Similarly one who *searches* for profit at the expense of others or actually looks to harm them, is going to find it rebounds on him in the end.

5. Trust in riches (v. 28).
Greed for gain and the misuse of goods have both been condemned, but now we are warned against something less obvious – the danger of *trusting* them. This is easily done because of the security they give (10:15). It is not that this trust is wrong but that it is misplaced. This whole section is geared to the consequences of our actions rather than their bare morality. The point is brought home by the tree imagery. Riches are like leaves in autumn – after a brief life they *fall*. *Righteousness*, however, is like the evergreen (cf. Ps. 1:3) – it survives the fluctuations of the market and all life's changes. For it is the gift of the righteous God and, like him and his promises, worthy of trust.

6. Neglect of family (v. 29).
We have already seen how those who harm others, or even fail to do them good through meanness, eventually *bring trouble* on themselves. But if they have a *family*, that will suffer too. This will in turn increase their own troubles. People expect their families to support and comfort them in old age. But one who has ruined his family will get nothing and *inherit only wind*. He himself may be driven into slavery, to *be servant* to one who has been more *wise* in handling his affairs.

CONCLUSION
The teaching of this chapter is here summarized in two principles.

1. The best way to do good in the world is to be righteous (v. 30). Trees exist for the benefit of all. They afford shade and bear fruit, and even when they die their wood is useful for building or fuel. The *righteous* man is like a *tree* (Ps. 1), in fact *a tree of life* (alluding to our original paradise). So *the righteous* person is a means of God's blessing on others. Righteousness makes a person *wise*, so that he does things which bring general benefit. Not only does he share his goods (vv. 24-27) but *wins souls*, for he is such a good advertisement for the righteous life that other people are won over to it.

2. All our actions have consequences for ourselves (v. 31).
This is probably the chief point to emerge from this chapter and so is prefaced with the word 'Behold' – 'see what I've proved!' That righteousness is profitable for this life has been shown repeatedly. But this is not always obvious: sometimes the *righteous* get a bad deal and *the ungodly* prosper. This may be why justice to *the ungodly and sinner* is prefaced with *how much more*. We have had enough teaching to convince us that retribution may not be immediate. It may be delayed, but it is ultimately inevitable, because God is righteous. Although mentioned by name only twice, God is a hidden presence behind every verse.

Questions
1. Does PROVERBS appeal too much to self-interest in commending righteousness? Does the New Testament correct this?
2. Micah (6:8) summed up righteousness in three principles. Can you illustrate these from this chapter?
3. Can you see from this chapter how righteousness is based on the character of God himself?
4. What social benefits result from the presence of righteous people in a community?

10

The Righteous and Wicked Contrasted
(Proverbs 12)

The majority of these proverbs are **contrasts** between the first and second parts of each verse, separated by *but*. The experts call this 'antithetical parallelism'. The exceptions are: verse 9, which is a 'better' saying, and even this has an implied contrast as the second part begins with 'than'; verse 14, which is merely confirming the truth stated in verse 13; and verse 28, which some emend to make it a contrast between the ways of life and death. In any case it rounds off the chapter rather than makes a fresh point.

So in this chapter the father or teacher is showing his son or pupil the reality of the world into which he is being launched. Not everyone walks the good way; some are set on evil. He needs to discern these and avoid their ways. To encourage him the advantages of righteousness are displayed in full. The same division exists in our world between 'believers' and 'unbelievers'.

We can consider this under: life-style, character and behaviour.

A. LIFE-STYLE (vv. 1, 3, 7, 9, 21).
The believer's life-style is contrasted with the unbeliever's.

1. The Disciplined Life (v. 1).
Here are two people with contrasting approaches to life. One we call 'teachable' because he is willing to be taught and if

necessary *corrected*. His is the way of *discipline* or 'training', which in PROVERBS is essential to acquiring wisdom (1:2), that is, knowledge put into practice. The more you practise what you hear, the more *knowledge* you acquire and the better understanding you have of life, yourself and your God (cf. 2:9f, 10:17, Ps. 119:97-100). The other one we may call 'obstinate'. He thinks he knows it all without being told. Most obnoxious of all to him is any criticism or *correction*. He thinks this attitude makes him look wise and important; in fact the opposite is the case. He is merely *stupid*, literally 'brutish' – he behaves like an animal impervious to reason (see Ps. 32:8f), or worse for some animals respond to training (Isa. 1:3). Those with this mind-set will always be ignorant (Ps. 92:6, 2 Thess. 2:10b, 2 Tim. 3:7).

2. The Secure Life (vv. 3, 7, 21).

These different approaches have different consequences. 'Obstinate' may appear stable but is merely self-opinionated and rejects godly teaching. This is *wickedness* and cannot endure, **verse 3**. His thoughts and ways come not from God but his own sinful nature. They are like the sand on which 'the foolish man' built his house (Matt. 7:26f). It looked secure but lacked the foundation necessary to survive even the adversities of life, let alone the judgment of God. 'Teachable', however, dwells in God and God in him. In Gospel terms he has roots in Christ (Eph. 3:17). He can be shaken but not uprooted. After the storm has passed his branches may be stripped bare or his stem stripped of branches, but his roots remain, and his branches, leaves and fruit will grow again in time (cf. v. 12, 10:25, Pss. 15:5b, 125:1)

Verse 7 takes this thought a little further. That was a state-ment of principle, this is a fact of life, the principle in practice. Literally it is 'overthrown the wicked' – we are given a preview of those who appeared in control, unassailable, suffering a sudden overturn and disappearing, taking their whole brigade with them. From a position of almost absolute power Haman overreached himself and hung on the gallows he had built for Mordecai, and left no descendants to perpetuate his name and line (Esther. 7:9f).

But the house of Israel went on, as God had promised David (2 Sam. 7:16, 26). For this is a promise not just to an individual but a family and people: *the **house** of the righteous*. It recalls the words of Jesus about his church in Matthew 16:18: 'The gates of death will not overcome it' because he is its foundation. Thus while verse 3 applies to the individual believer, this is for the whole church.

In **verse 21** the principle and its practice are made into a **promise**. The word *harm* ('evil' in KJV) means harm resulting from sin, that is, judgment. *The righteous* may suffer not for his own sins but because he is enmeshed with *the wicked* in this world and suffers along with all mankind. But the *harm* is not total or final – he survives and emerges from it, like Job. This is even clearer under the Gospel, for the new covenant makes no promises about material prosperity or exemption from want and injury in the way the old did. The believer is to **expect** tribulation (Acts 14:22) knowing God will turn it to his good (Rom. 8:28-35, 1 Pet. 1:6-9).

We could be equally sceptical about the statement on *the wicked*. Even under the old covenant they often thrived, as Asaph complained (Ps. 73:3). But there is no security in their prosperity (Ps. 73:18-20). God is just and he must restore the moral balance of his creation. Many indeed do find they 'fall into their own trap' (1:31), that justice overtakes them. But even if it doesn't they shall not escape the righteous judgment of God who 'will give to each person what he has done ... on the day when God will judge men's secrets through Jesus Christ' (Rom. 2:6, 16).

3. The Realistic Life (v. 9).

Here is a saying needing some cultural adaptation. To us someone who *has a servant* is hardly a *nobody*. However, in the social class addressed here, status was measured by the number of servants, so that someone with only one was a *nobody*. But at least he was being realistic and leaving enough money to buy *food* for himself and his family, whereas he who spent more than he could afford on servants and left his family with *no food* was putting status symbols above the necessities of life. Which was living in the real world and which in a pretend one?

In today's world *servants* are not human but mechanical – the household appliances that help with our washing, cooking, cleaning, gardening and travelling. The unrealistic person puts all his resources into these in order to keep up with or ahead of the Joneses, but deprives his family of their basic needs. Surely it is better to have enough to eat than to go without food in order to maintain an unrealistic status in society? You can't eat your dishwasher or your Daimler!

Question
What does the New Testament say of a Christian who is obsessed with his image in the world? See 1 John 2:15-17.

B. CHARACTER (vv. 2, 4, 8, 10, 12, 15-17, 19, 22-23, 25).
The man of God and the man of the world differ from each other not only in the way they live but in what they are, as we see here.

1. Kind or crafty (vv. 2, 4).
Since only God is *good* in an absolute sense (Matt. 19:17) the *good man* (v. 2) is he who like God acts lovingly, kindly and generously to others. The new covenant *good man* loves not only his friends and neighbours but his enemies, and does them good because he is like his Father (Matt. 5:43-47). He has no inherent goodness; it comes from the life of God in him, the 'heart in every thought renewed and full of love divine ...' (Charles Wesley). When God sees his likeness in one of his creatures what can he do but show *favour*? Do we not glow when we see our children bearing our likeness? Do we not delight in them and freely give them of what we have? God's *favour* is similar: he lets us enjoy his company (Job 33:26), he lavishes his blessings on us (Ps. 84:11) and above all gives us his Son, and all that goes with him (Rom. 8:32).

The *crafty man* is the opposite; he seeks to harm his neighbour. *Crafty* is literally 'man of plots' for he devises schemes for doing others down. He is a real Absalom (2 Sam. 15:3). *Plots* is the plural of the word for 'discretion' in 1:4, 8:12, basically a good quality but perverted to evil purposes, as in the originator of craftiness (see Gen. 3:1). But thankfully what has been *per*verted can become *con*verted and the 'man of plots' become one who makes plans to bless others, e.g. Saul of Tarsus (Acts 9:1f, Rom. 1:13).

Verse 4 turns us from the man's character to the woman's. Remarks about women in PROVERBS are usually from the man's point of view because it is about the upbringing of sons who would grow up to look for wives. These must put *noble character* before attractiveness (11:22, 31:30). *Noble* is literally 'strong', not in the sense of domineering but of self-control: not susceptible to sloth, waste, squandering and temptation (see 31:10-25). Solomon underlines this by mentioning the important place she has in her husband's life. If her character is 'strong' she will be his crown – he will be 'happy as a king' (Matthew Henry). But if weak she will disgrace him, she will be like an incurable disease causing weakness, pain and ultimately ruin.

2. Wise or Foolish (vv. 8, 15, 16, 23).

In **verse 8** it is the common sense aspect of *wisdom* that is in view, that capacity for seeing a situation clearly and coming to a right decision. Such people are found useful, *praised* even by the ungodly, and promoted. Thus was Joseph by Pharaoh (Gen. 41:39), Daniel by Nebuchadnezzar (Dan. 1:19f) and the shrewd manager by Jesus (Luke 16:8). On the other hand those who can't think straight are *despised*. The term *warped* does not necessarily have a moral connotation, which is why NIV avoids the word 'perverse' used by KJV. Of course, those who have good sense will not just make good decisions about worldly things (like the shrewd manager) but make right moral choices, and above all choose Christ. 'The fear of (trust in) the Lord is the principal part of wisdom'. Such may not get much praise from sinners but will be commended by Christ at his coming (Luke 12:42-46).

Verse 15 takes the matter further by showing us what makes the wise *praised* and the foolish *despised*. The main trouble with the *fool* is that he doesn't know that is what he is because he always thinks he is right. While he remains self-opinionated he will never be any other than a fool because he is blind to himself and thinks he doesn't need *advice*. Sooner or later he will have an accident.

The only way to become *wise* is to *listen* and check your thoughts with those of others. We must get out of our narrow subjectivity and see ourselves as others see us, admit we may be wrong and someone else knows better. This may involve humiliation and this we hate. But even the great Moses, the man with whom God spoke face to face, was prepared to listen to the priest of Midian, his father-in-law, and take his advice (Exod. 18:14-24), and so was called 'more humble than anyone else on the face of the earth' (Num. 12:3). David, the anointed King, listened to a mere woman and avoided disaster (1 Sam. 25:23-32). But the typical Pharisee won't listen to the one who was greater than Moses and David, and Jesus showed us why: he was totally ignorant of himself and thought himself a splendid fellow. Only those who first listen have anything worth saying, even to themselves (James. 1:19).

Verse 16 shows how the difference between these two types betrays itself in the way each reacts to an *insult*. To the self-opinionated *fool* any disagreement is *an insult* (literally 'humiliation'). He doesn't just **feel** *annoyance*, which is natural, but **shows** it, and *at once*, without stopping to consider whether he has understood the remark correctly or whether it may be true. Saul's anger flared up against his son before he even knew the facts (1 Sam. 20:30f) and Nabal was angered by a peaceful request for hospitality (1 Sam. 25:10). Alas even the godly are found guilty of this. Moses may have been 'more humble than any man on earth' but when the people accused him of bringing them out of Egypt to die in the desert, he cursed them and struck the rock from which came their water supply (Num. 20:10f).

Haven't we all behaved like this? If we can't help feeling hurt by criticism and rudeness we can help showing it. The word *overlook* is literally 'conceal' and the way to learn this art is by learning to *listen* (v. 15) to what the person is really saying, not to what we fear he might be saying (James. 1:19). Above all we must **love** the person, for 'love covers (same word as *overlooks*) all wrongs' (10:12). For further details see 1 Corinthians 13:5-7.

Verse 23 indicates another difference between these two types. The self-opinionated *fool* doesn't know 'there is a time to be silent and a time to speak' (Eccles. 3:7, cf. Prov. 11:13).

So he *blurts out* what he thinks is *knowledge* but it comes over as *folly*. He just wants to show off and is totally insensitive to the company and the occasion. So the response he gets is not 'that's interesting', but 'this man talks like an idiot'. The *prudent man* doesn't glory in his *knowledge* and think himself clever. He waits until he has digested it and understands it better. Silence may not mean ignorance but greater knowledge – of what should be said, to whom and when. Christians can do harm by blurting out precious words to those not in a right condition to receive them (Matt. 7:6). Let us cultivate the wisdom that uses *knowledge* in a way that commends it, not in a way that makes it – and us – look foolish.

3. Honesty or Acquisitiveness (v. 12).

All translators and commentators on the Hebrew agree there are problems with the text, especially in line 1, and some come up with alternatives in order to make line 2 follow more naturally. Literally it reads 'the wicked (man) desires the net of evil men'. The original warning about the ways of the wicked in 1:10-19 said they aim to catch their victim in their *net*, rob him and share the spoil. The meaning therefore is that all who are *wicked* at heart would dearly like the proceeds of a night's robbery, whether or not they have the courage to do it. Because they are *wicked* at heart they see righteousness as unprofitable, and think the only way to prosperity is by theft and force. They can gain in one night more than a life-time's steady honest work can realize.

In fact the reverse is true. It is the outcome of *plunder* that is uncertain. Will it come off? Will you be caught? Will your companions share out fairly? How will you use the proceeds without being detected? The other way may seem unattractive but it has the guarantee of God's word which says it is a root which *flourishes* or 'bears fruit'. This is because *the righteous* trusts God and is content with the earnings of honest work.

4. Truthful or deceitful (vv. 17, 19, 22).

Commending truth and condemning lies occurs frequently in PROVERBS, teaching us how precious truth is to God but how common lying is among us.

Verse 17 is basic, bringing out **the essential difference** between the two. Superficially it appears to state the obvious, but there is more here than meets the eye. It establishes two big principles.

(a) *What we say expresses what we are.* Literally it reads 'he who breathes truthfulness', showing that truth comes from within (Matt. 15:18, 12:34). By nature our 'heart is deceitful' (Jer. 17:9), taught by 'the father of lies' (John 8:44) who deceived our first parents into lying to God. But God who 'desires truth in the inner parts' (Ps. 51:6) can deliver us from this false evil being and fill us with 'the Spirit of truth' (John 14:17) so that henceforth we 'speak the truth' (Eph. 4:15, 25).

(b) *Love of truth is inseparable from love of justice*: *gives honest testimony* is literally 'reveals justice'. This takes us into the law court where truth and falsehood can be a matter of life and death, and which is the setting of the ninth commandment on which this saying is based. Here one witness speaks the truth because his sole concern is for justice – that the defendant be condemned if guilty and acquitted if innocent. The *false witness* has other motives, such as fear or self-interest, and *tells lies*, literally 'reveals deceit' – that is, he shows the falseness of his heart, from which, as Jesus said, 'come evil thoughts ... false testimony' (Matt. 15:19). He whose nature is not right will not be concerned for righteousness or for truth.

Verse 19 commends truth for its enduring nature – it 'stands firm' (NEB) *for ever*. 'What is true will always be true' (Henry) – it cannot change. How it is received makes no difference to its intrinsic rightness. This will one day be acknowledged, although perhaps not until eternity: 'Heaven and earth shall pass away but my words will not pass away' (Matt. 24:35).

In contrast, lies have only a short life-span – literally 'lasts only while I wink', the briefest measurement of time in the ancient world (cf. 1 Cor. 15:52). At its lowest this means lies are often exposed very quickly, as David predicted of those who falsely accused him (Ps. 52:1-5); as Gehazi found to his cost (2 Kings 5:25-27) and even more drastically Ananias and Sapphira (Acts 5:3-10). In a scrape we tend to resort to the lie, but it is a very short term solution. 'Truth will out.' 'Lies have no feet.'

What applies to the words applies to their speaker. He who has *truthful lips* 'stands firm' *for ever*. Even if denounced as a liar now, he will like Job be vindicated 'in the end' (Job 19:23-27). Truth and life go together, being inseparably bound in him who is 'the way, the truth and the life'. Those who have the truth have eternal life because they stand on him whose words 'are the words of eternal life' (John 6:68). But the one with *the lying tongue* builds his life on what will crumble away and take him with it.

Verse 22 reveals what lies behind these proverbs – God's personal approval or otherwise. The language is strong: *detests* and *delights* represent opposite poles of God's reaction to our words, our deeds and ultimately ourselves. Various things are said to arouse God's *detestation* (see 6:16-19 where *lying* comes at the top of the list and features twice). Nothing reminds God of the devil and the first sin more than this. The devil 'is a liar and the father of lies' – and of liars too, for in this way they show they 'belong to (their) father the devil' (John 8:44). Lies not only produced the first sin but disrupt society more than anything else. Paul tells us to 'put off falsehood and speak truthfully ... for we are all members of one body' (Eph. 4:25), here not the body ecclesiastical but the body politic. Society can only function where there is trust, and there can only be trust where there is truth.

Conversely, nothing more *delights* him than truth. He is the God of truth and his Son is the truth, so that those who are truthful are objects of his love. He sees the stamp of his own image on them. Literally it reads 'who act truthfully'. Truth is not just factual accuracy (there are times when this is impossible) but the way we live. Paul even used truth as a verb in Ephesians 4:15 which literally reads 'truthing it in love'. It is possible to be a George Washington and not be what John calls 'walking in the truth' (2 John 4, 3 John 3-4). This requires believing him who is the truth and living in him, on which depends our eternal destiny (Rev. 21:8).

5. Consideration or cruelty (vv. 10, 25).

(a) *To animals* (**v. 10**).
Animals were much more prominent in the economy of ancient Israel than in ours. Life could scarcely go on without

them. From them came wool and skin for clothing, milk and meat for food, sacrifices for worship and above all the work of ploughing fields and carrying burdens. So this verse is not a charter for animal rights, nor a motto for the conservationist lobby. It is about how a man treats *his animal* rather than the animal kingdom in general. It is an appeal to common sense. If you want the maximum return from your animal treat him well. Let him feed as he works (Deut. 25:4), give him the rest you give yourself (Exod. 23:12). Cruelty is counter-productive and foolish. The wise man 'knows the condition of his flocks and gives careful attention to his herds' (27:23).

But there is more than worldly wisdom here. Since it is about *the righteous man*, there is a moral aspect. The animal is not just your servant it is God's creature. What is done to the creature is done to the Creator, who cares for all his creatures (Ps. 36:6, 147:9). The believer who is remade in God's image will therefore treat animals as God does. Literally it reads 'he knows the life of ...' – he considers their feelings which, although less than ours, are real. So it doesn't condemn the butcher or medical researcher, nor pest control. But it does condemn the *cruelty* that comes from a *wicked* nature. Line 2 is peculiar and may be a figure of speech ('oxymoron') saying that the unbeliever's nature inhibits **true** kindness and is just a cover for inward heartlessness. So his *kindest* acts are a mere show. Does it explain why the activist in this field can damage or destroy property and hurt or even kill humans in the course of allegedly protecting animals?

(b) *To humans* (**v. 25**).
One who has the sensitivity to *care for the needs of his animal* will also sense when his neighbour is weighed down with anxiety. Depression is no new problem – the uncertainty of life in every age breeds the anxiety which causes it. Most Israelites lived by farming and were dependent on climatic conditions, the uncertainty of which meant they lived with anxiety. This no doubt explains the number of references to it in PROVERBS (14:10, 15:13, 17:22, 18:14), not to mention PSALMS. Economic uncertainty is still the major cause of depression, with personal relationships a close second.

Nor has the cure changed much. Where we speak of 'trauma counselling', they spoke of *a kind word*. This may be the good news the sufferer has been waiting for (15:30, 25:25), or in the absence of this a word of encouragement to *cheer him up* (v. 18, 15:23, 16:24, 25:11, 27:9). We who live on this side of Calvary know how Jesus entered into this condition as well as the other effects of sin. In Gethsemane 'he began to be deeply distressed and troubled ... with sorrow to the point of death' (Mark 14:33f). How well this qualifies him as our best trauma counsellor! He is a 'high priest... able to sympathize with our weaknesses ... who has been tempted in every way just as we are' (Heb. 4:15f). This he does not only directly but, in the case of those whose hearts are too heavy even to come to him, through their friends who have learned 'to know the word that sustains the weary' (Isa. 50:4).

Question
Since none of us is perfect, let each of us ask:

(a) how kind, wise, honest, truthful and considerate am I?

(b) how much craft, folly, acquisitiveness, deceit and cruelty is there in me?

(c) what am I doing to free myself from (b) in order to become (a)? See 1 John 1:8f, Ephesians 4:20-5:2.

C. BEHAVIOUR (vv. 5-6, 11, 13-14, 18, 20, 24, 26, 27).

1. Making plans (vv. 5, 20).
Verse 5 takes us into the very mind of the *righteous* and *wicked*, or believer and unbeliever. The unbeliever's mind is 'carnal' (Rom. 8:5-8), controlled by his sinful nature; the believer's mind has been 'renewed' by the Spirit (Eph. 4:23) who controls it. So the believer's mind is always turning to ways in which he can do good. *Plans* is literally 'thoughts' and conveys the idea of straightforwardness or openness. One who seeks good has nothing to hide.

By contrast the unbeliever thinks deviously. His *plans* are plots. *Advice* conveys the wrong idea, for he is not seeking to guide someone else but thinking of how he can use them for his own advantage. Most translate it 'counsels', which is misleading; 'designs' (NEB) or 'intentions' would be better, in the sense of a carefully laid plan by which he can appear to be doing good when actually seeking to exploit, hence *deceitful*. To succeed in this requires careful thinking out. Herod in Matthew 2 had a carefully laid plan for killing the infant Christ. What is not open and plain smacks of evil, and the believer is delivered from it.

Verse 20 spells out what v. 5 hinted at by specifying *plotting* and *deceit*. This is how one who is out to exploit his neighbour has to operate. He has to cover what is in his *heart*, to make plans in such a way he won't be found out. This way of life inevitably creates tension; not for him the *joy* of the other. He is always on edge, suspicious, trusting no one. By contrast we see one with totally opposite thoughts, seeking to *promote peace*. The Hebrew SHALOM means general welfare, total good. God seeks to do us good, to give us good things to enjoy and inward peace. For this he sent his Son, the Prince of Peace. Those after his heart devise schemes to do likewise – to provide needs and preach the gospel of reconciliation. Such have minds free from tension and anxiety; they can operate openly without looking over their shoulder. So they find only *joy*.

2. Speaking words (vv. 6, 13, 14, 18).
This theme will come up time and again in PROVERBS. The above verses show something of the power that lies in mere words, to help or harm.

Verse 6 *speaks of* their power to destroy or deliver. In the mouth of *the wicked* words are (literally) 'an ambush'. This refers not only to a deliberate plot to shed *blood*, such as we find in 1:11-19 or Absalom's plot against David in 2 Samuel 17:1-4, or that of the Jews against Paul in Acts 23:12-15, but also to any false accusations designed to ruin a reputation or secure a legal condemnation, such as the Jews did with Christ (Luke 20:20-40, Matt. 26:59-66). Even common gossip can ensnare and destroy another.

One who is *upright* will not only avoid this but use his power of speech to *rescue* those ensnared by *the words of the wicked* (cf. 11:9, 14:3). Mordecai's plea to Esther and hers to Artaxerxes saved the Jews from Haman's plot of genocide

(Esther. 4:7-14, 7:4-6). Christ frequently escaped the Jews' attempts to trap him with trick questions by the wisdom of his answers, and promised the same wisdom to his disciples when in similar situations (Luke 21:15, cf. Acts 4:8-12). Church history abounds with instances of this. We who are not in such dire straits may prove the truth of this saying by defending another against gossip or even speaking for him in court. Words are powerful not only to destroy but deliver.

Verse 13 gives the other side of the coin: **the power of words to damage or save their speaker**. Line 1 is even plainer in 18:7: 'a fool's mouth is his undoing and his lips are a snare to his soul'. *Sinful talk* brings God's judgment down on it. The Psalms speak of how God judges lying speech (5:6), proud words (59:12) and malicious talk (64:8). Nor are these idle threats. Daniel's accusers were proved liars and ended up in the lion's den into which they had thrown Daniel (Dan. 6:24). The Jews' imprecation against Christ, 'His blood be on us and our children' (Matt. 27:25) came terribly true in AD 70.

The same applies where *sinful talk* enters our ordinary conversation. Rudeness arouses anger and may lead to blows, while slander may take the utterer of it to court. Even if this doesn't happen, such words are recorded by God to be recompensed at the final judgment (Matt. 12:36f). That statement also says, 'By your words you will be acquitted', a good comment on *a righteous man escapes trouble*. The words which acquit us at God's judgment seat are our confession of Christ, by which we are 'saved' (Rom. 10:9f). Meanwhile in the present, honest, gentle and kind words save us from the pitfalls of the rash. 'A gentle answer turns away wrath' (15:1), which Gideon proved true when he faced the wrath of the Ephraimites (Judg. 8:1-3), as did Abigail when confronting a vengeful David (1 Sam. 25:23-34).

Verse 14 takes verse 13b further by pointing out that right words not only save from *trouble*, but can be a positive blessing. Those who through words teach others learn themselves; those who bless others are blessed themselves. In this way they are *filled with good things*. Line 2 is unusual, for instead of a contrast it is a confirmation, made by comparing words with *work*. We all know how much we gain from diligent *work*, but it is less obvious that good words benefit speaker as well as hearer. This is why we tend to speak carelessly, not considering the harm our words can do others or ourselves, nor the pleasure we can derive from speaking *good things*. Let the fruits of our labours encourage us to think before we speak, to fill our hearts with good will and pour it into our words. We ourselves won't be emptied, but *filled* and *rewarded*.

Verse 18 relates not only to the above but to verses 16-17. A wise man may *overlook an insult* (v. 16) or even *a lie* (v. 17) but he feels it *pierce like a sword*. David felt this when his enemies accused him, as did Moses when the people complained against him. Malicious words, whether in the form of lies, insults, threats or complaints were equated by Jesus with murder (Matt. 5:21f).

But words have equal power to *heal* as to wound and can even heal the wounds that very tongue has caused. These are words which reason, comfort or soothe. Those best equipped to speak them are those whose ears have been opened by the Sovereign Lord, who gives 'an instructed tongue to know the word that sustains the weary' (Isa. 50:4f). They are those in whom 'the word of Christ dwells richly' (Col. 3:16) who speak 'what is helpful for building others up according to their needs' (Eph. 4:29).

'The tongue can be death or life, poison or medicine, as it is used' (Henry).

3. Doing work (vv. 11, 24, 27).

This is a favourite subject in PROVERBS, e.g. Ch. 10 (point C) where it was connected with wealth and prosperity. Here we have both repetition of points already made and fresh insights.

Verse 11, like verse 9, encourages realism and discourages pipe dreams. But whereas verse 9 was about spending money, this is about earning it. Ploughing, hoeing, reaping and mowing year in year out may be tedious, but they are a reliable way of earning a living. Besides, what is the alternative? A more exciting scheme to get more money more quickly? This may be dreamed up, as NIV takes it (*he who chases fantasies*) or be suggested or offered by someone else, as KJV thinks ('he that follows vain persons'). Whichever it is, it is gambling not godliness. For it was God who called man to this task (Gen. 2:15), and the Fall, although it made work harder and less productive, didn't abolish it (Gen. 3:19, Isa. 28:23-26).

Work, then, be it manual or mental, agricultural or technological, is honoured by God and need not be seen as humdrum by man. Speculators show they don't understand God's ways for man, they lack *judgment* or 'understanding'. They will only learn when their *fantasies* fail them and they end up in *poverty* (see 28:19). Although the character of work has changed, the basic calling remains and so does the truth of the proverb. The plight of the unemployed, their sense of futility as well as their struggle to survive, only strengthens the point.

Verse 24 develops this. The hard worker will not only have *abundant* **food** (v. 11) but will **rule**. This is probably meant metaphorically. The hard worker will get on, he will be promoted. The lazy man will not be trusted with responsibility but made a drudge. Our 18th and 19th century commentators take this in an absolute sense. They lived in times when there was work to do, when the hard-working apprentice was assured of becoming a master. But in our cruel, commercial, technological age what is the victim of redundancy to make of this? Let him try not to be cynical. Unemployment need not mean inactivity and uselessness. An energetic person will find something useful to do, even if he doesn't get paid for it. There is no other way to maintain self-respect. This is particularly true for the Christian, who is never redundant in Christ's service. His promise of promotion to the diligent doesn't depend on market forces (Matt. 24:45, 25:28).

Verse 27 has some textual problems. The word for *roast* is unique in the Old Testament and is most likely a technical hunting term, which some translate 'pursue'. It describes the half-heartedness of *the lazy man*, who manages to entice his prey from its lair but can't be bothered to chase it. This is the sluggard's whole approach – he never finishes what he starts (cf. 13:4, 20:4, 26:15). The result is that he has nothing.

The contrast with *the diligent* in line 2 needs the subject and predicate reversing to give 'a precious possession (for) a man is diligence'. This makes an appropriate contrast, bringing out that the best thing in life is a diligent, industrious, persevering spirit. This is the key to a satisfied life, as 13:4 puts it: 'the desires of the diligent are fully satisfied'.

4. Choosing friends (v. 26).
This is literally 'searches out his friend', meaning he is very careful whom he chooses for his confidant and adviser (the word is used of a close friend in 19:7, Judg. 15:2). He doesn't want one who will make excessive demands on him (11:15) or who will *lead him astray*. This marks the contrast between the *righteous* and *wicked* in this area. The *wicked* has no such confidant or adviser and is left to go his own *way*. Since he lacks principles and follows his own judgment and desires he goes *astray* (cf. James 1:10f).

All this teaches us that *friendship* is best entered not casually but carefully. In choosing friends we have a duty, to ourselves not to let the demands of *friendship* lead us *astray*, and to our friend to help him go the right way. Jesus, our supreme example, discerned the nature of his friends, even the one who betrayed him. He never withheld his friendship from sinners (Matt. 11:19, Luke 15:2), but used it to turn them from *the way of the wicked* so that they would not continue to be led *astray*.

Question
Put these four activities together in your mind: planning, speaking, working and socializing, and reflect on how large a part of your daily life they occupy. Do these verses lead you to make any changes in or adjustments to your life in these areas?

D. A Concluding Commendation of Righteousness (v. 28).
Some try to make this into a contrast like almost every other verse in the chapter and read *immortality* as 'to death' instead of 'no death' (which in Hebrew involves only a tiny vowel change). Line 2 then becomes 'there is a well-worn path to death' (NEB) which contrasts with the first part, *the way of righteousness* which leads to *life*. This would form a summary of the two ways of life set out here and their consequences for time and eternity.

On the other hand, verses 9 and 14 are not in antithetic form and this verse, like them may simply be a concluding commendation of *the way of righteousness*. It has two consequences:

1. It makes for the good life, the happy prosperous life that results from following the *life-style*, cultivating the *character* and performing the *activities* set out here;

2. It doesn't end when life ends, for there is 'no death' (*immortality*) but a higher life to follow. In other words, it is groping for what Christ brought us – 'life to the full' and 'eternal life'.

11

Following the Instruction of the Wise
(Proverbs 13)

All the themes touched on in this chapter have already cropped up. Some are repetitions, others develop their subject.

1. **Discipline and training**: verses 1, 10, 13, 18, 24 (cf. chs. 10, 12).
2. The right and wrong use of **words**: verses 2-3, 5, 17 (cf. chs. 10, 12).
3. Good and bad approaches to **work**: verses 4, 23 (cf. ch. 10).
4. The **security** enjoyed by the righteous: verses 6, 14 (cf. ch. 12).
5. **Money** matters: verses 7-8, 11, 21-22, 25 (cf. chs. 10, 11).
6. The way to **happiness**: verses 9, 12, 19 (cf. ch. 11).
7. Human **relationships**: verses 15, 16, 20 (cf. ch. 12).

A. DISCIPLINE AND TRAINING (vv. 1, 10, 13, 18, 24).

Verse 1 pinpoints what is the main subject of the chapter. If we are to 'follow the instruction of the wise' we must begin by listening to what they have to say. Ideally this starts in childhood in the home, because we come into the world in a state of ignorance ('simple', 1:4) with a bias to 'folly' and sin (22:15). This makes it hard to *heed ... instruction*:

(a) because we are opinionated by nature, think we are right and don't need teaching (12:15);

(b) because some of the teaching will be in the form of correction (*rebuke*), which we find offensive (9:7f). If we find it hard to be directed in the right way, it will be harder to accept we are going the wrong way. But all depends on doing so: the character we develop, the life-style we adopt and the company we shall enjoy (for it is only wilful, headstrong cynics who are drawn to mockers).

Verse 10 continues to warn us against our natural tendency to ignore our teachers. The question is whether *only* goes with *pride* or *quarrels*. KJV is alone in opting for 'only by pride comes strife', and commentators on it tend to explain that *pride* is the ultimate source of all *quarrels,* although other factors may come in. RSV and NEB emend RAQ (*only*) to REQ ('brainless' or 'heedless'), which contrasts well with *those who take advice,* but the economic writer of PROVERBS is unlikely to put two words as similar as *pride* and 'heedless' together in a clause of four words.

Experience as well as Scripture teaches us that pride invariably leads to contention (e.g. Judg. 12:1-4, 1 Kings 12:10-16, 2 Kings 14:10, Luke 22:24). This applies to our church disputes, which we excuse as 'clash of personality', whereas the truth is that two proud, opinionated people are competing to have their own way. The best way to avoid *quarrels* is to be humble enough to *take advice* from others who see things more dispassionately and know that quarrelling won't solve the issue. Only listening to the instruction of the wise will do that.

Verse 13 further emphasizes what verse 10 said about heeding *instruction.* Hidden in the terms is the fact that what the wise speak is the word (*instruction*) and *command* **of God**. So this is not a teacher threatening detention but a man of God warning of the consequences of disobeying him. The *scorn* is not necessarily laughing out loud, but simply failing to take it seriously enough to act on it. For the 'word' he *scorns* is that which alone can save him from disobedience and offer him the *reward.*

As Bridges observes, since God is holiness he will not be trifled with, and since he is grace he will not be served for nothing. The opposite of *scorn* is *respect,* which means taking the word to heart as coming from God himself, even though it reaches you via man. Instead of being *ruined,* such are *rewarded.* This is not a doctrine of merit, for the New Testament gospel of free grace only offers life to those who respond to it with 'the obedience of faith' (Rom. 1:5, 6:17). For the *reward* see verse 14.

Verse 18 takes us on to the consequences of *heeding* or *ignoring* instruction. It is a striking instance of where God's ways are not ours. It is rebukes, *discipline* and *correction* that make us feel *shame*, especially in front of others. They strike at our self-image and offend our pride. We are afraid that lowering ourselves in our own esteem will lower us in the eyes of society. The reverse is the case – it is *honoured*. Accepting criticism graciously is the fruit of humility, an attractive quality in the eyes of most people. To be respected for humility is surely greater *honour* than the kind of respect pride gains.

There is also an economic argument: the threat of *poverty* is held over those who won't bend to *discipline*. This would be very real in Old Testament Israel. Children who did not accept the discipline every Israelite parent was expected to impose tended to drift into wickedness and become socially unacceptable. Such would have difficulty finding employment or doing business, and so fall into *poverty*. Certainly he couldn't count on God's blessing in terms of material prosperity. Now God has other means of *honouring* those who submit to *discipline*, not the least being the assurance it gives us and others that we are truly his: 'Endure hardship as discipline; God is treating you as **sons**' (Heb. 12:7).

Verse 24 brings us back to the family circle (v. 1 cf. 10:1) and the discipline of the young (1:2-4) by the parents. None was better qualified for this than Solomon, who was taught not only by David (4:3-9) but by God, who even threatened him with the rod (2 Sam. 7:14)! It is interesting that in his book Solomon refers to **divine** discipline before **parental** (3:11f). This is the key to the whole subject as it shows the spirit in which discipline is to be administered to children. Love is the motive for discipline and even punishment.

To unbelievers it may be inexplicable that you show your child love by causing him pain, but this is because they are ignorant of what the Bible teaches about the nature of a child as it comes into the world. Through imputed sin 'folly is bound up in the heart of a child' (22:15). A loving parent will want to make this 'young fool' wise and so will use the means God has given. To withhold it is not love but mere fondness, in fact love of self rather than of the child, which is what the verse means by *hates*. To discipline a child we must first discipline ourselves – control our natural weakness, indulgence, desire for affection and popularity. If parental discipline is lacking in our society it is because self-discipline is absent. The consequence – juvenile delinquency – is all too obvious. We are, however, warned against over-severity which tends to 'exasperate ... embitter ... discourage' them (Eph. 6:4, Col. 3:21). Scriptural discipline is not that which comes from our pride and anger, but from 'the training and instruction of the Lord'.

Questions
1. Do you think *the rod* is to be taken literally or as a metaphor for a non-corporal form of punishment which will encourage the child to 'heed instruction'?
2. If the latter is the case what does it teach us about how God gains greater obedience from us as his children (see Micah 6:8f, Hebrews 12:5-11)?

B. THE RIGHT AND WRONG USE OF WORDS (vv. 2-3, 5, 17).
One of the chief parts of wisdom is the right use of the tongue.

Verse 2 is about the good or harm our words may do to others. 'Jaw, jaw is better than war, war,' said Churchill. To discuss disputes and negotiate a fair settlement of issues is better than resorting to *violence* – that way everyone loses. Which course of action is chosen will depend on character and disposition. The *man* in line 1 is clearly the opposite of him in line 2 – a faithful, righteous or good man, who will have good counsel to offer and will look for long-term solutions in which everyone has a fair deal (*good things*).

Even if he fails he will not go unblessed for good words profit the speaker himself (12:14). He **may** fail, not because he is a poor speaker but because he is up against an *unfaithful* (treacherous) person, who is out for himself and his party, but has no principle other than self-interest. He is not interested in peace except on his own terms and at heart he has a *craving for violence* and ends up like those described in 1:11-19.

Verse 3 develops the point in 2a that words affect the speaker himself. Whether or not they succeed, good words profit the speaker, whereas *he who speaks rashly* harms himself. 'Careless talk costs lives' was a memorable World War II slogan, and this might include the life of the careless talker. So the violent man, even if he doesn't commit violent actions, will speak *rash* words likely to provoke violence or an action for slander. His weakness is his lack of self-control. He 'opens his mouth wide' (as *speak rashly* is literally) and lets it all out. He doesn't control the flow of his words, so that a deluge pours out as when the sluice gates are opened. But it is himself he drowns.

So if we value our *life* ('soul') we will learn to *guard* our *lips* and weigh our words. They are like the city gates of old times – if they are secure so is the city. Words, as James said, are like the bit in the horse's mouth or the rudder on the ship (James 3:3f) – they determine the whole course of life, now and in eternity. Who can tame this wild beast (James 3:7f)? How can we learn self-control? David recommended prayer: 'Set a guard, O LORD, over my mouth; keep watch over the door of my lips' (Ps. 141:3f).

Verse 5 refers to the use of words for deceit or slander, both of which are *false*. *The righteous* man is essentially one who deals fairly with others and will therefore *hate* misleading or abusing them (11:27). *The wicked*, however, thrive on deceiving and exploiting others (12:5, 6, 12) and thus *bring shame and disgrace* on themselves. The word for *shame* is derived from 'stink', referring to behaviour that disgusts. Jacob complained that his sons' treacherous slaughter of the men of Shechem had made him 'a stench to the Canaanites' (Gen. 34:30). The message is thus not just about behaviour but attitude. What do we *hate*? What disgusts us? What gives off a bad smell? The mark of *the righteous* is that they *hate* what God hates (6:16-19, 8:13).

Verse 17 draws our attention to one use of words which was very important in the ancient world where the human messenger was virtually the only means of communication. A *messenger* conveyed news (Job 1:14), acted as an intermediary (Gen. 32:3-6) and negotiated deals: about produce, stock and land. A king's envoy would be responsible for threatening war or suing for peace. Much depended on his being *trustworthy* – to abuse this would bring trouble on his master, himself and the whole nation. If he was true to his trust he would do much good. *Healing* suggests that this is about reconciliation: of individuals, families or nations. A *messenger* was a high calling and a great responsibility.

Questions
1. What are the implications of this teaching on WORDS for the 'information technology' of our day?
2. Apply verse 17 to our testimony to or preaching of the gospel. Refer to Matthew 5:9, 2 Corinthians 5:20, 1 Corinthians 4:2, 2 Timothy 2:2.

C. Good and Bad Approaches to Work (vv. 4, 23).

Verse 4 is about *diligence* or lack of it. We have met *the sluggard* before (6:6-11, 10:4, 12:11, 24) and will do so again (26:13-16). Here, as usual, he is contrasted with the hard worker (*diligent*). The Hebrew has 'soul' for both *craves* and *desires*, used here not as in verse 3 for *life* but for 'appetite' (AMP). On the lowest level both have an 'appetite' for food, but the one who doesn't work for it goes hungry (cf. 2 Thess. 3:10). Both may desire prosperity, to be *fully satisfied* (literally 'made fat'), to have abundance. But to attain this requires more than dreams, as we saw in 12:11. The Hebrew is dramatic: *the soul of the sluggard craves and – nothing*! We get *nothing* without desires, but neither do we get anything with no more than desires.

Verse 23 is about good and bad management. As it stands in NIV this verse suggests that a *poor man* by hard work may make an unpromising piece of land, perhaps bought cheaply, prosper, but lose it all at a stroke through *injustice*. This seems to contradict verses 21-22 and the general teaching of the old covenant. An alternative is to go back to the KJV's 'there is that is destroyed for want of judgment'. This forms a better contrast with the first part of the verse, suggesting that one who has an opportunity for prosperity may fail through bad management. The words 'there is that' (or 'there is one who') are nearer to the Hebrew word used, and the jarring note following the optimism of verses 21-22 is removed. However, it is possible NIV is right in saying that industry is no guarantee against exploitation.

Questions
How would you apply these points to spiritual 'work' or life:
    (a) to salvation itself (cf. Rom. 4:2-5 with John 6:27-29, Luke 13:24);
    (b) to growth in grace (Heb. 6:11, 2 Pet. 1:5-11)?

D. THE SECURITY ENJOYED BY THE RIGHTEOUS (vv. 6, 14).

Verse 6 tells us that *righteousness* gives security to those who practise it, as in 10:9, 30; 12:3, 7, 21. This does not mean they **trust** their *righteousness*, (unacceptable under both covenants), but that their eyes are upon pleasing God – they 'hate' what he 'hates' (v. 5), and so enjoy his protection (Eph. 6:14).

There is no such security for those who walk in *wickedness*. They are left to the mercy of those whom they make their enemies. The natural vindictiveness of humanity means they are unlikely to be shown much mercy. But they can't complain, for it is their own behaviour that ultimately *overthrows* them. God simply gives them up to their overthrowers – their victims, their victims' friends or the authorities. This is an uncompromising statement of divine retribution which restores the moral balance of society. When Thales, a wise old Greek, was asked what was the greatest rarity in the world, he replied, 'To see a tyrant live to be an old man.'

Verse 14 shares with us what a satisfying experience it is to enjoy this security. It is all part of the *teaching of the wise*. *Teaching* is literally TORAH, as in 1:8, indicating the teacher is one who has himself been taught the word of God, which has made him *wise*. One who 'respects' (v. 13) this *teaching*, who is attentive, interested and obedient to it, will enjoy two blessings:

(a) *Refreshment*, for a *fountain of life* is spring water, always clear, fresh and cool, unlike tank water which has long been stored. O for that preaching in our day which is to the soul what a cold shower or glass of water is to the body after a hot night!

(b) *Safety*. The Word not only has its doctrines of grace but its warnings about the world, flesh and devil who are always out to trap us, stop us reaching heaven's gate and bring us down to eternal *death*. It not only tells us what *the snares* are, but makes them abominable to us, so that we turn from them.

For further study consider the New Testament teaching on the eternal security of the believer in Romans 8, from the points of view of

(a) the fact of it, verses 1-4;

(b) the peace it gives, verses 31-39.

E. Money Matters (vv. 7, 8, 11, 21, 22, 25).

Although 'money' as such does not feature in all these verses, they all concern material well-being. The place of this in our lives and our need for a wise approach to it is reflected in the fact that almost a quarter of the chapter is devoted to it.

Verse 7 at first sight seems to be a re-run of 12:9. However, in the latter the contrast was between building an image and living in the real world. Here it is between two forms of pretence or deceit. For in spite of KJV's translation 'maketh himself rich', there is little doubt the term means 'play' or 'act'. The subject of line 1 is indeed similar to 12:9b in that he has delusions of grandeur and is trying to impress.

But what about the subject of line 2? We could be generous and say he is avoiding ostentation, not parading his riches. But he could do this without going to the extreme of feigning poverty. So it is likely he is being crafty and trying to mislead, perhaps to avoid the attentions of thieves and professional beggars; but more likely because he is mean and evading his responsibilities to the needy (3:27f). We must appear what we are. Neither riches nor poverty are things to be ashamed of. But riches bring responsibilities and poverty should make us swallow our pride.

It is not easy to decide what is in view in **verse 8**. It may refer to Exodus 21:28-30, the law which allowed the owner of a mad bull which habitually gores people to death, to 'redeem his life' by paying whatever is 'demanded'. Such payment would be beyond the reach of *a poor man*. However (apart from the fact that he is unlikely to own a bull!) to say he *hears no threat* scarcely fits.

So most translators take it to mean that the rich man is vulnerable to blackmail and *threat* because he is known to be able to pay up (e.g. Jer. 41:8). The *poor man* is not worth the bother and so *hears no threat*. If we compare it with verse 7 we may make more sense of it. One who *pretends to be rich* may suffer what a real rich man suffers, while he who hides his riches will escape the attentions of kidnappers and blackmailers. Unfortunately this sounds like an encouragement to deceit, whereas it is probably a word of consolation to the genuine poor man who doesn't have to pretend. Poverty isn't all bad news (15:16f, 16:8, 17:1).

Verse 11 gives us two ways of making money and two ways of using it. It can be **made** *dishonestly* (literally 'by vanity') or *little by little* (literally 'by hand'). This seems like a contrast between earned and unearned income. The latter might be made *dishonestly* – by theft or sharp practice; by gambling, which fits 'vanity' quite well, indicating a very easy way of making money; or more respectably by inheritance. It is all comparatively easy money. As for its **use**, 'easy come, easy go'. For the type of person who lives by easy money is the type who is not very careful in its use. We use best what we value most, and we value most what we gain the hardest. So one who works for his income and obtains it *little by little* will want to *make it grow*. So he will save or, better, invest it either in his work or the money market. The wise person doesn't envy one who wins the lottery, makes a killing on the stock market or receives a legacy. These may raise the problems of verses 7-8!

Verse 21 is a shining example of the black-and-white world of PROVERBS in material matters: the *sinner* is punished and the *righteous* prospers. This is because PROVERBS is based on the Law, which, as we have often seen, relates prosperity to morality. This verse even personifies evil as *misfortune* and good as *prosperity*. The first relentlessly *pursues the sinner*, the second *rewards the righteous*. All this is backed up by the teaching of the prophets (Isa. 3:10f) and by specific examples of this poetic justice, beginning with Cain (Gen. 4:10-12) and continuing throughout Old Testament history. It applies both to whole nations (Ezek. 14:13) and individuals (Ezek. 18:4). There are agonizing exceptions to this (Job, Asaph in Psalm 73) but these only prove the rule.

When we turn to the New Testament we find this outlook only in the mouth of ignorant Jews (John 9:2) or outright pagans (Acts 28:4). Does this mean God is not 'the Judge of all the earth' after all? No, the New Testament position is that God, as well as just, is long-suffering and tolerates sin in order to give time for repentance (2 Pet. 3:9). This does not mean he forgets justice, but he has reserved it for a final day of reckoning, when punishment will be meted out and rewards allotted (Rom. 2:7-10). So it is still true that *evil pursues the sinner*; although it may lag behind him it will eventually overtake him; he will find no hiding place from it. So too the *righteous* may pass his days in affliction but none of his good deeds or his sufferings will be forgotten on that day (Matt. 10:42, Heb. 6:10).

Verse 22 begins where verse 21 left off. Here we see **how** *misfortune pursues the sinner* and *prosperity rewards the righteous*, who not only prospers himself but provides for his children, who build on it and hand it on to their children and so on. But the *sinner's* descendants don't profit from his wealth; though he is a miser and *stores it up* it finds its way into the hands of *the righteous*.

Such a statement raises problems for us. A century of socialism has altered our view of inherited wealth. We think it better everyone should work for his living. In any case, isn't this 'the Protestant ethic' (cf. 2 Thess. 3:10)? As for line 2, it is inexplicable. It hasn't happened to me, we say, or anyone I know! However, if we take it in the context of Old Testament Israel, it makes more sense. For one thing, most business was family based. Sons continued to farm the father's estate rather than go elsewhere and into another profession. To take over a farm running at a loss would be a curse. God promised so to prosper the righteous that their descendants would prosper too.

Our society is different. Unless we are blue-blooded we encourage our children to make their own way and become independent of us. The family business is almost a thing of the past. What they inherit from us is a good start in life, an upbringing in decency, self-control, kindness and above all godliness. Through our high taxation we contribute to their education so that they can prosper materially. The second part of the verse was literally fulfilled in the Israelites 'spoiling the Egyptians' (Exod. 12:36) and Jacob outstripping Laban (Gen. 30:42b-43), but we can only apply it in a general and long-term manner: the children of God inherit his blessings, especially his new creation, while the unbeliever will be left with nothing. Perhaps the nearest equivalent is 'the meek inherit the earth'.

Verse 25 (cf. 10:3) reflects the covenant between God and his people, by which he undertook to bless their crops and herds so that they would always have sufficient (Ps. 34:10). However, if they were unfaithful to him they might lose this provision and experience hunger (Deut. 28:47f; 32:24). That this was no idle threat was proved on several occasions when, because of idolatry, God allowed their enemies to invade and besiege their cities (e.g. 2 Kings 6:24f). Although on such occasions no doubt *righteous* and *wicked* suffered alike, God could make a distinction (Isa. 65:13f).

The New Testament position is not that God withholds provision from the wicked but that he supplies both alike (Matt. 5:45). This does not mean there is no difference, for the *wicked* can **feel** want even when not actually enduring it, because they are governed by greed not need; as 10:3 says, God 'thwarts their craving'. So it comes down not to amount but attitude: the *righteous* are free from anxiety (Matt. 6:25), thankful for basics, *content* with enough (1 Tim. 6:8) and generous even with their pittance (Luke 21:1-4). In this sense, *the stomach of the wicked* is certainly empty.

For further consideration: survey these verses on money matters and try to work out ways in which our use of money reflects our basic character.

F. THE WAY TO HAPPINESS (vv. 9, 12, 19).
The word of God is not all rules, but reflects God's understanding of our emotional nature and shows us how to be happy.

Verse 9 refers to happiness in terms of a *light* that *shines brightly*. In a country with long nights and very inefficient artificial light this is an apt illustration. This *light* is God's word itself (6:23, Ps. 119:105) which is like the sun in the sky, bringing a brightness which increases as the day proceeds (4:18, Ps. 19:4b-5). So those who listen to wise instruction are happy because they know where they are going and can even direct others. *The wicked*, however, have only a *lamp*, manufactured not created, perhaps a candle, oil lamp or even electric torch! These are dim compared to daylight and last only until the fuel runs out. It represents those who are self-taught and haven't followed the Word and its teachers. They derive little pleasure from their light, which will fail them just when they need it (Isa. 50:10f, Matt. 25:8). The light of reason is like a *lamp* – useful in a dark world but giving 'no future hope' (24:20).

Verse 12 seems clear on the surface: having something to *hope* for gives pleasure at first, but the longer the fulfilment is *deferred* the more the pain outweighs the pleasure. Correspondingly, the longer the delay the greater the joy when it is *fulfilled*; indeed it is the nearest thing to paradise that this world affords – *a tree of life,* like life from the dead. The question is: what is the message? Is it a **warning** not to set our heart on anything in this uncertain world lest we only make our *heart sick*? Is it a **counsel** to be patient and put up with delays? Is it an **encouragement** to be patient and bear up in times of disappointment because of the assurance of ultimate fulfilment when the pleasure will cure the *sickness* of waiting?

Possibly it is all these. It is exemplified by Abraham and Sarah laughing at Isaac's birth after a quarter of a century of waiting (Gen. 21:6f); Jacob's reunion with Joseph after a similar period of waiting (Gen. 46:30); the return of the exiles after seventy years in captivity (Ps. 126:1-3, cf. Ps. 137); Simeon holding the infant Messiah in his arms (Luke 2:29f), and the disciples seeing Christ after his resurrection (John 16:22; 20:20). So perhaps the lesson for us is to set our hopes on what God has promised, as in the above examples, especially on the renewal of creation and our own final glory (Rom. 8:19-25; 1 John 3:2). The pain of watching for this *hope* to be *fulfilled* will not make our *heart sick,* but be positively enjoyable (cf. 11:23).

Line 1 of **verse 19** is a virtual repeat of verse 12 – the pleasure we have when dreams become realities. Line 2 then spells out what we were groping towards in verse 12 – that this promise is conditional. Even then it does not express it by means of the usual contrast, which has made some suggest we have two separate sayings here.

If we take it as it stands it is saying that not everyone finds line 1 to be so: either their dreams don't come true or if they do they disappoint. This is because they are unworthy desires: either they are desires for something *evil*, or an inordinate craving for something good. The Teacher (Ecclesiastes) found his achievements 'meaningless' (Eccles. 2:11). The whole nation experienced this when they craved meat in the desert, which was not wrong in itself but done in a resentful untrusting spirit, so that along with the meat God sent 'a wasting disease' (Ps. 106:15). So in this matter what we need is wisdom to discern what is worthwhile and the self-control which keeps our desires in moderation. *Fools* are those who have not learned this.

Question
Is it true in your experience, of yourself and others, that a Christian is happier than a non-Christian?

G. Human Relationships (vv. 15, 16, 20).
PROVERBS is about teaching wisdom to the young, not only for their personal success but their contribution to the well-being of society. They need therefore to learn how to relate to others.

Verse 15 is about the social effects of heeding the instruction of the wise. Those who do so acquire *good understanding* (literally 'prudence', a quality which PROVERBS is concerned to cultivate, 1:3). By it one learns the art of dealing with people in a reasonable way and thus *winning* their *favour*. This contrasts with those who have not been taught the Word, who are called *unfaithful*, that is 'faithless' (RSV) or even 'treacherous' (RV) because they are not trustworthy. Saying that their way ... *is hard* has caused problems, since the word used means 'enduring' (cf. NIV mg, which unaccountably adds a 'not'!).

The clue lies in Deuteronomy 21:4 which uses the word of an uncultivated valley, so dry and hard it is unploughable. The idea is that these people are impervious to the feelings and conditions of their neighbours; their *ways* of treating people are unsympathetic and do not *win* their confidence but are *hard*. It does not mean **they** find life *hard* (as KJV and its commentators have it) but that they give others a hard time. The difference a Bible education makes! It even cultivates social graces!

Verse 16 continues to speak of our relationships and dealings with others. 'Understanding' (v. 15) and wisdom make a *prudent man*, that is, one who has the art of using his *knowledge* in a practical way, especially in his relationships. *Every prudent man* ensures he understands a matter before he *acts* on it, especially if it involves discussion or negotiation with others. If he does not, he will *expose his folly*. For *a fool* is one who is either ignorant of the area he is venturing into or has not prepared himself for it. The way he handles it and the people involved soon show this. Bible-believing people should be best of all at handling others, for they have the biggest advantages – God's own knowledge and wisdom.

Verse 20 echoes the truism that we become like the company we keep, for good or ill. *Suffers harm* is best translated 'becomes evil'. This explains why the early part of PROVERBS contains so many warnings against associating with criminals (1:11-19) and prostitutes (2:16-19). What is not so obvious is that we ourselves have the choice of our companions, and the choice we make says much about us. One who chooses to *walk with the wise* already has the wisdom to discern who are *the wise* and to desire their company.

This is why the parent has the duty of instilling wisdom into his offspring. He will learn the difference between righteous and wicked, between *wise* and *fools*, and will be drawn to the righteous and the wise. This incipient wisdom will increase and he will *grow wise*. For wisdom is to be acquired not only in youth but throughout life (1:5). When the child becomes a parent, if he has not become *wise*, how are his children to learn 'the beginning of wisdom'? What a blessing is the church where our *companions* are those who have been 'made wise for salvation' and where we can 'sharpen' each other 'as iron sharpens iron' (27:17).

For further consideration

1. Reflect again on the 'understanding' and 'knowledge' of verses 15-16: do you think these are the key to good relationships at home, work and church? Does this explain family and other breakdowns?

2. Apply verse 20 to Christian fellowship. How have other Christians helped you become wiser? See 2 Timothy 3:15, Proverbs 27:17.

12

The Wise and Foolish Compared
(Proverbs 14)

Not only is the contrast between Wisdom and Folly the specific subject of ten of these sayings, but it underlies most of the others. As usual, some Proverbs touch on more than one subject and this will be indicated by bracketing a verse which has some connection with the subject under discussion but is dealt with more fully in another section. We will begin with those specifically on Wisdom and Folly, then see how the principles apply in other areas.

A. THE WISE AND THE FOOLISH (vv. 6-8, 9, 15-17, 24, 29, 33).
Since the main purpose of the book is 'attaining wisdom ... giving prudence to the simple' (1:2, 4), it is no surprise that much space is again given to this. Not that these sayings are mere repetition, for they add much to what has already been said.

1. Who needs Wisdom and who has it? (vv. 6, 7, 33).
In a word – everyone needs it but not everyone has it.

(a) *Everyone recognizes the value of Wisdom.* **Verse 6a** tells us that even the cynic (*the mocker*) would like to be wise, to appear cleverer than others, to say things they haven't thought of, to be different, so that people admire him for his *wisdom*.

Verse 33b makes a similar point, although not everyone agrees with the niv's interpretation of a rather obscure piece of Hebrew. Some think it means that the wise (*discerning*) keep their thoughts to themselves (*in the heart*) whereas fools blurt them out (*let them be known*) to show everyone how wise they are. Others go with the Septuagint and supply 'not': 'wisdom is not known in the heart of fools' (RSV). However, even though it makes a more intelligible contrast, it seems unlikely a copyist would omit 'not' from his text by mistake. A good principle of textual criticism is to opt for the harder reading, since it is more likely an editor would simplify a text than make it harder! Taking the Hebrew as it stands makes it not so much a contrast as a commendation of Wisdom. *Even among fools* it is recognized – they are forced to admit that what the wise say is best in the end.

(b) *The cynic will never attain to it.* The mocker (**v. 6a**) would like to be thought wise but his approach is against him, not because he is stupid or ignorant but because he won't take that essential first step – to trust God (1:7). He only believes what can be proved by sense or reason and *mocks* the supernatural. He is intellectually proud and will not 'receive the kingdom of God as a little child'. So although he may be 'always learning' he will 'never be able to acknowledge the truth' (2 Tim. 3:7). The 'little child' is the one who believes in order that he may see, not vice versa.

(c) *It must become part of our very nature* (**vv. 6b, 33a**). The wise person is the *discerning* person (1:5; 10:13), that is, one who has learned certain basic moral and spiritual principles and judges everything by them. The more he does this the more *wisdom reposes* in his heart, becomes part of his very nature. Then he finds *knowledge comes easily to him*. Lest we think we shall never rise to such heights, let us remember that in our Gospel days 'Christ has become for us wisdom from God' (1 Cor. 1:30). It is not brain-power, education or experience that make us wise but 'Christ dwelling in our hearts through faith' (Eph. 3:17). The newest believer in Christ is wiser than the most learned cynic.

(d) *It won't be found in the conversation of cynics* (**v. 7**). This verse is best read not as a command but an observation: 'When you go *away from a foolish man you will not find knowledge.*' You can spend hours in his company, but if he lacks that 'discernment' which is at the heart of Wisdom you will have learned nothing of any value. You could teach him more than he can teach you, if he would only listen. But he is one of those 'pigs' who if you feed them 'pearls' only rubbish them and get cross with you (Matt. 7:6).

Now we see how to identify and distinguish the wise from fools.

2. How to identify the wise and the foolish (vv. 8, 9, 15-17, 24, 29).

Many marks are given in PROVERBS, of which this chapter concentrates on one. The wise are thoughtful, cautious and patient – they 'look before they leap'. Fools are thoughtless, hasty and impatient – they 'rush in where angels fear to tread'. Our chapter first lays down a principle then illustrates it.

(a) *The Principle* (**v. 8**). The wise (*prudent*) are those who *give thought to their ways* (cf. 15:28; 21:29). They have been taught the principles of the Word of God, that way of life which pleases him. *Wisdom* in PROVERBS is about the way we live. As sinners this does not come naturally to us, we have to be taught it by his Word and those called to teach it to us. So in deciding on a particular course of action, the *prudent* weighs up the situation in the light of these principles. Fools, however, are guided not by principle but pragmatism: will it work? ... make me richer or happier? Although he may indeed become a richer and happier man than the wise, in fact he has fallen prey to the *deception* of his own heart, which lies to him, telling him that only material things are real and that this life is the only one there is. This was how the rich man of Luke 12:13-21 came to grief: he acted on impulse, without deep thought and purely materialistically. Although his decision seemed wise, it turned out to be folly.

(b) *The application of the principle* (**vv. 9, 15-17, 29**). Here are some examples of matters which require careful thought.

(i) **Sin (v. 9).** *Fools* don't take *sin* seriously. Since their lives are based on pragmatism rather than principle, they are only concerned when their plans don't come off or (if they involve breaking rules) they are found out. They will never *make amends*, you will never get an apology or restitution out of them. Since the word for *sin* can refer to 'the guilt-offering', it suggests there were those in Israel so unconcerned about sin they would never bother with atoning sacrifices. This folly is repeated today by those who laugh at the doctrine of substitutionary atonement (cf. 1 Cor. 1:23). They are mocking the only way of their salvation. In contrast, *the upright* take *sin* seriously and seek to avoid offending others by promoting *goodwill* among themselves. If they should *sin* they are sorry and seek to put it right by apology and restitution to the offended party (Matt. 5:21-26), and by repentance towards God (1 John 1:9). You can know the wise from the fool by the thought he gives to sin.

(ii) **Belief (v. 15).** Another mark of the fool (*simple*) is credulity. He will swallow what sounds plausible and jump at an offer that looks attractive without taking careful thought as to the character or standpoint of the speaker, or the value of the offer and the conditions of accepting it. For Wisdom is not merely theoretical, it is practical: *a prudent man gives thought to his steps,* he 'looks where he is going' (RSV). Again we need sound principles on which to assess what people say to us and particularly what they invite us to do. Nowhere is this more important than in spiritual truth. People are always going round with new teachings backed up by spectacular stories designed to convince the *simple* (2 Tim. 3:6f). The mature believer who is *prudent* will 'prove all things' (1 Thess. 5:21) and 'test the spirits whether they are from God' (1 John 4:1). Only when he is convinced it is the Word of God will he believe unreservedly and act unhesitatingly. 'To believe every word of God is faith; to believe every word of man is credulity' (Bridges).

(iii) **Behaviour (v. 16).** This verse continues the thought of verse 15. One who *gives thought to his step*s is aware that *evil* is abroad and seeks to avoid it because he *fears*. The question is, what does he fear? Since *the Lord* is not in the Hebrew it may simply mean he *fears* the consequence of some careless action. However, the name of *the Lord* is so often coupled with *fear* that it is not unlikely this is what is meant (1:7). This sense of his relationship to God enables him to control his passions. The *fool* lacks this – he is *hotheaded*, quickly excited by his plans and choices; the more you try to talk sense into him the more he 'rages' (KJV) and the more *reckless* he becomes. One of the fruits of the Spirit is 'self-control' (Gal. 5:23), of which the knowledge or *fear* of God puts us in possession.

(iv) **Temperament (vv. 17, 29).** One of the most vital areas in which wise thoughtfulness is needed is that of our natural temperament. Some of us have short fuses and none has one of unlimited length. Self-control has to be learned and the learning process requires *understanding*: of ourselves, what our temperament is; of other people, their meaning and motive; and especially of the awful consequences of losing our temper and doing *foolish things* which harm others and shame us. It is impossible to lose your temper without *displaying folly*, showing how stupid you are.

However, not everyone who can control his temper is wise in the Biblical sense. He may be *crafty* – suppressing his anger while planning a more effective way of revenge than just lashing out wildly as the *quick-tempered man does*. The damage done by the latter may be slight (unless he is armed with a gun!) whereas the former is set on a final solution. This is why he is *hated* where the *quick-tempered man* is merely despised. Nevertheless, both are fools in the Biblical sense for they lack the essential principle of Wisdom – the fear of God (1:7). It is this that suppresses both quick temper and smouldering hate – more, replaces them with love. God who is love is also 'patient' (2 Pet. 3:9) and 'slow to anger' (Ps. 103:8). Those who are his are like him, and 'love is patient ... not easily angered' (1 Cor. 13:4f).

(v) **Money (v. 24).** Thought is also needed in handling money and other material *wealth*. Where this is done the man of *wealth* will be honoured, like one who wears a *crown*. This sounds strange in modern ears, but under the Law prosperity was God's blessing on the righteous and wise. A person of wealth must be wise or God would not bless him with it (8:18). Solomon was given riches because he was wise enough to ask for wisdom to fulfil his high calling. Even one of more modest means was esteemed wise for he took care how he used them and was never in want. Those with nothing were regarded *fools*, either because God had not blessed them with prosperity or because they had wasted it, thus displaying to the world their folly and their ungodliness.

Under the Gospel we don't measure God's blessing and a person's worth in pounds and pence. The world may judge thus and we shall have to expect that. But with believers the wisdom of knowing, trusting and obeying God makes us rich towards him, even if poor materially (2 Cor. 6:10, cf. Rev. 3:17f).

Question
Our Lord's contrast between wise and foolish is best seen in his parable of the Ten Virgins (Matt. 25:1-13). To what did the foolish not give thought? What is he saying we should give thought to and what is the consequence of not doing so?

B. WISDOM AND FOLLY IN THE HOME (vv. 1, 11, 26).
The home, parents and family are frequent themes in PROVERBS. This is not surprising, since the book is chiefly a manual on parenthood. These verses touch on fathers, mothers and children.

1. Two kinds of father (v. 11).
Although *uprightness* and *wickedness* are not confined to males, we may take it that here they refer to the character of the head of the *house*. Ultimately the survival of a family depends on the conduct of its head in the eyes of God who can *destroy* or make it *flourish*. The verse indicates that it is morality not prosperity that determines its continuance. *The wicked* has a *house*, which seems stable, strong and permanent, yet it falls; *the upright* only has a *tent* – frail, vulnerable and temporary, yet it *flourishes*. Not that the verse is really about fabric – these are simply metaphors for the family itself: one rich, the other poor. The rich would be expected to continue for generations, but the poor will almost certainly die out. Yet because the latter honours God, he honours it and sustains it, whereas the other flouts his laws and his family is cursed with extinction.

The above of course is in an old covenant setting, where the continuance of the family name meant more than anything else except the covenant itself (Gen. 19:32, Num. 27:1-4, Deut. 25:5f). This required obedience to God, particularly from the head of the *house*. In our Christian age, names in themselves are less important and only ancient or aristocratic families take them to heart. In its place we might put a family's happiness and unity, and the care and love of its members for each other. For this much depends on the integrity of the head of the household.

2. Two kinds of mother (v. 1).

The Bible in both Testaments emphasizes the importance of the woman's role in the home. A stable family needs not only an upright man but a wise woman. An upright man may be weak, unskilled or simply unfortunate; he may be sick and even die. Yet a woman who is wise in the Biblical sense of trusting God (1:7) and running an efficient home (31:10-31) can bring her family through this. On the other hand, a home may have much going for it and the husband may be a good man, but if she is wasteful and negligent (foolish) she can undo all his good work. The high calling of the woman to the domestic sphere needs reinstatement because of its weakening under the influence of feminism. A woman is free to pursue any career, but need not look on her home as her prison but the vocation for which she is best qualified, since she is, like her first parent Eve, 'mother of all living' (Gen. 3:20).

3. The children of the home (v. 26).

Here we have the happy effect on the home of a combination of the man's uprightness and the woman's wisdom. Both these are covered by the expression *fears the Lord*, for this is both the beginning of wisdom and the way to righteousness. Such homes enjoy the special protection of God – they are a *secure fortress* against evil. Those who benefit most from this are their *children*. Although this promise applies in a different way under the Gospel, it is still true. The best thing parents can do for their children is to maintain and develop their own relationship with God. They have of course many other responsibilities, but this above all attracts and guarantees the blessing of God.

Exhortation. Look up Psalm 127:1 and reflect on the need for the Lord's personal help in home-building. How much of your prayer life (personal, domestic and public) is devoted to this matter, for your own family or that of relatives and friends? Will you from now let these proverbs guide you in prayer and practice?

C. WISDOM AND FOLLY IN RELIGION (vv. 2, [9, 26,] 27, 30).

Although PROVERBS is essentially practical, its teaching is religiously based (1:7). But not all religion is true and even one that is factually true can be falsified by foolish behaviour. Some of the differences can be learned from these verses.

1. What wise religion is (vv. 2 [9]).
In a word, it is moral, that is, it guides our *walk* and *ways*. Just as there can be no true morality without religion (for morality is derived from God's holiness and our creation in his image), so there can be no true religion without morality. No one can claim he believes in God (*fears the Lord*) who lives unrighteously, for he *despises* what pleases God and practises what he hates. He is being *devious* – claiming a holiness he doesn't live out. He fails to take sin seriously and declares he is a fool (see v. 9). This applies to the self-righteous Pharisee, who denies God's grace and the 'Christian' libertarian, who denies his holiness, as much as to the atheist who denies his very being.

2. What wise religion does (vv. 27, 30 [26]).

(a) *It gives life* (**v. 27**).
A religion which practises righteousness out of sheer love for God (*the fear of the Lord*) is a living religion, it does for the spirit what water does for the body – keeps it vital. This is because true religion is a personal relationship with God who is himself *the fountain of life* (see on 10:11, 13:14). Those who have him derive such joy and satisfaction from this relationship that they discern and avoid those temptations (*snares*) which, whatever their short-term gains, end in disaster (*death*, cf. 2:16-18, 22:5, Eccles. 7:26). To us who know Christ this is even more meaningful. Faith so unites us with him that he lives in us as 'a spring of living water welling up into eternal life' (John 4:14). His Spirit dwells in us and brings forth fruits which allow no place for those 'works of the flesh' which drag a person down to eternal death (Gal. 5:16-25). As Revelation 20:6 puts it, 'the first resurrection' (regeneration) delivers us from 'the second death' (hell).

(b) *It gives peace* (**v. 30 [26]**).
This is not the famous Hebrew word for *peace* – SHALOM, in fact it is better translated 'a healthy mind'. However, this is

impossible without general contentment and freedom from *envy*, which is only given to those who have the life of God within them (v. 27). Only the God of peace can give us *peace* (cf. v. 26).

The emphasis here, however, is on the physical effects of this peace, for in the Hebrew the phrase *life to the body* begins line 1, and *rots the bones* line 2. The word 'psychosomatic' was unknown to the ancient world but the idea is there. According to PROVERBS, bodily health is promoted by faith in and obedience to God (3:7f), the knowledge of his Word (4:20-22) and even a suitable marriage (17:22a). On the other hand, discontent with our lives combined with jealousy of another's has a debilitating effect and acts 'like cancer of the bones' (GNB, cf. 17:22b). So true religion is the wisest course to follow in this life.

Question
Since the New Testament does not guarantee the Christian immunity against disease and accident, is there still any truth in the idea that the true religion outlined in these verses makes for bodily health?

D. WISE AND FOOLISH TALK (vv. 3, 5, [23,] 25).
The subject of talking has been touched on in every chapter since 10 as well as in the Prologue. Here are some telling contrasts between two ways of talking.

1. Foolish Talk is Proud Talk (v. 3).
The Hebrew text of line 1 reads 'In the mouth of fools is a rod of pride' (cf. KJV, RV). The emendation *to his back* is thought to give a better contrast with line 2: *a fool* blurts out everything that comes into his mind and gets himself into trouble, whereas *the wise* is more restrained and gracious in his speech (cf. 10:13; 13:3; 18:6). This, however, may not be the meaning. 'The rod of pride' may mean that in his pride the *fool* lashes others with his tongue, always accusing and condemning any who don't go along with him. The *rod* is not that of 13:24 – a hard stick, but of Isaiah 11:4 – the flexible switch which sprays blows over the whole body of its victim, which depicts the unrestrained

anger of the *fool*. This would make line 2 mean that *the wise* speak in such a way as to be able to *protect* the victims of this savage talk – themselves or others. This idea we had in 12:6.

2. Wise Talk is Truthful Talk (vv. 5, 25).

As with most references to the *truthful* or *false witness*, these verses are about bearing *witness* in court (cf. 12:17). The only qualification required of a *witness* is that he is *truthful* or 'trustworthy' (13:17), one whose word can be relied on. A known liar is useless because he (literally) 'breathes lies' **(v. 5)** just as one who 'gives honest testimony breathes faithfulness' (12:17). Truth and falsehood are not just things said on a particular occasion but inherent in character. **Verse 25b** reads literally *a false witness is deceit* – not an occasional deceiver but deceit personified. This is because lying originated with Satan (John 8:44) who taught it to Adam (Gen. 3:4), since when it has been endemic in the human heart (Jer. 17:9, Rom. 3:4) and can only be cured by regeneration (John 8:32). This is not to say that everyone who is not a Christian lies in court! The 'common grace' of God preserves most people from becoming compulsive liars. However, those who lack saving grace are more vulnerable to the lying spirit – 'everyone has his price'.

The seriousness of the matter is brought out in **verse 25a** – life and death may hang on a *witness's* testimony. Under all judicial systems, old and new, the most vital piece of evidence is the living *witness*; circumstantial evidence rarely stands up on its own. A defence witness can provide an alibi that can *save lives*, just as a prosecution witness can secure a condemnation.

3. Foolish Talk is Idle Talk (v. 23).

While this verse is discussed in the section on 'Work', it is also relevant here. It describes one who talks when he should be working. It is not an injunction to silence, but a warning against evading the job in hand by wasting time talking about what is irrelevant to the job. In an agricultural society everything depended on getting through the work of that day or season: ploughing, sowing or reaping. To put it off meant losing the crop and consequent poverty. The work was straightforward, there was little to discuss and small talk only held up the process.

For reflection
1. See how many of today's occupations you can think of which are pursued mainly by talking. Do you think we would be better off without some of these, or with some curtailed?
2. What about the work of the Gospel? Think of ways in which word and action can balance each other.

E. WISDOM AND FOLLY IN THE WORK PLACE (vv. 4, 23).
The subject of hard work and its counterpart – laziness – already aired in 10:4f, 12:11, 24, 27 is here further developed.

1. The economics of work (v. 4).
This is a warning against false economy. A farmer persuades himself that if he doesn't buy any *oxen* he will save himself both the initial outlay and the cost of feeding and the labour of maintaining them. But this is the fool's economics. The wise man realizes he himself cannot do the work *the ox* can do; he will always be scraping a living, whereas if he buys some *oxen* and fodder, their work will bring a *harvest* which will feed him and them, with some over. The work he puts into their care is more than made up by what he saves in using them to pull the plough. This is sound economics in any age and type of work. Investment in the appropriate equipment will more than pay for itself, and the effort put into maintaining it will be saved in its efficiency.

2. The effort of work (v. 23).
Sound economics is no substitute for *hard work*. But combined together they *bring a profit*. We have been advised about work being diligent and *regular*; here we are warned against the danger of wasting time with *mere talk*. Talking can be time-consuming and 'time is money' when it should be spent in doing the job in hand.

For consideration.
Look up Paul's use of *oxen* as a picture of the Christian ministry (1 Cor. 9:9-11). What would Paul say

(a) to the church which, like the farmer in verse 4, is doubtful if it can 'afford' a minister?

(b) to a minister about the way he spends his time?

F. WISDOM AND FOLLY IN THE EMOTIONAL LIFE (vv. 10, 12, 13).

Although PROVERBS is primarily about the practicalities of life, it does give some guidance in understanding the emotions.

1. The wise approach to the emotions (vv. 10, 13).

What emerges here is the essentially private nature of the emotions. There is no greater proof of our individuality than our innermost feelings. Like our fingerprints (digital and genetic) our emotions are peculiar to ourselves. However well we know and trust another, there is a private area that is impenetrable. 'Everyone knows where the shoe pinches', goes the saying, or in more Biblical language, 'who among men knows the thoughts of a man except the man's spirit within him?' (1 Cor. 2:11).

Verse 10 warns us that *none of us can fully **share** either the joy or **bitterness** of another's feelings*. The wise person will realize this and tread carefully when in touch with one who is excessively depressed or euphoric. This doesn't mean he won't express sympathy with the former or congratulate the latter (see 12:25 and Rom. 12:15). It means he will avoid unsympathetically telling the sorrowful to pull himself together or jealously dampening the exuberance of the happy. The person feeling the emotion also needs to know how to handle it wisely. He shouldn't try to shut out the sympathizer with, 'How can you know what I feel?' for most experiences are common to us all (see James' advice in 1:2-12).

Verse 13 reveals another dimension of the subject, *warning us against judging by outward appearances*. This particularly applies to our approach to the apparently euphoric. There is a certain temperament we call Stoical which 'keeps a stiff upper lip'. The wise will perceive that although his friend is full of *laughter*, he may be 'whistling in the dark' to keep his spirits up and avoid becoming a bore. The wise one may know of a problem which will make his *joy end in grief*. So he won't be deceived by outward cheerfulness and think the problem has gone away, but will gently and sensitively try to share in it (Gal. 6:2). The friend too if he is wise will realize he can't laugh away his problem, but must face it realistically and talk it over with one he can trust, who is likely to be the wise one who sees through his *laughter* to his aching *heart*.

2. The foolish attitude to the emotions (v. 12).
The warning here is not to judge by appearances – not this time another's situation but one's own. The fool is the one who lets his emotions determine his decisions. He takes *the way that seems right*, going by what he feels. He thinks only of the short term and doesn't investigate *the end*. He is like a traveller setting off along a road that looks straight, firm, free from hazards and rather attractive, as far as he can see it. But he doesn't study his map to see what happens when it goes out of sight!

In these subjective days this kind of folly is applied to ethical and spiritual matters. It is said there are no moral absolutes – what is wrong for some or in a certain situation may be right for others or in different circumstances. Nor is there but one way to God; there are many options and each has to find the way that suits him. 12:15 comments: 'the way of a fool seems right to him.'

Meditate on the emotional life of Christ; his own deep feelings which he could share with none but the Father (Matt. 26:36-39); his divine knowledge of all our emotions (1 Kings 8:39; Ps. 44:21); and his ability to enter into them to the full (Heb. 2:18; 4:15f.).

G. The Destiny of the Wise and the Foolish (vv. 14, 18, 19, 22, 32)
Verse 12 warned against failing to think ahead to 'the end' of a course of action. These verses spell out how differently things turn out according to whether our decisions are wise or foolish.

1. There are rewards and punishments (v. 14).

This verse establishes that the way things turn out is related to the course of action chosen: people are *repaid* or *rewarded for their ways*. The Hebrew begins with those three words to show they are emphasized. PROVERBS is strong on the idea of rewards and punishments (e.g. 13:21), as indeed is the Bible generally, which describes life as a harvest, with sowing and reaping (Hosea. 8:7, 10:12f, Gal. 6:7-10). God does not need to intervene in judgment, simply to let us have our way and suffer or enjoy the consequences (Ps. 106:15, Rom. 1:24, 26, 28). There is no injustice in this for God has made known right and wrong. *The good man* here is he who has been true to what he knows, and the *faithless* is he who knows the right way but does not choose it, literally 'the backslider in heart'. This is developed in the next two verses.

2. Rewards and punishments are according to character and intention (vv. 18, 22).

These two verses tell us more about the two kinds of people described in verse 14 and how this affects their destiny.

(a) *Their character* **(v. 18)**. Although the theme of this chapter is 'the wise and foolish', these terms are not always used. 'The wise' is also 'the righteous' and 'the foolish' also 'the wicked', for these are moral and spiritual terms. 'The good man' of verse 14 is the wise man, and 'the faithless' is the fool. Here they are called *simple* and *prudent*. *The simple* is basically the very young or uninstructed (1:4), who has no standards by which to regulate his actions. The purpose of PROVERBS is to make *the simple prudent* by teaching them. A mature person who is still simple is either untaught or has been *faithless* to his teaching, whereas the *prudent* has learned to live by his teaching. The difference in their destinies is spectacular: one becomes a fool, the other a king; one inherits the fool's cap (*folly*), the other the king's *crown* – that is, one lives a life without God's help and blessing, the other is honoured and promoted.

(b) *Their intention* **(v. 22)**. Between character and action lies intention. Our actions are not mere knee-jerk responses to situations, there is a thought process which leads up to them.

This may be brief or long but it is there. If we do *evil* it is because we 'devise' (*plot*) it; if we do *good* it is because we *plan* it. The *plots* and *plans* may not be elaborate, but what we do has first passed through our mind. Just as *intention* is the fruit of *character*, so *destiny* is the fruit of *intention*. The 'faithless' or 'simple' (the fools) *go astray* – they follow a course that leads to disaster; 'the good man' or 'prudent' (the wise) *find love and faithfulness* – others treat them as they treat others and God himself blesses them (which is the next theme).

3. Rewards and punishments are real (vv. 19, 32).
The idea of recompense can be made to sound insubstantial – 'pie in the sky', but it is in fact very real, as we see here.

(a) *The wise triumph over the foolish* (**v. 19**).
What is hinted in verse 18 is now spelt out – the life based on God's Word is superior to that which despises it. This happens in a number of ways:

(i) there are situations in which the ungodly have to admit they have been wrong to despise the godly, who turn out more fit for leadership than they: Genesis 37:5-11; 42:6, Psalm 49:14;

(ii) there are times when the ungodly need the help of the righteous: 2 Kings 3:12, and even beg for their lives: Exodus 8:8, Esther 7:7;

(iii) the ungodly are often found admitting the godly were right after all: Acts 16:39, Revelation 3:9;

(iv) those who have worshipped false gods and opposed the worshippers of the true God are found coming to join them, especially through the preaching of the Gospel: Isaiah 60:14;

(v) at the last day the godly will participate in the judgment of the ungodly: 1 Corinthians 6:2.

(b) *The wise, unlike the foolish, are never forsaken* (**v. 32**).
Some modern translations (RSV, GNB, NEB) follow the Septuagint and emend *in death* to 'in/through/by his integrity' because it gives a sharper contrast to line 1, which they translate 'by his wickedness the wicked is brought down'. This however is not the point, which is that *the wicked are brought down* to despair

when a major *calamity* befalls them. They think it is the end of the world, at least of *their* world. But the righteous can face both the trials of life and *death* itself with 'hope' (KJV). Because God is their *refuge* in life (v. 26), so he is in their death.

For consideration. Are you the victim of oppression, misjudgment or failure, or do you pray for anyone who is? Consider Job and his hope in God as his vindicator (Job 19:25-27). Apply this to the increased hope of believers through Christ's resurrection: e.g. Paul facing execution (Phil. 1:21-23, 3:21); and his encouragement to Christians in their trials (1 Cor. 15:55-58).

H. WISDOM AND FOLLY IN FRIENDSHIP (vv. 20, 21, 31).
Here is another subject which affects our daily lives.

1. The world's (the foolish) way of friendship (v. 20).
The innate selfishness of human nature indisposes it to true friendship. No one wants to be friends with *the poor*: he has nothing to give you and may expect you to give to him. The emphasis of the Hebrew, which puts *even his neighbour* at the beginning, is best brought out by GNB: 'No one, not even his neighbour, likes a poor man', though he sees him every day and is aware of his need. 19:7 goes further: he is 'shunned by all his relatives' – even the thickness of blood is diluted by a poor relation! *The rich* seems better off, having *many friends*. But are they *friends* or scroungers? See 19:4, 6.

Thank God there are exceptions to this cynicism, that 'there is a friend who sticks closer than a brother' (18:24). Ruth remained with Naomi in her destitution and Jonathan was David's friend when, far from enriching him, it put him in danger of his life. True friendship is seen in Christ, 'the friend of sinners' – a term of abuse but one he gloried in. Those he befriends share his Spirit, lose their selfishness and become gracious, willing to share their goods with the poor and their gospel with the rich and so bring about that equality described by James in 1:9-11.

2. God's (the wise) way of friendship (vv. 21, 31).

The world's way of friendship may appear wise, but it is really foolish, for it involves despising another human being and God calls this *sin*, **verse 21**, for reasons we shall see in verse 31. The word for *sin* is the one which means 'missing the mark' or 'falling short' (Rom. 3:23), for not only does he fall short of God's requirement but 'misses' the *blessing* promised to the *kind*. That *blessing* is promised many times in Scripture, but nowhere better than in the words of Jesus at the end of his public ministry. To those who had shown this kindness he promised they would hear him say, 'Come, you who are blessed by my Father, take your inheritance, the kingdom prepared for you since the creation of the world.' The reason? What they did in being *kind to the needy* they did to him who owned them as his 'brothers' (Matt. 25:34, 40).

Verse 31 tells us why the world's friendship is *sin* and why those who are *kind to the needy* are 'blessed'. It is because God is as much *their Maker* as he is that of the rich and they are as much his image and the objects of his care. To *oppress* them is to show *contempt for their Maker*, as if to say, 'These didn't come from your hand so I can treat them as I like', or 'These don't bear your likeness so they don't deserve any respect', or 'You haven't looked after them so why should I?' But God takes their part, his Son became one of them (2 Cor. 8:9) and identifies with them. This will emerge at the last day when he will say to those who *oppress* them, 'What you did not do to them you did not do to me', and to those who are *kind*, 'What you did to them you did to me' (Matt. 25:40, 45). So whatever anyone thinks, to be *kind to the needy honours God*, and those who honour him he will honour.

Question
How would you answer the charge that this teaching, especially as it appears in Matthew 25:31-46 is salvation by works?

I. Wisdom and Folly in Politics (vv. 28, 34, 35).

If there is such a thing as a 'theology of politics', then PROVERBS has much to contribute to it. Some are 'royal proverbs' because they mention the king (vv. 28, 35), others are more general (v. 34). There is no subject on which Solomon was more qualified to speak, since the wisdom God gave him was primarily for governing (1 Kings 3:7-14). The subject has already been aired in 8:15f and 11:10f, 14, and is here taken further.

1. The size of the population (v. 28).

The *glory* of a ruler does not lie in outward trappings like titles, clothes, palaces, ceremonies and servants, for these are nothing without a people to govern. *A large population* means more trade and therefore more revenue, better national institutions and a larger stronger army. Rulers who realize this govern wisely and justly, so that people are encouraged to stay in the land, or even immigrate to it, to have large families and work hard. Where this takes place it indicates the nation is ruled wisely; but where the population declines, then trade diminishes, poverty and misery increase and the government's folly is exposed. Either it is too weak, or oppressive to the point of tyranny. The foolishness of this can be as readily exemplified in recent regimes as in those of Bible times. The graveyards of the world contain not a few *ruined princes*.

2. The moral character of the nation (v. 34).

A nation needs not only wise leaders but *righteous people*. Large numbers are no use if they are wicked or foolish. In Israel the principle that applied to the individual – *righteousness* brings prosperity and *sin* leads to ruin – holds good for a nation (Deut. 4:6, 26:19, 28:1). Israel's history proves this: their periods of prosperity and victory were those in which they followed the example of a godly king, such as David, Solomon and Hezekiah. Defeat and recession occurred when kings like Rehoboam and Manasseh led the people off the rails.

The saying applies equally to non-covenant nations, being about *a* (not 'this') *people*, and *any people*. The prophets preached that those nations which practised injustice and unrighteousness would fall victim to the justice of a righteous God (Jer. 18:7-10, Amos 1 and 2). The history of the last four centuries before Christ shows how these prophecies were fulfilled in the fall of the great empires: Assyria, Egypt, Babylon, Persia and Greece. The course of the world's history from then till now is much the same. Nations based on freedom, justice and morality flourish, whereas those which decline into *sin* fall into *disgrace*. Today we tend to judge greatness by a nation's economy or defence, hence our categories of 'First' and 'Third World'. God has a different standard, which it would be wise to follow and foolish to ignore.

3. The wisdom or folly of the legislators (v. 35).
Between 'the king' and 'the people' lie the king's counsellors. To attain national greatness and avoid disgrace requires good and wise administrators (*servants*). In the case of a monarchy a wise king will appoint like-minded *servants*, and dismiss those whose work and behaviour bring *disgrace* on the whole nation (20:8, 22:11, 25:5, 29:12). David, a righteous man himself, knew he could not exercise good government without men of integrity to assist him (Ps. 101:4-8). Had the Persian emperor listened to Haman his empire would have been stained with the disgrace of genocide, whereas his replacement by Mordecai preserved its reputation for justice (Esther. 8:2).

Question
How does all this help you to assess the fitness of those who put themselves forward for election to local and national government and thus enable you to use your vote in accordance with Biblical wisdom?

13

Living Before the All-seeing God
(Proverbs 15)

There are more direct references to *the Lord* in this chapter than in any previous one. This sets its tone and reminds us that our behaviour is not to be governed by what others see and think but by what he approves who knows everything about everyone.

A. THE ALL-SEEING GOD HIMSELF (vv. 3, 8, 9, 11, 25, 26, 29, 33). The first two verses state plainly that he knows us thoroughly.

Verse 3 means that because God is omnipresent (*everywhere*) he is also omniscient: his *eyes ... are ... keeping watch*, he knows everything that is going on with everyone. This 'seeing' is not mere voyeurism but the basis of his general care and provision. He makes no distinction between *the wicked* and *the good*, for he causes his sun to rise and his rain to fall on both (Matt. 5:45, Acts 17:24-28). But as regards whom he personally fellowships with here and especially hereafter, he is more particular. Wickedness has to be confessed and forsaken. Being unwilling to do this unbelievers find the idea of an all-seeing God terrifying (Gen. 3:8); whereas those who know him find it a comfort (Gen. 16:13, 2 Chr. 16:9, Ps. 139:17f.). We know he is not *keeping watch* to check up on us but to protect and attract us.

Verse 11 goes further to show that God's knowledge is not confined to persons and their actions but reaches our thoughts (*hearts*). These are inaccessible to the wisest humans

(Jer. 17:10) but *open* to him whose knowledge is greater even than that of the *hearts* he sees into (1 John 3:20). The proof? *Death* and *destruction lie open before him.* SHEOL (*Death*) is the abode of the dead and ABADDON (*destruction*) is the abode of the wicked and a name for the devil himself (Rev. 9:11). None is further from God than the dead, the damned and the devil, yet he knows them – how much more *the hearts of men*! The way he deals with us and ultimately judges is based on this knowledge (Ps. 7:9, Heb. 4:13).

For further study read Christ's letters to his churches in Revelation 2–3 and see how many times the phrase 'I know' occurs.

1. The all-knowing God sees us at prayer (vv. 8, 29).

These verses assume that praying is not confined to believers (*the upright, the righteous*) but even practised by *the wicked*. Evidently there were those in Israel who came into this category and who went so far as to make *sacrifice to the Lord*, so these verses cannot refer only to pagans. Indeed we find the prophets rebuking the whole nation for continuing to offer sacrifices while living in disobedience to the God to whom they offered them (Isa. 1:11-13, 66:3, Jer. 6:20).

To us under the Gospel our *sacrifice* is 'spiritual worship' (Rom. 12:1) and may be included in the term *prayer*. Not all prayer is acceptable to God, for what he chiefly regards is the condition and character of the one who prays. When he refused Cain's *sacrifice* it was not because it differed from Abel's but because *he* differed: whereas Abel was 'a righteous man' (Heb. 11:4), Cain 'belonged to the evil one' (1 John 3:12). The same applies to *prayer*. Disobedience renders prayer unacceptable (28:9, Ps. 66:18) because *the Lord is far from the wicked.*

The prayer of the upright pleases him because he to whom 'the hearts of men lie open' (v. 11) sees they are not trusting their sacrifice or prayer but the sacrifice God has provided in his Son which alone makes a person righteous (Rom. 4:24f.); also that through Christ they 'offer their bodies as living sacrifices to God' (Rom. 12:1). Because this prayer *pleases him* he *hears*.

2. The all-knowing God sees how we live (v. 9).

The repetition of *detests* connects this with verse 8 and confirms that when God refuses a sacrifice or prayer it is not because he disapproves the form of the sacrifice or the prayer. The sacrifice may keep all the rules of Leviticus and the prayer may be in the very words of Jesus (Matt. 6:7-13). What God requires is a humble heart (Ps. 51:17) and an obedient life (Micah. 6:6-8).

However, this saying applies equally to those who did not sacrifice and to those now who don't pray. They may avoid the sin of hypocrisy, which only religious people can commit, but not professing godliness does not excuse their moral conduct. God takes account of what the Bible calls *the way* and we would call life-style. This describes the direction in which our lives tend, what we *pursue, the way* we follow. There is a *way* that belongs to those who do not know God which *the Lord detests*; there is another *way* which *he loves*. He doesn't expect us to perform this perfectly, only to have it as our supreme aim (Phil. 3:12-14).

3. The all-seeing God knows our attitude (v. 25).

God looks behind our way of life to our attitude to life. The juxtaposition of *the proud man* with *the widow* shows what pride is – self-reliance, trusting in achievements and possessions, acquisitiveness, always looking for more, but in a cowardly way, for there is a hint that he increases his property by stealing from the defenceless *widow* (Matt. 23:14), craftily moving her *boundary*-stone (23:10f). This attitude – to self, to material things, to others who are there to be used and exploited pitilessly, and to God himself, for whom such have no need or place – is abhorrent to God (16:5), who shows what he thinks by tearing them *down*, and with them all they have built up and boasted in, ruining, not only themselves but theirs, since *house* includes family (v. 27).

The attitude of mind God approves is illustrated by *the widow*, who, realizing her weakness and vulnerability, depends on God and his promises (Ps. 68:5) and lives by prayer (1 Tim. 5:5). You don't have to be a widow to do this! What counts is attitude.

4. The all-seeing God knows our thoughts (v. 26).

Closely allied to attitude are *thoughts*, for our attitudes are formed by the way we think. The term used indicates what is in view is not day-dreams or idle *thoughts* but deliberate plans (RV: 'devices'). It is a mark of *the wicked* that he is always conspiring how he may better himself at someone else's expense (12:20; 14:22). This is where he differs from the righteous person whose 'plans are just' (12:5). The good person doesn't keep his thoughts to himself but expresses them in *words*, for he has nothing to hide (Hebrew reads 'words of pleasantness'). He is not plotting to deceive or exploit others but do them good, so he speaks 'pleasant things'.

Few take *thoughts* seriously. We are appalled at acts of sin but take little trouble controlling the *thoughts* that give birth to them. To God, however, *thoughts* are as words, and words as deeds. If they are loving *thoughts* they are *pure* to him, but if malicious they are as *detestable* as the offering of a holy sacrifice by a wicked man (v. 8).

5. The all-seeing God knows our relationship with him (v. 33).

This is not only the climax but a summary of the previous points. For worship, behaviour, attitude and thoughts are parts of *wisdom* which produces a whole person not just a knowledgeable mind. That *wisdom* can only be learned in a personal relationship with God, for which the Old Testament term is *fear*, which to us means knowing, trusting, loving and obeying – the ingredients of a personal relationship with God. It is these attitudes not intellect or ability that produce *wisdom*. Indeed those who pride themselves on their mental or manual skill debar themselves from attaining *wisdom*. We have already seen what the Lord thinks of the proud (v. 25). Such may receive *honour* from man but not from God. Those he esteems and honours as his sons and friends are those who humble themselves before him (22:4; 29:23; Isa. 66:2). This was the way of Christ (Phil. 2:5-11) and it is enough for the servant to be as his master.

To ponder. A famous mediaeval devotional book was called 'The Ladder of Perfection'. Can you see in verse 33 four steps up that ladder? Compare it with 25:6f and Luke 14:7-11.

It is from the mouth of this all-knowing God that the remaining precepts come. Although all have been touched on in previous chapters, how much more vital they now seem!

B. THE WORDS GOD WANTS TO HEAR (vv. 1, 2, 4, 7, 23, 28, 31).
The God who sees all we do hears all we say. What he likes are:-

1. Gentle words (v. 1).
Here is a situation in which someone speaks to us in *wrath*, complaining, criticizing or condemning. Everything now hinges on the *answer* we give. If we reply in kind (*harshly*), we will *stir up* that hot pot until it boils over, for the Hebrew for *anger* is a fiercer term than that for *wrath*. But if we 'keep our cool' and give *a gentle answer* the heat is taken out and we divert the stream of lava so that it trickles away ineffectively. When the Ephraimites angrily complained to Gideon that he hadn't involved them in his campaign against Midian, he replied that their victory had outshone his (Judg. 8:1-3) and all was sweetness and light. But when the same tribe complained to Jephthah that he hadn't asked their help against Ammon, he flared up and blamed them for not responding to his invitation to do just that, and the result was a minor civil war (Judg. 12:1-4).

The greatest example of all is Jesus before his unjust accusers: 'When they hurled their insults at him, he did not retaliate; when he suffered he made no threats' (1 Pet. 2:23). The Spirit who was in him is in us, as a Spirit of 'peace, patience ... gentleness and self-control' (Gal. 5:22f, cf. 1 Cor. 4:12f).

2. Wise words (vv. 2, 7).
To be able to speak *wise* words it is necessary to be a *wise* person. For this two things are needed:

(a) to have *knowledge* – of what is true, right and good, for in Scripture *knowledge* is not mere fact or philosophy but is of practical, spiritual and eternal value;

(b) to make a right use of that *knowledge* by *spreading* it, literally 'scatter' like seed, as the Jerusalem Christians did when they were 'scattered' by Saul's vendetta (Acts 8:1, 4).

The fool is he who has no *knowledge* in his *heart*, that is, of the things of God, the essentials of life. So he really has nothing worth saying. What he does say is 'not right' or 'reliable' (better than *not so*). This doesn't stop him talking, but what comes out of his mouth? Only *folly*, that is, his ungodly opinions or mere gossip, for *gushes* means 'spews' or 'vomits'.

3. Healing words (v. 4).

The idea of the *healing* property of words (10:11, 12:18) presupposes that our hearer has been wounded in *spirit* – perhaps disaster has befallen him, someone has upset him or God has convicted him. 'The wise' (the believer) has the means of *healing* such – not just giving him the sympathy pill to make him feel better, but transforming his misery into paradise – *a tree of life* (see on 3:18). This refers to a restored relationship with God, suggesting his basic trouble was spiritual.

But words in the mouth of a *deceitful* man have the opposite effect. This is not necessarily a flagrant liar, but one who being misled himself can only mislead others. Can the blind lead the blind? He will have no constructive advice to offer and, like Job's friends may make things worse by ignorance and tactlessness so that one already wounded in *spirit* is utterly *crushed*.

4. Apt words (v. 23).

For a word to be *apt* two things are needed:

(a) that it should be an accurate reply to the question asked or the situation faced which hits the nail on the head (Isa. 50:4);

(b) that it should be delivered at the appropriate moment – *timely* (Ecc. 3:1). Christians have the very word that another needs, but if we catch him in the wrong mood or when he is preoccupied with something else, it will fall flat or even annoy him. There is satisfaction (*joy*) in coming up with the right answer, *the apt reply*. But there is even more in right timing, for the *joy* is felt by hearer as well as speaker. If Paul had told the Philippian gaoler to believe on the Lord Jesus Christ when he was locking him up, he might have laughed at or even beaten him. But telling him this as he was about to fall on his sword was as the French say, 'le mot juste'.

5. Well-chosen words (v. 28).
It would be so good to be able to speak gentle, wise, healing and apt words, but how? Here is the answer: pause, consider the question, weigh up the situation and arrive at the answer in your heart before you let it out of your mouth. As verse 2 said, it is the fool who speaks off the top of his head. The scum always floats to the surface and folly will always be first out. Because the fool is wicked he will have little to say that is not evil (Matt. 12:35). The righteous has 'good stored up in him' but he too can react hastily and sin with his tongue (Ps. 39:1). It was to Christians James wrote that we should be 'quick to listen, slow to speak' (James 1:19, not to mention chapter 3!).

6. Plain words (v. 31).
This does not mean a person qualifies for membership of 'the society of the wise' (NEB) by willingness to hear their *rebukes*, but that those who want to hear words that promote spiritual life will go to *the wise*, who are both able and willing to give them. As we saw in the Prologue, the greatest gift to be derived from wisdom is *life* (3:13-18). This means more than long, healthy, prosperous life, it is 'life to the full' (John 10:10), the life of God himself, called 'a tree of life' (v. 4, 3:18), paradise, where man and God lived together in love. To enjoy this we need to be instructed in plain words, to be shown our faults and how to remedy them. Only those already made wise for salvation will have this knowledge and be able to give it.

Consider the place of prayer in learning to speak words which please God. Refer particularly to Psalms 19:14 and 141:3.

C. THE DISCIPLINE GOD WANTS US TO ACCEPT (vv. 5, 10, 12, 19, 32).
Discipline is at the heart of PROVERBS from the beginning (1:2f) since it is the road to Wisdom and thus to life. We tend to find it irksome, but the all-seeing God knows this and here warns us against refusing it.

1. Why it is foolish to refuse discipline (vv. 5, 32).

Verse 5 reminds us that *discipline* begins at home and is the *father's* or parents' responsibility. We all begin life in a state of simplicity, ignorant of how to live the good life (1:4). We tend rather to the bad life and therefore need *correction*. One who *spurns* this will degenerate from being merely 'simple' to becoming a *fool*, that is, wilfully ignorant and disobedient (Ps. 14:1). So the first step on the road to the good disciplined life is to *heed correction*, for that in itself constitutes *prudence*. Once that first step is taken we are well on the way to maturity and wisdom: 'The child is father of the man.'

Verse 32 goes further to show us why one who *ignores* or rejects *discipline* is a fool – he undervalues *himself*. His concern is for his immediate physical comfort and satisfaction, and anything involving pain, hardship and effort goes against that. But 'life is more than food ... and clothes' (Matt. 6:25). We are in the likeness of God, made for eternity (Eccles. 3:11). One life has greater value than the entire cosmos (Mark 8:36) and is only equalled in value by the 'precious blood of Christ' (1 Pet. 1:18f). One who accepts *discipline gains understanding* of his real value.

2. The kind of person who refuses discipline (vv. 12, 19).

What puts us off the discipline which is really in our own interest? Why are we such fools? There are two kinds here.

(a) *The scornful (*v. 12*)*.

This is a type that crops up frequently in PROVERBS: 1:22, 9:7f, 13:1, 14:6, 9. He doesn't take life seriously; he is a fun-lover, a playboy, contemptuous of those who have standards and fear God. It's not just that he won't *consult the wise*, he won't be found in their company (the word *consult* is added). This is because he *resents correction*, he doesn't like being told he's on the wrong road – whether this is stated explicitly or he is just made to feel it because his conversation is different from that of *the wise*. He cannot face the truth about himself and finds the easiest way out is to laugh off anything that gets too near the bone, e.g. 2 Chronicles 18:7, Amos 5:10, John 3:20, 2 Timothy 4:3. We all know people like this and how hard it is to get under their skin. Only by God's grace are we not among them.

(b) *The slothful* (**v. 19**).

This is another character we have met before (6:6-11) and will meet again (19:24, 22:13, 26:13-16). Some of those verses depict him as one always making excuses for his lack of achievement. The same is probably the case here: 'He plants his own hedge and then complains of its hindrance' (Bridges). He doesn't want to make progress if this involves effort and interferes with his pleasure. It is probably because of this dishonesty and self-deceit that *the sluggard* is contrasted not with the energetic but *the upright*, the honest man. From the beginning he has accepted the 'discipline of instruction and correction' and knows that any effort is worth while. The chief hindrances to the disciplined life are thus both blemishes of character and closely connected. Someone who finds such a life too much bother is usually one who fails to take it seriously.

3. What happens to those who refuse discipline (v. 10).

Ultimately discipline cannot be avoided. If we won't *discipline* ourselves we will have to be disciplined. One who won't control himself but robs and wounds has to be restrained. This applies to the ways of God: if we *leave the path* (of righteousness) we shall find he blocks or makes our way unpleasant (13:18). But he does this, not out of pique because we have refused him, but to lead us back to *the path* of the upright, to his level and pleasant 'highway' (v. 19). Everything depends on our reaction to these experiences. If they bring us to our senses and we turn back, all is forgiven and all will be well (Isa. 1:15, 18f). But if we remain obstinate then worse awaits us: if we *hate correction* so much we shut our ears against it, then we *will die* (Isa. 1:20), we won't enjoy the 'life to the full' which consists in a happy relationship with God, but will live in spiritual death (1:28-31).

Think about it. It is clear that in our society discipline is in decline: personal, family and social; and we know the consequences. Although Christians aren't going down that road, do you think we lack *spiritual* discipline? If so, in what ways?

D. GOD KNOWS WHAT WE HAVE IN THE KITTY (vv. 6, 16, 17).
The subject of money, wealth, possessions and prosperity or their lack has cropped up several times in various forms. Here is how we who live under the all-knowing God look at it.

1. Where there is much (v. 6).
The teaching of PROVERBS, as of the Old Testament generally, is that where there is righteousness there is prosperity, partly because the righteous work hard and waste little, but chiefly because God blesses them and theirs (8:21, 10:22, 13:22, 21:20, Ps. 112: 3). Abraham walked with God and became a rich man in spite of his nomadic life (Gen. 13:2). This is not an infallible rule, as we shall see, but a norm. There is still much truth in it, although not as much as the 'Health, wealth and prosperity gospel' people claim. It may be true in the American Bible belt but not the Third World, where there are many poor sick Christians. The force of the saying lies in its comparison with *the wicked*, who may have just as much *income* or maybe more, but it *brings them trouble*. Thus it is not the *amount* that is at issue but the use made of it and the effect it has on the family generally. With *the wicked* it breeds greed, jealousy and strife; but for *the righteous* God 'adds no trouble with it' (10:22) and the whole *house* shares in it.

2. Where there is little (vv. 16-17).
Godliness did not always mean prosperity and wealth even under the Old Covenant. In any case these are relative terms. If a *little* is enough then it is *great wealth* to one who has nothing. God's promise is that those in covenant with him will not be left to starve (Ps. 37:25). The righteous who trusts (*fear of*) *the Lord* has something many a wealthy man lacks – contentment, freedom from both restless covetousness and nagging worry. Likewise the family that only has *vegetables* but feeds on *love* has something better than roast beef (literally 'fatted ox'). An atmosphere of *hatred* can destroy the taste and give only indigestion.

There may be a distinction in the settings of the two verses. **Verse 16** may refer to the day-to-day household income and expenses of a family, whereas **verse 17**, with its use of the word *meal* (literally 'portion') may indicate a guest being entertained. He shouldn't be offended if he is given only a *meal of vegetables*; the *love* being shown him more than compensates for the plain fare. (v. 27 is relevant but included with Section G).

Consider. Let us who live in an affluent society – with supermarkets, a bank card to pay for the shopping, fridges and freezers and all the cooking utensils – ask ourselves about our real values. Is our trust in God and our love for each other more to us than the quantity and quality of the food on the table?

E. THE ALL-KNOWING GOD SHARES IN OUR EMOTIONS (vv. 13, 15, 18, 30).

Although God is said to be 'impassible', he well knows our emotional life (14:10, 13) for he made us as we are and in Jesus entered into it (Heb. 4:15). The ancients classified the emotions as 'Four Temperaments': sanguine and melancholic, choleric and phlegmatic. We have all four here in their appropriate contrasts.

1. The sanguine and melancholic (vv. 13, 15, 30).

The sanguine is the one with the *happy* or *cheerful heart*, the melancholic the one with *heartache*, who is *wretched* (v. 15). The points made here are:

(a) *How temperament affects personality (***v. 13***).*
This is so much the case that even *the face* registers our state of *heart*. *A happy heart* will produce *a cheerful look* (v. 30) or smiling *face*. It goes without saying that a melancholy person will not be able to help looking miserable, however hard he tries (Neh. 2:2). He lacks that 'light in the eye' (as *cheerful look* is in Hebrew) which the sanguine cannot hide. But worse – his *spirit is crushed*, he has lost all confidence and hope. Since it is 'a man's spirit that sustains him' (18:14), the melancholic will have great difficulty finding the motivation and strength to continue, may become mentally ill and seek relief in suicide.

(b) *How temperament affects circumstances* (**v. 15**).
Here is someone whose *days* are *wretched* because he is *oppressed* – not necessarily by enemies but perhaps by a personal affliction connected with health, family or work. This is where the sanguine temperament scores – he not only survives but even enjoys life. He lives as though life were one long party (*continual feast*). But what hope has the melancholic who can hardly cope with normal life, let alone adversity? We read of Naomi, whose name means 'pleasant', changing it to Mara ('bitter') because of her afflictions (Ruth 1:20f), whereas Habakkuk, in circumstances not utterly dissimilar, says he 'will rejoice in the LORD' (Hab. 3:17f).

(c) *How the sanguine can help the melancholic* (**v. 30**).
It is generally agreed that this means the heart and health of the melancholic is refreshed by the *cheerful look* and *good news* of the sanguine. The latter has a 'light in his eyes' (as the Hebrew reads) which is infectious and to which only the most depressed do not respond. He also has a more positive attitude to life. His approach is, 'It isn't all bad news'; he is able to show the sufferer the silver lining and give him hope of better times ahead. This ministry not only *brings joy to the heart* but *health to the bones* – it makes him feel better all over.

2. The choleric and phlegmatic (v. 18).
Here are two other temperaments: the fiery *hot-tempered man*, who is never far off the boil; and the placid or *patient* man, who has his temper under control. The former is a threat to any company, especially a family or local community (yes, and a church too!), which is why PROVERBS is always warning us against him (6:19, 10:12, 22:24f, 26:21, 28:25, 29:22, 30:33). He is provocative and confrontational; if there isn't an argument or a fight he'll soon start one. The other is one of the greatest blessings to any society (yes, and a church too!), for he not only refrains from provocation but brings a *quarrel* to an end if he can. 'Blessed are the peacemakers' (Matt. 5:9) – and a blessing too.

Questions
1. What are the weaknesses of the 'Four Temperaments' theory? Does it oversimplify our complex psychology? Is it correct to attribute these differences, as they did, to body chemistry?
2. What effect does the gospel have on temperament? Can it make depressives into happy people, and warmongers into peacemakers? See Isaiah 61:1-3 and 11:6-9.

F. THE ALL-KNOWING GOD SHARES HIS KNOWLEDGE (vv. 14, 21, 22).
The knowledge spoken of here is derived from knowing God himself.

1. Knowledge needs seeking out (v. 14).
The difference between the wise and foolish is seen in their approach to *knowledge*. One is wise, not because he is more intelligent or learned than the other, but because he is *discerning* enough to realize the limits of his *knowledge*. The fool however is satisfied with what he knows: he *feeds on* it, thinking it sufficient. This would be fine if what he knew were true and good, but it is in fact *folly*, mere fiction. Israel was like this when they *fed* on the optimism of the false prophets who told them peace was round the corner, when it was the Babylonians hiding there (Isa. 30:10). Worse, when they persuaded themselves that the idols they made were real gods (Isa. 44:20).

The main thing our learning should teach us is how little we know, for this creates an appetite for real, better and perfect *knowledge*. Nowhere is this truer than in *knowing* God himself:

> We taste thee, O thou living bread,
> And long to feast upon thee still;
> We drink of thee, the fountainhead,
> And thirst, our souls from thee to fill (Bernard of Clairvaux).

2. True knowledge leads to godliness (v. 21).
This verse begins where verse 14 ended, but doesn't end there. It is based on the connection, which runs through the Bible, between knowledge or wisdom on one hand, and morality on

the other. He whom the Bible calls 'a fool' is by no means stupid; he may be cleverer than most. But his skills are devoted to the pleasure of sin – sin's *folly delights* him, which is why he 'feeds' on it. But, however clever he is, he *lacks judgment,* he fails to perceive where true *delight* is to be found, that righteousness is in his best interest and brings greater joys than sin.

The other, however simple and uneducated, has an *understanding* of the main thing – that a *straight course* is the best *course.* He is the one who turns out to be wise, as the 'Wisdom' books keep saying (14:6, Job 28:28, Ps. 111:10). The wisdom of the New Testament is the same (Eph. 5:15, James 3:13), but more glorious, for wisdom becomes not just a way of life but him who is 'the way, the truth and the life,' who, being wisdom personified, is our life (1 Cor. 1:30). True *understanding* is to perceive Christ and be led in his way.

3. Knowledge has social value (v. 22).

This saying qualifies the previous one which may sound as though acquiring knowledge and understanding makes us self-sufficient. Life is not so simple. Our knowledge may enable us to form the right 'purposes' (better than *plans*), but is not adequate to make these purposes *succeed.* For that we need *advisers,* the *counsel* of friends, and they need us. The relevance of this principle to politics has already been mentioned (11:14); it is equally necessary in churches (Acts 15); but here it refers chiefly to the individual. Even those of us who have Christ for our wisdom are not infallible. We don't know everything, we lack experience, we see things from our own perspective. Consulting others will provide us with a *course* correction.

Question
Do you think the present craze for 'counselling' as an expertise, even a profession, is altogether good? Do you think it would be better shared out among us and practised by all? See Proverbs 27:17, Hebrews 10:24f, 12:15.

G. This God Knows All About Our Families (vv. 20, 27).

The subject of the family has featured in every chapter since 10. For Israelites this was the most important part of their lives, for it impinged on their covenant relationship with God and their tenure of the land, as the Fifth Commandment states (Exod. 20:12).

1. The children (v. 20).

This is where we came in (10:1)! But it is not a straight repeat: the *foolish* man here is said to *despise his mother*, which is probably the reason for her 'grief' in 10:1. A later proverb adds 'when she is old' after saying that the father 'gave life' to him (23:22). This paints a picture of a rebellious child who outgrows his mother, thinks he outknows her, despises her and as she ages forgets she bore and nursed him. This is said partly to comfort the parents with the assurance that God knows what they are going through, but chiefly as a warning to children who refuse instruction and discipline. Later proverbs speak of the dire punishments awaiting such (20:20, 28:24, 30:17). Although this refers to the Sinai law code (Exod. 21:17), it is a reminder for all time that the all-seeing God takes account of each child's behaviour and he will have to answer to him for it.

2. The father (v. 27).

This is not the lazy father who neglects (11:29) or who brings other *trouble to his family*, but one overzealous for profit to the point of *greed*. Indeed his *greed* leads him to break the rules and take *bribes*. This was forbidden under the Law (Exod. 23:8) and, although the penalty is not specified and death is not mentioned, something of the sort is implied in *will live*. See also Deuteronomy 16:19f which did not necessarily mean the magistrates inflicted the death penalty on such fathers, but more likely refers to the curse of God, as in Deuteronomy 27:25, cf. Habakkuk 2:9f. What this meant, not only for the offender but his family is seen in the terrible story of Achan (Josh. 7 – *trouble* has the same root as 'Achan'). On a positive note our proverb is telling us not to be anxious lest, if we fail to make gains by fair means or foul, we shall lose out. In fact the opposite is the case: *he who hates bribes will live*. If we trust God enough to obey him, he will look after us, which is the heart of the covenants old and new.

Consider a similar balance between fathers and sons in Ephesians 6:1-4.

CONCLUSION: A MATTER OF LIFE AND DEATH (v. 24).

Although not the closing verse it fitly rounds off these sayings which relate to the all-seeing God. It is to him that belong the issues of life and death. To live by his wisdom is not just good, it is *life* itself. Like Moses (Deut. 30:15) PROVERBS sets before us two *paths* – life and death – and urges us to choose *the path of life*. There are two reasons for this:

(a) *the path of life leads upward* – it contains the highest and noblest things; it is blessed by him who because he sees all things is over all things, and it ends with never-ending *life* in his presence (although this is probably reading back from the New Testament);

(b) it is the only way of avoiding *going down to the grave* (SHEOL). Although all must go *to the grave* in the physical sense, the idea includes darkness, fear and separation from God. It was with this in mind that the father urged his son to keep away from evil company, from those whose practices take them down the road to death (2:18, 5:5, 7:27). It is not the will of our Father in heaven, who sees and knows all things, that any of his little ones should perish in this way.

14

Living Under The All-Sovereign God
Proverbs 16

This chapter emphasizes the Lord in his sovereignty by beginning and ending on this note (vv. 1-9, 33). The intermediate verses show how we can all benefit from this, from the King (vv. 10-15) to the labourer (v. 26) and even the pensioner (v. 31)!

A. THE EXTENT OF GOD'S SOVEREIGNTY (vv. 1-5).
First a number of areas in which God reigns supreme.

1. God's Sovereignty over our thoughts and words (v. 1).
Here is the perfect balance between human freedom and divine sovereignty. Man has freedom of thought through the gift of reason. He can also put his thoughts in order, for *plans* is literally 'arrangements', a word used of setting a battle array (Gen. 14:8) or laying a fire (Gen. 22:9). But thoughts, however good and logically ordered, do not achieve anything; they have to be put into words in order to address the situation or communicate with the people in question. This *reply of the tongue* does not come about without God. However, the distinction between the two parts of the verse shouldn't be pressed too rigidly, for **God** also has access to our thoughts, and **we** have some freedom in our choice of words. The verse taken as a whole means that no purpose of man that enters into *the heart*, can come to anything without God's involvement in some part of the process (cf. v. 9, 19:21).

2. God's Sovereignty over our ways (v. 2).

This verse is about our actions or *ways*, which carry into effect what began as thoughts and words (v. 1). In this area as in the other we are not competent to make a right assessment. We are unable to view our actions objectively and therefore can see nothing wrong with them; to us they are pure and clean (*innocent*), cf. 21:2. In themselves they may indeed be good, but God also takes account of the *motives* that lie behind them. These we are even less qualified to judge, for we have a heart that deceives us (Jer. 17:9f.), either into ignoring motivation altogether or persuading us it is good. This is where the sovereign God comes in, for he not only **knows** our motives (5:21) but *weighs* them (21:2, 24:12), that is, passes judgment on their merit. Those who accept this will not always be 'justifying themselves in the eyes of men' like the Jews (Luke 16:15), but examining themselves and praying he will purify their motives, as David did (Ps. 19:14).

3. God's Sovereignty over our affairs (v. 3).

The NIV may be getting ahead of the train of thought when it advises us how to make our *plans succeed*. For this is not the same word as 'plans' in verse 1; 'your thought shall be established' (KJV) is a more literal rendering. This follows well from verses 1 and 2, which may have unsettled our minds by showing us our thoughts are unreliable (v. 1) and scrutinized by God (v. 2). This was not God's intention in inspiring these sayings. His wish is for our peace of mind, to free us from anxiety, uncertainty and indecision (Ps. 94:19, Isa. 32:17, John 14:27, 16:33). The way to achieve this is to entrust (*commit*) all our affairs (*whatever you do*) *to the Lord*. This applies to our daily routine, to impending and unusual events, to decisions not yet made and anxieties real or imaginary. Turn all these thoughts into prayers by thinking them in God's presence 'and the peace of God ... will guard your hearts and your minds' (Phil. 4:6f); you will have a sense of security, an assurance that in all the above matters which occupy your mind, he will be working for your good (Rom. 8:28).

4. The Sovereignty of God over all things (v. 4).

Here is the proof that committing our thoughts, plans and ways to God will give us peace of mind – the fact that nothing and nobody is outside his control. This is the most absolute statement of God's sovereignty in this section, possibly even in the whole book; it ranks alongside Paul's teaching in Romans 9 (especially verses 14-24) and Ephesians 1 (especially verse 11). It sets God forth as the beginning and end of *everything*. He began all things, for 'has made' is preferable to *works out*. When he made them he had a purpose or *end* in view, which was that everything should bring him the glory due to him (Rev. 4:11). Because of evil there are some who fail to do so during their span of life – *the wicked*. Nevertheless he will not be deprived of his glory even in their case, for he has appointed a day in which he will call all to account and demonstrate his sovereignty in judgment, even though it means *disaster for the wicked*. This is the God to whom we 'commit' our affairs (v. 3) and who will establish our thoughts!

5. God's Sovereignty over the greatest (v. 5).
This enlarges on verse 4b in two ways. **First**, it specifies what kind of wickedness is in view, which is pride: *all the proud of heart*. The discussion has been about realizing the inadequacy of our decisions and the impurity of our motives. *The proud of heart* won't do this, nor acknowledge God's right to scrutinize let alone judge them. So, however righteous, pious or abounding in good deeds a man is, if he is *proud* of himself *the Lord detests him* – a strong word – 'abomination', which AMP translates as 'disgusting, hateful and exceedingly offensive'. This aversion of God's to pride is frequent in Scripture (6:16f, 8:13, Job 40:12, James 4:6). But why is it worse than other sins? Because it is a direct challenge to God, a denial of his right to observe and punish; it 'contends with him for supremacy' (Bridges).

This leads to the **second** way in which this verse enlarges on verse 4b – what will happen on 'the day of disaster'. *Unpunished* or 'acquitted' is a legal term; it depicts God on his judgment seat saying to the *proud*, 'Guilty!' Whatever their good points or the esteem in which society has held them, God has no place for them in his kingdom. The *proud* man will ultimately find himself in the company of those whom he has all his life despised and condemned (Rev. 22:15). Nothing is as *sure* as this (see on 11:21.)

Question
What other areas come under God's sovereignty?

B. How to Live Happily Under a Sovereign God (vv. 6-9).
How can I escape being 'punished' on 'the day of disaster'
(vv. 4-5) and enjoy the peace of verse 3? By acquiring attitudes
which are the opposite of pride, such as those mentioned
here.

1. Loving loyalty to man and reverence for God (v. 6).
First cultivate *love and faithfulness to man* and *fear of the Lord*.
This may sound like salvation by works, for human qualities
are made the means of *atonement*. It is however in keeping
with the Old Testament teaching that performing the
Levitical sacrifices without obedience is worse than useless
because God rates moral and spiritual qualities higher than
ceremonies (1 Sam. 15:22, Micah. 6:6-8). Nor is it foreign to
New Testament teaching, even though the Levitical sacrifices
have been replaced by the sacrifice of Christ. A mere mental
assent to substitutionary atonement which does not bear fruit
in loving loyalty to others and humble obedience to God is
not the faith which saves (James 2:14-17). The expression
is therefore an example of the fruit of an act being put in
place of the act itself. He who obeys God by trusting in the
atonement he has provided and proves his faith is genuine by
his relationship with God and man will certainly *avoid* the *evil*
of eternal punishment on the last day.

2. Pleasing God rather than man (v. 7).
If this verse sounds simplistic we must bear in mind that the
PROVERBS were originally intended for those growing up in
a society in which God was universally acknowledged and
his law accepted by all. Because of their struggle to live even
at subsistence level, rivalry between farmers or smallholders
could break out and lead to nastiness (a scenario used by
Jesus in his famous parable in Matt. 13:24-30). Under the old
covenant one who refrained from hostility and practised
godliness enjoyed God's blessing: his farm and family alike
prospered (Deut. 28:1-6). Those who observed this would think

it in their interest to be on good terms with these favoured ones. To some extent this applied to the surrounding nations who frequently found it better to trade peaceably with Israel rather than fight costly wars against them.

As with 3:3-4 this is not so straightforward in these gospel days, when the godly are mixed socially with the ungodly. In fact our very godliness provokes them to vent their hatred of God on us, as Jesus warned (John 15:18, 16:1-4) and as the early church soon discovered (Acts 4:1-3). Thus the believer has to face a sterner test than his Old Testament counterpart – not to compromise his principles in the interest of peace, but remain loyal to his God. In this way he may win his 'enemy' over (Rom. 12:17-21), but if not he knows he needn't fear him, for 'if God is for us, who can be against us?' (Rom. 8:31).

3. Contentment (v. 8).
This qualifies the bald statement of verse 7. Even under the Law it didn't always happen that God prospered the godly man and impoverished the wicked. A man may have *righteousness* but *little ... gain* (literally 'increase') and another *much gain* but which he has acquired dishonestly or by oppression and thus *with injustice*. What price the promise of God in such circumstances? In what ways was the first *better* off than the second? 21:6 reminds us that whereas temporal wealth is fleeting, righteousness is for ever. This is even more so where wealth is gained by dishonesty or tyranny, for what is obtained without labour is spent carelessly or lavishly, not earned for the purpose of keeping alive but to enjoy luxury; and once the taste for this is acquired it is insatiable and demands further dishonesty or oppression to finance it. One who lives like this can never have the contentment which is one of the greatest blessings of life, *better* than the restless pursuit of wealth for its own sake (1 Tim. 6:6-9).

4. Submissiveness (v. 9).
The sovereignty of God is no mere philosophy, it is about life, both in its totality and its details. Life is here compared to a 'journey', as NEB translates *course*, which we with our God-given intelligence *plan* in our minds. We work out where we

want to go and how to get there, then take *steps* to fulfil our *plans*. But while free to follow our reason, we can ultimately do nothing without the consent of God's providence. He may prosper these *plans*, redirect or stop them altogether. For he too has *plans*, which take into account things we either don't know because we lack foresight, or we don't choose because they are unwelcome. But he is the one with the greater power and it is his 'purpose that will stand' (Isa. 46:10, Prov. 19:21, 20:24, 21:30). Our best course is to cooperate with him by submitting our thoughts to him so that our plans coincide with his, and by committing our lives to him as we go out to fulfil them (cf. v. 3).

Question
Is it restricting or enriching to live under the sovereignty of God? In what ways?

C. THE EARTHLY REPRESENTATIVE OF THE SOVEREIGN GOD (vv. 10-15).
From the general to particular positions and situations, beginning at the top with government, based on five things.

1. Justice (v. 10).
The basic and primary duty of one who holds the reins of government is to administer *justice*. A commitment to *justice* is more essential in his case than anyone else's because of his high position. To say *he speaks as an oracle* is not to attribute infallibility to him. It is to say he is there as representative of the sovereign God, whether he knows it or not (Rom. 13:1), which was written with reference to the Roman emperors! Because of this he is highly regarded by his people who expect him to make right decisions. This trust he must not *betray* by allowing opinion, profit or partiality to obtrude themselves into his decisions.

This does not mean monarchy is the only divinely ordained form of government. What matters is not its form, but its basis and aim – *justice* for all. Since governments and politicians are human and therefore sinful and fallible, we need to pray God will govern their thinking (21:1) so that they will fulfil their responsibilities efficiently. The King of Israel was committed to the divine Law (Deut. 17:18-20), but in the majority of nations conscience and custom have to do duty. All the more reason for us to pray for them (1 Tim. 2:1-2).

2. Integrity (v. 11).

11:1 has already established God's personal concern about *honest* trading. Here is the reason: accurate weights and measures are part of his Law (Lev. 19:35f, Deut. 25:13-16). *Scales* must be correctly adjusted and *weights* (literally 'stones', which the merchant carried around *in the bag*) must correspond to a fixed standard. God did not dictate what these measures were – they were fixed by the King and his government (see 2 Sam. 14:26). It was for them to appoint inspectors and for magistrates to punish offenders. Thus although this verse does not mention the King, the editor was probably right in placing it between two 'royal' proverbs. If 'justice' is the King's main duty, little is more important than enforcing it in the vital everyday activity of trading. In fact *honest* is the same word as that translated 'justice' in verse 10. So living under God's sovereignty is not such a bad thing! Every society, however ungodly, knows it must agree on such things as its standards of weights and measurement and the value of its currency, if its economy is to be stable and individual traders and their customers are not to be cheated.

3. Morality (v. 12).

It is not clear whether this is to be taken as a statement of fact, as NIV does, or a warning, as KJV does: 'It is an abomination for kings to commit wickedness'. The former is saying that Kings abhor doing evil because it is inconsistent with their office, whereas the latter is warning them against evil because it puts their throne in danger. Perhaps we should place it somewhere between the two and see it as an instruction or encouragement to governors to maintain that justice which is basic to their office (v. 10) and without which their reign would be unstable.

For it was certainly not a 'fact', even with the Kings of Israel and Judah, few of whom seemed to *detest wrongdoing*.

As for their *throne* being *established* the unrighteous seemed to fare no worse than the *righteous*. However, they had to rely on brute force rather than the goodwill of the people. Surely this is how it applies today. Democratic governments rely on the support of the population, which they lose if they become corrupt and immoral. Corrupt governments on the other hand are *established* on force: bodyguards to protect the dictator, police with arbitrary powers of arrest, imprisonment without trial and death for political crimes. This is not the Bible's and therefore not God's idea of security. A tyrant may think his security perfect, but only one breach is needed for him to be stretched out on the tarmac, dead.

4. Honesty (v. 13).

What was said of verse 12 applies here – that it is advice rather than fact. For there are plenty of examples, even in Israel and Judah, of Kings murdering prophets who told them *the truth*, and too few who made resolutions such as David's in Psalm 101:5-7. However, we must bear in mind the context – that justice is the basic principle of good government (v. 10) and can only be administered where *truth* reigns. The correct facts must be known for a right decision to be made in any area of government. So a ruler who is concerned about justice will appoint counsellors he can trust to give accurate reports and *honest* opinions (cf. 14:35). One who is surrounded by flatterers and liars will make many misjudgments both in legislation and administration. He may survive a long time but it will be at the expense of justice.

5. Power (vv. 14-15).

These 'royal' proverbs are addressed not only to kings but their subjects. No doubt Solomon was partly preparing his sons and later generations of his dynasty for their kingly office, but chiefly he is compiling a manual of wisdom for all the people. It was as necessary for the humblest citizen to know about *kings* as it is for us to know about our government, since it affects our lives so much. In no area is this more important than that of **power**. Of course, the one in view here is the ancient oriental despot with his immediate power of *life* and *death*. *This* is brought out strikingly in some vivid metaphors. His *wrath* is *a messenger of death* – he has but to storm and his servants will rush out and kill someone, as Henry II's knights did when they heard him say, 'Who will rid me of this turbulent priest?' (Thomas à Becket, Archbishop of Canterbury). *His favour*, however, *is like a rain cloud in spring*. Spring was the time of the barley harvest, on which the year's bread supply depended. Without rain the barley would be very thin, so when *a raincloud* appeared in the sky it *meant life* and was heralded with joy. The smile on the *face* of a *king* was like this – it indicated that an offender or suspect, perhaps a whole community, was pardoned or favoured.

There are still autocrats in the world and we should pray for those who have the misfortune to live under their rule, that they will be made *wise* to *appease it*. At the same time let us realize that even under our democratic system, where our vote has power to elect or dismiss the government, while it is still in office it has power over us, and this power affects at least the quality of our lives, if not our actual existence. So we too need to be *wise*, in the exercise of our vote, the expression of our opinion and the extent of our cooperation.

Refer back to 14:28, 34, 35 and see what this section in ch. 16 has added to Proverbs' 'theology of politics'.

D. QUALITIES VALUED BY THE SOVEREIGN GOD (vv. 16-24, 31, 32).
In these verses we are treading familiar ground, in fact it has been suggested they are chapters 1–9 in a nutshell. Be that as it may, the fact that they are commended by the God who is sovereign over us all, kings included, elevates them to a higher plain.

1. Wisdom and Understanding (v. 16).
Wisdom's supremacy is, of course, the great theme of PROVERBS: 3:13f, 4:7, 8:10, 11, 19. But this verse has its own contribution, if only because of the perfect parallelism of the poetry.

(a) *Gold* goes with *silver* to cover all precious metals then in use, which were universally accepted as currency.

(b) *Wisdom* and *understanding* go together and interpret each other: *wisdom* is more than knowledge of facts; it means *understanding* those facts, so that one who *understands* a few basic facts is better than one who has a vast store of knowledge but little *understanding* of how to use it. However ill-educated, he is a wise person.

(c) *Get* is balanced by *choose*, for we are free to *choose* which of the many things on offer we will seek to *get*. There is nothing wrong with *gold* and *silver* – they can do much good – but *wisdom* is *much* better, so *much* better that we are urged to prefer it by the use of the word *how*! If this is the sovereign God's estimation of it, let's put it top of our list.

2. Vigilance (v. 17).

He who is wise is also *upright*, for he values his *life* and therefore does all he can to protect it from *evil*. Some limit this to meaning that integrity is the best way to stay out of trouble, but this doesn't seem to go far enough. *Life* is NEPHESH (soul), which is our whole being and which Jesus said is worth more than the whole world (Matt. 16:26). It is vulnerable not merely to mishaps but to falling into moral and spiritual *evil*. In order to *avoid* this state of affairs we need two things.

(a) *To choose the right way*, the *highway*, so called because it was raised above ground level to avoid the pits and bogs. Such is the way of wisdom or 'holiness' (Isa. 35:8) which God has shown us in his Word.

(b) *To walk it vigilantly*, by keeping *guard*, for dangers lurk even for those who have chosen God's Word for their way (vv. 18f). We must not only walk *the highway of the upright*, but walk it uprightly, on the lookout for foes (Eph. 5:15, 1 Pet. 5:8); above all keeping company with him who can 'keep you from falling' (Jude 24).

3. Humility (vv. 18-19).

If the main point here is to commend humility, it is first necessary to condemn its opposite – *pride*. We have already seen how 'the Lord detests' this attitude (v. 5) and will not leave it 'unpunished'. This will certainly happen on the day of judgment, but it is not unlikely 'the day of disaster' will come long before that. For verse 18 reads as if proud words and deeds are the actual harbingers of *destruction*. One who overreaches himself and climbs too high puts himself in great danger. But being full of self-confidence he doesn't heed this, which makes him even more vulnerable. It was when Haman thought he was at the height of his power and about to receive the Emperor's accolade that he was commanded to give way to Mordecai whom he had despised (Esther. 6:6-14). It was while Nebuchadnezzar's arrogant boasting 'words were still on his lips' that he heard his doom pronounced (Dan. 4:31f). The same fate befell Belshazzar in the following chapter. Nor is this confined to unbelievers. Peter's boast of undying loyalty to Jesus was quickly followed by his denial of him (Matt. 26:33-35, 69-75). Churches are warned not to make a recent convert into an elder 'or he may become conceited and fall into the condemnation of the devil' (1 Tim. 3:6).

Anything is better than that, even sharing the lot of those *oppressed* by *the proud*. We need not envy them as they *share* their *plunder*, for they won't enjoy it for long. However, humility is not a matter of being materially poor and physically *oppressed*. It is an attitude of mind called here *lowly in spirit*. To envy the great, strong and rich is to be as *proud* as they. Humility is a sense of unworthiness at being entrusted with riches or greatness, a feeling of gratitude that we are kept alive. It is such, said Jesus, that God blesses (Matt. 5:3). It is such who are about to receive honour (15:33, 18:12, 29:23). That 'honour' is to enjoy the favour of God (Pss. 34:18, 138:6, Isa. 57:15), or in Gospel terms to be admitted to 'the kingdom of heaven' (Matt. 5:3).

4. Faith that obeys (v. 20).

This is the last thing the proud man will do; he won't *heed instruction* from another, for he is the one who gives the orders. As for *trusting God*, he is so self-confident he needs no such prop as religion. But anyone who has taken to heart the principles of God's sovereignty in verses 1-5 will realize how much he depends on God for his prosperity and happiness. *Instruction* is just what he needs because he is ignorant of the best way; so not only will he **listen** to it but **practise** it (both are in *heed*). But more than outward prosperity he wants assurance of God's personal favour, which might not coincide with *prosperity* (v. 19). This he has not by works, only by faith. So even the Old Testament with its strong stress on law and works, continually appeals for *trust in the Lord* and promises true happiness to those who do so (29:25, Pss. 2:12, 32:10, 40:4, Isa. 26:3f, Jer. 17:7). The New Testament enlarges on this by showing how faith gives us a share in the atoning sacrifice of Christ and lifts us up with him into heavenly realms (Eph. 2:4-9).

5. Gentle persuasion (vv. 21-24).
A beautiful picture of an able advocate for God and his truth. It originates in hearing and believing God's teaching (v. 20) which bears fruit in those qualities described in verses 16-20. To become such is to be *wise in heart* (**v. 21**). The beauty and glory of this is seen in the picture of *the fountain of life* in **verse 22**, which is not an artificial fountain but a spring bubbling from the ground unceasingly for the benefit of all around.

One thus equipped grows into a *discerning person* (**v. 21**), one who knows how to run his own life and is thus qualified to counsel others, which requires a gift of speaking. His *wise ... heart* teaches him this too, for it *guides his mouth* (**v. 23**). What is a gift of speaking? It is a combination of two things. **First**, *pleasant words (vv. 21, 24)*, words which are *sweet to the soul* (**v. 24**), that is, they sound good, they are both kind and sensible, well-meant and apt. **Second**, *effective words* which 'persuade', for *instruction* in verses 21 and 23 is literally 'persuasion' (see NIV mg). Because they represent the teaching of God they do good, they are *healing to the bones* (**v. 24**). *The bones* are the basis of the body's strength, so that these *pleasant ... healing words* restore mental, emotional and spiritual strength to one who is flagging.

The illustration of *honey* (**v. 24**) is aptly chosen for it both tastes sweet and does good. Not everything that tastes good is good for us. Words can be listened to like music – pleasing to the ear but producing no change (Ezek. 33:31f). Our Lord spoke both pleasantly and persuasively, as was prophesied beforehand (Ps. 45:1, Isa. 50:4) and testified by his hearers (Luke 4:22, John 7:46). Those who learn of him also become gentle but effective persuaders. Paul's aim was so to grow spiritually that he would be able to 'persuade men' to be 'reconciled to God' (2 Cor. 5:11, 20). But one who does not learn of God has no chance of achieving this. *Fools* (**v. 22**) are those who don't heed wisdom (1:7) yet set themselves up as teachers. But what do they teach? Only the folly that is in their minds, for line 2 reads literally 'the instruction of fools is folly'. 'If a blind man leads a blind man, both will fall into a pit' (Matt. 15:14).

6. Persistent righteousness (v. 31).

This saying is to be understood in the light of God's promise under the old covenant that obedience is rewarded with long life. It is addressed mainly to the young who are apt to admire youth and strength and despise the elderly for their weakness (20:29). When they see *grey hair* they should see it as *a crown of splendour*, the proof and reward of God to one who has lived *a righteous life*. This was why the Law required respect for the old (Lev. 19:32) – it was an indirect way of recognizing that God values *righteousness* above physical strength. kjv wrongly inserts 'if' ('if it be found ....'), for there is no implied contrast between a godly and an ungodly old person. Old age **proved** *righteousness*. There was virtually no such animal as an old sinner! The situation is not quite the same in Gospel days. Age of itself tells us nothing about a person's moral or spiritual life. It is the way he views it and employs it that is significant. Does he see it as the evening before the dawn of eternal glory? Does he use it to continue to 'bear fruit in old age' (Ps. 92:14)? Or does he just whinge about it and slip into total inertia?

7. Self-control (v. 32).

From the standpoint of values this is similar to verse 31. As the wisdom of the ancients placed persistent goodness above (temporary) physical strength, so did it place self-control above heroism. In answer to the question, 'Who is the strong man?' the uninstructed would say, 'He who by his strength and heroism *captures a city*.' Wisdom would reply that in fact it is harder to control your passions than lead an army or wield a sword. Gideon won a great military victory over the Midianites, but his greatest moment was when he suppressed his anger and returned a gentle answer to the unfair provocative criticism of the Ephraimites (Judg. 8:1-3). This point is frequently made in PROVERBS: 14:17, 29, 15:1, 18, 17:27, 19:11, 25:28. It is confirmed by Christ in Matthew 5:5 and by the apostles – Paul in Romans 12:21 and James in 1:19. We who live under the gospel are in a better position to practise it, with the example of our Saviour (1 Pet. 2:21-25) and the ministry of the Spirit (Gal. 5:22f).

Question
Is your belief in the sovereignty of God helping you become the sort of person described in these verses or is it having the opposite effect?

E. WHAT DISPLEASES THE SOVEREIGN GOD (vv. 25-30).

1. Self-delusion (v. 25).
This is a straight repeat of 14:12, although in a different context. There it occurred in a study of the contrast between the wise and foolish in relation to the emotions. The fool tends to be led by his feelings and his judgment rather than by fixed principles. Here we are thinking of life under an all-sovereign God, of what he approves and disapproves. We have already been advised that this God sees through our self-assessment to our real motives (v. 2). We tend to skate over or justify them, but he takes them seriously, he 'weighs' them to reveal their worth.

Here we see what makes this such a serious matter. To be wrongly motivated and yet not know it can send us in a direction that ends in disaster. This is not what God wants, but it is the sure outcome of self-delusion and self-deceit. Nowhere is this more so than in the matter of salvation. We who are blinded by sin, ignorant by nature and easily duped by the devil will find *a way that seems right* and convince ourselves we are prepared to meet *death*. But it is *a way* we have thought up or learned from others. God is sovereign in salvation and only his *way* leads to life.

2. Starvation (v. 26).

Nothing could contrast more with verse 25 than this. The life of *the labourer* is simple, he has no time for complex motives, nor is there a choice of ways before him. He is *driven* by one motive – *hunger*, which like hanging concentrates the mind. He knows but one way of satisfying it – *work*. For the setting is the subsistence farming common in that age and widespread in the Third World today. What place has the sovereign God in this? We can see it as the outcome of his original sentence on sin, that keeping body and soul together would be hard going (Gen. 3:17-19). At the same time we can see the awful predicament of one so taken up with working for 'food that spoils' that he has no space to 'work for the food that endures to eternal life' (John 6:27). Yet it is not God's will that anyone should starve to death for want of food (Ps. 145:15f) nor that he should go to eternal death for want of the knowledge of the Gospel and the opportunity to come to faith in it (2 Pet. 3:9). But God's sovereignty does not mean he provides these personally and directly. He uses the better off to share with the abject poor (Isa. 58:7) and those who know him become his witnesses to others (Acts 1:8). So we can see this as an implied call to 'feed the hungry' and 'rescue the perishing'.

3. Mischief-making (vv. 27-30).

From the evolution of the gentle persuader (vv. 20-24) to the evolution of the mischief-maker. As the harm he intends increases so his mind becomes more perverse and his methods more vile.

(a) *Destroying a good name by slander (v. 27).*

He begins by being called simply *a scoundrel*, literally 'man of Belial', one with no good in him. He is jealous of the good man and wants to destroy his good name. So he *plots* (= 'digs') *evil*, that is, he lays a trap to catch his victim as a hunter does with an animal. He works hard, like a digger, to unearth some scandal and expose him. When he has found a story which has the slightest whiff of smoke he fans it into a *fire* with inflammatory language which *scorches* his victim's reputation in the eyes of the public. James warns us against going down this road in 3:6.

(b) *Breaking friendships by spreading rumours (v. 28).*
But he is not satisfied. He has damaged his victim's good name before the world but his *close friends* remain loyal. He must break this up and '*spread* strife' (rsv) between them to turn them against each other. Being unable to win loyal friends himself he is jealous of anyone who succeeds. So he starts a whispering campaign (*gossip* = 'whisperer'). His approach here is less public because it has no basis in truth but is sheer rumour-mongering. He just throws out a casual remark knowing it will be exaggerated in the telling. So he is called 'a man of falsehoods' (*perverse man*). He has these lies conveyed to his victim's friends to *stir up* suspicion and mistrust, hoping to break up the friendship.

(c) *Enticing into a life of crime (v. 29).*
The victim is now isolated from society and friends, but as yet is not in trouble with the authorities and may in time recover. His enemy must finish him finally. Rumours and scandal are not enough – he must have concrete evidence against him, so must lure him into crime. To do this the 'man of Belial' (v. 27) and 'the man of falsehoods' (v. 28) becomes *a man of violence,* one who aims at the physical punishment or even the execution of his enemy. How he does this we are not told, but 1:10-14 and 2:12-15 have extended descriptions of enticement.

(d) *Persevering to the death (v. 30).*
Since this verse does not begin as do the last three with 'a man of', it is not a further stage in the campaign but a description of the man's determination utterly to destroy his victim. His total commitment to this is seen in his body language, especially *his eye* and *his lips.* The word used is not *wink* but 'shut' which may indicate his total concentration on what he is doing. neb has 'narrowing' the eyes – a common way of expressing evil determination, often accompanied by *pursing the lips,* which adds to the picture of a set face reflecting a determined mind. The mouth, like the eyes, is very expressive. 'If looks could kill,' we say. *Bent on* is in the perfect tense, literally, 'has finished' – he won't give up until his aim is accomplished and his victim finished. Although he may keep himself in the background, his plan may be read in his face muscles.

Turn to 6:12-19, what does God think of the mischief-maker?

CONCLUSION: THE SOVEREIGNTY OF GOD'S WILL (v. 33).

We have learned much about what the sovereign God approves or disapproves from this chapter. However, we frequently have to make decisions about matters too local or particular to be laid down in Scripture. God had to keep his Word within reasonable dimensions if it was to be of value to the common man. To cover every contingency would have required books larger than the Jews' Mishnah and Talmud and put us in the hands of priests and professors. Under the old covenant the problem was solved by *casting lots* (which may have been identical with 'Urim and Thummim'). By this method officers were chosen for the Temple (1 Chron. 24-25), the truth was brought to light (1 Sam. 14:41), offenders were brought to justice (Josh. 7:16), arguments settled (Prov. 18:18) and the land of Canaan divided among the tribes (Num. 26:55). In this way the Israelites were able to believe that the resulting *decision* was *from the Lord*. This was because of their belief in the sovereignty of God and his will (as in verses 1-4).

The last recorded occurrence of the use of the lot is in fact the last recorded event before Pentecost – the choice of a twelfth apostle in place of Judas (Acts 1:26). The coming of the Spirit made infants into grown sons (Gal. 4:3-7) who have more direct access to the mind of their Father. Our belief in the sovereignty of his will moves us to consult him in prayer before making our decisions, to seek the leading of the Spirit, and above all to develop our understanding of the moral and spiritual principles of the New Testament set down to guide our footsteps in his way.

Question
As a result of studying this chapter are you any clearer on 'the will of God' and how to discern it?

15

Goodness, Wickedness and Foolishness
(Proverbs 17)

References to God are confined to verses 3 and 5 and *Wisdom* is totally absent. But three themes recur in sharp contrast with each other: goodness, wickedness and foolishness. So we will follow these in turn, bringing out the characteristics of each.

A. GOODNESS (vv. 1-3, 6, 9, 10, 17, 22, 27, 28).

1. Peaceful love (v. 1).
Here are two families at the dinner table. One has a few scraps of bread and nothing to drink (*dry* does not refer to the bread but the lack of wine); the other has roast meat, possibly the remains of the *sacrifices* (NIV mg) they have just offered. This shows they have large flocks and herds, whereas the first has no animals and probably offered loaves to the priest, which was why they only had the odd *crust* left. Which is *better*? 15:16f. and 16:8 have already given the game away: it all depends on the relationship of the eaters with God and each other. The first are enjoying God's blessing and each other's company, which makes up for the lack of food. The others are only together because of the special occasion, and their underlying jealousies and grievances soon surface. The resulting *strife* affects both appetite and digestion and takes the enjoyment from the *feasting*. The writer therefore describes the food not as 'peace offerings' but literally 'strife offerings', because their behaviour has altered the whole nature of the

meal. Here is something to take to heart at our parties and Christmas dinners: which comes first – the peace or the plenty; the lashings of food or the love?

2. Wise conduct (v. 2).
There are many ways of praising wisdom. Here is a very practical one, seen in a domestic setting, where it scores over privilege. The son, who has all the advantages, so abuses them by his attitude and behaviour that he is disinherited. How he 'causes shame' (*disgraceful*) we are not told, possibly by the sort of conduct described in 19:26. His disgrace means a complete role reversal: he now has to 'take orders' (NEB) from the *servant*, who eventually takes his share of the father's *inheritance*. It puts a different slant on 11:29 (which referred to the father) and was tragically fulfilled in Solomon's own son, Rehoboam, who lost ten of the tribes he had inherited from his father to Solomon's former *servant*, Jeroboam (1 Kings 11–12). It could have been avoided had he paid attention to the wisdom he was taught. After all he had a head start over *the servant*, being more likely to have been taught wisdom by his father.

3. Heart purity (v. 3).
Your *heart* is the real you, your character and personality. It has become diseased through sin, 'beyond cure' by man (Jer. 17:9), but when we bring it to Christ he heals it through his atoning blood and the gift of the Spirit (Acts 15:9). Since defects of character and sometimes actual sins remain, the work of purifying has to go on. *Gold* and *silver* extracted from rock is valuable, but to realize its full worth it has to be heated in a *crucible* in the case of *silver* or a *furnace* in that of *gold*. The impurities cannot endure the heat and are destroyed; the precious metal melts but remains and quickly solidifies. It is to a similar process that *the Lord* subjects the personalities of those he 'excavates' from the world. The world does not willingly yield us up to him and turns against us. God allows this as his way of **proving** (*tests*) our genuineness by bringing us safely through, and **improving** our character by purging our self-love and worldliness (Isa. 48:10, Zech. 13:9, 1 Pet. 1:7). Those who want to 'grow in grace' are not only willing for this

process but even ask him for it (Ps. 26:2). It is the 'pure in heart' who are truly 'blessed' with the vision of God (Matt. 5:8).

4. Family pride (v. 6).

The Old Covenant promise lies very much behind this saying. A man who lived to see his *grandchildren* was doubly blessed – with long life and with progeny, both of which were marks of God's approval (Pss. 91:16, 128:5f). He could die in the knowledge that one of his chief prayers was answered – his family name would continue. For the *children* themselves their greatest blessing was to have *parents* in whom they could take *pride* – respected in the community, prosperous in business and thorough in bringing them up. Under the New Covenant, while these things are still important, our blessedness does not depend on them, and some of the choicest saints have come from bad homes, or died young and childless. But as far as we can let us make homes where old and young respect and delight in each other.

5. Discreet silence (v. 9).

We have been warned before about 'stirring up dissension' in 6:14, 19; 16:28 where it was deliberate, out of malice, jealousy and hatred. But it can also be done through sheer indiscretion: someone hears of an *offence*, *repeats the matter*, finds it comes to the ears of the offended party and *separates close friends*. The gossip is not necessarily a malicious person; he may just be a nosey-parker who likes to be first with the news. But he can do as much harm as the 'scoundrel' of 6:14 or the 'perverse man' of 16:28. The trouble with him is that he lacks real love. He may be well-meaning, kind and friendly up to a point, but doesn't have the sensitivity to others' feelings which is a mark of *love*.

Love 'keeps no record of wrongs ... does not delight in evil ... always protects' (1 Cor. 13:5-7). So it is very discreet about what it passes on. One bursting to tell something he has heard will consider the people concerned, especially if they are *close friends* and will *cover over an offence*. This is not to be taken to the extent of 'concealing evidence' in the case of a crime. Nor is it to be applied to sin which is serious enough to bring the church or gospel into disrepute. Such matters we have a duty to report, but to the proper authorities. This is not lack of *love*, since harm is done if the *offence* is not dealt with.

6. Wise sensitivity (v. 10).

Nowhere does the difference between wise and foolish appear more clearly than in their response to *rebukes* and punishment. *A man of discernment* needs just a word of *rebuke* to change his ways, whereas *a fool* is not altered by *more than a hundred lashes*. The plagues of Egypt didn't change the mind of Pharaoh, but David was convicted by one word from Nathan: 'You are the man!' This is because the *fool* is essentially ignorant. He doesn't know right from wrong or good from bad, and certainly doesn't know himself (12:15). On such a one corporal punishment is wasted. This is why it is important to impart wisdom from an early age, before character is formed and habits acquired. It also advises us to be discerning in administering discipline, which should be adapted to the character of the one concerned. Someone who has learned to know himself, *a man of discernment*, also needs to learn how to judge character and act accordingly.

7. Constant friendship (v. 17).

True friendship is not only sharing the good times, having fun together, but showing *love*, and *love* is constant *at all times*, even in the *bad times*, when there is no fun to be had, when things or people turn against us, even when we let our friend down or become cold to him. This only serves to deepen the *friendship* into *brotherhood*: from *a friend is born a brother*, who is bound as if by ties of blood, not broken by *adversity*. Such was Ruth's love for Naomi (Ruth 1:16) or more famously that of David and Jonathan. From their first meeting, when David was in the King's favour, 'Jonathan loved him as himself' (1 Sam. 18:3). But when Saul turned against him and Jonathan stood by him, David began to refer to him as 'brother' (2 Sam. 1:26).

You never had such a *friend*? But you have – Jesus came to be 'the *friend* of sinners' (Matt. 11:19), to call us 'no longer servants but *friends*' (John 15:13-15); in fact 'he was not ashamed to call us *brothers*' (Heb. 2:11-18). His *friendship* comes to us, not only directly, but through our human, especially Christian, *friends*. *We* can be a *friend and brother*, one who carries burdens and even restores a fellow-Christian who has fallen into sin (Gal. 6:1-2).

8. A happy heart (v. 22).

Long before the word 'psychosomatic' was coined, the idea was in Scripture (cf. 15:13). For the God who made us knows we are not machines but creatures with emotions which are integrated into our whole being. Just as a healthy body makes us feel in good spirits, so *a cheerful heart* can make a sick body feel better; it is *good medicine*, literally 'is good for health'. In the same way, despondency and depression tend to sap our energy and affect our health; they *dry up the bones. The bones* are the body's framework, its supports. So the meaning is that a melancholy person tends to lack determination, resolution and energy; he can't work his way out of depression. This doesn't mean that all he needs is cheering up by jovial companions or humorous entertainment. This in fact can be counterproductive. The basic cause of *a crushed spirit* is separation from God, the weight of guilt and prospect of judgment. Its restoration therefore comes from the 'good news of great joy' (Luke 2:10), that one has been sent among us 'to comfort all who mourn ... to bestow on them ... the oil of gladness instead of mourning' (Isa. 61:2f).

9. Self-control (vv. 27-28).

Here is another occasion when silence is the better part of discretion. In verse 9 the occasion was the temptation to pass on the news of a dispute between two friends. Here it is provocation – a taunting remark or unjust accusation. The natural reaction is to reply in an angry or abusive way; the *wise* one is to *keep silent* and *show restraint* (14:29, 16:32). He who does so is *a man of knowledge* who has learned his lessons well. For this is no mere theoretical matter – it involves controlling our temper, literally being 'of a cool spirit'. The *man of understanding* 'keeps his cool'.

Verse 28 is best seen as hyperbole with a touch of irony. The very thing the fool **can't** do is *keep silent*, especially under provocation (14:29b, 15:28b). Suppose in a hypothetical situation he managed to do so he would pass for a *wise ... and discerning* man, for he has acquired one of the highest parts of wisdom – to *hold his tongue*. As James said, one who succeeds in doing this 'is a perfect man, able to keep his whole body in check' (James 3:2). The fool will never be that.

Compare these nine qualities with the nine fruits of the Spirit in Galatians 5:22f. Do they help you understand the practical nature of those fruits and make you want to 'live by the Spirit'?

B. WICKEDNESS (vv. 4, 5, 7, 8, 11, 13, 15, 19, 20, 23, 26).
Nine forms of goodness are contrasted with nine of wickedness.

1. Itching ears (v. 4).
The world says 'we are what we eat', the Bible says 'we are what we listen to'. There will always be people who spread lies and *malicious* gossip because this will always attract an audience. If nobody *listened* they would keep quiet, so the hearers share the responsibility and show they are as bad as the speaker, the *wicked ... liar*. They only *pay attention* because they want to pass the tale on and cause more trouble. So it is not only *evil lips*, that are reprehensible but false ears.

From the spiritual standpoint there are those who *pay attention* to false teaching, in order to justify their own views or conduct. Ahab listened to false prophets because they told him what he wanted to hear – victory (1 Kings 22:6-15). Jeremiah found the people would not listen to his warnings but only the flattery of the false prophets who said they had nothing to fear from the Babylonians (Jer. 5:31). Today the world grasps at false teaching because it accords with its own views, flatters its pride and encourages its irresponsibility (2 Tim. 4:3, 1 John 4:5).

2. Heartless contempt (v. 5).
All *contempt* for others is reprehensible because all are made by God in his image and deserve respect. To *mock the poor* is therefore to despise the God who made them. This does not mean, as some commentators of former days suggested,

that God made them poor. True, the providence of God plays a part in the fortunes of all of us, but to sing

> The rich man in his castle,
> The poor man at his gate,
> God made them high or lowly
> And ordered their estate

is to overlook human responsibility: our duty to provide for ourselves and share with others. Poverty may be due to fecklessness or others' neglect of those who are *poor* through no fault of their own. The latter appears to be the case here with the reference to *disaster*. Someone of a *contemptuous* spirit is likely to take a 'serve you right' attitude to misfortune. But as Jesus warned and Paul after him, we are judged by the criteria with which we judge others (Matt. 7:1f, Rom. 2:1-4). In the Old Testament nations which *gloated* over Israel's downfall were warned of their own impending overthrow (Ezek. 25, Obad. v. 12). The New Testament is if anything more severe, saying that if material want doesn't arouse our pity and practical help then we ourselves are outside the love of God (1 John 3:17). 24:17f enlarges on this.

3. Lying leaders (v. 7).
Normally how we speak expresses what we are (10:11-14, Matt. 12:34f). Here the opposite is the case: we have *a fool* – not the usual term in PROVERBS which describes one ignorant and uninstructed, but NABAL, the worthless person who refuses instruction and lives for himself and his low vices. We would expect to hear filth, abuse, lies and blasphemy coming from his mouth, but lo and behold he is making 'a fine speech' (NEB), 'eloquent' (NIV), exalting virtue and encouraging people to follow it. Yet who will take it seriously when his life belies it? An unlikely scenario, but this is the point, for the sting is in the tail – the *ruler* (literally 'noble', NADIB to balance NABAL) who has the right to address the people, lay down principles of behaviour and exhort people to follow them because he is trusted and respected, yet is found *lying* to them (cf. 16:10). Whereas the *arrogant fool* only creates a minor sensation, the

lying ruler overturns the fabric of society. In our democratic system someone may come to government who is not up to the job, but if he is honest this compensates to an extent. The worst situation is one who lies to Parliament, press and people. Some are exposed but we fear others get away with much. Lord, give us honest politicians!

4. Bribery (vv. 8, 23).

(a) *Its power* (**v. 8**).

If a 'ruler' (v. 7) is deceitful he is probably also bribable; this may even be the way he has reached his position. Although *charm* is literally 'precious stone', it is clearly not just the monetary value of it that is in view, but the idea that a bribe 'works like a charm' (NEB) or 'like magic' (GNB). It gives success on every side: it gains a way into the highest circles (18:16), it pacifies an enemy (21:14) and can even buy off the magistrate (v. 23). Although bribery is not specifically condemned here, the very use of the word is enough, in view of the Law's prohibition (Deut. 16:19). Verse 7 moved us to pray against dishonest politicians; this verse will do likewise regarding those who are in politics for self-advantage. They are vulnerable both to bribing others and being bribed themselves.

(b) *Its wickedness* (**v. 23**).

The *wickedness* of the *bribe* lies both in its means and its end. It has to be given and received *in secret*, literally 'out of the bosom', a picture of the briber taking money from under the folds of his cloak and the bribed slipping it into a pocket inside his cloak. What has to be done secretly is usually (though not always) bad (Eph. 5:12) and this is certainly the case with bribery. The end in view here is probably worst of all – *to pervert the course of justice*, because it involves one who of all should be trustworthy – the judge or magistrate, whose chief qualification is that he 'hates dishonest gain' (Exod. 18:21). Judges are supposed to be impartial, to be guided only by facts and evidence. But money 'blinds' them to the truth and encourages them to 'twist the words of righteousness' (Exod. 23:8). Nor is it just an abstract concept of 'justice' that suffers: a criminal or oppressor is set free to continue in his ways and increase the sufferings of his victims. But God sees what is done *in secret* and will expose and punish it openly. We find it exemplified in Samuel's sons (1 Sam. 8:3) and Judas Iscariot (Mark 14:10f) but refused by Paul to the covetous Felix (Acts 24:26).

5. Rebelliousness (v. 11).

Line 1 can be taken as NIV does or reversed: 'A rebel seeks only evil', which is a more natural expression than 'seek rebellion'; also the word *only* doesn't seem appropriate, since *an evil* man has a longer agenda than *only rebellion*. It might, however, be an emphatic way of saying 'wicked people are always stirring up trouble' (GNB). Is the *rebellion* against God or the government? If it is against God *a merciless official* will need to be translated 'cruel messenger' or even 'angel of death' (cf. 16:14), 'destroying angel', such as God sent against rebellious Israel (Ps. 78:49). However, if this were the case why is God's name not used? Also the context of various forms of antisocial behaviour best fits the idea that this is someone rebelling against the state. David had suffered from this in the cases of Absalom and Sheba, and Solomon's own reign began with the rebellion of Adonijah. All were put down *mercilessly*. The point seems to be that a person motivated by *evil* will not be open to negotiation (cf. v. 10); only force and strict justice will avail. It is a sobering thought in these days of terrorism and guerilla warfare.

6. Base ingratitude (v. 13).

Is this the full height of wickedness? To *pay back evil* for evil is condemned (20:22, 24:29, Rom. 12:17), so what of *paying back evil for good*? 'To render evil for evil is brutish, but to return evil for good is devilish' (Henry). Yet it is common: Saul did it to David (1 Sam. 19:4, 24:17); but David himself did it to Uriah and suffered the consequences specified here: 'The sword shall never depart from your *house*' (2 Sam. 12:10). God makes no exceptions: because David had suffered this himself did not excuse him – perhaps it rendered him more culpable since he knew what it felt like. Let none of us feel we are exempt, for we belong to a race under a curse for ingratitude to God (Rom. 1:21). So endemic is this spirit that when the most favoured nation in the human race refused that 'higher gift than grace ... God's presence and his very self' it brought a terrible curse on itself (Matt. 23:38, 27:25). Although this was fulfilled in AD 70 with the destruction of Jerusalem and decimation of the nation, there is a sense in which it continues in that particular blind hardness to Christ which characterizes the Jews (Rom. 11:25). However, non-Jews need not be smug, for if those who bask in the light of the gospel reject the offer of Christ, they may not only suffer judgment themselves but deprive their families (*house*) of the knowledge of salvation, perhaps for generations.

7. Perverting justice (vv. 15, 26).

(a) *The verdict (*v. 15*).*
The words are deliberately chosen to emphasize perversion, since they completely reverse those of the law: 'Acquitting the innocent and condemning the guilty' (Deut. 25:1). The main reference is to administering justice, in which judges or rulers are God's representatives, whether in Israel (Exod. 23:6f) or among the Gentiles (Rom. 13:1-4). No doubt bribery lay behind the practice (v. 8): a rich man by paying the judge could get a poor innocent punished for his own crime or get his enemy condemned. This happened in Israel and Judah's declining days (Amos 5:7, 6:12, Ezek. 22:27-29). Jesus himself was condemned to let a guilty man, Barabbas, go free. In God's eyes there is nothing to choose between *condemning the innocent and acquitting the guilty*, for he *detests them both.*

But what we may not do to each other he can do for us – not *condemning the innocent* for there is no such person, but *acquitting the guilty*. This he does with no breach of justice, indeed through the plainest act of justice ever performed – the punishment of his own Son, which was just because he willingly stood surety for sin of the world, 'made sin for us' (2 Cor. 5:21). In him we see sin getting its full wages, see Romans 3:25f. Nor does he need a bribe to *acquit the guilty*; he does it 'freely by his grace' (Rom. 3:24).

(b) *The sentence* (**v. 26**).
The Hebrew begins with 'also' which may connect it with
verse 15 or verse 23, both of which refer to the perverting
of justice. Whereas verse 15 refers to the verdict this refers
to the sentence. Under the Law punishment might be in the
form of a fine (Exod. 21:22) or a beating (Deut. 25:2f). RVmg
and RSV translate *punish* here as 'impose a fine'. To do this
to an innocent man is not only unjust but causes him great
hardship. It would be done by the type of judge or ruler in
view in verse 23, one who puts gain before justice and is
utterly callous – a tyrant who rules men for what he can get
out of them, if not by bribes then by unfair fines. As for line 2,
Henry and Bridges follow KJV ('strike princes') and think it
means people rising against their rulers for imposing **just**
punishments, which would be as much a perversion of justice
as rulers imposing **unjust** punishments. However, it is more
likely that the word 'noble men' (*officials*) refers to nobility of
character (cf. Isa. 32:5-8) and is thus parallel to line 1. It is all
about abuse of power, either for financial gain or increase of
authority.

8. A quarrelsome spirit (v. 19).
Verse 14 speaks of quarrelling as folly because it leads to
unforeseen trouble; this verse denounces it as *sin*. For what
we have here is not someone finding himself in a dispute
he never sought, but one who *loves a quarrel* for the sake of
it. He is cantankerous, he can't have a conversation without
it becoming an argument, a discussion without making it
a controversy or a dispute without turning it into a lawsuit.
The reason is pride which is what makes it *sin*. His *high gate*
may be a metaphor for the permanent division from others
which his quarrelsomeness raises up; or for his ostentation,
which bolsters his case by a claim to superiority; or for
his underlying paranoia which craves excessive security.
Whichever it is, it stands for pride, and 'pride' as we have
been told, 'goes before *destruction*' (16:18). The proud man
sets himself apart and makes enemies. His display of riches
and his state-of-the-art security system invite burglary. Pride
is a challenge to man and God and suffers the consequences.

9. Dishonesty (v. 20).

Here is a beautiful description of a very ugly person. The beauty lies in the rhythm and balance of the poetry: the *perverse heart* is balanced by the *deceitful tongue*, and *does not prosper* (literally 'not good') but *falls into trouble* (*literally* 'evil', the opposite of 'good'). There is also development of thought: the *perverse heart* expresses itself in the *deceitful tongue*; the heart aimed to *prosper*, but the words spoken caused it to *fall into trouble*. It is the mini-saga of the deceiver. He wants to do himself 'good' but cares not how he achieves it so long as he *prospers*. Since his *heart* is not directed by righteousness but by sin, it devises a dishonest way because this seems quickest and most lucrative. When he puts his plan into action his *tongue* comes into operation. But it is all lies and deceit, and although it appears to *prosper* for a while, it eventually gets him into *trouble*. Why? Because *the Lord detests men of perverse heart* (11:20) and will bring his judgment on them sooner or later (6:12-15, 18:6f, Ps. 18:26). Mortals are deceivable, not the God of Truth.

Review these nine forms of Wickedness. Can you see they are all 'social' sins? Do you think these are still the sins that break relationships and disrupt society or are there more modern ones?

C. FOOLISHNESS (vv. 12, 14, 16, 18, 21, 24, 25).

Interspersed among the fruits of goodness and wickedness are some of the marks of the fool, to which can be added insensitivity (v. 10).

1. Ungovernable (v. 12).

One of the most famous of all stage directions is in Act 3, scene 3 of Shakespeare's 'A Winter's Tale': 'Exit pursued by a bear'. Humorous as this seems to us, it was a real danger in the ancient world where *a bear* could appear out of nowhere and if *robbed of her cubs* would ferociously attack the first person she met, whether or not he had anything to do with their loss. There is little exaggeration in the use of this scenario as a metaphor for *a fool in his folly*. This is perhaps the strongest statement on the *fool* in the whole book. Often he is merely a nuisance, fairly harmless and his own worst enemy, but here he is a dangerous menace. This is because he is *in his folly* – 'busy with a stupid project' (GNB), in pursuit of satisfying a lust or on a mission of vengeance. He will hear no objection or suggestion and woe betide anyone who gets in his way. His self-will and passion soon burst into rage and anyone around may as well confront *a bear*. This is he who is impervious to the severest punishment (v. 10).

2. Provocative (v. 14).

This is about petty provocation and describes a minor misunderstanding or disagreement whose consequences are not foreseen, but turn out worse than giving in to the original cause of the bother. If you open a sluice gate or *breach a dam* you have lost control of the water, cannot see the outcome or retrieve the situation. Even if the pocket or pride is hurt, the cost is less than if the dispute is left to run its course. An out-of-court settlement is cheaper than the damages and costs the court may award, a scenario Jesus appealed to in his wise words on anger (Matt. 5:25f). How wise was Abraham to nip in the bud the quarrel between his shepherds and Lot's (Gen. 13:8), Gideon to refuse to argue with the Ephraimites (Judg. 8:1-3) and the apostles to settle the dispute between the Hebrew and Grecian widows by appointing seven wise men to resolve it (Acts 6:1-3). Our world today is strewn with the casualties of quarrels that began over trifles and escalated into major wars. How can this be avoided? See James 3:6, 14-16. The comment on verse 28 is also relevant here.

3. Mindless (v. 16).

NIV and NEB are on their own in placing the words *to get wisdom* after *no desire*; most others place it where it is in the Hebrew sentence – after *the hand of a fool*. 'Of what use is money in the hand of a fool since he has no mind' or 'Why should a fool have a price in his hand to buy wisdom when he has no mind?' (RSV). This does not mean there were professional 'wise men' who would teach wisdom for a fee, for education was home-based. It has a more general meaning: Wisdom cannot be bought with money in the way most other things are. It requires the right attitude of mind (*desire* means 'heart' or 'mind') – an attitude which puts it above things like money (2:4f, 8:10f). Wisdom is not a list of principles and precepts which can be learned by rote like other knowledge. It is an approach to everything in life and therefore begins deep in the mind with a willingness to be taught the right way. This is what a *fool* lacks – he is mindless.

4. Rash (v. 18).

We have been warned before about the danger of *putting up security* (6:1-5, 11:15) and will be again (20:16, 22:26f). It is repeated here partly to qualify verse 17, which does not advocate giving financial guarantees to all and sundry, for *neighbour* is not the 'friend' who has virtually become a 'brother', for whom you would even lay down your life and who would lay down his life for you. The last thing he would do is to bind you to an agreement which would impoverish you and your family. Your *neighbour* is but a slight acquaintance and may even be exploiting your generosity. You certainly have an obligation to your *neighbour* but not to the extent of pledging yourself to what you may be unable to fulfil. Another reason for including it here is because aspects of Foolishness are under consideration and this is one of them. This is why it begins *A man lacking in judgment*, which is not said in the other verses on *putting up security*.

5. Hurtful (vv. 21, 25).

Verse 21 makes the same point as 10:1 and 15:20. It comes in here because folly is one of the main themes of the chapter. Talking of folly, Solomon is saying, those who suffer most from it are parents. If it is *a son*, when he was born there was great rejoicing, for sons were God's greatest blessing to his people (Pss. 127:3-5, 128:3b): they would take over the family business and continue its name. But if he turned out *a fool*, the *joy* would soon turn to *grief*. If he behaved like the *fool* in this chapter – ungovernable (v. 12), provocative (v. 14), mindless (v. 16), rash (v. 18) and worst of all impervious to discipline (v. 10) – then to hand the family name and business over to him would undo all the good work done by the parents (Ecc. 2:18). How vital then for us to begin early the task of 'giving prudence to the simple, knowledge and discretion to the young' (1:4), backed up with the firm discipline designed to counteract the folly innate in all sinners (22:15) and surrounded by prayer. Solomon knew *grief* over a foolish son (Rehoboam), as did his father David (Absalom), and as had both Samuel (1 Sam. 8:3) and Eli (1 Sam. 2:27ff) before them.

Verse 25 steps up the hurt of verse 21 in two ways. *First*, he hurts both parents. Verse 21 had the father in view whereas this verse brings the mother *who bore him* into the equation. As both parents share in bringing a child into the world, so both are affected if he disappoints them. Neither can blame or pass the responsibility on to the other. Better they share the *grief* and thus help each other bear it, while exploring ways of changing things. *Second*, the anguish caused is greater: the word for *grief* in verse 25 is not the same as that in verse 21. It has the sense of 'provoked' as in Deuteronomy 32:19 where 'the LORD was provoked by his sons and daughters' (the Israelites) and in 1 Kings 15:30 where Jeroboam 'provoked the Lord to anger' with his idol shrines. Thus *the father* here is not quietly grieving but boiling with rage over his son's behaviour. The feeling in the mother's heart on the other hand is one of *bitterness* – she has suffered the pains of childbirth and the hardships of nursing, but gladly because 'sons are a heritage from the LORD' (Ps. 127:3), only to wish she had never done so. Eve's exultation over the birth of Cain (Gen. 4:1) must have turned to *bitterness* when he became a murderer. Children who go their own way with scant regard to their parents' feelings have no conception of the hurt they cause them.

6. Distracted (v. 24).

Here is an important contrast between the wise and foolish. One has the power of concentration, he can sustain his undivided attention on one thing; the other is continually distracted, he can't set his mind on something but is always changing it; he quickly tires of one occupation and looks for something else. Why? Because the *fool* lacks a real aim in life, he has nothing to focus on, no centre to which to relate everything else. He can't distinguish what is important from what is less relevant. To the author of PROVERBS one thing is above all others: *wisdom* 'is supreme, therefore get wisdom. Whatever else you get (mg) get understanding' (4:7). Then everything else falls into place. So he who doesn't 'pay attention to wisdom' and *keep* it *in view,* is not only a *fool* now but will be one all his life. To us *wisdom* is Christ, who saves from the folly of sin and unbelief. So the believer will *keep* Christ *in view* at all times, do all things in his name (Col. 3:17) 'so that in everything he might have the supremacy' (Col. 1:18).

Personal application. Whereas the Lord has delivered us from the works of Wickedness mentioned here, are we at least on the brink of Foolishness? Spend a few moments in self-examination on the above points. After all, Paul does warn Christians against being 'foolish' (Eph. 5:15-17).

16

Some Matters of Importance
Proverbs 18

There is no single theme in this chapter, but underlying it is the whole subject of the character and conduct of the wise. No one can get far in life before coming up against the issues touched on here: companionship, depravity, words, fairness, security. There are some profound observations on these points.

A. COMPANIONSHIP (vv. 1, 22, 24).
Here is more useful counsel on personal relationships.

1. Unfriendliness (v. 1).
This is the life story of the loner. *Unfriendly* is literally 'he who separates himself'; this person is antisocial, he has little time for anyone else. This is because he is *selfish*, he has his own *ends* in view and the company of others interferes with them. This brings him into conflict with conventional wisdom – *sound judgment* – for in order to justify being different from others he has to criticize and condemn normal thinking and behaviour. The word for *defies* is strong, literally 'breaks out', suggesting that from his ivory tower he issues scornful denunciations of the lives and views of his fellow-citizens. This type of person is introduced here as one not to emulate, for the truth is, not that he is superior to others, but that he can't form relationships.

2. Over-friendliness (v. 24a).

The chapter ends on the subject on which it began, but with the complete opposite of the loner. There is little agreement on the translation of line 1, but KJV's 'a man of friends must show himself friendly' is only supported by NKJV. RV's 'He that maketh many friends doeth it to his own destruction' is followed in various ways by most other translators. The meaning is a little obscure but it probably describes one who has many companions, that is, a good mixer who treats all alike and is 'every man's friend'. At first this great socialiser seems the ideal, yet we are told he *may come to ruin*, because in adversity he has no one to whom he is close enough to command his loyalty, no one such as the second part of the verse describes. It is possible to have so many friends you have no real friend!

3. True friendship (v. 24b).

Having seen the 'too little' (v. 1) and the 'too much' (v. 24a) we now have the 'just right'. True friendship is giving yourself unreservedly to the interests of another. It is unrealistic to attempt this to everyone you are on friendly terms with. True friends are brought together by a combination of circumstances and that mysterious chemistry that creates a bond between two people which can be *closer* than the ties of blood and qualify for the name *brother*. David's brothers virtually disowned him but Jonathan took up his cause. Jesus was rejected by his brothers but John, 'the disciple Jesus loved', stayed with him to the end. True friendship is more than affability, it is commitment (17:17).

4. Marriage (v. 22).

This is the ultimate in friendship, involving as it does a more formal and public expression of total and life-long commitment than that made to 'a friend'. It is one of the Bible's finest commendations of a *good* marriage. God gave the man a companion like himself when he and creation were still perfect. How much more does he need one in a world of evil! She is one of the *good* things that still remain through *favour from the Lord*. He has not utterly withdrawn his gifts and knows how much we need the support, care and sympathy of a companion. But this is no longer automatic or a right – it is a gift of grace (*favour*) which has to be sought – we have to *find a wife*. Not all women make *good* wives, as the book has shown (11:22), nor are all *good* women necessarily compatible. So prayer, observation and thought have to go into the matter lest it turn out unhappily, as in 19:13, 21:19, 25:24, 27:15. PROVERBS, like the Old Testament generally, looks at marriage from the man's point of view. But the New Testament redresses the balance with its requirement of love and tenderness from the husband: Eph. 5:25-33, Col. 3:19, 1 Pet. 3:7.

For further thought. Are you a loner or a socialiser? We are not responsible for our chemistry, but we are also 'new creatures in Christ'. He had the perfect balance between kindness to all (Matt. 5:45) and giving his life for his sheep (John 10:15); he can restore the balance to our personalities.

B. Depravity (vv. 3, 9, 23).
Here are three of the many features of the depraved person.

1. The Sinner (v. 3).
If verse 1 was the life-cycle of the loner, this is the life-cycle of the sinner or 'wicked person' (the Hebrew term is personal rather than the abstract *wickedness*). The idea is that where you find someone devoted to *wickedness* you find other things follow: *contempt*, for the confirmed sinner always regards the righteous as stupid, because of his restricted life-style and fear of punishment; *shame*, for as he progresses along the path of evil the wicked person has to perform his actions in secret or under cover of darkness (1 Thess. 5:4-7); and *disgrace*, for however much he gets away with in this life, he is under the eagle eye of God and will answer to him at the judgment when he 'will awake ... to shame and everlasting contempt' (Dan. 12:2). This is why the Bible warns us against starting down this road, for it is a slippery slope.

2. The Sluggard (v. 9).

We have had several warnings about the dire consequences of laziness (6:6-11, 10:4, 12:24, 27). Those were about one who neglected his own business and came to poverty. This is about one who works for another, for work here means 'commission'. One who through laziness fails to discharge this promptly or efficiently is no better than (*brother to*) an enemy who actively opposes (*destroys*) the job. Although his motive is different, the effect is the same. The master's feelings in the matter are vividly described in 10:26. The application to our service of Christ is unmissable: to fail to fulfil his calling and our duty is as bad as to oppose him, for 'he who is not with me is against me and he who does not gather with me scatters' (Matt. 12:30). At his judgment he will make no distinction between the 'unfaithful manager' who 'wasted his master's possessions' (Luke 16:1) and the 'lazy servant' who 'hid his talent in the ground' (Matt. 25:25, cf. 24:45-51).

3. The Harsh (v. 23).

This reads like a simple comment on a social evil, that *the poor* has to beg from the *rich*, only to be refused *harshly*. But in view of the many other proverbs on the contrast between *rich* and *poor* there is more in it than meets the eye. For one thing, it shows the effect of social conditions and position on character. Poverty produces a humility that makes one willing to beg favours, whereas prosperity tends to breed an insensitivity which reveals itself in rudeness. This led Christ to use poverty to describe the humbleness of spirit that characterizes those who are blessed with acceptance into his kingdom (Matt. 5:3), whereas those who trust in riches are excluded (Mark 10:24f). For another, it implicitly commends those who respond kindly to the pleas of the poor (see 14:21), and rebukes those who, although they can well afford it, brush off the *poor* as if they are vermin, see 17:5.

Ponder. It is amazing what evils lurk in our natures long after we have come to repentance. Let us follow David and ask God to 'see if there is any offensive way in me' (Ps. 139:24).

C. Words (vv. 2, 4, 6, 7, 8, 15, 20, 21).

This popular subject receives further treatment here. It surveys the differing uses of the tongue and their consequences.

1. Foolish words (vv. 2, 6, 7).

One who *delights in airing his own opinions* (**v. 2**) can appear knowledgeable and wise, and even gain a great following, but he lacks *understanding*. This is because he can't be bothered to go thoroughly into the matters on which he expresses his opinion (v. 15); this is too much trouble and he *finds no pleasure in it*. After all, if he does, he may discover he was wrong and have to eat his words, which the self-opinionated will never do. He may have begun as a loner (v. 1), critical and contemptuous of conventional wisdom. He must be different in order to draw attention to himself. It is important for us to check our *opinions* against those of others, past and present. Opinionated people are a menace in churches: they won't be taught, they breed a critical spirit and are in danger of forming a party. We should all realize we are not adequate in ourselves and need the checks and balances of social intercourse and, if teachers, of wide reading.

Verses 6-7 show that the self-opinionated *fool* doesn't have his own way for ever. He soon provokes disagreement, which leads to *strife*, but being a controversialist he quite enjoys this (20:3). However, provocative words can lead to blows: *his mouth invites a beating* (14:3). He may get the best of the argument but he comes off worst in the fight and so *his mouth is his undoing*, literally 'ruin, destruction'. This may mean he is such a well-known nuisance no one will take his part, or that he is brought before the authorities for brawling and given his due punishment (19:19). Whichever it is he has only himself to blame. No one set out to get him, he himself laid the *snare* which brought 'ruin' to his *soul*, that is, himself, his life (10:8, 14, 12:13, 13:3, Eccles. 10:12). James, well versed in PROVERBS, put it in a nutshell: 'what a great forest is set on fire by a small spark' (James 3:5).

2. Wise words (vv. 4, 15).

The two parts of **verse 4**, as often with proverbs, are parallel, so that it is *the words of ... wisdom* that are here in view throughout. Line 1 speaks of their source – they come from the depths of the mind and are therefore like *deep waters* (cf. 20:5). Wisdom is deep (Job 28), it is what God is (Rom. 11:33). Those who know God and are taught by him from his Word are admitted to those counsels which 'no eye has seen, no ear has heard', but which 'God has revealed... to us by his Spirit' (1 Cor. 2:9f).

Line 2 describes the *communication* of this wisdom, which is compared not to an ocean or well but a *fountain* from which flows a *bubbling brook*. This is how others come to share 'the depths of the wisdom and knowledge of God' – when those who are taught by the Spirit speak what they have heard. Such are like the *bubbling brook* flowing from a *fountain* – they refresh and revive those they speak to (10:11, 13:14). So Paul exhorts us, 'Let the word of Christ dwell in you richly' – meditate deeply upon it – then, 'Let your conversation be always full of grace' (Col. 3:16, 4:6).

Verse 15 tells us how this ability to speak wisely is *acquired*. It takes us back to the first nine chapters, which are chiefly an encouragement to cultivate wisdom. Quick reminders of this frequently occur (see on 15:14a). This verse goes further and is a good summary of the teaching and exhortations of chapters 1–9.

(a) *Cultivate* a *discerning heart* by appreciating the value of *knowledge*. This is what the parents try to instil by their patient instruction, part of which is to praise wisdom above all else (3:13-18; 4:5-7; 7:21-27; 8; 9:10).

(b) *Approach* it with earnestness, *seek it out*, don't wait for it to come to you. *Knowledge* lies deep down on the ocean bed or in the bowels of the earth and has to be delved out (see on verse 4).

(c) *Give* it rapt attention – the *heart* will not *acquire* it unless *the ears* listen to it with concentration in order to understand and retain it.

3. Wicked words (v. 8).

The *gossip* is worse than the fool – he doesn't blunder into trouble with his eyes shut, he really means to cause it. This is why *gossip* was forbidden by the law (Lev. 19:16). We have already met him in 16:28 where he is out to divide his victim from his friends by spreading rumours. Here we see how he manages to be so successful – he never lacks a ready audience. As 17:4 pointed out, the listener to malicious *gossip* is as 'wicked' as the one who speaks it. The way rumours are received is graphically described here. They are *like choice morsels*, those titbits which don't need chewing or stick in the throat but slip easily *down into a man's innermost parts*. We find no difficulty in concentrating on the *gossip's* tale, we lap it up like a cat the cream. Nor do we find it hard to remember, indeed the term (literally) 'inner rooms' has the sense of a storeroom where things are retained to be brought out later. In this way the listener to *gossip* assists him in carrying out his cruel schemes.

4. Their consequences (vv. 20-21).
The power of words for good or ill has already been illustrated in the above verses. Here it is pictured as a farm or garden. *A man* grows *fruit*, vegetables or grain so that at *harvest* time his *stomach* may be *filled* and he may be *satisfied*. He takes great care over this work – it is *life or death* to him. If his *harvest* fails or his *fruit* is bad he will starve and die. If it is good and plenteous he will *eat its fruit* and be *satisfied*. Since his very *life* depends on it he will put his heart and soul into his work, he will *love it*. We are being asked to put as much *loving* care into what we say. If we did but realize the consequences (*fruit*) of our words we would certainly do so. There is great satisfaction in speaking what is true, edifying, informative, understanding, instructive, sympathetic, comforting and even rebuking. But lies, misinformation, blasphemy, cursing, boasting, vilifying poison the soul of the one who speaks them and ensure he will be 'condemned' on 'the day when we must account for every careless word we have spoken' (Matt. 12:36f).

Response. PROVERBS scratches us where we itch; that is why it harps on about things common to us all which crop up most days of our lives. What is more common than talking? There is no other possible response to these verses than to take more care in what we say. Reading books or listening to sermons on the subject have only a limited value. We must listen to ourselves for a change!

D. Fairness (vv. 5, 13, 16-19).
Justice crops up frequently in PROVERBS in various ways. Since God is a righteous God, justice is bound to be part of his revealed wisdom. It applies from the top down: from the magistrate (17:15, 26) to the man the in street, who is most in view here.

1. Misjudging (v. 5).
This may at first sight seem a straight repeat of 17:15, 23, 26. However the different terms used give us another slant on the subject. It speaks not of 'acquitting the wicked' (17:15) but showing *partiality*, literally 'lifting the face', that is, going by appearances. Although it seems to be addressed to the magistrate, this can and does apply outside court and is so used by James in his famous passage on how we receive visitors to our services (2:1-9). If we 'show special attention to' the well-dressed visitor but treat the tramp roughly we are guilty of discrimination or partiality. The term James uses – 'favouritism' ('respect of persons' KJV) is the Greek equivalent of the Hebrew 'partial' or 'lift the face'. The Hebrew for *deprive* is 'thrust aside', recalling the treatment of the poor man in James' passage. We all make judgments and discriminate to an extent. But we are warned by Christ against judging by appearances rather than by facts (John 7:24).

2. Prejudging (v. 13).
If verse 5 warned us against misjudging, this verse warns us against prejudging – giving an *answer* without *listening* to the statement. The Mosaic law forbade this in legal or official disputes (Deut. 13:14), but our verse probably refers to more mundane situations. Most of us are better at airing our own opinions than listening to the other person's (v. 2). Either we give him no chance to speak, interrupt him before we've heard him out, or just don't hear what he's really saying. While the immediate effect is to make the other person appear foolish

and shamefaced, the proverb is saying that the real *folly and shame* belong to the one who has jumped to the conclusion. People may think him clever (especially if he is a media person interviewing a politician!) but by Biblical standards he is guilty of the *folly* of prejudice and should feel *ashamed*. How much better our conversations with other Christians and our church meeting discussions would go if we followed this simple precept! Perhaps it would help to remember how our Lord was victim of this folly and shame (John 7:51f).

3. Bribery (v. 16).

It is not agreed among the authorities whether the *gift* here is a bribe or a present, whether *the giver* is doing something unlawful and underhand, as in 17:8, 23, or merely courteous. While the word gift is not the same as 'bribe', they appear to be equivalent in 21:14, and the verse could therefore refer to a person who bribes a servant or lesser official to get him a hearing from a *great* man. Also, the next two verses are on legal matters and the right and wrong ways of handling them. Others connect it with the oriental custom of bringing presents to a superior out of respect, of which the Bible gives examples: Abraham (Gen. 24:30-33) and Jacob (Gen. 32:13, 20, 43:11).

Our very uncertainty about the correct interpretation is, as Kidner says, 'a reminder that the boundary line between the two (bribery and courtesy) is thin.' Probably the deciding factor is whether the gift is made surreptitiously (as in 17:23, 21:14) or openly, as in the examples quoted. Which of these applies here we are not told (only GNB and NEB commit themselves to the second interpretation). It all depends on whether we have a good motive for wanting our *gift* to *usher us into the presence of the great*: is it to plead for justice for ourself or others, or to gain an unfair advantage?

4. Hearing both sides (v. 17).

We have been warned against misjudging (v. 5) and prejudging (v. 13); now we are taught how to avoid this unfairness: hear both sides of the question. The setting is probably the law court: the prosecution *presents* a very plausible *case* against the accused; a verdict given at this point would probably be 'guilty'. However, the defence is permitted, not only to *present* its own *case*, but to examine the prosecution witnesses. From this it may emerge that they were mistaken or lying, causing the judge to arrive at a different verdict. A good example in the Bible of this principle is Paul's trial before Felix in Acts 24. Although we know more about the details of the Roman legal system than about Israel's, its basic principle is laid down in Deuteronomy 1:16: 'Hear the disputes between your brothers and judge fairly.' This is a principle that applies out of court: settling a quarrel between our children, not believing a piece of gossip without hearing from the person concerned, deciding between political parties or different points of view on ethical or social matters, and last but not least considering both sides of a theological dispute!

5. The final court of appeal (v. 18).
If this also is in a court setting (only GNB is prepared to use the words 'in court' in the actual translation), then it envisages a situation in which the arguments are equivocal and even the judge is unable to decide between the two *opponents*. Since these are *strong*, which presumably means they are important, resourceful and have a large following in the community, if they tried to *settle the dispute* by force, there would be general disruption. A way must be found to *keep* them *apart*. Israel had the means of appealing directly to God – the use of the *lot*, or 'Urim and Thummim'. This has already been explained in 16:33 and it clearly implies that the parties concerned, however sure of their case and whatever their power to back it up, mutually agreed to accept the verdict of the *lot* as the will of God. We can scarcely expect this to happen in a modern court of law! For one thing, neither the contending parties nor the judge and jury think of themselves as acting for God, and for another *the lot* has ceased to be God's means of making known his will. The usefulness of such a verse to Christians is therefore limited. The 'penalty shoot-out' comes to mind, but this has no equivalent in litigation! The fact is that God reveals his will now, not through *the lot*, but by the principles of his Word. Let Christians settle their differences around the Bible.

6. Avoid causing offence (v. 19).

Perhaps this verse is placed here to back up the need for fair dealing so prominent in this chapter. Where injustice is done the consequences are serious and protracted. The disputants here are *brothers*, meaning relatives or close friends. Scripture and experience both testify to the fierce and enduring hatred that can exist between those who once were close, but because one has *offended* the other, a *dispute* has broken out which nothing and no one can resolve. In Scripture we have Cain and Abel, Jacob and Esau, Joseph and his brothers and Amnon and Absalom. History and current life tell us that most murders are domestic and that once relatives fall out they can keep up the *dispute* all their lives. They are like a *fortified city* or *the barred gates of a citadel*, doing all in their power to shut the other out.

Alas that the church is not free from this! Our denominational divisions prove that once Christians disagree they set their *dispute* in concrete by separating, forming a new institution, erecting a building and so on. They refuse fellowship and even publicly vilify the other party, to the disgrace of Christ's name. They persist in perpetuating the division even when its original cause is forgotten. We cannot expect to see eye to eye on everything (even Paul and Barnabas didn't) but we can avoid disagreeing in such a way as to cause offence to the other or take it ourselves.

Think over the advice this chapter gives on conducting relationships by comparing these points with those made about Companionship in A. Do these speak to you about any of your own relationships at the present time?

E. SECURITY (vv. 10-12, 14).

This is a favourite subject in PROVERBS. Here are three different approaches, with a P.S. about the awfulness of no security.

1. The name of the LORD (v. 10).

The Prologue frequently spoke of Wisdom as a sure means of security (1:33, 2:7f, 3:23-26). The Proverbs themselves tend to stress *righteousness* as the way (10:9, 24, 30, 12:3, 7, 21, 13:6,

14:32). Once only is personal relationship with God seen as security (14:26). Here that idea comes into its own – it is *the Lord's name* that is *a strong tower*, that is, what he has revealed about himself and his character, especially his power, love and faithfulness, which qualify him as our best protector. But the illustration not only indicates what *the Lord* is, but that we have a responsibility if we are to avail ourselves of his ministry. A city's fortress is not where people live and work, but there for refuge in emergencies, so that the citizens can *run to* it *and be safe*. Thus there is no automatic security in having wisdom and being *righteous* – we have to exercise them. The *running* describes faith and prayer (29:25, Pss. 91:2, 56:3, Isa. 26:4), which give direct access to God who responds by warding off the danger. *Safe* is literally 'lifted high', as if one who trusts God is not only behind thick walls, but above the range of the enemy's weapons.

2. The wealth of the rich (v. 11).

The verbal similarities as well as the theme indicate that this verse is to be compared with verse 10. *The rich* man feels he is more secure than 'the righteous', as in 10:15 he felt more secure than the poor man. 'The name of the Lord' is only words but he has tangible money and goods. 'The righteous' has 'a strong tower' but *the rich* has a whole *fortified city*. 'The righteous' is placed in a room at the top of the tower which will have steps up to it and which an enemy can climb, but *the rich* is behind *an unscalable wall*. True as all this is, the *security* of it is something *they imagine*. He might accuse 'the righteous' of living in an unreal world, trusting a God he can't see, hear or touch, while *the rich* has visible money and solid city walls. In fact, money, goods and fortifications are vulnerable commodities (Matt. 6:19). Even if he retains them throughout his life they won't keep him from death and the judgment of God (Luke 12:19-21). On the other hand, God is eternal and faith which rests on him is for ever (Isa. 26:4).

3. The *heart* of the *proud* (v. 12).

This verse combines 16:18a and 15:33b, and its two parts are connected by *before*, as is best brought out by AMP: 'Haughtiness

comes before disaster and humility before honour.' This emphasises the contrast between 'haughtiness' and *humility* on the
one hand and 'disaster' and *honour* on the other. We are still
on the subject of security. The person here is secure in himself,
a big element in pride, which says, 'I don't need anyone to
look after me, I can take care of myself'. Since this puts him off
his guard he is likely to suffer a *downfall* or be overcome. The
opposite of pride is *humility* which is a sense of inadequacy
creating dependence. This is the one who 'runs to the strong
tower' when he is afraid, and is 'exalted' to the top floor and
given the *honour* of the Lord's personal protection.

4. Insecurity (v. 14).

Here is a good reason for not seeking security in yourself
(v. 12). This can hold while health lasts and even endure in
sickness, for we all have a built-in courage in our *spirit* that
sustains hope and confidence in the face of adversity (cf. 15:13,
17:22). But this prop is itself vulnerable and subject to being
crushed. One's *spirit* can only *bear* so much and if the power
of endurance is lost there is nothing to 'raise it up' (as RVmg
translates *bear*). If the buttresses of the crumbling building
themselves crumble, there is nothing to hold them or the
building up. So, however good our health or comfortable our
circumstances, we must not give way to a 'proud heart' (v. 12).
While the intended answer to the question *who can bear?* is,
'No one', the Bible as a whole shows there is one who can
even heal *a crushed spirit*. Luther said, 'It is as easy to make
a world as to ease a troubled conscience.' But he who made
the world can, especially as he himself endured *a crushed spirit*
(Mark 14:33). Paul was able to speak of him as 'the God of all
comfort who comforts us in all our troubles' (2 Cor. 1:4).

Application. This is a good area for a little psychoanalysis.
Am I a fairly 'sanguine' person (15:13)? If so, why? Is it
temperament (v. 14), self-confidence (v. 12), material well-
being (v. 11), or trust in God (v. 10)? If you are not sanguine
tell yourself you don't need the first three, only the last, and
that it is open to all believers.

17

The Good, The Bad and The Ugly
(Proverbs 19)

People come in a variety of types, as our title says, our experience proves and the Bible teaches. Here are a few to look out for, as examples or warnings, as the case may be.

A. THE FOOL (vv. 1-3, 19, 29).
Here are some more points to add to those already mentioned.

1. Perverse (v. 1).
The first thing this chapter says about the fool is that he lacks a sense of values. Although the word 'rich' is not used here (except in a couple of ancient versions), the contrast of *the fool* with *the poor*, plus the almost identical proverb in 28:6 lead most expositors to the view that the *fool* here is a rich man. But he has acquired his riches by *perverse* methods: he despises honest work, faith in God and all who live that way, for they can still end up *poor*. So he has no patience with them; if they seek his charity he 'answers harshly' (18:23). How many are living thus in this present commercial age! Perhaps the believer is tempted to do so. It may make him 'better off' but not *better*, for God's wisdom sets more store on righteousness than riches, on trust than on treasure (Matt. 6:33). Temporarily he may look foolish and be despised, but the future is his (Matt. 16:26).

2. Impetuous (v. 2).

It is a pity NIV has omitted the opening 'also' which establishes a connection with verse 1 and shows we are still talking about the fool. Here he is not compared to the 'blameless poor man' but considered on his own merits, so we have simply *not good* instead of the comparative 'better'. We see that the root of folly is *zeal without knowledge*, that is, desire or ambition which has not been submitted to instruction to discover whether it is a good desire and if so what is the best way of fulfilling it. The fool is too busy satisfying his desire to stop and study, listen or think. The result is he *misses the way*, like one who drives too fast down the motorway and overruns his turning. PROVERBS frequently warns against rashness: 1:16, 14:29, 21:5, 29:20, and the rest of the Bible is strewn with examples of its consequences: Joshua who suffered defeat at Ai (Josh. 7:3-5), Saul who lost his kingdom (1 Sam. 13:11-14) and the old prophet who lost his life (1 Kings 13:11-24). Worst of all, the Jews' ignorant zeal led them to crucify their Messiah (Luke 23:34, Rom. 10:2) and later to persecute his followers (John 16:2f). Time spent in study, thought, prayer and taking advice is never wasted. Even popular lore advises 'more haste, less speed' and 'look before you leap'. But today's world is strewn with the wreckage of thoughtless fanaticism.

3. Blind (v. 3).

The first line is another way of saying what verse 2 said – that one who cannot be bothered to think and listen before he rushes into an action goes wrong and thus *ruins his life* through *his own folly*. Yet because he is blind to himself he blames God, not with quiet bitterness but burning *rage against the Lord*. He accuses God of injustice when he himself is the unjust one; he left God out of his plans, but when they go wrong it's all God's fault. This has been the story of all our lives since Adam disobeyed God and blamed him for creating Eve, who herself blamed God for allowing the serpent to tempt her. The darkest blindness of all is to fail to see that if we would only accept the blame and confess our folly to him, he would not only forgive our wilful ignorance (Luke 23:34) but rebuild our ruined lives (Hosea. 14:4-7).

4. Culpable (vv. 19, 29).

Behaviour of the kind described in verses 1-3 is intolerable. It does harm, especially to the weak (v. 1), it causes disruption through its thoughtless haste (v. 2) and is dishonouring to God (v. 3). Sooner or later it will lead the fool into crime, for the *hot-tempered man* will overstep the mark, hurt someone and have to pay compensation (*penalty*): see Exodus 21:22. This may put him into severe financial difficulties, not only because he has a heavy fine to pay but because he may be ostracized so that people shun his business. On the other hand we are to beware of being too soft-hearted and bailing him out, for he won't learn his lesson. He is in bondage to his bad spirit and will repeat his crime, so that you will have to *rescue him again*. Moreover, each time the severity of the punishment increases – from fines to 'judgments' (*penalties*), possibly some sort of 'community service' or the surrender of his property, since there were no prisons. As a last resort corporal punishment is inflicted: *beatings for the backs of fools*. The fool is incorrigible.

For further thought. Does this drive you into the 'bring back the birch' lobby? If so, consider: should we not restrain ourselves from giving way to the same rage as the fool feels towards us and God? Should it not rather turn our thoughts to the God who alone can *rescue* any of us from the folly of our ungodly self-confidence and the impatience and bad temper it produces?

B. The Lazy (vv. 15, 24).

Warnings against sloth have been occurring at regular intervals (6:9-11, 10:4, 12:27, 15:19), and more are to follow. They are not straight repeats but differently phrased, although the general thrust of them is that laziness makes one poor. But the lazy man tends to brush this aside and claim he is only resting and will start work soon. So **verse 15** comes as the answer to that, stressing the addictiveness of this particular weakness. Although love of sleep is part of sloth, *brings on deep sleep* probably means mainly that it becomes a habit from which it is almost impossible to rouse oneself. Even the prospect of starvation does not register.

Having tried the serious approach he turns to ridicule in
verse 24. In 10:4 the lazy man couldn't be bothered to go and
find food, in 12:27 he couldn't take the trouble to cook it, and
here, having done all this (or had it done for him!) he is too
lazy to eat it! We are meant to laugh at the picture of a fool
with a meal in front of him, his hand about to pick up a morsel
but dropping off to sleep in the process. A caricature, but if
serious warnings won't work, perhaps ridicule will.

Give some thought to the place of ridicule in teaching
or counselling. When is it justified? How should it be used?
Compare Jesus' mockery of the Jews in Matthew 11:16f with
the soldiers' mockery of him in Matthew 27:27-31; also that of
the priests in verses 41-43.

C. THE LIAR (vv. 5, 9, 22, 28).
The frequency of references to lying, especially in court, shows
it was then as now a serious social problem.

1. His true nature (v. 28).
This is not the little fib that slips out to cover something
shameful, but is premeditated and prepared as with witnessing
in court. It is exemplified by those who witnessed falsely
against Naboth (1 Kings 21:10, 13), Stephen (Acts 6:11-13) and
our Lord himself (Matt. 26:59). These instances show how
deliberate lying against another is a *mockery of justice*. This is
emphasised by the second line which uses the language of
gluttony. The *corrupt witness* lies because he **enjoys** seeing
his victim suffer. It also applies outside court in the form of
sharing juicy morsels of scandal which, even if they have some
basis in truth, give a totally false picture of someone and bring
him into disrepute.

2. His baseness (v. 22).
It is better to translate with RSV 'what is desired in a man is
loyalty', which fits best with the punch line *better to be poor
than a liar*. The *liar* here is not just the one who gives false
witness in court but who lies generally to or about his friends.
He is guilty not only of sin against God but of disloyalty to his
friends; he breaks the bonds of friendship. This is something

a person should be far more ashamed of than being *poor*. The *poor* can be honest and keep faith, which is more admirable than wealth or position with dishonesty, as verse 1 has already mentioned.

3. His doom (vv. 5, 9).

It is not just lying itself but the doom which awaits it that needs repeating. Here are two almost identical statements within a few sentences of each other. The only difference is that what **verse 5** says negatively **verse 9** says positively: instead of *not go unpunished ... free* it has *will perish*. In case there is any doubt what the punishment of verse 5 is, it is spelt out – *perish* means death. The rules of testifying in old Israel are set out in detail in Deuteronomy 19:15-20: more than one witness to a crime is required in case one is lying maliciously to make his enemy suffer; but if his testimony is found to be false he himself receives the punishment the accused would have received, even death. But lies do not always come to light in court. This does not mean we have to qualify these statements, for many times God has said he will personally deal with liars who escape detection, whoever they are: national leaders (Isa. 9:14-16), prophets (Jer. 23:16-32), pastors (2 Pet. 2:1-3), people (Rev. 21:8) and devils (Rev. 19:20).

Question
What makes lying such a serious social evil? (Eph. 4:25).

D. The Friend (vv. 4, 6, 7, 17).

Our fall into sin has affected our relationships with each other as much as anything else, making apparent friendship often nothing but self-seeking. Yet true love can still be in the heart that seeks to please the Lord.

1. Cupboard love (vv. 4, 6, 7).

The mercenary nature of much friendship has already been brought to our attention in 14:20 and is here described at greater length. **Verse 4** succinctly states the effect of this on rich and poor respectively in almost identical terms to 14:20 but with a different scenario: here is one who has recently come into *wealth* and with it a wealth of *friends*; the other has been struck by poverty and been *deserted* by his former *friends*. The son in Jesus' parable was popular when he was throwing his inheritance around, but as soon as it was spent no one wanted to know him (Luke 15:13f). Both aspects are expanded in **verses 6-7. Verse 6** describes the life of a wealthy man, for the *ruler* or 'noble' is probably well-off and can bestow favours and even offices. This attracts self-seekers who, according to Delitzsch, 'stroke his face', pretend affection and offer to be his *friend*, to vote for him, canvas his cause, obey his orders. Joseph, previously shunned by his family, was fawned on when he became rich and powerful (Gen. 42:6), as was Job before he fell on bad times (Job 29:24).

This is contrasted with the pitiful picture of one struck down by poverty, **verse 7**: *his relatives shun him* and *his friends avoid him*. He has *relatives* and had *friends* but his poverty has brought out the real character of their friendship. Not only can they no longer get anything out of him but if they continue his friends he will try to get something out of them, which will never do. How heart-rending is the ending, as he follows them around *pleading* for their help while they keep out of his way, as Job experienced after disaster struck him (Job 19:13-22). Let us not see this as the cynical outburst of an embittered pauper but, (a) as an arrow with which to wound the selfish, and (b) a comfort to the friendless poor, that the divine author of this book knows their plight.

2. Constant love (v. 17).

Here we have the opposite spirit to the above: one who cleaves to *the poor* because he is poor. His heart and hand work together, for he gives to him, not to get him off his back or salve his own conscience, but because he feels for him – *kind* denotes compassion and pity as well as generosity. Without this feeling, 'charity' does not live up to its name (cf. 1 John 3:17). Feeling is not enough, it must be expressed in practical help to qualify as 'love' in the way the Bible defines it (1 John 3:18, James 2:15f).

How can we suppress that selfishness that spoils relationships (vv. 4, 6f) and become generous? By seeing how *the Lord* identifies himself with *the poor*: 14:31, 17:5. What we don't do for them we don't do for him and vice versa. It is on this basis that we who profess godliness will be judged or *rewarded* on the day of Christ (Matt. 25:40, 45). This is why our verse speaks of kindness to *the poor* as an investment. What we *lend to the poor* may seem to put them in debt to us, but the Lord does what he advises us not to do – 'stand security' for them. *The poor* cannot repay the debt but *the Lord* can and will – with interest, as *lend* implies. The Old Testament sees the *reward* as prosperity in this life, while the New Testament places it in the next (Matt. 10:42). However, those who give for the Gospel's sake are assured they will on no account be losers (2 Cor. 9:6-8, Phil. 4:17).

For further thought. Meditate on the way the Bible turns our thinking and ways on their heads. When we have money to invest we demand collateral or go to the company or bank which seems most secure. We lend to the rich at the highest rate! Yet what rivals God's security and who can offer his interest rates (Matt. 19:21)?

E. THE WISE (vv. 8, 11, 16, 20, 25, 27).
Very few chapters of PROVERBS pass without mention of its chief subject: wisdom. This is the overall theme that binds the others together, the glorious white light that breaks down into the many colours that comprise the practical details.

1. Value (v. 8).
Everyone *loves his own soul* (life) and wants to do the best he can for himself. But not everyone realizes what that best is – to *get wisdom*. Perhaps some have the wrong image of it and think of it as vast learning requiring hard work and great intelligence. But the word used here is literally 'heart', that is, 'sense' or *understanding*, putting it into the practical rather than the intellectual realm. It is learning to live so as to get the best out of life, which is why PROVERBS is full of practical advice. But having found it we need to 'keep' (*cherish*) it. Wisdom is not a certificate given at the end of a course but a way of life pursued to the end. Only this guarantees we will *prosper*.

Under the old covenant the way to get on was to keep the laws by which Israel was governed. Being God's laws this pleased him and attracted his blessing; and being the nation's code, obeying them was the way to fit happily into society. Under the Gospel *wisdom* is Christ, and the *prosperity* that allegiance to him attracts is that of enjoying the love of God in prosperity and adversity.

2. Fruit (v. 11).

It is not only the individual who benefits from the acquiring of wisdom but society. For *wisdom gives ... patience*, literally 'makes him slow to anger'. Even the wisest will feel provoked but he won't give way to it, he will control it. This was an important qualification for *wisdom* in the ancient east, as several sayings have already shown (14:29, 15:18, 16:32, 17:14). This is why to *overlook an offence* is *to his glory* – it enhances his reputation for *wisdom*. Our culture has reversed this way of thinking. To us what is humiliating and a disgrace is to let an insult, blow or *offence* pass; this shows weakness rather than strength. In bygone days a duel was called 'a matter of honour', the only way to recover lost honour. But God's *wisdom* is that 'it is to a man's honour to **avoid** strife' (20:3) not to court it. For this is God's own way: when Moses asked to see the glory of God he heard him proclaim himself as 'the LORD compassionate and gracious, slow to anger' (Exod. 34:6). For of his many *glories* this is chief:

> Great God of wonders, all thy ways
> Are matchless, Godlike and divine,
> But the fair glories of thy grace
> More Godlike and unrivalled shine.
> Who is a pardoning God like thee,
> And who has grace so rich and free? (Samuel Davies)

3. Acquisition (vv. 16, 20, 25, 27).

Verse 20 reminds us of the normal way of becoming *wise*. There is nothing new here; this has been the book's message from the beginning. PROVERBS is a book of *advice and ... instruction* for teachers or parents to set their children on the right road. There is no quick way to wisdom; as he grows the child must *listen* to all he needs to know. Since he is a free being he must willingly consent to (*accept*) what he hears in order to become *wise*. Those who patiently do this *will be wise at the end* – not meaning *the end* of life which would hardly make it worthwhile, but meaning eventually, when grown up. The Bible doesn't countenance the 'instant enlightenment' offered by modern cults. It knows it is dealing with people whose state in sin has blinded them to and hardened them against the wisdom of God, yet made them eager to learn worldly and foolish ways. Only long exposure to sound teaching can change this.

This is why the warning of **verse 27** is added. The Hebrew is somewhat cryptic and there are three possible interpretations: (a) *stop listening* to that teaching which will cause you to err from *the words of knowledge* (KJV only); (b) *stop listening to instruction* if you are only going to *stray* from it, that is, if you hear but don't do (RV, RSV, AMP); (c) that of NIV (also in NKJV, GNB, NEB). The first is a warning against listening to false teaching, the second is ironic, a challenge: 'Don't come to my class at all if you're not going to do what I say', the third a warning against giving up learning when you've only just started. The third follows well after verse 20, which hints at the need to persevere in learning to *the end*.

Verse 16 reminds us that *mere listening* is not enough – it must lead to obedience. Whether the *instructions* (Hebrew MITZVAH = commandment) are the parent/teacher's or God's matters little since the parent/teacher under the old covenant stood in place of God. The point is that they are *instructions* about ways – behaviour, on which all depends. To be *contemptuous* of them means to fail to bring them under the searching light of the *instructions* or 'commandments'. Here *the end* means the final curtain, for obedience is a matter not just of happiness or misery, prosperity or poverty, but life or death (3:1, 13:13, 15:32, 16:17).

Verse 25 spells this 'end' out in its gory details – the consequences of not listening to instruction or of turning from it to error. The error may be serious enough to constitute *mockery*. In the original setting this could simply mean disobedience to parents, refusal of their instruction. Since the parents were teaching God's law it was a serious thing to disobey them, in fact an infringement of the Fifth Commandment, punishable in the way described in Deuteronomy 21:18-21. Even if the offender was so foolish he was incorrigible (15:5, 17:10) an example would be set to others, especially the *simple*, who were most susceptible to the influence of the *mocker*: they would see that following him would get them into the same trouble. This would be a valuable, if elementary, lesson in *prudence*. Those who learn it become *discerning* – between good and evil, truth and error – such will not need *flogging*, though they may need the occasional *rebuke*. But because they have a positive attitude they will *gain knowledge* by it and become wiser.

Question
How would you transfer these principles to the modern home, classroom or society?

F. THE ORDERLY (vv. 10, 12-14, 18, 21, 23, 26).
Orderliness is a fresh topic, but it receives the full treatment and touches on most areas in which it is needed.

1. In the personal life (vv. 21, 23).
We who are made in God's image have what other creatures lack – the power of reason and imagination, through the use of which we make *plans* for ourselves in things small and great (**v. 21**). Originally this process harmonized with *the Lord's purpose*. Our unilateral declaration of independence from God has brought these into conflict: we make *plans* to suit ourselves rather than to fulfil *the Lord's purpose*. This is the basic cause of the disorder that reigns in the universe and in our own minds. If we are to have any peace we must first acknowledge that *the Lord's purpose* is better than our *plans* (Rom. 12:2) and that it *prevails* ultimately, even though ours may appear to do so for a while (see on 16:1, 9).

    Verse 23 describes a life in which order has been restored in one who has accepted the truth of verse 21. He who believes God's will is both sovereign and good is one who has *the fear of the Lord*, for this is different from fear of anyone or anything else. It means revering in a spirit of trust and love the God who is both great and good. This resolves the conflict between our will and his that the Fall brought about, and thus restores order in the *life*. This order is enjoyed in two ways. First, it gives satisfaction, *one rests content*, an expression which crowns a beautiful picture, for it means 'he does not go hungry to bed' (Delitzsch). Hunger is normal in the morning or at the end of the day's work, but being unable to satisfy it by bedtime is the ultimate in human misery. This illustrates the emptiness of a human soul in conflict with God. Second, it brings security, *untouched by trouble*, which continues the picture of going to bed, meaning he is not afraid of being awakened by terror in the night (Ps. 91:5). 14:26 has already spoken of the security that lies in a right relationship with God, for true fear conquers all other fear, as Tate and Brady's paraphrase of Psalm 34:9 brings out:

> Fear him, ye saints, and you will then
> Have nothing else to fear

or even better, 'perfect love drives out fear' (1 John 4:18).

2. In the domestic life (vv. 13, 14, 18, 26).

If the ultimate source of order or disorder lies in the individual soul, its most common expression is in the home, the relationship between husband and wife, parent and child.

(a) *Husband and wife* (**vv. 13b, 14**).
Sin brought disorder not only into the soul but also into the marriage relationship, as God said to the woman at the Fall: 'Your desire will be for your husband and he will rule over you' (Gen. 3:16). Man would use his superior strength to exploit the woman's attraction to him and may reduce her almost to slavery. The one weapon she has to fight back with is the tongue, and its power lies not in the occasional fierce outburst over some big issue but the constant nagging over trivialities day in and day out. Which is worse, the roof that blows off in a gale once in a generation or the roof with the slight leak that wears us down with its incessant *dripping*? An Arab proverb identifies three things which make a home intolerable: 'tak, nak and bak' – a leaky roof, a wife's nagging and bugs!

But does it have to be like that? Is there no alternative? Yes, for there is such a thing as a *prudent wife*. She is *prudent* enough to realize that to be *quarrelsome* is counterproductive, for she will drive her husband away from her (21:9, 19). She will therefore seek to please him rather than cross him, which will deprive him of the need to abuse or exploit her and encourage him to love her, then both will be happy. But such is the effect of sin there is no way of guaranteeing a wife will turn out to be *prudent*. It is not like inheriting *houses or wealth*, which are matters of custom and law and can be predicted and expected. A *prudent wife* is made so by God's grace and brought to a man in his providence. While a man can't be sure of choosing such a wife, he can ask God to provide him with one.

If all this seems one-sided, this is because it is the upbringing of **sons** that is in view in PROVERBS and they who are being instructed in the best way of living. But a woman may equally have a *quarrelsome* husband who wears **her** down, not with words but blows. She can pray for a *prudent* husband and if she also is *prudent* all will be sweetness and light.

(b) *Parent and child* **(vv. 13a, 18, 26)**.
Solomon's collection began with the *foolish son* (10:1) because his chief object is to teach and discipline the child out of his inborn ignorance and folly. It is the parents who suffer most if this is not achieved, as we are frequently reminded: 15:20, 17:21, 25. But now we are told they will suffer not just 'grief' but *ruin* (**13a**), a warning fully justified, as we shall see. But first we must face the strong call to apply ourselves to this task in **verse 18**. Solomon may have in mind the parent who is finding the child unresponsive, even rebellious, and is inclined to relax his discipline. His advice is, 'Don't, *for in that* (only) *there is hope*', for it is the prescribed way of purging the folly out of him (22:15) and moulding him into a wise son (29:15) who will bring you joy (29:17).

Line 2 is more difficult. KJV's 'Let not thy soul spare for his crying' has very little support. There is certainly a reference to *his death*, but what is not certain is whether it means 'don't get carried away and beat him to death' or 'don't leave him to a life of crime for which he will be executed, *making you a willing party to his death* because you didn't stop him going down that road'. There is something to be said for both although the second fits well with 23:13f whereas the first has nothing comparable, nor is it certain that corporal punishment is in view anyway.

The urgency of the matter is brought out in **verse 26** which shows what may happen if discipline is neglected. He may develop into a violent criminal, for some translate *rob* by 'do violence', suggesting it is not mere laziness that impoverishes the family but some delinquent act. The *mother* is *driven out*, either by fear and want or literally turned out by the son. The resulting *shame and disgrace* fall on everyone: the parents who have failed in the upbringing of their son and the son who is loathed by society and eventually brought to book. These are both no doubt extreme examples of domestic disorder but they are warnings of the unlimited possibilities of neglecting careful upbringing.

3. In national life (vv. 10, 12).

When these two verses are brought into juxtaposition they show a sharp contrast between an orderly and a disorderly state. The **disorderly** state is one with an unsuitable leader (**v. 10**). The second is the punch line and probably refers to an ambitious or discontented subject or courtier who usurps the throne, perhaps by assassination, as Zimri did with Elah (1 Kings 16:9f). Such a one cannot handle his new-found power which goes to his head, as it did with Zimri, and makes him a tyrant, even a butcher. Line 1 throws this into relief: a *fool* cannot handle *luxury*; he doesn't know when to stop, makes himself drunk and sick, lazy and gluttonous and so on. It takes a wise man to use luxury in moderation and make it do good in his community. Power too needs wise handling, for it tends to corrupt. Those who come to it suddenly without preparation tend to abuse it. This is illustrated by those who replaced the Czar of Russia after the Revolution. Such things are intolerable and cannot last (30:21-23).

Order in the state needs the right people at the top (**v. 12**). The **orderly** state is one where those who govern devote themselves to their proper functions: protection and provision, the defence of the realm and its economy. They are given power to protect the people from their enemies, to whom they should appear like a *raging lion* whose roar deters any predators from attacking his lair. They also command the nation's resources so that all are well cared for: fed, housed and healed. Such rulers are like *dew on the grass* – refreshing and invigorating. The settled and prosperous nations of the world are those where the rulers use their power justly and compassionately. Those who treat their own people as if they were enemies and bestow their *favour* on outsiders who happen to share their ideology or aims create misery and discontent and invite revolution. This explains the state of many nations in today's world.

Reflect on 1 Corinthians 14:33, 40 – the God of order and the way he orders his creation and his church.

18

Things To Avoid and Things To Seek
(Proverbs 20)

Most individual proverbs contain two parts, the second contrasting with the first. Also, in the collection as a whole, one proverb contrasts with another. Wisdom is a balanced discipline: it tells us what to avoid and what to seek. When we are advised to **avoid** something this implies we should **seek** its opposite. For example, verse 22 both discourages vindictiveness and encourages patient faith. So some of these verses belong to either or both sections.

A. THINGS TO AVOID.

1. Intoxication (v. 1).
The Bible does not require prohibition or total abstinence (only priests were absolutely forbidden: Lev. 10:9), but it does warn that intoxication is not wise. Even godly men fell through drunkenness, such as Noah (Gen. 9:21-23), Lot (Gen. 19:31-36) and later the leaders of Israel: its princes (Hos. 7:5), priests and prophets (Isa. 28:7). It states the dangers plainly here and in 23:19-21, 29-35, 31:4-7. The New Testament goes so far as to exclude drunkards from the kingdom of God (1 Cor. 6:10, Gal. 5:21). This no doubt applies not to occasional drunkenness but what we call alcoholism. You cannot be controlled by spirits and the Spirit at the same time; you must make your choice (Eph. 5:18).

This verse is one of the most vivid statements on the subject. The Hebrew by using the definite article before *wine* personifies it and presents *wine* and *beer* as two bosom friends whose companionship is best avoided (see NEB). Strong drink takes away your self-control (*led astray* = 'stagger'). This affects people in different ways. Some act the fool (*mocker*), others become violent (*brawler*); both do things they afterwards regret. Liquor promises happiness, an escape from misery or dull routine into realms of bliss. But it leads to a worse hell than the one you tried to escape, as the AA will tell you (not the motoring organization! – that too, considering the numbers killed by drunk drivers!). Man made in God's image was endued with wisdom. If drink makes him behave worse than a beast he is *not wise*, not even human.

2. Quarrelling (v. 3).

For warnings against quarrelling see 14:29, 16:32, 17:14 and 19:11. It is one of our commonest human weaknesses and has the most serious effects; it marks one of the clearest differences between wise and foolish. Not everyone shows his folly in sloth, lust or dishonesty, but **every fool** *is quick to quarrel*. It is so easily done: jealousy makes an insulting remark and pride is quick to reply. Its *honour* has been impugned and must be defended, if necessary by blows. But in the wisdom of God *honour* comes not from defending your reputation or fighting your corner but controlling yourself, giving way and forgiving the injury (19:11). The word *avoid* has the idea of sitting still, remaining calm under a hail of insults or blows. The wisdom of the world sees this as weakness and dishonour (James 3:14-16). But, as Bridges puts it, 'An evil world is a fine theatre for the display of the grace of God in the fruits of "the wisdom that is from above"', that is, peaceableness (James 3:17f). It takes far more strength to control your temper than to beat your enemy to pulp, for the latter is common to man, the former God-given.

3. Laziness (vv. 4, 13).

Sloth is another common human weakness (6:6-11, 10:4f, 19:15, 24, 26:13-16). In 10:4f the *sluggard* had done everything necessary to produce a *harvest* but at gathering time sleep overcame him and he gained nothing from his labours. The scenario in **verse 4** begins 'after harvest' (= *in season*), the time of the autumn rains when the land was soft enough to *plough* and sow. But the lazy man feels he has earned a rest. Since he expects a *harvest* presumably he does the sowing but omits *ploughing* first. But seed sown on unbroken ground won't germinate. Such a man may go out and *look* for a harvest but he will *find nothing*.

While the chief application of the saying is practical – to get a good result we must do a thorough work – one thinks of Christ's parable of the sower (Matt. 13:1-23). That three of the crops were poor was due to a lack of *ploughing*. The seed of the gospel will not produce the fruit of faith without a prior or accompanying work of repentance. When the final *harvest* is reaped (Matt. 13:36-43) such will *look* for a share because they did part of the work, but since they omitted the vital part they will *find nothing*.

Verse 13 tells us how to avoid this situation: *do not love sleep*. Not because there is anything wrong with *sleep*. It is God's gift and must have existed before the Fall, since he made day and night from the beginning and surely *sleep* is night's purpose? What we are warned against is *love of sleep* for its own sake. It is a principle that applies to all the good things of life: food, drink, sex, leisure and so on. There is use and abuse in all these. The eyes were not made (v. 12) to be kept closed most of the time! Those who do so are themselves the chief sufferers for they *grow poor*. If we practise regular hours of going to bed and rising we shall enjoy our sleep more and be well-fed as well.

4. Dishonesty (vv. 10, 14, 17, 21, 23).

(a) *In selling* (**vv. 10, 23**).
The Hebrew reads 'a stone and a stone, an ephah and an ephah'. A stone was used as a *weight* (the word survives in our Imperial system) and an ephah was the name given to the quantity of meal which would supply an average family. It refers to pre-coinage days, the age of the barter system. The cheat used the lighter weight for what he sold and the heavier for what he took in exchange. The difference couldn't be detected by the eye of the victim, it would need to be checked against a standard

weight. But it didn't escape the eye of God who is as really in the market as among the saints and angels in glory. Although *the Lord* has nothing to buy or sell he *detests* cheating because it is really stealing, the innocent lose out and what is done against them is done against him (see on 11:1 and 16:11). Nor is he impotently sympathetic but will reckon with such thieves and liars. In spite of the clarity of the Law on the subject (Lev. 19:35, Deut. 25:13-15) and the diligence of parents who used Solomon's textbook, it became rampant in Israel (Amos 8:5, Micah. 6:10f) and was a contributory factor in the downfall of the nation. The almost verbatim repetition of **verse 10** in **verse 23** shows how necessary this warning was. Although we have a better method now and inspectors to check the scales, there are still ways of beating the system for those determined enough. The use of money is not the answer, for the love of it is the root of all kinds of evil and is common to man. But God will still reckon on the final day with all 'the deceitful' (Rev. 21:27).

(b) *In buying* (**v. 14**).
It's not only the seller who can cheat but *the buyer* too. In those days there were no fixed prices but sales were transacted by bargaining (as in eastern bazaars today). In this case the deceit is of a psychological kind: *the buyer* undervalues the goods, points out their faults, complains about the price and appears uninterested. Yet in his heart he wants them, and having forced the price down, quickly disappears from the scene and *boasts about his purchase* and the bargain he has won by his cleverness. In fact he is admitting to deception and will have to answer for it as much as the seller who used false weights. Possibly this was intended as a warning to naive farmers who were a prey to merchants buying up surplus stocks for a fraction of their value. But our modern society uses deceptive psychological techniques: try selling your car to a dealer or your watch to a pawnbroker! Where money is concerned the human heart is dominated by covetousness (Luke 12:15).

(c) *In begging* (**v. 17**).
This probably refers to the professional beggar or confidence trickster who makes up a convincing tale to extract money or

goods from the naive. It does not mean the *food ... tastes sweet* **because** it is obtained deceitfully, but that getting it freely and through cleverness adds to the enjoyment. This is true of sin generally – there is pleasure and pride in it (Heb. 11:25). Adam and Eve **enjoyed** the fruit of the tree of the knowledge of good and evil (Gen. 3:6f), but only while eating it. Sins are like rich food which is enjoyable in the eating but makes you sick (Job 20:12-14). In fact this saying makes the pleasure of sin even more short-lived, suggesting it has only a sweet coating, and once that has been sucked off underneath is *gravel*, which you only want to spit out. So it is not speaking of the ultimate 'wages of sin', but the remorse that comes on the conscience when the pleasure is over (5:3f, 9:17f); this is true of all sin.

(d) *In inheriting (*v. 21*).*
This must refer to *an inheritance gained* not only *quickly* but dishonestly, for such as Joseph, Mordecai and Daniel had a sudden rise to wealth through the providence of God. But *an inheritance was gained* prematurely and fraudulently by Absalom who seized the kingdom while his father still lived, and by Ahab who not only had Naboth murdered but took a property from his family. An example that applies more commonly is that of the Prodigal Son who obtained his rightful inheritance by emotional blackmail (Luke 15:12). The main force of the saying lies in the close juxtaposition in Hebrew of *in the beginning* and *but the end*. How short-sighted we are where material things are concerned! If only we can lay our hands on this sum of money or that piece of property all will be well. We fail to take into account they will not benefit us unless God permits, for he is able to 'curse our blessings' (Mal. 2:2) and in this way judge our dishonesty or just our covetousness (28:20). We may not live to enjoy the *inheritance* (Luke 12:16-21) or fritter it away (13:11) and end up in poverty (28:22), leaving our family destitute (13:22).

5. Unsecured loans (v. 16).
In previous warnings against *putting up security* (6:1-5, 11:15, 17:18) the message has been addressed to the one standing surety. Here it is addressed to a third party, perhaps one who

has been asked to help the one who put up the security and has had to pay it, leaving himself destitute. Solomon's advice is – don't lend to him without some security. *The garment* is specified because it might be all he is left with. Normally this could not be held for more than a day because it doubled up as his bed-covering (Exod. 22:26f). But this is an extreme case: he has under-written another's debt without any security and done it for a *stranger*, not someone he knows and trusts. Most translators and interpreters prefer the reading 'foreigners' to *a wayward woman*. This makes line 2 simply a reinforcing of line 1. While we are to be generous with what we have, we are not expected to ruin ourselves for someone who has foolishly ruined himself. Some bond of trust has to be there first.

6. Trusting the talkative (v. 19).

Line 1 is like 11:13 except that the words come in a different order here and depict one whose interest in life is to get you to share your secrets with him so that he can go and tell them to someone else. The Hebrew tells us he 'walks about' as *a gossip*. He can't keep at home and mind his business, he must be into someone else's and the more private it is the better he likes it – not because he wants to sympathize, advise or help but because he is addicted to *gossip* as a gourmet is to 'choice morsels' (18:8). As soon as he leaves you he is 'walking off' to his friend to share the juicy bits. Line 2 is equally vivid for *talks too much* is 'opens his lips' or as we would say, 'He can't keep his mouth shut.' There is no such thing as *a confidence* with him and the only safe course is to keep **your** mouth shut or talk about the weather. Wouldn't it be better if we talked more about the gospel? What blessing can we expect in churches where people pay so little attention to the word of God that as soon as it is finished they're talking to their neighbour about someone else?

7. Disrespect for parents (v. 20).

The Fifth Commandment promised 'long life', that is, happiness, prosperity and a peaceful end to those who honour their parents. Those who do the exact opposite can only expect the exact reverse of the promise. Indeed the Law specifically prescribed death for this offence (Exod. 21:17). However, God may not wait for the process of law to take effect, especially if the authorities are negligent or lenient, as they often were in such matters. The vivid metaphor indicates a sudden cutting off either of the offender's well-being or his very life. *His lamp* was shining happily like a candle but is suddenly *snuffed out*, it doesn't gradually burn down and flicker away. We are of course in the old covenant here, where Israel's continuance in its land depended on the transmission of the Law from generation to generation. This made respect for and obedience to parents essential for Israel's continuance as a nation. Under the new covenant the survival of the church and gospel is not jeopardised because a child rejects its parents. Nevertheless it is still a serious sin for the person concerned and is classed among all the other sins in Romans 1:29-31, about whom it is said they 'deserve death' (Rom. 1:32).

8. Vindictiveness (v. 22).

Nothing is more certain in this fallen world than that we shall suffer *wrong*, sometimes unjustly. It is just as certain that our first reaction will be *'I'll pay you back for this'* (cf. 24:29). While this is natural and can often plead justice in its favour, it is not according to the wisdom of God. The law of Moses forbade it (Deut. 32:35). The law of experience discourages it, for vindictiveness harms you more than your adversary (cf. 17:13); 'He that studieth revenge keepeth his wounds open' (Bacon). The law of love reverses it (25:21; Rom. 12:17-21). The law of faith dispenses with it, for if *wrong* has been done to us God can nullify and turn it to our good. David was a man unjustly persecuted and he both practised and preached *wait for the Lord* (Pss. 40:1; 27:14). *Wait* means trust patiently, go on trusting and expecting until he *delivers* you from the harm done and turns it to your good (Ps. 37:5f). Our example is Christ who suffered everything his enemies hurled at him without retaliation (1 Pet. 2:23) because he trusted God (Matt. 27:43). God didn't immediately take him down from the cross and destroy his murderers, but did something better, something which enabled him to 'endure the cross' (Heb. 12:2). Let us do likewise (1 Pet. 4:19). 'Revenge is sweet' but patience, faith and love are sweeter.

9. Rash commitments (v. 25).

Under the old covenant you could *dedicate* things voluntarily
(lit. 'say, "a holy thing"') as well as compulsorily (Num. 30:2).
This was to accommodate one who in a spirit of thankfulness
for a great deliverance or particular blessing wanted to
show his gratitude practically. But in his euphoria he doesn't
consider whether he will be able to go through with it. This
was a problem because, although the *vow* was voluntary, it
was not retractable. It was too late to 'enquire' (*consider*) how
he would pay it. Thus he ensnared himself or fell into a trap,
having made a commitment he can't fulfil. While we do not
have that system we are invited to make commitments. The
time to *consider* their implications is before they are made
(Luke 14:25-33). Otherwise we may find ourselves unable or
unwilling to go through with them and build a greater barrier
between us and God than before.

Questions
1. As you have read through these verses have your eyes been
opened to any weaknesses in yourself that you were unconscious of before? If so, what will you now do about them?
2. Have these verses helped you understand the people you
confront in your daily life and to be more careful whom you
trust?

B. THINGS TO SEEK.

1. An understanding of human nature (vv. 5, 9, 11, 12, 24, 27, 29, 30).
This and the question of good government are the principal
themes in this section, indeed in the whole chapter.

(a) *The difficulty of understanding human nature* (**vv. 5, 9, 24**).
We are first reminded that this is not easy. We are complex
beings and find it hard to understand ourselves let alone
others.

(i) *Understanding others* (**v. 5**). What we do and what we
are come from what we think – *the purposes of a man's heart,*
which *like deep waters* are hard to fathom. Those who graduate

from the folly of childhood to become *men of understanding* learn the art of *drawing them out*. For God knows what is in a man (John 2:25), since he made us in all our complexity and observed how sin affected us. His word is full of human psychology and those grounded in it will understand human nature better even than the professional psychologist.

(ii) *Understanding ourselves (vv. 9, 24)*. We won't begin to understand others until we have some understanding of ourselves. This is difficult, but the basic things are common to man, so that what is true of me will be true of others.

(ii.1). *Indwelling sin* (v. 9). This saying is put in question form: *who can say?* in order to evoke the answer 'none'. It states the universal sinfulness of the human heart, in keeping with the general teaching of Scripture (Rom. 3:10). It is however put in the first person singular because each of us individually has to realize and acknowledge this. Although we were made *pure, clean, without sin* we have fallen from this and corrupted our every faculty (Rom. 3:13-18). This alone explains why we are as we are and do as we do; there is no way we can understand ourselves or others without taking this into account. People who are bewildered by the treachery, selfishness and violence of others have never faced this essential factor.

(ii.2). *Divine providence* (v. 24). Although we have each 'turned to his own way' (Isa. 53:6) God has not utterly given us up. While he allows us short-term freedom to choose what *steps* we take (cf. 16:9, 19:21), he himself *directs* their outcome without revealing what this is. This makes it impossible for anyone to *understand* 'the direction his life is taking' (GNB). Who at the age of 70 can say he saw at 17 what course his life would take?

Seeing these two things in our lives helps us understand others.

(b) *The main phases of human development* (vv. 11, 29).
Human life is not constant but passes through various stages.

(i) *Childhood* (v. 11). It may be fashionable in some circles to see childhood as a period in which little can be expected: 'He's only a child', 'You can't put an old head on young shoulders'.

True as this is, it can be overemphasised. The sin which is common to all (v. 9) quickly expresses itself in *conduct*, especially in relationships with parents and other children, so that *even a child is known by his actions*. Adult behaviour is not expected of a child but he is supposed to obey, love and trust his parents and be friendly and kind to other children. This would qualify as *conduct* that *is pure and right*. PROVERBS sets out to cultivate this by guiding parents in how to 'train a child in the way he should go' (22:6).

(ii) *Manhood* (**v. 29a**). The word used for *young men* describes those who have grown out of the childishness of boyhood. They have reached the peak of their *strength* – their chief *glory*. It is the time of life when the beauty of their physique is at its best, and during which they will accomplish most, at least in a physical sense. If they become believers in Christ they will dedicate their *strength* to him and be useful in his service. 'I write to you young men, because you are strong and the word of God lives in you and you have overcome the evil one' (1 John 2:14).

(iii) *Old age* (**v. 29b**). The *glory* and *strength* of youth gradually fade, but give way to another *splendour* of which *grey hair* is the outward emblem. If manhood has been well spent it will have developed experience, wisdom and character. The old are therefore still essential to society, although able to achieve less physically. In fact the two stages are complementary: the younger to bear the brunt of the work and the older to set an example of righteousness (16:31) and to impart the wisdom that comes from experience.

(c) *The chief faculties of human nature* (**vv. 12, 27**).
Certain things are constant through all these periods, prominent among which are the outward sense organs and the inward sense of right and wrong, or conscience.

(i) *The senses* (**v. 12**). Sight and hearing are our most precious senses. What sort of life is it that is lived in total darkness or complete silence, to have *eyes that* do not *see* or *ears that* do not *hear*? Those who have to live like this deserve sympathy. But many more fail to use their eyes and ears to acquire knowledge and understanding, which is what *the Lord made them both for*.

Some are so deaf and blind in their minds they acknowledge gods who can neither see nor hear and reject the God who created these faculties (Ps. 115:4-7). Of them the psalmist says, 'Those who make them will be like them and so will all who trust in them.' The modern evolutionist attributes these faculties to some spontaneous force in matter itself. Only the God who made the physical senses can open the eyes and ears of the heart to him.

(ii) *Conscience* (**v. 27**). It is probably safer to go, as most translations do, with NIV mg: *the spirit of man is the Lord's lamp*. The reading in the main text would make *the lamp of the Lord* his word or Spirit or both, which is true (Ps. 119:105, Heb. 4:12f) but probably not what is meant here. The idea of God's knowledge of our inmost thoughts and motives has already become familiar to us (15:3, 11, 16:2, cf. 21:2) and here we are told a little more about it. God who himself is Spirit and made us in his likeness has endued us with *spirit*. Thus *our spirit* is his witness within man by which he *searches out his inmost being* – thoughts and motives. We too are conscious of our thoughts and motives. Unlike animals we have self-consciousness by which we know ourselves (1 Cor. 2:11) and conscience by which we pass judgment on ourselves (Rom. 2:15).

(d) *The benefit of afflictions (v. 30)*. It sounds like an advertisement for corporal punishment, and of the severest kind, for the word for *blows* has the sense of 'cutting', as RV translates: 'blows that wound'. *Beatings* describes the repeated flagellation of the persistent offender. This was the way of the ancient world, believing as they did in the effectiveness of corporal punishment, which not only deterred the wrongdoer from his *evil* practice but changed his *inmost being* or character. Since the Bible does not specifically command corporal punishment – certainly not with the severity described here – this may be taken metaphorically for 'chastisement', as in Isaiah 1:5. The afflictions of life, especially the world's hostility against believers, are like parental chastisement – they make us better people (Heb. 12:4-11).

2. Faithfulness (v. 6).

Few of us are what we think, appear and *claim*. This is not necessarily hypocrisy, which is, as the word indicates, deliberately wearing a mask to hide what you really are behind what you would like people to think you are. This is simply a mistaken self-image, which we all share because of the blinding effect of sin. It applies particularly in the area of sociability – the theme of this verse. We all see ourselves as friendly, trustworthy, dependable and kind. But in practice this only works out with those we like or to whom we owe something, and when and how it suits us. *Unfailing love* is what God is, and which he shares with us in the work of regeneration. Delivered from our self-image we are renewed in the image of Christ, and 'put on', among other things, true and faithful 'love' (Col. 3:9-14). So this is not the despairing cry of a good man left alone among the wicked (as in Ps. 12:1, Eccles. 7:28) but a statement about human nature.

3. Righteousness (v. 7).

This confirms that verse 6 was not a cry of despair but the truth about man without God. This verse is about one on whom God has laid his hand and accepted as *righteous*. This is a private transaction between him and God but it is made known publicly by his *blameless life* (part of which is 'unfailing love', v. 6). But it is also seen in *his children*, who are *blessed* with the same relationship with God and live the same *righteous ... life*. This cannot be taken as an absolute promise, for it didn't always happen even under the old covenant. The New Testament clarifies the reason: *righteousness* is not transmitted by blood, but is God's gift through repentance and faith (John 1:12f). Rather it is a way of encouraging the believer to live a godly life in the hope *his children* will follow on. It also encourages the *children* of believers to appreciate the benefit of having believing parents and to seek to walk in their ways.

4. The gift of communication (v. 15).

There are two ideas in *lips that speak knowledge*: wisdom and communication. 3:15 and 8:11 have spoken of wisdom as of greater value than precious stones. Solomon could truly say this for when presented with a choice between the two he went for wisdom rather than *gold* (1 Kings 3:5-15). His book, based on his thoughts, conversation and decisions, reveals the many valuable uses of wisdom. For Solomon had another gift – the ability to communicate his *knowledge* so that others benefited from it. What skill went into composing these pithy sayings, so true and so aptly expressed! We live in times when wisdom is Christ and all that pertains to him (Matt. 12:42). All who believe and know him are truly wise (2 Tim. 3:15), but not all have the added gift of being able to speak of Christ with the attractiveness and appeal which draws others to faith. This is *rare* compared with *gold and rubies* which are plentiful. Let those who have this double gift prize and use it; those who lack it seek it, and all of us pray God to raise up a generation of preachers of whom it will be true.

5. Good advice (v. 18).

Twice already we have been advised to *seek advice*: 11:14, 15:22 warned us that failure to *seek advice* meant failure in the project contemplated, be it a private affair (15:22) or national conflict (11:14), whereas trouble taken to consult others guaranteed success and victory. This verse speaks neither of failure nor success but is a simple instruction to *seek advice* and *obtain guidance*. NIV makes both parts imperative, though the Hebrew of line 1 is indicative: 'purposes (*plans*) are established by counsel'. The suggestion is that our brain-waves, while they sound brilliant to us, may be quite unrealistic because we've not taken all the factors into account. Others will point these out and we shall either modify our *plans* or abandon them altogether. If this is so in our own personal lives how much more in matters which affect a whole nation! The riskiest and most costly course a nation can contemplate is *war* (24:6). It is easy to start one, but its length, effect and final outcome are unforeseeable (Luke 14:31). It needs the combined wisdom of the greatest minds to arrive at a right decision. We who know Christ have the greatest mind of all to consult and the promise of his guidance (James 1:5) which may come through others and not directly to us.

6. Good government (vv. 2, 8, 26, 28).

From personal to general good. Each of us is affected by society and this is very much determined by who governs it. PROVERBS assumes monarchical government but the principles apply equally to democracy. In the New Testament we find the same teaching 1000 years later, that government exists 'to punish those who do wrong and commend those who do right' (1 Pet. 2:14, cf. Rom. 13:3f).

(a) *Punishing wrongdoers* (**vv. 2, 8, 26**).
Three stages in this process are described in this section.

(i) *Detection* (**v. 8**). Solomon speaks here as the one who 'built the throne hall, the hall of justice where he was to judge' (1 Kings 7:7). His father David believed he was given supreme power in order to administer justice (Ps. 101:6-8) and had taught this to his son (2 Sam. 23:3f, Ps. 72:1-4). His first task was to detect the lawbreakers *with his eyes*. Before they could be *winnowed* or separated from society like chaff from wheat they had to be seen to be chaff. How this was done in Solomon's day we don't know, but it developed into our vast network of police and espionage.

(ii) *Opposition* (**v. 2**). To identify lawbreakers is not enough; they must be shown to have offended, not just against the law but the people, whose well-being the law safeguarded. The *king's wrath* expressed the people's hostility and is vividly illustrated by *the roar of a lion*. He was supreme in the animal kingdom and anyone who valued *his life* did not arouse his anger. *Life* may be at stake in breaking the law. The wording of the saying may reflect a time when the King had an arbitrary power of life and death, although in ancient Israel only certain crimes attracted the death penalty. Although this may have been abolished among us, someone who faces long-term imprisonment or even spends his life in crime as an enemy of society, may be said to *forfeit his life*.

(iii) *Punishment* (**v. 26**). This verse describes the punishment of *the wicked* with greater detail and vivid imagery. They are dealt with in the drastic way in which harvesting is done. When the crop has been gathered grain and chaff have to be separated. This was done by crushing the heads by *driving the* *threshing wheel over them.* The separated chaff was then blown away so that only the grain remained, which was done with the *winnowing* fork and fan, a vivid picture of the punishment of criminals, the breaking up of their gangs and their separation from society. In the New Testament the harvest process illustrates the final judgment of Christ (Matt. 3:12, 13:40-42).

(b) *Encouraging well-doers* (**v. 28**).

This verse does not contradict the need for clear just laws firmly executed, for *faithfulness* is one of the guardians of *the throne*. But there is another: *love*. *Love* not only guards his person (*keep a king safe*) but *his throne*, the whole institution of government itself, whoever administers it at a particular time. Justice can be exercised in a cold and even terrifying way, which deters crime and rebellion but creates antagonism and discontent. It needs to be tempered with clemency, so that people's hearts are won as well as their bodies. For the majority of the people are not criminals or plotting to overthrow the government. Police states may be orderly and hard to topple but they create an atmosphere which is likely one day to boil over and destroy the governors, as we know from regimes in eastern Europe, Africa and central America. Law-abiding people need encouragement to keep them that way.

Questions

1. Do these verses direct your mind to areas which you have been neglecting or in which you are deficient?
2. Does the first section (understanding human nature) show you something of what Biblical psychology is?
3. Does the final section help at all in distinguishing the vital functions of government (law and order) from those that attract most publicity (economy, employment, etc.)?

19

The Sovereignty Of God In Judgment
(Proverbs 21)

While it is true that only six of the thirty-one verses mention God by name, the thought of God dominates the chapter. The virtues commended here are the qualities God favours and rewards, and the vices are what he detests and judges.

A. ATTRIBUTES WHICH LIE BEHIND GOD'S JUDGMENT.
God is qualified to be supreme Judge because he is both righteous (morally perfect and wholly just) and sovereign (all-powerful to execute his judgments).

1. His Sovereignty.

(a) *Over the highest authorities* (**v. 1**).
We have heard how the common man is under the sovereign rule of God (16:1, 9, 20:24); but the authorities are not exempt – the highest of the high have one higher. Other proverbs have spoken of the power of a king over his subjects and the terror this inspires (16:14f, 19:12, 20:2), but even he is not outside God's control. Nor is it just the outcome of the *king's* decisions ('steps', 20:24) but the working of his *heart* that *is in the hand of the Lord*. God can move his *heart* to do his people good as readily as a farmer can dig a channel (*watercourse*) to irrigate his fields and make his crops grow. Pharaoh favoured Joseph and his family (Acts 7:10), Artaxerxes financed the second temple (Ezra 7:11-27) and later permitted Nehemiah to return

to Jerusalem (Neh. 1:11, 2:8). Perhaps this explains why a staunchly Romish king, Henry VIII, furthered the growth of Protestantism.

(b) *Over the hearts of all* (**v. 2**).
This is a virtual repeat of 16:2 (see comments) but appropriately follows verse 1, which to an extent it explains: the *heart* which *the Lord* 'directs' is the one he first perceives; he knows what it thinks and evaluates (*weighs*) these thoughts. This is true not just for the king but for every *man*, for in the Hebrew *the heart* is plural. The point is the difference between the way we see ourselves and the way he sees us. We judge ourselves by what we do (our *ways*) which we can manipulate to cover our real feelings from others who only 'look at the outward appearance' (1 Sam. 16:7). But God 'judges motives' (GNB). The Pharisee in Luke 18:9-14 appeared very religious but Jesus knew he was full of pride in himself and contempt for others. This verse is therefore a call to face and repent of those bad motives which are a barrier to God's blessing. If we are willing, God will open our eyes to ourselves, not to drive us to despair but to lead us to him whose blood can cleanse our consciences (Heb. 9:14, 10:22).

(c) *Over human wisdom* (**v. 30**).
The words *that can succeed* are supplied and *against* is literally 'face to face with'. This may, therefore, mean that human *wisdom, insight or plan* are as nothing to *the Lord*. He alone truly understands the issues, perceives the whole situation and determines what to do. This means that the *plans* our *wisdom* and *insight* come up with should be submitted to his will which is all-embracing. What shouldn't happen, though it does, is that our *wisdom* and *insight* are used to *make plans against* him. Such attempts and their failures permeate the pages of Scripture: Pharaoh (Exod. 1:8-12), Balak (Num. 24:10), Athaliah (2 Kings 11:2) and Sanballat (Neh. 6). Satan is behind this and employs men, especially political and religious leaders to execute his plans (Rev. 13). But they inevitably fail (Rev. 20).

(d) *Over mighty armies* (**v. 31**).

Man's authority (v. 1), ways (v. 2) and wisdom (v. 30) reach their height when he goes to *battle*, on which he expends his greatest resources. *The horse* was the most powerful weapon of the ancient world, equivalent to the gun, tank and missile of later times. When it was *made ready for the day of battle, victory* was virtually guaranteed. The nation which relied on infantry was doomed. But this was to reckon without *the Lord with whom victory* ultimately *rests*. There have been surprising reversals in the history of warfare, from Abram's defeat of the kings of the east (Gen. 14) to the Vietcong's victory over the USA in 1970. God can give men up to war (Rev. 6:4) or intervene to end it (Ps. 46:9f).

Questions
1. In view of verse 1 what can you as a Christian do for nations that are poor, oppressed or even at war? See 1 Timothy 2:1-4.
2. Apply verses 30-31 to 'the war against the saints' led by Satan and his army, angelic and human, by referring to Ephesians 6:10-18.

2. His Righteousness.
In verse 12 God is called 'the Righteous One' because of which certain human attitudes are commended and others condemned. We first look at these before coming to the ways God judges them. Some verses contain both virtues and vices and could therefore appear in either or both of the following sections.

(a) *What God favours*
(i) *Obedience* (**vv. 3, 27**). This does not mean *sacrifice* was not *right and just*, since God himself instituted and required it as the way by which repentance was expressed and faith laid hold of his forgiveness during the period between the Fall and Calvary. But like all ritual it could be performed without repentance and faith. As **verse 27** says, it could even be offered by *the wicked*, the rest of whose life was the opposite of *right and just*. This was why God refused Cain's offering (Gen. 4:5) – not because there was anything wrong with it but because

of what was wrong in him (1 John 3:12). In fact it could be done from utterly false motives, such as using it as a cover for a secretly sinful life. To *sacrifice* in this spirit was not merely to do what was not *acceptable* but positively *detestable* (15:8). For *sacrifice* was intended as part of a total life of obedience and love to God. It could not stand up on its own and where this was attempted the wrath of God fell both on the disobedient life and the *sacrifice* (1 Sam. 15:22, Isa. 1:11-17, Hosea. 6:6, Micah. 6:6-8, Mark 12:33).

Although the sacrificial system is abolished we still have ceremonies in this gospel age: baptism, the Lord's Supper and other services. Apart from a life of obedience these are worthless, even sinful. Further, since offering sacrifices is replaced by trusting the Christ of Calvary, to claim 'Christ died for my sins' but continue in them unrepentant – what could be more *detestable*? Not even confession to a priest of sins to which one returns.

(ii) *Carefulness* (**v. 5**).

Usually it is sloth that is contrasted with *diligence* and put down as the road *to poverty* (10:4, 13:4). But here it is the opposite – *haste*. Haste is waste. Not that it is always bad, and sometimes it is essential: fires, accidents, illnesses call for quick response. But in these cases it is absolutely clear what has to be done. What is in view here is a longer-term project: a job of work, even a whole career. These call for careful *plans* if they are to *lead to profit*. One who rushes in impatiently to get the job done may be enthusiastic and energetic, the opposite of the sluggard, a workaholic, but if he hasn't *planned diligently*, his efforts will fail, however *diligently* he works, and only *lead to poverty*. Time taken in *planning* is not wasted, in fact in the end it saves, not just time, but perhaps the whole situation.

(iii) *Peace* (**vv. 9, 19**).

We were introduced to the *quarrelsome wife* in 19:13, whose nagging was as pleasant to listen to as 'a constant dripping'. **Verse 9** takes us a stage further: her victim can stand no more and takes his bed up on the roof (which was flat in an oriental house). Since this was both dangerous and exposed to the elements this is probably hyperbole, like 'I'd sooner be dead!' So too is the next stage depicted in **verse 19**. On *the roof* he is still within earshot and has to come down sometimes. Nor does his action seem to have improved her *temper*, which has got worse. The only answer is to go where he is out of reach and *live in the desert*. With all its privations and dangers no man would actually do so.

Although this conjures up a humorous picture it is making a serious point. Previous sayings on *quarrelling* (13:10, 14:29, 16:32, 17:14, 19:11) have been addressed to the quarreller, advising him to control himself in view of the serious consequences of his bad *temper*. Here the matter is seen from the point of view of the victim and his sufferings. Thus, although such sayings are a lesson to the son on choosing a wife (see on 12:4), they can be taken more generally. What if the *quarrelsome* person won't control him/herself? The only course is separation, at least temporarily. Although not an ideal solution, *it is better*, says our verse, than living in continual strife. Abram used it to resolve the dispute between Lot's herdsmen and his (Gen. 13:8f), as did Paul and Barnabas (Acts 15:39f). Whole nations, such as India and Ireland, have found it *better* to partition their country than keep together those who won't live together in peace. In our fallen state some relationships appear beyond reconciliation.

(iv) *Wisdom* (**v. 22**).
Our image of *a wise man* may be of one who is good at talking but ineffective practically. This example from war shows this to be far from the truth. Here is a commander with an inferior force seeking to take a seemingly impregnable *city*. Everything has its weak point and with patience and skill he locates it. Then he shrewdly deploys his forces so as to exploit the weakness. What was a small breach in the wall grows until the entire *stronghold* is *pulled down*. The Old Testament has many examples of this: Abram's victory over the eastern emperors (Gen. 14), Joshua's over Jericho (Josh. 6) and Ai (Josh. 8), Gideon's over Midian (Judg. 7) and some less famous ones in 2 Samuel 20:14-22.

There may be a deeper meaning than just military strategy, which is hardly suitable for the young! What is destroyed here is *the stronghold in which they trust*, so that he is saying wisdom is more powerful than self-confidence, because its first principle is trust in the almighty God (Ps. 18:29). The New Testament directs us away from our human enemies to our spiritual ones and shows that with the weapon of faith we can overcome their ideas and arguments, for these are the *strongholds* from which they attack our gospel (2 Cor. 10:4f, Eph. 6:10-18).

(v) *Self-control* (**v. 23**).

Of the many allusions to controlled speech 13:3 is nearest to this: 'He who guards his lips guards his life', for it draws attention to the harm we can do *ourselves* by unguarded words. Deceitful, provocative, insulting or blasphemous speech not only harms the hearer but gets the speaker into trouble. While we should chiefly consider the effect of our words on our audience (18:21), there is nothing unworthy in a man seeking to *keep himself from calamity*, especially as *himself* is literally 'his soul', that is, his very life, which can be endangered by foolish talk (12:13). The remedy is simple (though not easy!): learn when to keep your *mouth* shut altogether (Eccles. 3:7, Matt. 27:14) and, when it is right to open it, teach your *tongue* to say only what is necessary (James 3).

Review these 'virtues'. What sort of rating does 'the world' give them? Will others be impressed if we have them? If not, why should we bother cultivating them? See Galatians 1:10, Acts 24:16.

(b) *What God detests.*
(i) *Pride* (**vv. 4, 24**).

Sin is what is foreign to God and therefore what he hates. His great aversion is *pride* (6:17, 8:13, Luke 18:14, 1 Pet. 5:5). *Pride* is vividly described here as *haughty* or 'uplifted' *eyes*, describing the way they look down on others in a superior censorious way. The Pharisee in the Temple 'stood up', no doubt with head and eyes lifted, listed his virtues and despised the tax-collector as an example of all the *sins* he did not commit. The tax-collector 'would not even look up', his *eyes* were directed downwards. The one 'exalted' and the other 'humbled himself' (Luke 18:9-14).

So much is clear. But what of *the lamp of the wicked*? Some translate 'ploughing' or 'tillage'; Delitzsch has 'husbandry' and sees it as metaphorical of the *proud* man's whole way of life. His *pride* taints everything with *sin* and marks him as a *wicked* man. If *lamp* is right this too could be a metaphor of the life he displays to the world. His conduct may shine impeccably and his life be happy and prosperous but because his *heart* is *proud* he has to be written down as *wicked*. This is the sin to which religious people are most prone, and in a particularly nasty form – spiritual *pride*, which despises the unconverted simply for being unconverted, as if **they** had become spiritual by themselves not by God's grace – grace so far denied to the unconverted.

This censorious attitude is so much the characteristic of the *proud and arrogant man* that he is soon labelled '*Mocker*' (**verse 24**). Although he obviously thinks he is the wisest man since Solomon, in fact wisdom is far from him (14:6). He gives the game away by his inability to control his temper with those who disagree or compete with him: *overweening pride* is literally 'wrath of pride'. Such a man was Haman (Esther 3:5), as was Herod (Matt. 2:16). But although he sets out to destroy his rivals, ultimately it is he who is destroyed (19:29, 21:11).

(ii) *Fraud (**v. 6**)*.
Another vice on God's black list is dishonesty. Chapter 20 exposed a variety of ways of making *a fortune by lying*. But it is not a real *fortune*, it does not truly profit. For one thing it is a *fleeting vapour* – insubstantial and insecure. Dishonest money is hard to hold on to because too many others want to get their hands on it: those from whom it was fraudulently obtained, your fellow-conspirators, the police. The temptation is to spend it quickly, which means you don't keep it long and what you get from it has little value. For another thing it leads to death. The margin gives the Hebrew as, 'A vapour for those who seek death'. Theft or fraud are crimes which in some ages and societies attracted the death penalty. Unrepented they certainly bring down the judgment of God. For this the fraudster is himself responsible and so can be said to 'seek death'.

(iii) *Violence* **(v. 7).**

If verse 6 was robbery by deception this is 'robbery' (KJV) with *violence* – a different method for achieving the same result. Also it has the same ultimate outcome – death, but again by a different method. Instead of his gains slipping away from him he is *dragged away* from them, presumably to be executed. Crime doesn't pay, cheats are cheated and the violent suffer *violence*. Why then do people do these things? Because *they refuse to do what is right*. Their parents taught them right from wrong but they chose wrong. This was Lesson 1 of PROVERBS: 'Don't join a gang of violent robbers for they end up receiving the treatment they hand out to others' (1:8-19). Even those whose parents never taught them know in their hearts that stealing and violence are wrong. It is their own sinful nature that entices them into it.

(iv) *Deviousness* **(v. 8).**

The sins of the preceding verses: pride, ambition, deceit and violence make a person *guilty* in the eyes of society as well as of God. He knows this, it shows in the way he conducts himself: he is *devious*. He cannot operate openly but must act craftily and stealthily. One who is *innocent* of these flaws has nothing to hide or fear, he can hold himself *upright* and operate in a straightforward manner. Who is happier of the two? The first thinks he is free because he recognizes no rules; yet his freedom has led him into bondage to *guilt*, the burden of constantly looking over his shoulder and sensing that a higher power is watching and will call him to account. *Innocence* is the best freedom.

(v) *Perversity* **(v. 10).**

Here we reach the bottom of the pit of sin. This *wicked man* is not an occasional or even habitual evildoer, *evil* is endemic in him, his 'soul' *craves evil*. 'Evil, be thou my good' is his motto. *Evil* is to him what the beloved is to a lover who loves with his whole soul in the way God is loved by the believer (Matt. 22:37). He will let nothing and no one stand in his way once he has set his mind on an *evil* scheme. Even *his neighbour*, 'who lives trustfully by him' (3:29), *gets no mercy from him*. This is no doubt a rare condition, for most criminals have some good in them even if they only show it to their fellows ('honesty among thieves'). A condition like this is akin to demon-possession. But it must have had a beginning. True we are all born sinners, but not entirely devoted to *evil*. 'Total depravity' doesn't mean we are as bad as we possibly can be, but that sin has affected every part of our nature. But we all have the potential to end up here, once we have set off down that road.

(vi) *Bribery* (**v. 14**).
The power of the *bribe* has already been described in 17:8, with examples of how it can buy off the magistrate (17:23) or gain access to the great (18:16). Here it *pacifies* an enemy, one who has been justly provoked by an insult or harmful act, or even one whose *anger* and *great wrath* are unjustified. Clearly there are thoughts of reprisals – a court action or beating up. *A bribe* seems the cheapest way of avoiding the ruin of the body or estate. But it was against the Law (Exod. 23:8) and had to be done *in secret, concealed in the cloak* to keep it from prying eyes.

  This is one of those sayings which simply state a fact without approval or otherwise. The morality of the matter we have to work out ourselves. We have all found ourselves on the wrong side of someone. If it is just a private tiff, *a gift* can be a way of saying, 'Sorry, let's make up.' But it won't require the cloak-and-dagger approach. If it is more serious it needs something more: a genuine grievance demands open apology and restitution; a breach of law requires a legal settlement; unprovoked threats or blackmail need reporting to the authorities or they will be repeated. The *bribe* attempts to settle by an appeal to covetousness which can never be a right or effective way of proceeding.

(vii) *Sloth* (**vv. 25-26**).
We have heard more about the sin of sloth than almost any other. Common to these sayings is that in the case of this sin the culprit is the chief sufferer. Here the story reaches its climax, for his sloth is *the death of him*. He wants the fruits that only *work* can produce but he can't make the effort: his mind wants to act but *his hands refuse to work*, as if they are paralysed by a disease. So his whole life is one of unsatisfied longing: *all*

day long he craves. What a contrast is *the righteous!* He has been saved both from sloth and the selfishness that underlies it. So he *works* diligently and has enough not only to satisfy himself but to *give* to the poor. The sluggard is continually *craving, the righteous* is continually *giving,* and that *without sparing.*

(viii) *Bigotry* (v. 29).

The *wicked man* is not only perverse (v. 10) but obstinate. He tries to cover his crimes by *putting up a bold front.* He appears a man of conviction and certainty, who could never do anything devious. But it is mere bluster; he has decided on his course and ignores all warnings and arguments against it. The *upright man,* the careful one of verse 5, looks at the total situation and *gives thought* to *his ways,* 'Considers he might be wrong' (Cromwell), listens to advice, heeds warnings and faces facts. Good examples of the difference are Bunyan's 'Obstinate and Pliable' in 'Pilgrim's Progress'. Alas it is not only *the wicked* who are obstinate. Bigotry is found in the *upright*: there are Christians so certain they are right they can't tolerate any who differ from them. This *bold front* can hide a basic insecurity and even fear.

Look out for these types in your daily newspaper – and your daily life. Then do what Psalm 139:23f, Matthew 7:3-5 and 1 Corinthians 11:31 tell you.

B. THE JUDGMENTS OF GOD.

1. Punishment.

God may intervene personally and directly, or just allow the consequences of the sin to take their course.

(a) *Direct.*

(i) *On Wickedness* (v. 12).

We have surveyed some of the marks of *the wicked,* all of which 'the Lord detests'. In particular we have seen his perversity (v. 10) and incorrigible obstinacy (v. 29). Here we are reminded that everything is done before the eyes of *the Righteous One* who *takes note* of all that goes on in *his house.* What can *the*

Righteous One, 'the Judge of all the earth' do other than bring such a one *to ruin*? He deserves it, he is a menace to others, an affront to *the Righteous One* and utterly unrepentant and incurable. What form the *ruin* takes is not specified: financial collapse, sickness and death in the family, the destruction of *the house* by fire, flood or tempest? Whatever way it happens evidently God is the instrumental cause, *the Righteous One* restoring justice.

(ii) *On Selfishness* (**v. 13**).
God's judgment falls not only on 'sins of commission' (downright wickedness) but 'sins of omission', such as ignoring the destitute. Ignoring is not the same as ignorance, for here their needs are evident: *the poor cry* out but this one *shuts his ears to their cry*. This means (a) he has no **feeling** for him, as John so poignantly puts it, 'He shuts his bowels from him' (1 John 3:17, Greek), he hardens his heart against him; (b) he refuses to **help** him, shuts his purse, hides his wallet, locks his larder. Even if he feels sympathetic he does nothing practical. He may say, 'Go, I wish you well, keep warm and well fed,' but does nothing about his physical needs (James 2:16).

Selfishness and uncharitableness are judged appropriately. The unloving who shut their ears, hearts and purses, find themselves shut out of God's kingdom, as Jesus warned in Matthew 25:41-46. They will cry out in protest but their cry is unavailing (1:28). Like the rich man they will cry out from hell for some relief, but since they refused to hear *the cry of the poor* in their lifetime, their *cry* after death *will not be answered* (Luke 16:23-26).

(iii) *On Apostasy* (**v. 16**).
Those who turned to crime in Israel were usually those who in youth had been shown *the path of understanding* but *strayed from* it. This is not just about a misspent youth, for it concerns *understanding* as well as behaviour and therefore means rejection of the God who constructed *the path* as well as *the path* itself. It is what is called 'apostasy' – turning from the doctrine and ethic previously embraced. This formed the subject of stern warnings in the Prologue, couched in language similar to this about *the company of the dead*, the

REPHAIM (2:18f, 7:26f, 9:18). While there may be a reference to the death penalty for apostasy, the thought is more on the eternal judgment of God on those who forsake his ways. The New Testament is no less severe with its warnings of the dire consequences for those who, having willingly and knowingly professed the gospel, reject it in favour of some other faith or philosophy (Heb. 6:4-6, 10:26f, 38, 2 Pet. 2:21f).

Question
Do you think God still judges by direct intervention? If so, can you think of any instances? Does Luke 13:1-5 affect your answer?

(b) *Indirect.*
The more common way in which God's judgment operates is by allowing sin to work itself out fully (James 1:15); as Paul put it 'God gave them over' to the consequences of their sins (Rom. 1:24ff).

(i) *On Violence* (**v. 7**).
This verse has already been explained but is listed here for completeness. It probably refers to a *violent* man being brought to justice, one of God's most frequent ways of indirect judgment.

(ii) *On Rebelliousness* (**v. 11**).
The *mocker* (cf. v. 24) is one who by constant disobedience and refusal of parental instruction becomes 'stubborn and rebellious ... a profligate and a drunkard' (Deut. 21:18-20). Dire punishment could be meted out to such: flogging (19:25), even stoning to death (Deut. 21:21). This had the effect of satisfying justice: 'Purge the evil from among you' and of deterring others: 'All Israel will hear of it and be afraid'. It is the deterrent effect of punishment that is stressed here. Modern penal theory tends to play this down, probably under the influence of those who favour treating the offender as sick rather than punishing him as culpable. This is unwise, for while punishment can be disproportionate, it is doubly effective according to our verse. 'The blow that strikes one

reaches two' (Bridges): the offender is corrected and the young deterred from following the example of those whose ways have brought trouble upon them. Thus the punishment inflicted by society represents the judgment of God.

(iii) On Extravagance (vv. 17, 20).

Here is another area in which the judgment of God operates indirectly – the luxuries of life. We are not forbidden to use what gives *pleasure* (1 Tim. 6:17) or to enjoy it for its own sake. *Wine* and *oil* indicate that festivities are in view here, for on such occasions *wine* was abundant and *oil* poured on the body to delight the sense of smell as *wine* did that of taste (cf. Ps. 23:5). What is wrong is the *love of pleasure* indulged continually instead of occasionally – a constant round of parties. In the economy of ancient Israel wealth might be acquired but never guaranteed, so that if you squandered it on a life of luxury you might never replace it and *become poor*. Such warnings are still needed and the words of Paul referred to above mention the uncertainty of wealth. The New Testament also stresses how love of riches leads to neglect of the soul which soon *becomes poor* (1 Tim. 6:9f).

Verse 20 poignantly describes the outworking of this indirect judgment on the love of pleasure for its own sake. The well-stocked *house* soon becomes bare. It was hard work in those days to acquire enough for the present, and to have supplies in hand needed a combination of *wise* stewardship and the blessing of God (see on 15:6). To do all this just to *devour* it *all* at once was *foolish* indeed. We can't help wondering how such a one was *wise* enough to stock up in the first place. So perhaps it refers to two people: the *wise* who made his *house* plentiful, and the *foolish man* (his son or successor) who hadn't worked and saved but just consumes it without thinking or keeping up the hard work (Eccles. 2:21). For us it is a timely warning against consumerism, the spirit of our age, which we Christians are in danger of sharing. We need to heed Christ's word about the superiority of spiritual to material stores (Matt. 6:19).

(iv) *On Lying* (**v. 28**).

False witness is another of God's pet aversions (6:19). It was against one of his Ten Commandments (Exod. 20:16) and could be punished by death (Deut. 19:16-21). So Solomon was on firm ground in saying such *will perish* (cf. 19:5, 9). Perjury is still a serious offence even if not punishable by death. However, there is a deeper shade of meaning here to which the contrast in line 2 draws attention. The Hebrew reads 'He who hears will speak for ever' (cf. NIVmg). Some commentators take 'hear' to mean 'obey', that is, either obey God's word in general or his command to speak truth in particular. But it might be more appropriate to understand 'hear' as 'hear all the evidence' or 'hear both sides of the case'. This agrees with the judicial context indicated by *false witness* – one who lies in court, although it can apply to any speech, even ordinary conversation. So the contrast between the two lines is that what the *false witness* says will be exposed and *perish*, whereas the words of him who has weighed up all the evidence will prevail. What an encouragement to us who battle against unbiblical theories of the origin of the universe, cults, false religions and Christian deviations! Truth will prevail because it takes all the facts into consideration (Matt. 24:35)!

2. Reward.

In judging the wicked God does not forget the righteous and duly rewards them. Here are some of their rewards.

(i) *Joy* (**v. 15**).

Although the Hebrew reads, 'It is joy to the righteous to do justice' and most take it that way, it is probably better to read it passively with RSV and NIV. The preceding verses have had much to say about divine judgment and human justice. Much of it may sound harsh and negative. The reverse is the case. We saw in verse 11 that punishment has a deterrent effect on wrongdoing. Here we are told this in different words: it *brings ... terror to evildoers*. In this fallen world there are those who don't respond to appeals to their better nature, which has been immobilized by habitual wrongdoing. They have to be cured by punishment and controlled by the fear of it. *The righteous* don't *enjoy* this in itself, for they are not sadistic; but it means that for one thing their sufferings at the hands of such people are diminished, which is a cause for rejoicing, and for another that order is restored and maintained in society, enabling them to get on with their lives. Is this teaching not identical to what we find in Romans 13:1-4?

(ii) *Deliverance* (**v. 18**).
This explains and is explained by verse 15: the 'justice' which 'brings joy to the righteous' and is 'a terror to evildoers' is that which falls only on *the wicked*. Some judgments make no distinction, but there are times when, in order to save his own, God gives up *the wicked* to judgment. Such a time was when Cyrus was raised up to destroy Babylon and repatriate Israel which had suffered at her hands. In this connection the Babylonians are called a *ransom* in Isaiah 43:3f. The same verse mentions Egypt, for when God visited Egypt with the ten plagues Israel was spared and eventually released from cruel captivity. In the gospel age God may judge the church's persecutors but spare the church and so get her enemies off her back. REVELATION has much on this theme.

(iii) *Progress* (**v. 21**).
As God is just to the offender so is he with the obedient. Verse 3 has already told us that what pleases God is not bare ritual but good behaviour, described here as *righteousness* (treating others fairly) and *love* (giving God our heart's devotion, cf. Micah 6:8), not just occasionally but as our whole way of life (pursues). Those who do so he richly rewards:

(a) with long *life*, one of the main marks of God's favour under the old covenant, which under the new covenant is seen more in terms of quality of life than number of years;

(b) with *prosperity* according to NIV, although the Hebrew reads *righteousness*, which some have thought a mistaken repetition and either dropped it (as LXX does) or altered it to *prosperity*;

(c) with *honour*, which in the Old Testament means the respect of others for our character and actions, but in the New Testament means being received into God's glory, however badly treated here. God is no man's debtor but richly rewards those who are faithful to him (Rev. 2:7, 11).

Question
What is your overall reaction to this consideration of God as Judge? Can you go along with David in Psalm 58:11?

20

The Importance of Knowledge
(Proverbs 22:1-16)

This half chapter forms the end of the main section of the book – the first and longest collection of Solomon's own proverbs.

Verse 12 forms a good summary of the purpose, not just of PROVERBS but Scripture itself – **to impart** *knowledge*. The particular contribution of PROVERBS is *knowledge of how to live*. One generation passes this *knowledge* on to the next with the help of this book, indeed of the whole Bible. But that doesn't mean it is all plain sailing. All around are those who continue what the serpent began in Eden – denying God's truth and spreading lies: about God, the world and the way to live. The *unfaithful* are those who have departed from the *knowledge* and ways of God and want to draw others with them. They would succeed but that *the eyes of the Lord* which see into all hearts *keep watch over knowledge* and see that truth does not die out. This he does by *frustrating the words of the unfaithful* – demonstrating that their assertions are lies. History is a succession of false teachings which hold sway over minds for a season but ultimately prove false. Where are the pagan gods of Greece and Rome now, or the heresies of the early church? So will be the fate of those teachings which at present deceive millions.

Now follow examples of words of knowledge and of unfaithfulness.

A. THE VALUE OF RICHES.

The Scriptures never say *riches* themselves are defiled (1 Kings 3:13, 10:23). But they are not the supreme good and in God's scale of values they rate below such things as follow here.

1. A good reputation (v. 1).

This doesn't mean we should court popularity for its own sake, which can be as insecure as wealth. It does not recommend self-consciously wondering what other people think of us and trying to get them to like us, for popularity can be a snare (Luke 6:26; Gal. 1:10). It means behaving in such a way that we cannot be reproached for inconsistency in our conduct (2 Cor. 8:21; 1 Tim. 3:2, 7). This applies particularly to money; we must be seen to be honest in the way we acquire it and wise in the way we use it. As Christians we bear Christ's name and his reputation is linked with ours; people may judge him by us (Rom. 2:24; 2 Thess. 1:12). Equally, like him we may be misjudged and gain a reputation we do not deserve (John 15:18-21; 2 Cor. 6:8). If so, may we have the Spirit of him who for us 'made himself of no reputation' (Phil. 2:7, kjv).

Those who follow wisdom 'win favour and a good name' (3:4).

2. Basic humanity (vv. 2, 7, 9, 16).

We have been told twice that the *poor* are as much God's creation as the *rich* (14:31; 17:5). In those cases it was to discourage *the rich* from despising and oppressing *the poor*. Here (**v. 2**) it is so that both realize there are more important things than riches. Both are in God's image and the poorest is richer than other creatures. *The rich* should say, 'The best thing about me is not what I have but what I am.' When he looks at *the poor* he will see, not a repulsive being, but one who has the beauty of God in him. How much more if he is a Christian! 'Here is a little Christ, here is my brother.' *The poor* will say, 'I may not have money or possessions but I have a dignity that raises me above all other of God's creatures.' If he is a Christian he will say, like Paul, 'I have nothing but possess everything. I am poor but make others rich' (2 Cor. 6:10). 'The richest billionaire, if he has not Christ, has less than I. I don't envy him' (James 1:9-11).

Verse 7 shows what happens where this principle of basic equality is ignored: *the rich* enslave *the poor* by making them dependent. They have to borrow to fend off starvation but have no means of repaying the loan and have to sell themselves as *servants* or slaves (see 2 Kings 4:1; Neh. 5:4f). Our Lord used this scenario as a parable on forgiveness (Matt. 18:21-35). In our capitalist system the debt trap is still with us and while literal slavery is no longer a means of repayment, many find themselves trapped into crime or prostitution by it. In the Third World whole nations are crippled by it. Debt is avoidable where it is entered to finance luxury, but where it is for necessities it deserves consideration not the dehumanizing attitude of much capitalism.

Verse 9 shows how the rich should look on *the poor* – with 'a good eye' (as *generous man* is in Hebrew). 'The heart looks out at the eye' (Bridges), a person's character can be read in his eyes, particularly in the way he looks at one in need. The *generous man* looks kindly and lovingly, but he who has 'a bad eye' (23:6; 28:22 – 'stingy') looks harsh and unsympathetic or even avoids catching *the poor* man's eye. As is the eye so is the hand with which the *generous man* will *share his food*. This suggests he is not rich and has only enough for himself, but his sympathy moves him to break his slice of bread in half and *share his food with the poor*. It is therefore not the amount he gives but the love which motivates him for which *he will himself be blessed*. What he gives to *the poor* he gives to God, or rather 'lends' (19:17), for the Lord repays him with interest (2 Cor. 9:6-11).

Verse 16 is the ultimate in inhumanity to *the poor*. NIV sees two people here but *and* and *both* are lacking in the Hebrew. This is probably one person, perhaps the loan-shark of verse 7 extracting exorbitant interest payments from the poor and using *his increased wealth* to *give gifts to the rich*, expecting long-term returns far exceeding his original gift. If God is on the side of the poor and against their oppressors, he opposes these and ensures **they** *come to poverty*! Before we glow with self-righteous indignation, let us recall the words of Jesus in Luke 6:32-35 and 14:12-14 and ask ourselves if those to whom we are most generous are those who reciprocate our gifts or hospitality.

3. Foresight (vv. 3, 5).

(a) *In relation to life in general* (**v. 3**)
Although this verse does not mention money, sandwiched between 'riches' (v. 1) and 'wealth' (v. 4), it invites the comparison. How valuable is foresight! It is easy to *see danger* when it's happening, but it takes *a prudent man* to see it coming and take evasive action. The expression *keep going* may mean the *danger* is evident but *the simple* refuses to face up to it. So the *prudence* in view here is not so much intellectual as moral. Both may be aware of impending *danger*, but one is guided by what is right and good, and the other by his own wishes. One takes *danger* seriously, the other makes light of it. So the prudence lies in the will and attitude. The gospel principle is: people can be warned to 'flee from the wrath to come' but a work of grace is needed to cause them to change their life-style to escape it and find *refuge*.

(b) *In relation to wickedness* (**v. 5**).
In addition to the troubles that may befall any of us, *the wicked* has some of his own. He is like someone who has taken a wrong *path*, not designed for the use of humans, in which the *thorns* have not been cut down, and worse – *snares* have been placed because this is forbidden territory. *Wickedness* was not the way intended for man; it leads him into entanglements from which it is difficult to extricate himself. What is more, God has put it out of bounds; sin is 'transgression', crossing the border between right and wrong. So to take that road invites his judgment. If you value your life *guard your soul*, 'shun evil' (3:7) and God 'will make your paths straight' (3:6).

4. Spirituality (v. 4).
Although the foregoing verses show that spiritual virtues are better than material gain, this doesn't mean they are opposites. We don't have to choose between them, as the ascetic holds. If we truly honour God he will give us sufficient *wealth*, a good name (*honour*) and a full *life*, long or short (cf. 3:16; 10:27; Matt. 6:33). Honouring God is a combination of *humility and the fear of the Lord*: in our eyes we are lowly and he is great;

the more we think of him the less we think of ourselves. This is not despising ourselves, for we realize how highly he thinks of us and how greatly he loves us, for he gave us his Son and beautifies us with his righteousness. This transforms our outlook on the world so that we look for and find *wealth, honour and life* in a different way. This is the principle behind the Beatitudes: the truly 'happy' are those who possess 'the kingdom' or 'the earth'. Who are they? The 'poor in spirit', 'the meek' (Matt. 5:3-5).

Question. Can you think of anything else which should come above riches in your scale of values?

B. EDUCATION OF CHILDREN (vv. 6, 15).
This lies at the heart of PROVERBS and cannot begin too soon.

1. The Need.
(a) *The child* himself needs it because as a child he is ignorant and has no means of acquiring knowledge unless he is taught it, or of learning good behaviour unless he is shown it. He is also in a state of *folly* which because of inborn sin is *bound in his heart*. He needs no instruction in how to be silly or disobedient! He has to be trained out of it. So his whole life may depend on the way he begins: 'start' is an alternative translation, meaning 'point in the right direction'.

(b) *The community* needs its children educated or its acquired wisdom and skill will die out and that community will decline.

(c) *The church* needs its young taught lest the gospel disappear from the earth.

2. The Method.
The way he should go means 'appropriate to his nature'. A *child* needs educating in accordance with his stage of development. The word for *train* later became used for 'catechise' because this is appropriate for young children who lack understanding but have great powers of retention. They also need simple rules about things they don't understand: that fire burns,

knives cut, cats scratch. If they break these they need *the rod of discipline*, which may be corporal if it is administered in love, for the child's sake, not to work off the parents' anger.

3. The Result.

In the short term he will mature as the *folly* is *driven far from him*. In the longer term he will stay on track all through his life. 'The child is father of the man' (Wordsworth). There are exceptions, but this is the norm. If a child is not *trained*, he is almost certain to grow up ignorant, foolish and ungodly. If he is *trained*, there is every hope of success.

Question. What particular follies do you think today's children are most prone to and how can they best be countered?

C. KEEPING COMPANY.

1. Whom to avoid.

(a) *The Scorner* **(v. 10)**. Divisions and disputes in families, churches and societies arise from different causes and are dealt with accordingly. The cause here is a very common one but less commonly diagnosed – the person with the attitude problem, *the mocker*. He hasn't a genuine grievance, there is no false teaching or unjust treatment to complain of; he simply stirs up *quarrels* and trades *insults*. Such people cannot be reasoned with or even warned. The trouble lies in their attitude and until they can see it in themselves they will not change and the *strife* will go on. Peace and unity are so essential in a church or community that a company cannot afford to wait for self-knowledge to dawn. He must be avoided. This is what Abraham had to do with Ishmael (Gen. 21:9f) and what Paul, taking his cue from that situation, advised the Galatians to do with the legalisers (Gal. 4:21-31). This procedure is authorised by the church's head (Matt. 18:17).

(b) *The Slothful* **(v. 13)**. Here is a man whose place of work is not on his own property but *outside*, out of town, in the fields, perhaps a farm worker, shepherd or goatherd. He foresees two problems: there may be *a lion* lurking in the fields or robbers lurking in the streets along which he has to pass to reach the fields. These fears are not as unreal as they sound to us. There were lions abroad in those times (1 Sam. 17:34), and that gangs of robbers roamed the streets is evident from 1:10-19 where the pupil is warned off joining them. But the chance of these happening to a man on his way to work was small, and there were ways of protecting oneself against them. The real problem is laziness, which we are repeatedly warned against in this book. The most deadly excuses are the plausible ones, for by these our deceitful hearts are easily convinced. This applies in the Christian life: God calls to obedience and service, and we reply, 'It's too difficult, and I am inadequate.'

(c) *The Harlot* **(v. 14)**. This is the first reference in this section (10:1–22:16) to a subject which dominated the Prologue, but it wouldn't be complete without a mention. Every time sexual sin is spoken of, the temptation begins with *the mouth* (2:16; 5:3; 6:24; 7:5). It is her voice and the words she speaks that first arouse lust. Once these are received the rest follows – they are the push into the *deep pit*. This is more than falling into a sin, for it leads to a deeper pit (2:18), which is why we are told it is the fate of those who are *under the Lord's wrath*. If we deliberately refuse the call of Christ in order to follow our own desires God won't strike us dead on the spot but 'give us up' to our own way, so that we bring his judgment on our own heads (Ps. 81:12; Rom. 1:24). Of ourselves we lack the will and power to resist strong temptation, particularly to sexual lust. We first need to be in fellowship with God, for 'the man who pleases God will escape her' (Eccles. 7:26).

2. Whom to choose: the person of integrity (v. 11).

Here we have the exact opposite to him of verse 10. He promotes justice and peace to such an extent that he even finds favour with *the king*, who may use him in local or national affairs. Far from stirring up quarrels and trading insults his *speech is gracious*, an indispensible requirement of one who has to represent *the king*. Nor is this mere affectation or professional tact – it comes from his *heart*, which is *pure*, free from that negative haughty attitude which marked 'the mocker'. How has he become like this? Not naturally, for to say he *loves a pure heart* means it has been cleansed of pride and selfishness and given the grace of sincerity. We needn't take this as Lesson 1 in 'How to get into politics'. Few rise to the top of the tree, but we are all to emulate this one rather than 'the mocker'.

Think it over. Turn the subject on its head and ask youself how good a friend and companion you make to someone else.

Concluding thought: the God who is for 'knowledge' and against 'unfaithfulness' will right all wrongs (**v. 8**).

An agricultural society would quickly get the picture here. The lives of these people were a cycle of sowing and reaping, which was as regular as the seasons. Just as certain is it that every act has its consequences. This is said to comfort the oppressed and warn the oppressor, for the *wickedness* here is that of cruel and unjust tyranny (*the rod of his fury*). Oppression may be political but here it is economic (v. 7). Tyranny has immediate and dire consequences for the oppressed, but let them not despair – in the long term it has worse consequences for the oppressor, who is *destroyed*. In this way Isaiah encouraged his contemporaries who faced the *fury* of Assyria. At first she was the *rod* of God's anger (Isa. 10:5), but having used her to chastise his people God would destroy his rod: 'Woe to the Assyrian', 'the voice of the Lord will shatter Assyria' (Isa. 30:31). 'The Judge of all the earth' does not tolerate injustice for ever.

The Sayings of The Wise
(Proverbs 22:17–24:34)

This section may be an edited version of 'The Sayings of Amenemope', an Egyptian book of wisdom in thirty chapters (cf. thirty sayings in 22:20). This plus 'The Sayings of Agur' (ch. 30) and 'The Sayings of Lemuel' (ch. 31) comprise 'The sayings and riddles of the wise' the editor said in 1:6 he would use. References to 'the Lord' are therefore editorial additions to a pagan book. Like the Prologue the style is more continuous than 'Solomon's Proverbs'.

21

The Values of Wisdom
(Proverbs 22:17–24:34)

The change from the proverbial style is immediate and apparent (**v. 17**): *pay attention ... listen ... apply your heart*. This speaks more directly from teacher to pupil – exhortation rather than observation. It is an example: (1) *to preachers* to speak more directly to their hearers, with less explanation and more exhortation; (2) *to hearers* to *pay attention* in the sense of *applying* the *heart* to what they hear, that is, taking God's message to *heart* and working it out in their lives. The following description of 'Wisdom's Values' is an encouragement to do this.

1. Wisdom will give you pleasure (v. 18).
The popular view is that hearing the Word of God is dull hard duty; but if you taste it you will find it *pleasant* (2:10, 3:15), sweet as honey (24:13f, Ps. 19:10). To do this you must let the words enter *your heart* (= 'belly'), for like food they need inwardly digesting to become part of your whole view and way of life. Then you will *keep* or 'remember' them (GNB) and speak of or 'quote' (GNB) them. You won't have to go away and look them up, they will be *ready on your lips* because they are in your mind.

2. Wisdom will encourage your faith (v. 19).
The Word of God calls for more than listening, considering, remembering and reciting. Primarily it is for believing, which

is more than believing what it says; it is believing the one from whom it has come – putting *your trust ... in the Lord*. This call to faith is immediate – *today* and personal – *even you*.

3. Wisdom will equip you for teaching (vv. 20-21).
Verse 20a may refer to the 30 chapters of the Egyptian book, although only GNB divides it into 30 actual *sayings*. However, others take the Hebrew word more literally – 'the third day' or 'the day before yesterday', meaning 'formerly' (NIV mg). This balances 'today' (v. 19): what he is teaching 'today' in the hearing of his pupil he has already written down for him (as Paul wrote down things he had already preached, 2 Thess. 2:5). There has been no change in the *counsel* he is offering – it is unchanging and will guide him 'today' as it did before. This gives the assurance that they are *true and reliable words*. For the pupil is evidently being taught so that he in turn can teach others. His preparation for this work is to be able to *give sound answers* to *him who sent him* to receive instruction and who may be sponsoring him. He will need to be examined and if he gives correct answers he will be on the way to becoming a teacher himself.

Reflect on: how Jesus prepared his disciples to become teachers (e.g. Matt. 16:13-19; Acts 1:3-8); how Paul prepared such as Timothy and Titus for teaching, and for training other teachers (e.g. 2 Tim. 2:1-7).

4. Wisdom will win you promotion (v. 29).
Wisdom includes learning to use ability and time diligently: *skilled* combines the ideas of talent, understanding and careful painstaking *work*. Both question and answer indicate the rarity of this combination: *Do you see...?* has the sense of 'you'll be hard put to it to find one!' This is why he is soon promoted from working for *obscure men* to *serving kings*. It was in this way that such as Joseph and Daniel came to the ears of their respective monarchs. PROVERBS frequently commends diligence as the way of the wise (10:4, 12:24) and denounces sloth as the way of the fool.

Reflect on how diligent service of Christ (Rom. 12:11) is noticed and commended by him (Matt. 25:14-25, 34-36).

B. THE PROHIBITIONS OF WISDOM (22:22-28).

Wisdom has its negative aspects, for its principal part is the fear of God who hates evil. Here are some of his chief aversions.

1. Oppressing the poor (vv. 22-23).

There is more than one detestable evil here: a) to rob (*plunder*) anyone is wrong; b) to rob *the poor* is to fail in the duty of providing for him; c) to *exploit the poor because they are poor* is to rob those who can least afford it, to deprive them not of luxuries but bare necessities. It is also a sin of injustice – aggravated by the inability of *the poor* to find anyone to speak for them *in court*. Since there were no lawyers in our sense of the word, this depicts a situation in which everyone was afraid to go against the rich oppressor lest he crush them too.

The appeal however is not so much to justice as to self-interest. *The poor* have a 'Defender' (23:11) more powerful than any friend or lawyer – *the Lord* himself whom the Scriptures everywhere assert to be on the side of *the poor and needy* (Ps. 68:5). *The Lord's* defence is not by words *in court* but practical action. Those who seek to 'deprive them of their livelihood' (NEB) he will 'deprive of their life' (RV, RSV). While it may seem such a warning applied only to a few, we have to remember that Israel was *plundered* by the Babylonians for this very sin (Ezek. 22:29-31). It is also intended as an encouragement to the vulnerable themselves, that they need not fear their oppressors.

Question
Few Christians today will be *plundering the poor* or find themselves unrepresented *in court*, so how does this apply today?

2. Befriending an angry man (vv. 24-25).

'The Proverbs of Solomon' warned us against both bad temper (14:16f, 15:18) and bad company (1:10-19, 13:20b). Here the two are brought together: *do not associate with a hot-tempered man, one easily angered*. We have been told that the bad-tempered are fools (14:17); here we are told that those who *make friends with* them share their folly. We easily make role models of those we keep company with, albeit unconsciously, and *learn their ways*. If their influence is bad it may corrupt us: 'bad company corrupts good character' (1 Cor. 15:33). **We** shall lose control of **our** temper. Worse, we shall share in the evil consequences of their behaviour and *get* ourselves *ensnared*, for 'a companion of fools suffers harm' (13:20). Bad temper 'stirs' up dissension (15:18) – exchanging insults, fighting, causing damage, committing crimes. The first lesson the parents gave the young son about to go into the world was to keep away from the local gang or he would commit their crimes and share their punishment (1:10-19).

Question
As a child were you guided about choice of friends and role models? If you have children, do you give them guidance?

3. Securing another's debt (vv. 26-27).
The bad-tempered are not the only ones to avoid becoming too friendly with. There are also those who want you to underwrite their debts. This does not refer to the poor, whom others have a responsibility to feed (v. 9) and if necessary to pay off their debts. It describes a request to secure a debt before it is undertaken, when the matter can still be looked into and advice given. That is the time to face up to all the implications, especially whether the debt is honourable and whether you can pay it if required. NIV follows LXX in making verse 27b a statement whereas in Hebrew it is a question: *Why should your very bed be snatched from under you?*, for it is such questions that need to be faced before *putting up security*. It was legal to take a garment (which doubled up as a *bed*) as a pledge (Exod. 22:26f), which means that one who takes over another's debt may lose his own garment or *bed* (cf. 27:13). See also comments on 6:1-5, 11:15, 17:18, 20:16.

Question: As Christians, how far do our financial responsibilities extend? Do you think the New Testament, with its appeals for sacrificial generosity and trust in God for our needs, alters the teaching of PROVERBS? See Galatians 6 and compare verse 2 with verse 5.

4. Invading property rights (v. 28).
When the promised land was divided among the twelve tribes, each tribe probably subdivided it among the families, which explains *ancient* and *forefathers*. Once allotted it was to remain in that family (Lev. 25:23ff); the law made it inalienable and God protected it (15:25, 23:10f). To encroach on this entailed his 'curse' (Deut. 27:17), from which the king himself was not exempt, as Ahab found when he took over Naboth's vineyard (1 Kings 21:19). The *boundary* of the land was marked by a *stone* so that ignorance was no excuse for encroaching on another's land. But the land-grabber would *move* or 'push back' the *stone* in order to enlarge his property, especially if he thought the owner too weak to prevent it – a situation possibly included in verses 22f. But such reckoned without God, the protector of both the poor and his own laws.

Question: Can you think of more subtle ways in which property rights might be infringed today? Are the ancient creeds and confessions like *boundary stones* defining the truth? Are Christians who alter them doing what land-grabbers did in Israel?

C. The Warnings of Wisdom (23:1-11).

1. Against love of luxury (vv. 1-3).
This passage is capable of different interpretations. It may simply be a lesson in table manners to the son of a middle or upper class family just beginning the social round. In this case the marginal reading of v. 1 is preferable: *note well* **who** *is before you* and behave accordingly – with restraint (v. 2) and even nonchalance (v. 3), as if you were used to rich food. Don't think eating with the great guarantees promotion. Attending the Queen's Garden Party doesn't confer a knighthood! *Deceptive* may have a more sinister meaning, warning that the rich and great employ their wealth to make lesser mortals dependent

so that they can use them to further their own ends. Daniel is a good example of how to resist this (Dan. 1:5, 8). Deliberate social climbing is to be avoided (Luke 14:7-14); it is a greasy pole – *deceptive*.

More likely it is a simple warning against love of luxury. Here is a hypothetical situation: imagine you are sitting with a *ruler* who loads his table with *delicacies*, rich *food* that is new to you. Don't be dazzled by it – *note well what is before you*, that it is only 'food for the stomach' which 'God will destroy' (1 Cor. 6:13); it has no lasting value. To acquire a taste for *delicacies* with all their expense is *deceptive*, it promises more than it can perform. Luxury can ensnare you if you're not careful and drive you to *gluttony*. But the temptation is strong and to resist it you must be ruthless: *put a knife to your throat* – threaten your appetite with death. This is the self-discipline Jesus advised in resisting strong temptation in Matthew 18:8f, cf. 1 Corinthians 9:24.

Question
Does this mean luxuries are altogether forbidden to the Christian? Where is the balance between self-denial and self-indulgence? See John 6:27, 1 Timothy 4:3-5, 6:17.

2. Against covetousness (vv. 4-5).
This warning follows the first well. Luxury needs financing, and *riches* have to be worked for. Although 'the Proverbs of Solomon' only condemn dishonest wealth and see *riches* as God's blessing on diligent effort, this saying is not necessarily contradictory. For one thing the aim in view is not to provide for the family and help the poor but to finance a life of luxury. For another, the effort put into this is excessive – *do not wear yourself out* is more than industry, it is obsession. *Wisdom* teaches you to *restrain* this impulse, as it does with regard to luxury (v. 2). Self-control is one of the benefits of acquiring *wisdom* (17:27f).

Again the basis of the warning is the long-term consequences. You may spend years accumulating wealth only to see them vanish before your very eyes: *cast but a glance and they are gone*. The closing metaphor is apt and poignant. The nest-egg you have laid with such trouble hatches out, *sprouts wings* and disappears into *the sky like an eagle*, never to be seen again, gone where you can't recover it (21:17, 20; cf. Matt. 6:19; Luke 12:15-21; James 5:4-6).

Contrast the good and permanent use to which wealth can be put when acquired through trust in God and blessed by him: 3:9f; 13:8, 11, 22; 15:6; 22:7, 9; 2 Cor. 9:6-11.

3. Against meanness (vv. 6-8).
There are some textual problems here: whether 'one with an evil eye' (6a) means *stingy* or malicious; and whether line 2 of verse 7 is, 'as he thinks within himself' (mg), or, *always thinking about the cost*. If he is a malicious man then whatever *delicacies* he lays on and however much he urges you to *eat and drink*, he is still hating you in *his heart* and hoping his food will choke you. If he is a *stingy man, his heart* is calculating how much of his money goes down with each mouthful, rather than how much you are enjoying it. It is not essential to choose between the two. The point is that meals are acts of fellowship and the host's feelings towards the guests are more important than the cordon bleu. The atmosphere in which the meal is eaten should be better even than the food (15:17). This is why when the guest realizes what his host actually feels towards him (v. 8) he will be emotionally if not physically ill. He will *vomit up* the *compliments* he paid his host for his excellent cuisine and the gratitude he expressed for the invitation. It is better to excuse yourself and *not eat the food of* one known to be a *stingy man*.

Consider yourself as a host(ess). What do you feel and think as the dishes on which you have lavished such expense, time and trouble disappear? See Romans 12:13 and 1 Peter 4:9, noting 'without grumbling' (or 'grudging').

4. Against indiscriminate counsel (v. 9).
Here is another though very different means of wasting words – giving advice (*wisdom*) to *a fool*. *To* is literally 'in the ears of', directly addressing him personally, not as one of a crowd, and doing so seriously and earnestly, then finding your words

thrown back in your face, *wisdom* answered with *scorn*. Solomon himself warned against this and its consequence: 'Whoever corrects a mocker invites insult; whoever rebukes a wicked man incurs abuse' (9:7). Our Lord's words in Matthew 7:6 are similar but more powerful, with their metaphors of what pigs and dogs do if you don't give them the food they like. But how are we to know before we speak what reaction we shall get? Only by experience. Is the person one who makes a joke of everything or resents any suggestions? This implies we shouldn't take it on ourselves to advise perfect strangers, but first get to know something of the character of those we speak to.

Question

How does this apply to the indiscriminate preaching of the gospel? Is it necessary that our hearers are in a right frame of mind or that we know what that frame is? Consider Paul's reception from the Athenians (Acts 17:32) and his comments in 1 Corinthians 1:22f, 4:10.

5. Against exploiting the weak (vv. 10-11).

The prohibition on this practice in 22:28 was general and universal. This is repeated here with special reference to *the fields of the fatherless*, that is, those who had no one to support or protect them or take up their cause, such as a young person with no experience who has not yet gained the respect of the community. It would be easy to take advantage of such and for a neighbour to *encroach* on his property by moving his *boundary stone* a few yards. But these allotments were of *ancient* date (see on 22:28) and came under God's supervision. One who had none to take his part came under the direct protection of God. As *Defender* or 'Redeemer' he played the part of the next of kin and guarded their land for them (Lev. 25:25, Ruth 3:12f, 4:1ff). If the dispute came before the magistrate God himself would 'take up their case' (22:23). Since he was *strong* the effect on the exploiter could be devastating (15:25, Exod. 22:22-24). This assurance was needed by the whole nation when their God-given land was seized by the Babylonians – and it was forthcoming (Jer. 50:33f).

Application. Are you being taken advantage of, exploited, with no redress? Find strength in the promise of God (Ps. 12:5). We are all vulnerable before Satan's attempts to get God to cast us away (Job 1:9-11). But like Job (16:19-21, 19:25-27) we have an advocate who pleads his own righteousness (Rom. 8:33f, 1 John 2:1f).

D. THE COUNSELS OF WISDOM (23:12-35).

These are more positive than the Prohibitions and Warnings, even though many are expressed in the negative: 'do not'.

Verse 12 is introductory and recalls the way virtually every section of the Prologue (chs. 1–9) began – with a call to 'pay attention' to what is about to be taught (e.g. 1:8, 2:1, 3:1, 4:1, 5:1, 6:20, 7:1, 8:1-6). It also prefaced the 'Sayings of the Wise' (22:17). This emphasises the importance to the child or pupil of these counsels and reminds us of our natural disinclination for moral or spiritual instruction. This is why our first need is to get ourselves into the right frame of mind: *apply your heart*, literally 'bring your heart in', call it back from whatever it is preoccupied with, stir up a desire to learn what wisdom has to say. You can smoke passively but you can't learn passively! There is little value in *your ears* hearing *words of knowledge* if *your heart* isn't in it. These counsels are not just facts to be examined on but practical duties to be carried out.

1. Parental discipline (vv. 13-14).

Whereas verse 12 was addressed to the child, this is for the parent. Whatever the explanation, it indicates that parents themselves need counselling in parenting. So far we have had two admonitions to use *the rod* of correction (13:24, 22:15) and one reference to the possibility of *death* if it is withheld (19:18). Here the two are brought together in the most powerful statement on the subject in the whole book. The parent is told (**v. 13**) *not* to *withhold* corporal *punishment* through fear the child *will die* under it, and encouraged to use *the rod*; there is no *if*, it reads 'you shall punish'. **Verse 14** goes further to say that in fact this is the only way to save him *from death*, which here means spiritual death, the fate of those who refuse instruction. For further discussion see comments on the verses referred to above.

Further study. The New Testament says little about parental discipline, but more on self-discipline (1 Cor. 11:32), divine discipline (Heb. 12:5-11) and church discipline (1 Cor. 5:5).

2. Parental happiness:

(a) *in early days* (**vv. 15-16***).*
Solomon's own proverbs began with this thought: that the happiness of those parents who teach their children the wisdom, or Word of God, is bound up with the way their children respond to it (10:1, cf. 15:20, 27:11, 29:3). A godly parent will enjoy seeing his child growing up strong, healthy and good-looking; getting on well at school, making good friends and exhibiting useful talents. But his supreme joy will be the discovery that his *heart is wise*, that he has done what verse 12 says and that the discipline of verses 13-14 has worked. How will he know? One way will be that the things he *speaks are right*. The connection between what *the heart* thinks and what *the lips speak* is also strong in PROVERBS (15:28, 16:23, 22:17f). This means not only that he doesn't tell lies but that he repeats the lessons he has learned, the truths of God's Word, not like a parrot but from the heart. Like the angels of heaven, the parent *will rejoice* from his *inmost being* when he hears him confess a personal faith in the Lord.

Apply this principle to those who teach their church members (1 Thess. 3:6-10, 2 John 4, 3 John 3f).

(b) *in old age* (**vv. 22-25***).*
This is not the parent speaking but the sage addressing the son about his duty to his parents. For when they are old parents do not have the same authority as they once did; they look to their children not so much for obedience as respect, put here negatively: *do not despise*, meaning highly regard. Their children should listen, not for their 'do's and don'ts' but for what their long experience of life has taught them. Their children may now have more knowledge and skill than their parents ever had, but there are lessons which can only be learned from living into old age. Let them remember that

though they may now have children of their own, their parents still love them as those to whom they gave life, which is how the passage begins (22a) and ends (25b). This love gives them a special claim on their children's attention.

Grown-up children who truly respect their parents will want to see them happy in their old age (v. 25) which is not a pious wish (*May...!*) but an exhortation to take pains to ensure their happiness: 'Make your father and mother proud of you; give your mother that happiness' (GNB). How can they best do this? Not just by seeing they are comfortable and provided for materially, important as that is, but that they themselves still continue in the way their parents taught them – the way of *truth, wisdom and righteousness*. They should appreciate the value of this even more now than they did as children (v. 23). *Buy* it means spare no effort, time and trouble to know *the truth* and live by it (Job 28:15-19). *Do not sell it* means value it so highly that nothing equals it, and to exchange it for anything would be loss (Matt. 16:26). This will give your aged parents more *joy* than all the home comforts even our modern age can purchase.

Pray for those elderly Christians whose children have disappointed them because, although they may have achieved worldly success, they have turned from the way their parents taught them (22:6).

3. Curing envy (vv. 17-18).

The lack of a verb in **verse 17** line 2 ('but only in the fear of the LORD all day') may mean that the word *envy* governs both clauses. It is saying: that consuming obsession (*envy*) with what sinners achieve by dubious methods, plus their freedom from the afflictions which befall the righteous – let it be directed towards cultivating a right attitude to *the Lord*; be obsessed with him, let zeal for his glory consume you. Then you will accept your lot gladly as his good will, count his blessings, trust his promises, rely on his power, and do this 'all day and every day'. Then your *envy* of *sinners* will turn into *hope* for yourself. When you compare yourself with the *sinner*, you tend to feel there is no *future* for you. In fact it is **he** who has no *future*, for his end is to be *cut off*, as David realized when he struggled with this problem in Psalm 37 (especially verses 1f, 37f). This *future hope* is probably not life after death, although this is true, but a good prospect in this life, which is the subject of this verse.

Question
Is there anyone you envy? Try to analyse your feelings: Is there a perverted or grudging admiration for him or her; personal resentment against him or her; discontentment with your own life due to covetousness? Can you look at Christ crucified and still feel like this?

4. Avoiding excess (vv. 19-21).
We have had warnings against gluttony, drunkenness, bad company and sloth. Here all are brought together, which may account for the opening appeal (**v. 19**). This in itself combines four familiar calls: pay attention, acquire wisdom, take it to *heart* and apply it to your life. This spiritual discipline is essential in view of the dangers from corrupt society. People who eat and drink well are often sociable and free with invitations to their cocktail and dinner parties. But if 'their god is their stomach' (Phil. 3:19) you are in danger of being sucked into the cult of excess. *Wine* and *meat* are both gifts of God all are free to enjoy, but in moderation, lest they master us and we come to live for them (1 Cor. 6:12f). This will not only destroy our spiritual life but have a disastrous effect on our whole being. If the weekend is 'lost' at wild parties, Monday is also lost recovering from the hangover. If this happens regularly it will breed a lazy attitude, then the job may be lost or the business ruined, and the end result – poverty. If this was a danger in ancient Israel where this teaching was known and believed, how much more in our secular society where it is not!

Question
How would you relate this to the reputation Christ had (Matt. 11:19) which he did not deny but rather gloried in (Luke 15:1)?

5. Avoiding immorality (vv. 26-28).

The way of wisdom is the best defence against the temptations of the flesh. As it guards from the dangers of social eating and drinking (vv. 19-21), so does it against that even deadlier peril – promiscuous sex (2:16-19). Although **verse 26** is often taken as God's call for our love, there seems no reason for giving it a meaning different from verses 19 and 22. *Heart* does not mean 'love' but mind and will, and so is similar to verse 19, that is, a further appeal to listen to his teaching in order to learn good behaviour. *Keep to my ways* is like 'keep on the right path' (v. 19), but with the further idea of making the father his example: 'Do as I do, not only as I say.'

The dangers of promiscuous sex here are threefold:

(a) it is irreversible, like falling into a *deep pit* or *narrow well* from which you cannot extricate yourself. Sex is a commitment which gives another a hold over you (1 Cor. 6:16);

(b) it is clandestine – like robbery it is done secretly and privately, and like robbery it deprives you of your substance. The only love in the prostitute is love of money – your money.

(c) it is infectious; being an act of *unfaithfulness* it involves treachery, deceit and lies all round.

Question

Are we good examples to our children or pupils in this area? Can we say 1 Corinthians 4:16, 11:1?

6. Concerning drunkenness (vv. 29-35).

Verses 19-21 warned against the dangers of social eating and drinking. Because the latter is the worse of the two it is given separate and more powerful treatment. Although it contains a dehortation (*Do not*, **v. 31**), it mainly uses the device of painting a picture of one who has become enslaved to drink. It intensifies its force with some searching questions (**v. 29**). Something has to be done to arouse the fool from his drunken torpor, make him face up to his decadence and think where it is leading. What real pleasure does he derive from this habit? Isn't it negated by the sorrow which makes him cry *Woe!* in his more lucid moments? Doesn't he utter more complaints than thanks? Hasn't he good reason for this when his uncontrolled state involves him in *strife*, from which he gets *bruises* and *bloodshot eyes*?

Let the drunkard use this as a mirror to take a hard look at himself. Let him see how he has got into this state: by spending most of his time with a bottle of wine by his side (**v. 30a**), *lingering* over his lunch and dinner and continuing late into the night, always looking for something stronger – *mixed wine* was spiced to increase its potency. He is totally addicted (**v. 31**): even its colour fascinates him, as does the way it *sparkles* when you pour it into *the cup*; then there is that delicious feeling *when it goes down smoothly*. He is so absorbed in present pleasure he gives no thought to or doesn't take seriously what will be *the end* of his carousing (**v. 32**). The illustration of a *snake bite* is chosen because it is both painful and poisonous: the hangover is painful and the system is being poisoned, with the disastrous effects described in verses 33-35. Here is one who appears to be in a state of delirium tremens (**v. 33**): he is shaking while half-asleep (**v. 34**), like one tossed about on a ship at sea, in fact as if *sleeping on top of the rigging*, where the motion of the boat is most violent. He also has the evidence in his flesh of the beating up he had in the drunken brawl (**v. 35**, cf. v. 29), yet the alcohol has so anaesthetised him he can't feel a thing! All he can *feel* is his thirst for *another drink*, which is there sleeping or waking, even when the bad dream is on. Alcoholism is not a modern problem, but this tactic is an old-fashioned solution!

Compare this passage with Psalm 104:15, John 2:1-10 and 1 Timothy 5:23. How can we fulfil those words without falling into the condition described here?

Chapter 24: Further Warnings and Counsels.

A. Warnings.

1. Against envying the wicked (vv. 1-2, 19-20).

On this warning against being drawn into the *company* of *wicked men* through *envy* see also 1:11-15, 3:31f, 23:17. This passage adds to the previous points the two chief reasons against *envy*.

(a) *The character and behaviour of the wicked* (**vv. 1-2**).
These are not men who occasionally get into *trouble* but are (literally) 'men of evil' – they and evil are inseparable. There always have been and still are people who seem incapable of doing anything important except what is wrong and harmful. It is in their very *hearts* which are always devising schemes which cannot be carried out without the use of *violence* (6:14). The believer is committed to saving and helping people, but if he attaches himself to *wicked men* he participates in or at least tacitly approves their actions. Even their conversation is all about their schemes (v. 2b), and merely to take part in this implicates a person. If *envy* was enough to make someone seek *their company*, it is likely to make him go along with the *plot*. In any case *wicked men* are not likely to let someone go away with their secrets unless he is committed to them; he must either join the operation or risk being silenced by the conspirators. It is best to deal with the *envy* before it reaches this entanglement.

(b) *Their future* (**vv. 19-20**).
Verse 19b probes a little deeper into the psychology of the righteous person's *envy of the wicked* by using the word *fret*, which means burn in anger (see Ps. 37:8). It shows how this dangerous entanglement with evildoers can begin in a commendable way – with a righteous indignation that they are enjoying the rewards of their *wicked* schemes and violent acts with apparent impunity. Their *lamp* is shining brightly while many righteous are struggling to keep theirs alight. Isn't this anger justified? But reflect a moment, you who believe God is in charge. Is your anger not really against him who has permitted this situation in his wisdom? It must therefore be a wrong indignation and if not suppressed will quickly lead to the jealousy which will ultimately take you into their company as a partner in their schemes. So look ahead to the *future*: what *hope* has the *evil man*? God is eternal and his righteousness will only be fully revealed when everything is wound up. 'Judge

nothing before the time ...' (see 1 Corinthians 4:5). Their *lamp*
has no oil and will fail them at the crucial time (Matt. 25:8).
Yours might seem to be flickering, but when he comes it will
burn brightly and you will go out to meet him (Matt. 25:6,
cf. Prov. 23:17f)

Question
Does this help you cope with your anger against the tyrants of
this world who swell their Swiss bank accounts while allowing
their people to struggle in grinding poverty?

2. Against folly (v. 7).
You become wise in the Biblical sense not by going on a course
of study but by undergoing a change of heart: from unbelief
(Ps. 14:1) to trustful love (1:7). A fool is unwilling for this
change and so puts *wisdom* out of his reach: *too high* is elsewhere
translated 'coral', very difficult to obtain and therefore very
expensive. So however hard or far he seeks *wisdom* (14:6, 17:24)
he will be unsuccessful. It consists primarily in the knowledge
of God for which in his natural state he is unfit (Ps. 92:5f). The
New Testament puts us all in this category for it says that all
who are unregenerate find the things of the Spirit foolishness
(1 Cor. 2:14). This is why the *fool* is unable to make a useful
contribution to public affairs. He may have much to say among
other fools (12:23, 15:2, 18:6f) but *in the assembly at the gate*
where serious discussions take place and the courts are held
he has nothing to say of any value. Thank God that through the
gospel fools are 'made wise' (2 Tim. 3:15), for 'Christ becomes
for us wisdom from God' (1 Cor. 1:30). Those in him are wise
and have something worthwhile to say.

Question
Does this mean that only Christians make good magistrates,
politicians and advisers?

3. Against scheming (vv. 8-9).
A lot of name-calling to put into two verses! *Schemer*, 'fool'
(better than *folly*) and *mocker*. This is the 'fool' of verse 7 in the
advanced stage of his *folly*: the dumb ass has become a real

troublemaker. Far from making a helpful contribution to society he *plots evil* against it. His *schemes* are denounced as *sin*, for they are intended to harm: spreading lies to destroy another's reputation (Isa. 32:7), fomenting quarrels (6:14, 29:8) or even plotting acts of violence (v. 2). He himself has the double-denunciation of *schemer* and *mocker*, for he not only *plots* secretly against people but openly abuses them. The expression *will be known* probably refers to his being publicly named, so that people will be on guard against him. This is not officiousness on the part of the authorities but carries popular support: *men detest a mocker*. As 22:10 says, the only way to maintain or restore peace and unity when such are abroad is to dissociate from them.

Question
We don't have the authority to ban people from *society*, but can you apply this to a church fellowship? cf. 22:10.

4. Against taking advantage (vv. 15-16).
In 1:10-19 the child or pupil was warned against joining a gang which 'lies in wait for someone's blood'. The warning here is against housebreaking and burglary rather than violence against the person, looking for an opportunity to break in when he is absent or off guard. What has to be remembered is that God's personal protection of the *righteous* applies not only to their person but their property. See Job 5:18-26 from which the words *seven times* are quoted. However often the house is burgled or even destroyed it will be restored. The justice of God sees to it that wrongs are righted and wrongdoers punished, in the long, if not the short, term. This may be of some encouragement to harmless Christians who suffer loss from thieves in these crime-ridden days. However, we should take the warning personally too, for we may be working indirectly for another's downfall even without physically touching them or their property.

Self-examination. Have you ever taken or are you taking advantage of someone's weakness or defencelessness for your own gain?

5. Against gloating (vv. 17-18).

This pair of verses follows naturally from the previous pair; even some of the verbs of verse 16 are repeated: *falls* and *stumbles* (translated 'brought down' in verse 16 by NIV). But it takes up verse 16b rather than the earlier part. Whereas the 'righteous' are promised recovery, 'the wicked' are given no such hope. But that does not mean that the 'righteous' who 'rise again' may *gloat* over their fall (see on 17:5b). To do this makes you just like *your enemy*, who probably *gloated* when he brought you down, and so arouses God's *disapproval* of you. This may apply either to personal enemies or national. Sometimes Israel fell under God's judgment at the hands of heathen nations; but when these *gloated* God turned the tables (Lam. 4:21f, Zech. 1:15f). This may be hyperbole, since *gloating* seems a far less serious sin than enmity against the people of God. But it shows God expects a higher standard from his own people than from his and their *enemies*. He particularly deplores bad attitudes, a lack of sympathy – something in which his people should differ from others.

Question
What is Christ's way of curing this bad feeling which can easily enter the heart of a Christian? See Matthew 5:43-48 (cf. 1 Cor. 13:6). Notice in Matthew 5:11-12 that what makes the Christian rejoice is the exact opposite of *gloating*.

6. Against rebelliousness (vv. 21-22).

There are a couple of textual problems here. In **verse 21b** is it *rebellious* (literally 'those who change') or 'those of rank' (cf. NEB)? They may come to the same thing, for 'those of rank' may be the ones agitating for 'change', like Korah and company in Numbers 16, Absalom in 2 Samuel 15 and the English barons in the time of King John. The other problem is with **verse 22b**, which reads literally, 'Who knows the ruin of both of them?', which sounds as if the revolt is successful and both God and king are overthrown! NIV evades the problem by transferring 'both' to **22a**, translating it *those two* and making it the subject instead of the object. A less drastic solution is to see 'both' or *those two* as referring to the *rebellious* noblemen **and** those who *join with* them. The words, *sudden* and *who knows?*, indicate an element of surprise at the failure of the rebellion and the punishment of the rebels.

What is clear and agreed is that the student of wisdom (*my son*) will respect and obey (*fear*) those who govern his country, and do so out of duty to God. Under the old covenant it was easy to see the connection between *the Lord and the king* because *the king* was *the Lord's* anointed, and even David, although himself anointed, refused to oppose Saul. But the New Testament teaches the same doctrine, in spite of the fact that this meant respecting and obeying such as Nero and Caligula (Rom. 13:1-7, 1 Pet. 2:13-17). Our Lord had told his disciples to 'give to Caesar what is Caesar's' (Matt. 22:21), even though the Caesar in question was the decadent Tiberius. The overthrow even of wicked rulers is God's responsibility not ours: Psalm 75, especially verse 7.

Question
In the light of this, how can you justify the words and actions of the apostles in Acts 4:18-20 and 5:29?

B. COUNSELS.

1. Wisdom as the basis of the family (vv. 3-4).
Here is an interesting picture of setting up a home. First it needs a *house*, which has to be *built* out of such materials as brick, wood and glass. These have to be fitted together on a firm foundation so that it becomes *established*. Then it needs *rooms filled* with furnishings and equipment, and finally decoration with *rare and beautiful treasures*. The use of the terms *wisdom, understanding* and *knowledge*, upon which this whole book is based, shows that more than materials, construction and decoration are in view here. For the *house* is the family that occupies it and its progress and happiness depend more on their relationships than upon bricks and mortar. Good relationships come: (a) from *wisdom*, from basing everything on the Word of God; (b) from *understanding* that each of us is made differently, so that we stop trying to make the others do things our way, but let them be themselves, thus keeping

the tension out of the atmosphere; (c) from *knowledge*, that is, knowing ourselves, where we fit into the family and what is our contribution to its welfare. These principles would save many homes from breaking up and enable those which stay together to live more happily and productively.

Apply these principles of family life to a church family. How can they help churches avoid dividing and promote better fellowship?

2. Wisdom as strength (vv. 5-6, 10).

Some translate **verse 5** as a comparative: 'A wise man is mightier than a strong man' (RSV). Whether this is correct or not, the idea is that wisdom is more effective than force, which is inadequate alone (see 21:22, Eccles. 7:19, 9:14-18). An exceptionally strong man may with difficulty carry a sack of coal home from the pit head, but a clever man invents a machine which has power to haul hundreds of bags any distance. In every walk of life careful thought avoids much effort and achieves far more than physical strength. In the moral and spiritual realms physical strength has no place. Only by knowledge of God and faith in his Word do we grow strong and persevere in the way of righteousness (Isa. 40:31, Col. 1:11).

Nowhere is this principle more applicable than in *waging war* (**v. 6**). Victory is not guaranteed by superior numbers or weapons; they have to be skilfully deployed. Many a victory has been won by inferior forces using superior strategy. So the *guidance* of *many advisers* is as vital as recruitment and armament. As for spiritual warfare, whether mastering our own sins or delivering others from the power of evil, physical force and 'the weapons of the world' are futile (2 Cor. 10:4f). On the other hand 'the full armour of God' (Eph. 6:10-18) never fails.

The individual too needs the *strength* that comes from wisdom (**v. 10**). Line 1 uses the perfect tense and the interrogative form: 'Have you been slack in the day of distress?', so it is an actual not a hypothetical situation. If so, the reason is, not that the *trouble* was too heavy, but *your strength* too small to bear it. If this sounds unsympathetic it may be addressed to the complacent who think they are strong but when under stress show their *strength is small*. But there is no need to crack under pressure for strength lies in wisdom not muscles and nerves. This brings us back to verse 5 and the promise of God through Isaiah (40:31).

See how the New Testament goes even further with the word to Paul that 'my power is made perfect in weakness' enabling him to testify, 'When I am weak then am I strong' (2 Cor. 12:9f).

3. Wisdom and responsibility (11-12).

It is clear that **verse 11** lays on the wise the responsibility of intervening to *rescue* one on the point of being put to *death*, but in what circumstances is less clear. It may be one who has been innocently condemned about whom we have vital evidence; or one who has been waylaid by thieves or avengers and is about to be murdered; or one in danger of a fatal accident. **Verse 12** limits the scenario to one in which no one else knows we have the means of *rescue* – that we witnessed the crime or can give the defendant an alibi; no one saw us on the scene when the victim was attacked or the accident happening. So as far as others are concerned we cannot be blamed for not getting involved. But there is one who *knows*, and *knows* the reason for our inaction, which is implied as cowardice, fear of what might happen to us if we intervene, especially where violence or risk are involved. Being a just God he won't let us get away with this; the secret will out (Rom. 2:16).

Question
Does this answer Cain's 'Am I my brother's keeper?' Can it apply to our responsibility to warn others of God's sentence of death and show them the way of salvation? (Ezek. 3:16-19).

4. Wisdom's sweetness (vv. 13-14).

Honey is used as an analogy for *wisdom* because it both *tastes sweet* and does *good*. It was what recommended Canaan to the Israelites (Exod. 3:8) and John the Baptist lived on it, perhaps by spreading it on the locusts (Matt. 3:4)! Not everything that tastes *sweet* does *good*, and not everything that does *good tastes sweet*! The best *honey* is straight from *the comb*, literally 'the drippings' (RSV), when it is most pure before anything has been taken from or added to it. It is this pure *wisdom* that the sage has in view – words that 'drip' from the very mind and mouth of God, before human interpretations have added to or taken from them. This is to your *soul* what *honey* is to your body (see on 16:24, 22:18).

(a) *It gives you pleasure,* it reveals 'the love of Christ which surpasses knowledge' (Eph. 3:19), it imparts 'the peace of God which passes all understanding' (Phil. 4:7) and fills you with 'an inexpressible and glorious joy' (1 Pet. 1:8).

(b) *It does you good.* As with 23:18 the *future hope* which *will not be cut off* is probably not the hereafter but the whole course of our present life. *Wisdom* is 'the fear of the Lord', living by faith in him, a way of life which guarantees his blessing.

Question
How does the analogy show that it is only experience of God that gives pleasure and profit (Ps. 34:8, Heb. 4:2)?

C. ADDITIONAL SAYINGS (vv. 23-34).
Verse 23a (*also*) makes this an appendix, either to the previous section or the whole book (LXX places it after 30:14). These are some of 'the sayings and riddles of the wise' referred to in 1:6.

1. On Justice (vv. 23b-25).
On the face of it, this refers to litigation. A judge is not to be influenced by the person of the one before him (**v. 23**) – *partiality* is literally 'know faces', that is, be influenced by the fact that the defendant is known to him, may be a friend or one who could help or harm him. He is to go by the truth, whether he is *guilty* as charged (**v. 24**). If he pronounces such *innocent* he becomes an enemy of the people who will *denounce* him, not just locally but universally. Surely the regard of mankind generally is more important than that of one individual? For even if he makes an enemy by condemning someone he will

not lose out, for he gains the approval of the *people* and God himself (**v. 25**).

Since justice was the responsibility of all the people of Israel (Deut. 1:17), the words have universal application. We all have to make judgments at times. Jesus' words in Matthew 7:1-6 are not against all *judging*, but against condemning in others what we allow in ourselves (cf. John 7:24). We are to be led by the Holy Spirit not our own prejudices (1 Cor. 2:15). We have to judge whether to accept the words or follow the example of those who come to us as teachers (1 John 4:1). Church members have to decide whether someone applying for fellowship is a true believer (2 Cor. 6:14). Perhaps this was what Jesus meant by 'dogs' and 'pigs' in Matthew 7. Right judgments are a blessing to us, our church and society.

Question
See the comment on 18:5 for further application.

2. On Honesty (vv. 26, 28-29).

The court setting of verses 23-25 is widened in **verse 26** to general conversation, which is to be as carefully regulated as testifying in court. This may refer not merely to malicious lying, which is covered in verses 28f, but to withholding unpleasant truths to avoid giving offence. It is tempting to give someone the *answer* they want to hear, which may mean avoiding contradicting or rebuking them in order to retain their friendship. To do this at the expense of *honesty* is not an act of friendship. It is like the *kiss* of Judas. The wise person knows this and is willing to receive rebukes (9:8). He will receive them as *a kiss on the lips*, which seals rather than severs the friendship. *Honesty*, like justice, is ultimately more acceptable than partiality.

This *honesty* is to be observed particularly in court, to which **verses 28f** return. An accusation or witness *against your neighbour*, must have a just *cause*, v. 28; there must be provable grounds for it. Otherwise it will be using the *lips to deceive*. Why should anyone want to do this? One strong motive would be revenge (**v. 29**). Perhaps he has done something like this to you and you see your opportunity to *pay that man back*.

But this is no excuse for breaking the ninth commandment. Personal vengeance has already been condemned (see on 20:22), but when it involves deceit it becomes even more reprehensible and utterly against the spirit of the people of God. Vengeance belongs to him alone, yet he has caused his mercy to triumph over his justice, and made forgiveness a righteous act by punishing sin in his Son. We who believe the gospel must think and live in the spirit of the gospel.

Self-examination. Take a moment to search your heart and life for any dishonest words and resentful feelings.

3. On Priorities (v. 27).

If we understand the *work* here as farming and the *house* as the family, then the advice being given to the young farmer is to get his farm under way before he marries and raises a family. He should make sure his *fields* are productive and making a profit lest he should have nothing from which to provide for his family. He himself can live in a tent or rented room while the *work* is getting established but he can't realistically take a wife and bring up children under those conditions. There are two parts to this preparation: *finish your outdoor work* means to get the ground ready for immediate use to meet present needs; and *get your fields ready* refers to preparation for the next stage, so that there is something to follow when you've exhausted what you grew. For us who aren't farmers, for the young we send into the world, the same principle applies: get things in the right order; make sure you can meet your commitments before you undertake them. Apply this principle to your discipleship (Luke 14:25-33).

Consider the matter of 'church planting' in the light of this principle. In an unevangelised community should pioneer evangelism and the winning of converts precede 'planting' a church?

4. On Sloth (vv. 30-34).

As well as the lesson itself, this passage shows that the two-line saying was not the only way of teaching wisdom; daily life itself could be instructive. Here a chance journey sparked off a whole train of thought. This therefore supplements 6:6-11, 10:4.

(a) *The Observation* (**vv. 30-31**). The wise keep their eyes open, they don't daydream or sleep-walk, they notice things. Here is a perfectly good *vineyard* planted in a *field*, protected by a *stone wall*. The owner had at some time expended money and labour. But he hadn't kept it up, and now *thorns* and *weeds* were choking the *vine*, which was not yielding as it should; and neglect meant the *wall* (probably a dry *stone* one) was collapsing.

(b) *The Lesson* (**vv. 32-33**). The wise think about what they *observe* and *learn a lesson* from it. Why is this *vineyard* neglected? The owner is a *sluggard*. He loves ease; he can't get up in the morning and when he does he decides it's too late to start work that day. Nor is he just ruled by his flesh; his thoughts are wrong, he *lacks judgment* (cf. 12:11). Perhaps he is an optimist or idealist. He hasn't taken to heart the reality of evil in the world. *Thorns and weeds* are as old as Adam, there as a judgment on human folly (Gen. 3:17-19). Adam and Eve *lacked judgment*, they made a foolish choice and we all suffer. But we must come to terms with the results of sin and try to mitigate them, to keep the *weeds* under control. That curse fell also on animal and human nature: beasts become savage and men dishonest, so that we have to secure our property against them. Belief in the perfection of mother nature and the goodness of human nature (so common today) will not prevent us being savaged or burgled.

(c) *The Conclusion* (**v. 34**). Whether or not armed robbery takes place, *poverty and scarcity* will surely be the end result of neglect. Better to learn this from looking over someone else's fence than from lying in bed and waiting for it to happen. In 6:6-11 Solomon observed the ant and came to the same conclusion.

Apply this to your spiritual life and the church: see 1 Corinthians 3:6.

Solomon's Proverbs (second set)
(Proverbs 25–29)

Here we have another clue to the literary history of this book. The original collection (chs. 10–22:16) was probably published in or soon after the reign of Solomon himself. 'The Sayings of the Wise' (22:17-24) were added later, then Hezekiah had another selection of Solomon's own proverbs copied by his men, who autographed it in this verse. Where they obtained these proverbs we are not told; possibly they were rediscovered by Hezekiah when he 'spring-cleaned' the Temple (2 Chr. 29). But neither he nor his copyists laid any claim to authorship. This is an example of the teamwork God uses in revealing and circulating his Word.

22
Kings and Commoners
Proverbs 25

A. ON KINGS: (vv. 2-7b).
'Hezekiah's men' were not mere copyists; they edited and arranged their material. Here they have brought together a number of isolated sayings about kingship to give a comprehensive picture of the power of governments. *The king* is beneath the *God* he represents, but above the people, who look up to him as he to *God*.

1. The King's Knowledge (vv. 2-3).
Verse 2 shows how the *king* is inferior to *God*. *God* doesn't need to *search out a matter*. 'Everything is uncovered and laid bare before (his) eyes' (Heb. 4:13). While there is much he has revealed: in creation, history, the Scriptures and Christ, there is much he has *concealed*: the method and process of creation (Job 38:4) and the way it functions (Job 39), the origin of evil and his permission of it, and his own essence (Exod. 33:20, Isa. 45:15, John 1:18). Yet it is part of his *glory* to veil his *glory* in order to exalt himself and humble us. *The king* doesn't share the divine omniscience; he has to study the art of politics, to acquaint himself with the state of his kingdom and the needs of his subjects, and winkle out those plotting against his throne.

Verse 3 shows the same *king* in relation to his people. To them he has something of the inscrutability of God. For while he publishes policies, issues laws and uncovers plots, he keeps much to himself. All governments have their state secrets, lest enemies discover their weaknesses or obtain advance knowledge of their plans, or lest greedy subjects gain access to privileged information and exploit it to their own profit. We are all aware of the danger of 'leaks' from the 'think tank'!

2. The King's power of appointment (vv. 4-7b).

The king is also inferior to God in that he needs advisers (which is what *the king's presence* means), whereas God is all-sufficient (Isa. 40:13f). But like God he has the authority to appoint whom he will to serve him. He is also like God in that the stability of *his throne* depends on *righteousness* (Ps. 89:14). This requires keeping away *the wicked*, those who would steer the ship of state on to the rocks of corruption and disaster because they lack the principles of *righteousness*. This high view of government is also seen here in likening *the king to silver*. *Silver* is never mined in a pure form and needs the heat of the furnace to *remove the dross* before it is fit *material* for the *silversmith* to make into an object of beauty. Many aspire to office who are unfit for government. These must be kept from the corridors of power if the state is to be the instrument of administering the justice of God (14:34). For further comments see on 16:10-15, 20:8, 28.

Verses 6-7 apply this principle to the hearer or reader (v. 7c belongs to verse 8). In view of *the king's* sovereignty in making appointments to office and the high standard required, an ambitious person should pause before trying to become part of his government (*the king's presence*) and to have *a place among great men*, that is, one of his counsellors. If he thinks you are trying to promote yourself he is likely to send you packing, which won't do much for your morale. Humility is a grace but humiliation a disgrace. This is the point made by Christ in his little parable in Luke 14:7-11, which seems to have this passage in mind. The moral he draws in verse 11 shows he is not advocating a crafty way of climbing the social ladder, but making a spiritual point, for although God's name is not used it is implied. The way to acceptance with him is to humble ourselves before him. This he tried to teach his disciples when they quarrelled over who would be his chief advisers when he set up his kingdom (Matt. 20:20-28). Greatness lies in serving not ruling, of which he is the supreme example, who 'came not to be served but to serve'.

Question
Assuming you yourself do not aspire to a political career, does this passage help in exercising your vote?

B. ADVICE ON DISPUTES (vv. 7c-10).
That disputes will arise between *neighbours* and even Christians is certain. They originated at the Fall when each blamed the other (Gen. 3:12f). We should do all we can to avoid them (17:14) but if they arise we need to try to resolve them.

1. How not to handle them (vv. 7c-8).
Don't just bark out, 'See you in *court!*' Consider whether you have a sound case, that you have rightly interpreted *what you have seen with your eyes*, that is, the incident that sparked off the dispute. Are you certain of winning the case in the end? For if you lose it the *shame* you thought to bring on *your neighbour* will fall on you.

2. How to handle them (vv. 9-10).
Try to settle it privately – *argue your case with* him (RSV adds 'himself'). At this stage don't bring anyone else into the dispute, for you may find yourself divulging personal information given by *another man* in *confidence*. To do this in a small community where everybody knows everybody is to break the social code and become guilty of a worse offence than the one your *neighbour* committed against you. You will get a *bad reputation* as a betrayer of secrets and wish you had never started the dispute.

See how Christ and the apostles apply these principles to church members by considering Matthew 5:25f, 1 Corinthians 6:1-6 (going to law) and Matthew 18:15-17 (settling disputes privately).

C. WELL-CHOSEN WORDS (vv. 11-15, 25).
A number of sayings on the best use of words has been brought together here, for words can bring peace and comfort.

1. The aptly-spoken word (v. 11).

The saying itself is a perfect example of what it is teaching, so easy on the ear, beautiful and soothing. Unfortunately the precise meaning isn't altogether clear. Does *aptly* mean the right word or the right time? Probably both, for the best advice, instruction or encouragement given in the wrong circumstances or when the hearer is in the wrong frame of mind to receive it hardly deserves the beautiful picture used to illustrate the *apt word*. This raises the other question as to what the comparison means. It conjures up a vision of a beautifully crafted silver dish of filigree work, full of 'Golden Delicious' apples. However, the *apple* had not then been introduced into Palestine, though it might be a poetic way of describing an orange or pomegranate. In view of what follows in verse 12, the likelihood is that it refers to jewels or ornaments, spherical in shape and golden in colour, whose intrinsic beauty is offset by their *silver setting*.

2. The wise rebuke (v. 12).

If words of comfort and encouragement need careful choosing, how much more do *rebukes*! 'No duty calls for more delicacy of feeling and meekness of wisdom' (Bridges). Our native pride indisposes us to be told we are wrong, especially if what is pointed out is not a misjudged action but a defect of character. Yet it is possible for a *rebuke* to be as admirable and acceptable as a pair of *gold earrings* or a necklace (*ornament*) of *fine gold* displayed in a jeweller's shop for passers-by to gaze at and covet. Two things are needed to bring about this happy result. The first is a *wise man*, who has not only a gift with words (v. 11) but an insight into human nature, combined with a loving sympathetic heart which won't antagonize the hearer. The second is *a listening ear* in the one at the receiving end, one who wants to know the right way in order to improve in character, and doesn't mind being told.

3. The faithful message (vv. 13, 25).

For the place of the *messenger* in the ancient world see on 13:17. A faithful one was like new life to both sender and receiver.

(a) *To the sender* (**v. 13**). The message may be instructions to do something vital and must be accurately and promptly delivered. Or it may be an enquiry to which the *master* is urgently awaiting the answer. We may imagine him sweating like a worker in the heat of *harvest*, who would refresh himself with melted *snow* from the mountains, which they stored in the clefts of rocks. A true prompt answer to his question would be a similar relief.

(b) *To the receiver* (**v. 25**). The picture is much the same but more generalized – not just the worker sweating at the harvest but any *weary soul* who has travelled, worked or just waited long without water. This fits the theme of someone longing for *news from a distant land*. Solomon himself was often in this position because he traded with *distant* parts and had no idea whether his ships would return safely until his lookout sighted them (1 Kings 9:26-28). Abraham had no idea of the well-being of the brother he had left in Haran until *news* came of how his family had grown (Gen. 22:20-24), which was important in connection with Isaac's need of a wife. Jacob thought Joseph lost to him until his sons brought the news 'Joseph is alive!' (Gen. 45:26). Paul did not repress his impatience for news of the Thessalonian Christians whom he had to leave so suddenly just after their conversion; news of them was 'life from the dead' (1 Thess. 3:5-8). How much more true this is of those who waited for news that the expected Messiah had arrived (Luke 2:10f and 25f)! The God who sends his messengers across the world is himself not indifferent to the way his message is delivered and received (2 Cor. 2:15f).

4. The empty boast (v. 14).

In sharp contrast to the faithful messenger who reports the truth is the boaster whose mouth is bigger than his hand. He *boasts* about his generosity but his promise exceeds his performance, to the great disappointment of those to whom he promised cash, goods, work or time. This is similar to the disappointment of expecting *rain* but seeing *only clouds and wind*. There is a more sinister undertone: man fell by believing a promise that he would be 'like God' if he accepted the proferred fruit (Gen. 3:5), the result of which was the loss of our godlikeness.

However, he who was God in flesh was not deceived by boastful offers from the same source (Matt. 4:8-10). We his followers need his wisdom, for the spirit of Satan is moving those who come among us with offers of great blessings if we will adopt their methods (2 Pet. 2:19, Jude 12). Never was this problem more acute, for today's 'ministers of Satan' have all the latest marketing technique at their disposal and a gullible generation to work on. They boast they can heal our sicknesses, lift our depressions, cure our addictions and crown it all with ecstatic experiences which will make us laugh uncontrollably. But what comes of it all? *Clouds and wind without rain.*

5. The gentle tongue (v. 15).
We have already seen how answering gently and refusing to be provoked can extricate us from awkward situations (see on 15:1). This can also work positively. Here is *a ruler* who won't *be persuaded* – perhaps to change a policy heading for disaster for one which will succeed better. To shout angrily at him will only make him stand more obstinately on his dignity. But there is more than one way to *break a bone*. *Patience* and calm reasoning can soften *a bone* and make it more pliable. How can we deal with those false teachers of verse 14? Do we simply refuse to listen to them or can we win them over? Strident controversy will only harden them and start a quarrel. Paul's way is better (2 Tim. 2:23-25).

Reflection. How can mere mortals like us learn to use words in the ways prescribed here? Two things are needed. See if you can work them out from Isaiah 50:4 and Ecclesiastes 12:10.

D. On Relationships (vv. 16-24, 26-28).
The remaining part of this chapter contains advice on this important matter, mainly telling us how to avoid spoiling our relationships. It uses astonishing similes to show what to avoid.

1. Over-familiarity (vv. 16-17).
This is not really about dieting, for as in verse 27 and 24:13 the saying about *honey* is simply a launching pad for a bigger

subject. In 24:13 it was wisdom, here it is visiting. In 24:13 no restriction was placed on *eating honey* because it was compared with gaining wisdom, of which we can never have too much. Here however we are advised to eat it in moderation, for *too much of it* will make you sick. This is obvious to everyone who has overindulged the sweet things of life. What is less obvious but equally true is that friendliness can have the same effect. Few translations bring out the verbal similarity between the two verses – the use of the same word in line 2 of each verse. NIV does it well: *too much of it* and *too much of you*. It is a good thing to converse with our friends and *neighbours*, but if we are always on their doorsteps it may be self-indulgence rather than friendship, insensitivity to their feelings, seeking an audience for our tales, or even tale-bearing, rather than to be helpful to them. What could be a happy relationship is ruined by overdoing it. Let's avoid making our friends 'sick' – of us!

2. False reporting (v. 18).
There is no surer way of destroying a relationship than by lying about a person. *False testimony*, as in the ninth commandment, refers to witness in court, but applies equally to conversation or writing. It may seem exaggeration to liken it to what are all weapons of murder, but unless it is publicly withdrawn or proved wrong it can murder a character or reputation, and along with that the person's living, family and happiness. The frequency with which it is referred to in PROVERBS (6:19, 12:17, 14:5, 25, 19:5, 9, 21:28, 24:28) shows how common it was even among those who subscribed to the commandments. What can we say of our permissive age, when huge fees are paid for scandal to print in newspapers?

3. Unreliability (v. 19).
There is more than one way of letting someone down. Although not as blatantly wicked as telling lies or spreading rumours (v. 18), to prove unreliable can be very hurtful. This is brought out by the vivid simile: chewing on *a bad tooth* or trying to walk on *a lame foot* is both ineffective and painful. It is *in times of trouble* we most need our friends. If they prove *unfaithful* then what sort of friends are they? 'A friend loves at

all times and a brother is born for adversity' (17:17). By nature we tend to be fair-weather friends, as he complained in 20:6, and it takes renewal in the image of Christ to make us what he is, 'a friend who sticks closer than a brother' (18:24). He himself knew what it was like to be forsaken in his hour of need (Matt. 26:56), as did David before him (Ps. 55:12-14) and Paul after him (2 Tim. 4:16).

4. Lack of sympathy (vv. 20-22).
What is the best way to cheer *a heavy heart*? Not to *sing songs* to it, at least not merry ones. We commonly think this the appropriate treatment but how often does it work? Nor should we expect it to, for will not the sufferer think we aren't taking his sorrow seriously? Whatever chemical reaction is produced by *vinegar poured on soda*, it is clearly *unproductive* or even *destructive*, like *singing songs to a heavy heart*. Worse, it is *inhuman*, for it is even compared to *taking off a coat on a cold day*. Our songs don't warm the heart of our sad friend, they only make it feel colder and him more isolated. True sympathy is 'feeling with' the person, not against him, treating the disease with the bacteria – as Paul put it, 'Rejoice with those who rejoice and weep with those who weep' (Rom. 12:15).

Verse 21 shows the real way of sympathy, which is practical – give the sufferer what he craves – not what suits you but what meets his need. This can be done not just to your sad friend but to your sworn *enemy*, literally 'him who hates you'. This verse goes further than any previous statement on the subject. The law required you to give back to your enemy what belongs to him, if you came across it accidentally, such as his animal (Exod. 23:4f); but this requires you to give what is *yours, your food and water*. The proverbs up to now have forbidden revenge on your enemy (17:13, 20:22) or secretly enjoying seeing him suffer (24:17). But this calls for open, positive action. It falls a little short of the teaching of Jesus to '*love* your enemies' (Matt. 5:44), which goes beyond emergency aid to seeking their total happiness.

All this is plain. The problem lies in **verse 22**. The *burning coals* have been variously interpreted: as bringing the wrath of God on him (cf. Ps. 18:8) – the vengeance which is God's prerogative; as making him burn with shame that he has hated one who is kind to him; as making him acceptable to God (which the priest did with the offering on the Day of Atonement by filling a censer with *coals of fire* [Lev. 16:12, see AMP mg]); and as purifying his mind of hatred like metal ore when placed in the fire. Since there is a *reward* from *the Lord* for it, it must mean some improvement is brought about in the *enemy*. Paul's interpretation is best: the 'evil' of hatred is 'overcome with good' (Rom. 12:21) – he ceases to be your *enemy* and becomes your friend.

5. Spreading slander (v. 23).

The *sly tongue* is probably that of the gossip, described in 11:13, 20:19 as one who betrays confidences, either because he enjoys talking about someone else (18:8) or because he wants to make trouble (26:20-22). It isn't clear whether the *angry looks* are on the face of the one he is talking *to* or *about*. Certainly PROVERBS would tell us to frown on those who bring gossip or slander to our ears. Yet it also faces the fact that many enjoy hearing it (18:8), so it may refer to the anger shown by the object of the gossip when he hears what is being said of him. This would fit the warning about gossip stirring up strife (26:20f). There is also a problem with the simile, since in Palestine *rain* doesn't arrive from *the north*! Dark clouds however do, so the idea may be: 'The *north wind brings* black clouds and *the sly tongue brings* black *looks*.' In the small closely-knit communities of Israel gossip could have far-reaching results – a word in secret might be the spark that starts a forest fire (cf. James 3:5f). In our local churches a conversation between two members may start a chain of events which will end up destroying the fellowship. Paul was concerned for this in Corinth (2 Cor. 12:20).

6. Domestic disputes (v. 24).

This is identical to 21:9 (see comments) and similar to 19:13 and 21:19, but in a different context. Following verse 23 it shows that open abuse can be as bad as secret gossip. The most tragic example of this is in the domestic scene for it puts asunder those God has joined. It causes private unofficial divorce, for the henpecked husband can't live with the *quarrelsome wife*. Since *the corner of the roof* or 'top floor back' was where the servants were accommodated, there may be a hint here of a role reversal. The woman has usurped the husband's headship with her sharp tongue, and the husband has become subject to her, contrary to the original order (Gen. 3:16b). This scenario is all too common in these days of 40% divorce. Is it due to ignorance of the nature of marriage, to lack of consideration as to how well-matched a couple is, to mistaking passion for love, to failure on the part of one or both partners to fulfil their side, or just to the triumph of self-assertion over companionship?

7. Compromise (v. 26).

In a dry climate where people are dependent on *fountains* and *wells* for their water, to find them *muddied* or *polluted* is a disaster of the first magnitude. In the realm of truth and morality compromise with error or sin are similarly catastrophic. 'The righteous man is a well of life' (10:11) and like Abraham he is a 'blessing' to others (Gen. 12:2); God is with him and he brings God into the lives of those among whom he circulates. But if he falters in his convictions or behaviour, if he concedes the arguments of the opponents of truth or adopts the ways of the ungodly he not only ceases to do good but does actual harm. *Polluted* water is not just nasty to the taste but poisonous to the body. What a challenge to Christians! We are 'the salt of the earth' (Matt. 5:13), our presence and influence in the world not only gives it the relish of goodness but preserves it from rottenness. 'But if the salt loses its saltiness', by *giving way to the wicked*, 'how can it be made salty again?' If *we* cease to be salt, where else will the world find any? If we allow poison into the *well* of truth where will the world go for the water of life?

8. Ambition (v. 27).

The advice on *eating honey* in moderation was given us in verse 16 in connection with over-friendliness. Here it is used as a warning against over-ambitiousness. There is a problem with line 2 in that the negative *nor* or 'not' (kjv etc.) is lacking in the Hebrew text. Many suggestions and emendations have been made to obviate this (e.g. RSV, NEB) but the negative seems the best way of matching the lesson with the simile. It implies that honour – a good reputation – is a worthy aim in life. But there is a danger of being overanxious about it and always drawing attention to it, to the extent of boasting. This is *to seek one's own honour*. We should just get on with our lives, do our duty to God and others, and let our reputation look after itself, or, as 27:2 says, 'Let another praise you and not your own mouth'. Continually harping on about your character and integrity will, like too much honey, make others sick as well as you!

9. Impatience (v. 28).

In 16:32 the *self-controlled* person was compared to a great general taking a city. Here the uncontrolled person is compared to the city which is taken, *whose walls are broken down*, leaving it open to invasion. *Self-control* is our defence against temptation and provocation. Lack of it leaves us at the mercy of blind impulse which is the sure way to defeat and possession by the enemy. But the situation is more serious. Inability to control ourselves is a sign of weakness of character and leaves us vulnerable all round. Self-discipline in today's society is at a premium. Many lack it and some despise it as Victorian. But lack of it is at the root of many of our problems: broken homes, delinquent children, unteachable youth, crimes like theft and violence, rape, promiscuity, drink and drug-addiction and so on. We have left ourselves without *walls* and who can foresee the end result?

Question
To what extent are the above blemishes in our own power to avoid and to what extent are they only attainable by Christians 'filled with (i.e. under the control of) the Spirit'? See, e.g. Romans 8:5-14, Ephesians 5:18.

23

Fools and Knaves
Proverbs 26

This chapter is entirely about bad characters: the foolish, the lazy, the quarrelsome and the malicious. There could be various reasons for this choice of subject. One would be to warn those trained in righteousness that not everyone is so favoured, that they will encounter such people and need guidance in identifying and handling them. Another would be to look to ourselves lest we become like them. Perhaps above all to be thankful God is showing us a better way.

A. THE FOOLISH (vv. 1-12).
Since PROVERBS is a book about wisdom, its opposite is never far away – folly. *Fools* and their follies are mentioned frequently, but this is the fullest treatment, probably because, as with the study of kingship in chapter 25, a number of sayings have been brought together by the editor. The emphasis is on what is *unfitting* to the fool – things good in themselves but in the hands of a *fool* at best ridiculous and at worst dangerous.

1. Honour (vv. 1-3, 8).
Snow and *rain* (**v. 1**) are good and essential things but not at the wrong place and the wrong time. *In summer* at *harvest* they are not merely unwelcome but actually harmful. It is right and good to give *honour* to those worthy of it – because of their office (parents, teachers, governors), their character or noble deeds. 'Give everyone what you owe him ... if honour, then

honour' (Rom. 13:7). But to do this to one who rejects normal behaviour and spends his time, money and strength on what is useless or even wrong is absurd, like putting 'a gold ring on a pig's snout' (11:22); worse, it is dangerous, for he is bound to abuse it and cause harm.

Verse 8 bears this out. *Giving honour to a fool* is like giving a madman a *sling* with a *stone* in it, or as we would say, putting a loaded pistol in his hand. Honouring fools may even be a judgment like *snow in summer or rain in harvest* (see 1 Samuel 12:16-18). For example, when God allowed Israel to set the wrong people over them it was a form of judgment (Isa. 3:12, Eccles. 10:5-7).

Verse 2 may be an example of how dangerous it is to put a fool in a place of honour, for he may abuse it by pronouncing a *curse* on the *undeserved*. In which case God will have to step in and stop it settling, like the *swallow* and the *sparrow*, as he did with Balaam's curse on Israel (Num. 23:8, Deut. 23:5), Saul's on Jonathan (1 Sam. 14:28) and Goliath's on David (1 Sam. 17:43f). Jesus took this further and forbade us cursing those who deserve it because they persecute us (Luke 6:28). Yet hovering in the background like a vulture poised to swoop on its prey, is God's own curse on our whole race, indeed the earth itself (Gen. 3:17f, Gal. 3:10). This he will not allow to *come to rest* on those in Christ, who has 'redeemed us from the curse of the law by becoming a curse for us' (Gal. 3:13).

Verse 3 prescribes the appropriate treatment for a *fool*: far from *honour* he needs punishment, not power laid **on** him but **over** him. He is like *a horse* from the wild (the oriental horse's breeding-ground) and needs taming and bringing into submission, and like a *donkey*, which although more docile, needs the *halter* to direct him (Ps. 32:9). So *the fool* lacks understanding and needs guiding. Even then he is unwilling to accept guidance and needs some coercion. The *rod* doesn't have to be literal. Whatever Jesus did in the Temple we can't imagine Paul laying into the Corinthian Christians with a stick (1 Cor. 4:21)!

Consider how careful we in the churches need to be about whom we appoint to office (1 Tim. 5:22, 3:1-7), and how careful all need to be about the role models we choose (1 Cor. 11:1).

2. Serious discussion (vv. 4-5).

Having considered appropriate and inappropriate ways of treating a *fool*, we now see the appropriate way to conduct a discussion with him. The apparent contradiction shows what a difficult and delicate matter this is. We have to avoid the Scylla of making ourselves look as foolish as him without coming to grief on the Charybdis of making him think he is really quite a wise guy. So there is a way not to answer (**verse 4**) and a way to answer (**v. 5**). This means the words *according to his folly* have two different meanings. In **verse 4** the idea is to avoid, not so much his question or assertion, as the way he expresses it: maybe scornfully, angrily, insultingly, even deceitfully. All these are no-go areas for the child of God. Jephthah did this with the Ephraimites (Judg. 12:1-6), but Jesus refused to 'repay insult with insult' (1 Pet. 2:23, 3:9). But that doesn't mean he never replied to questions or accusations. The wisdom with which he answered the taunts of the hostile Rabbis is one of the most astonishing parts of his ministry. He did it in such a way as to bring out the foolishness of their clever questions and remarks in contrast with the truth he brought out. He made these controversies a way of exposing his enemies and at the same time of giving positive teaching. Thus he fulfilled **verse 5** and is an example to us of how to *answer a fool according to his folly*.

Further study. See our Lord in controversy in Matthew 12; 15:1-20; 21:23-27; 22:15-32. Lest we say this is beyond us, read how a man just coming to faith tackled the clever ones in John 9:26-33.

3. Taking messages (v. 6).

This is the fourth proverb in the book about messengers, showing their importance for communication in the ancient world (see on 13:17). This probably explains the strong language used here to deter us from employing a *fool* in that capacity. *The fool* either won't reach his destination or if he does will garble the *message* or forget it altogether. Since you employed him to save your own *feet*, this will be like *cutting* them *off*. To speak of *drinking violence* sounds exaggerated, but probably describes the opposite to the effect a 'trustworthy messenger' has. In 25:13 he was compared to an iced drink at harvest, for by faithfully delivering the message and bringing back the answer he revived the spirits of the sender. But if he gets it all wrong it causes you suffering and even trouble, like drinking vinegar (10:26) or poison.

Apply this to those sent with the good news of salvation. If they turn out *fools*, consider the damage they do and the grief to God who sends them. Read of the spies who came back from Canaan with a negative report and its devastating consequences (Num. 13).

4. Wise sayings (vv. 7, 9).
There is more to wisdom than repeating *proverbs* parrot-fashion. Wisdom consists not only in knowledge but character and behaviour, which is precisely what the *fool* lacks. We have all heard unbelievers quote the Bible and felt it doesn't ring true. For one thing he does nobody any good. It is like a *lame man's legs*, which may look all right, but if he tries to use them he falls flat. So a *proverb in the mouth of a fool* may sound accurate but in the ears of his hearers it will fall flat. For another thing he may actually harm himself (**v. 9**). Alcohol anaesthetizes from pain (23:35), so the *drunkard* doesn't feel the *thornbush* and makes no effort to extricate himself or the thorns and may end up with a poisoned hand. So for someone to quote the word of God but not follow it is to bring condemnation on himself (Matt. 12:37).

Consider the devil's quoting of Scripture in the light of these sayings (Matt. 4:6).

5. Employment (v. 10).
Uncertainty about the nature of the original text of this verse has led to a variety of translations and interpretations. Most agree that line one is the simile and line two the punch line. In accordance with the theme of the passage the point is that a *fool* is as unsuitable for employment as he is for taking messages (v. 6). You are as likely to get your job done well if you grabbed any *passer-by at random*. It is a matter of chance,

like firing arrows indiscriminately into a crowd. Some are bound to receive *wounds*; similarly if you *hire a fool* trouble is sure to come of it. It might be hard to fit this advice to today's employment regulations, but no one can quarrel with the wisdom of being careful to whom you entrust an important piece of business.

Apply this to the Lord entrusting his business to us.

6. Repentance (v. 11).

A dog because of its voracious appetite may eat something which upsets it and which (if dogs have such feelings) it will regret. But once it has *vomited* it up it feels better, and if nothing else is on offer it may *return to its vomit*.

Temporary or false repentance is like this. We can get so deep into sin it disgusts us. The effects of drunkenness, promiscuity, drug addiction, occultism and so on can eventually sicken us, make us wish we'd never started them and even move us to give them up. But if self-disgust is the only motive it is not gospel repentance. It may make us feel better for a while but will leave us in a vacuum. The only way we can fill it is to return to what satisfied us before, which the proverb likens to *a dog's vomit*. Peter uses it in connection with antinomianism in the churches – 'Christians' who embraced the gospel but never truly believed it as 'the way of righteousness' and therefore returned to their former ways (2 Pet. 2:17-22). The repentance the gospel calls for abandons sin, not merely because it debases our humanity but because it offends God and separates us from him. *The fool* doesn't see this and is merely satisfying a temporary whim.

Consider Christ's little cameo on exorcism in the light of this (Matt. 12:43-45).

7. Conceit (v. 12).

Strictly speaking this is not about the *fool* as he has been described in this chapter. As v. 11 indicates a *fool* may come to realize his folly and want to be saved from it, even if for the wrong reasons. The one in this verse may not be into that sort of folly. He may be a good speaker (v. 7), a reliable messenger (v. 6) good in debate (vv. 4-5) and worthy of honour (v. 1). His trouble is he knows it and thinks this passes for wisdom. It may do in the eyes of the world. But the wisdom of PROVERBS begins with 'the fear of God' (1:7), which includes a sense of failure and sin in the intellectual, moral and spiritual realms. This puts him in worse case than the *fool*, whose *eyes* are at least partly open to his condition. He may even come to realize what he is in God's *eyes*. There is no *hope* of this in the totally blind man.

Question
Consider the words *Do you see..?* as if addressed to you personally: (a) as a window through which to observe someone you know; (b) as a mirror to see whether this is true of you.

B. THE LAZY (vv. 13-16).
This is another subject which has already been explored, especially in 6:6-11, 24:30-34, and is now summarized under four heads in a tongue-in-cheek fashion.

1. His Excuses (v. 13).
We have already been confronted with this idea and there is no need to repeat what was said on 22:13. The matter is to do with going out to work. *The sluggard* won't admit his real reason for staying in and covers it with excuses. This one amounts to 'it's too dangerous!' There are always dangers in going out, even in our day when there are no *lions* (unless one escapes from the Zoo!). We might be mugged, run over or hit by falling masonry. But when everyone else braves them, why should one be excused? The workshy can always find reasons for not working.

2. His Incurability (v. 14).
This is the true explanation for his absenteeism – he is too fond of sleeping (see 6:9f, 24:33). So much so that he is hardly more able to get out of *bed* than *a door* is able to break away from its *hinges*. The only movement he can make is to *turn* over, which leaves him in the same place as he was before, just as a *door* moves only within the orbit of the space it occupies. This is a good illustration of the Bible's use of humour in the form

of exaggeration. It is hoped scorn will achieve what ordinary methods have failed to do. If only we would look at or listen to ourselves sometimes, and even laugh at ourselves!

3. His Weakness (v. 15).
This is almost identical to 19:24, to which you are referred. This proverb is bolder: instead of the vague, 'He will not even bring it (his hand) back to his mouth', we have the blunt *he is too lazy*, literally 'weary'. In spite of all the sleep he's had! We can have too much sleep, but be more tired than if we'd had too little. The picture is again exaggerated – the idea of someone taking hold of the food on his plate and dropping off to sleep is absurd. But the point again is to get *the sluggard* to look at himself and laugh; then cry with shame and pull himself together.

4. His Self-image (v. 16).
How justified our author is in caricaturing *the sluggard* and holding him up to ridicule! He simply does not see himself. He believes the *answer* he gives to those who challenge him about **not** working is *wiser* than the *answer* of *seven men* to the question as to why they **do** work! Here is one who of all qualifies for the stricture of verse 12. He is worse than a fool, for he cannot see himself.

Now consider the opposite of laziness – diligence: in the daily routine (Eccles. 9:10), in spiritual growth (Rom. 12:11f) and in devotion to the family of God (Rom. 12:9, 13).

C. THE QUARRELSOME (vv. 17-22).
Although the quarreller is not termed a fool, yet the way the subject is handled shows the foolishness of quarrelling. The way quarrels arise brings this out.

1. Meddling (v. 17).
The expression *seizes a dog by the ears* probably means you are trying to pull it off another dog with which it is fighting. The result would be that the bared teeth will bite you. Intervening in a *quarrel* on which you happen as a *passer-by* is similarly dangerous. It is likely to make things worse. But in the Gospel

age are we not supposed to be 'peacemakers' (Matt. 5:9)? The interesting thing is that Jesus himself refused to become involved in a domestic dispute (Luke 12:14) and the apostles counselled against meddling (1 Pet. 4:15) and arguing (2 Tim. 2:23). This shows that peacemaking requires more care and preparation than is possible for the mere *passer-by*, who knows neither the parties nor the full facts of the matter. Before we can successfully reconcile we need enough information to make a right judgment and the confidence of the parties concerned.

2. Joking (vv. 18-19).

We are all too familiar today with maniacs firing off automatic guns into crowds to miss the force of the imagery of verse 18. But to compare this to a practical joker (v. 19) seems far-fetched. The point lies in the unintentional hurt caused by an impulsive action. The *madman* had no just complaint against his victims, but hadn't thought about the consequences of giving way to his impulse. No more has the practical joker. He has seen his chance of a bit of fun and taken it without thinking of how it will go down with his *neighbour*. To the latter it isn't funny but hurtful and may spark off a quarrel or at least sour the relationship.

3. Gossiping (vv. 20-22).

These verses establish a connection between *quarrelling* and *gossiping*. *Gossip* serves both as *kindling* for *strife* (v. 21) and the fuel for sustaining it (v. 20). *The gossip* may not intend to start a *quarrel* – he may just enjoy telling tales; but he ought to realize he is making trouble, for who is going to be happy to have his private business discussed? How much worse is one who keeps the *quarrel* alive by spreading more *gossip* (v. 20)! As we have already seen (18:8) it isn't difficult to do this since there are few who don't enjoy a tasty piece of scandal (v. 22). Our hearts are highly inflammable! But Christians should be among this 'few'. Much as we may enjoy talking about each other, we need to control this form of entertainment (which is about all it is) because of the harm it does to our relationships (see on 16:28).

Read again James 3, especially verse 6, which uses the same illustration of fire to describe the effects of gossip or contentious words.

D. The Malicious (vv. 23-28).
The characters in this chapter are on a sliding scale and with the last we reach the bottom of the ladder.

1. His Hypocrisy (vv. 23-26).
The purpose of this passage is to warn the youth or disciple that people are not always what they seem and we should guard against taking them at face value. They may come to us with *fervent lips* (v. 23) professing friendship and love, and *charming* or 'kind' *speech* (v. 25) offering us their help. But the words, smiles, handshakes and kisses may be just *a coating of glaze* (v. 23). If the vowel pointing of the Masoretic text is right the *glaze* was made from 'silver dross' (kjv), a deposit left after refining silver. Spread over earthenware this gave the look and feel of silver but soon wore off. The same is true of the malicious person. His words are a *disguise* (v. 24) and a *deception* (v. 26) covering *an evil heart* (v. 23) filled with *seven abominations*, that is, a whole set of evil intentions: *deceit* (v. 24), fraud, theft, destruction of your reputation, blackmail and even violence.

Like the glazed pot, the veneer of kindness soon wears off and *his wickedness* is *exposed*, not just to you privately, but publicly too (v. 26). Hatred is too powerful an emotion to be hid for ever. So the punch line is *do not believe him* (v. 25), that is, don't commit yourself to him on first impressions. Give it time, check him out. This is not meant to encourage us to cultivate a suspicious nature. There are too many Christians who see the spiritual equivalent of 'reds under every bed'. Rather it is another lesson in wisdom – growing out of the naivete of immaturity which goes off with every stranger who offers sweets. It means always remembering man is a fallen creature and that 'just as Eve was deceived by the serpent's cunning, your minds may be led away from your sincere and pure devotion to Christ' (2 Cor. 11:3). Which of us has never been 'conned' at some time?

2. His 'come uppance' (v. 27).
Malice is even more publicly exposed when it receives its due recompense. Of the two illustrations here, the first is common in Scripture (a Reference Bible will give many allusions). The

second is unusual, although Psalm 7:16 says, 'His violence comes down on his own head'. The idea may be of throwing a *stone* up a cliff or steep slope, a dangerous thing to do if you're standing at the bottom! You may intend hitting someone higher up, but the law of gravity means you may come off worst.

Poetic justice is a popular theme in wisdom literature (JOB is full of it) and fiction. How much of a reality is it? A life of crime or even a personal vendetta is fraught with danger, and the malicious man often comes off worst. But to 'get away with murder' is common, and which of us has not harmed another out of hatred in a way never traced to us? There is no perfect justice in this life: the guilty escape and the innocent suffer unjustly. But the final administration of justice will be perfect. For it will be conducted personally by God. He has the true facts and all of them, and being free both from guilt and vindictiveness has the right to judge and the ability to do so impartially. It is the New Testament rather than the old that spells this out most clearly, e.g. Romans 2:12-16.

3. His Harmfulness (v. 28).
Verse 27 sounded like the last word on the subject, which it will be in the end. Meanwhile we live in 'the real world' where verse 27 does not always apply. We cannot be sure our enemies will be struck down before their plots succeed. They may *hurt* us. This will stir our enmity against them which will in turn make them *hate* us even more and *work* for our utter *ruin*. So this is an even severer warning against the hypocrite than before. Here he is described as *flattering*: coming to us with praises when his intention is to *hurt* us. It is the *flatteries* that are the lies, but since we love praise they put us off our guard. So it is even more important to guard against credulity (v. 25a). In a way it is good that verse 27 comes first since it takes the bitterness out of this statement. We can take this treatment if we know it will turn out right in the end.

For your encouragement trace this malicious treatment through the life of our Lord: the secret malice of his enemies (John 8:40, 15:23-25), their flattery (Matt. 22:16), false friendship (Luke 22:47f) and plotting of his ruin (John 10:31-33).

24

The Attitude Question
Proverbs 27

Chapter 26 was on behaviour, Chapter 27 is on attitudes and relationships.

A. BAD ATTITUDES (vv. 1-4).
These come first, since good relationships are impossible until inner attitudes are corrected. They are in descending order.

1. Boasting (vv. 1-2).
Two aspects of this are mentioned here.

(a) *Boasting about the future (v. 1)*. This is directed to one so confident about what he is going to do that he announces and even brags about it. Such people are annoying because they are claiming a control of the future which none of us has. The future is God's province, even the very near future – *tomorrow* (James 4.13-16). Not only do we have no control over it, we cannot even foresee it, as line 2 says. This must not stop us preparing and providing for it, or verses 23-27 would be nonsense; but we mustn't presume all will be as we wish (Isa. 56:12, Luke 12:19f), nor fear it's sure to be worse (Matt. 6:34). Positively it challenges us to make the best use of today, both for our material life and our salvation (2 Cor. 6:2).

(b) *Boasting about ourselves (v. 2)*. This is for one who *praises* himself for what he is and has done, and so refers to the past and present rather than the future. It is right to do things that will elicit *praises*, but the *praising* is to come from others

(v. 21, 25:27). 'Praise is a comely garment but another must put it on you' (Bridges). Self-*praise* is the fruit of pride and self-love, which we hate in others but tolerate in ourselves. So instead of joining in the chorus of *praise* we are leading, others will dislike us and find fault with the very things we are boasting of. Self-*praise* is therefore foolish, as Paul observed in 2 Corinthians 10:12. If this sounds like an appeal to self-interest, turn to what Jesus said in Matthew 5:16: the Christian does praiseworthy things to get *praises* for God (cf. John 12:43).

2. Provocation (v. 3).
The boaster is irritating but not destructive, like the next two attitudes. *Provocation* from *a fool* is heavier than the weight of *stone* or *sand*. For it isn't 'anger' (KJV etc.), which may be justified and can be appeased. It is an attempt to provoke anger for no reason; so there is no case to answer, nothing to grapple with. However, the *fool* soon wearies of it, unlike the jealous.

3. Jealousy (v. 4).
This far surpasses the *cruelty* of *anger* and the *overwhelming* flood of *fury*. It is not just intolerable, it is irresistible. For it is not blurted out, but cherished within. It contemplates the destruction of its object and doesn't rest until that is achieved. Even Christ was destroyed by it (Matt. 27:18). So serious is it that the Law had a special ceremony to resolve it (Num. 5). It does more harm among Christians than most other problems and James has severe things to say about it (3:14-16).

Question
Are these attitudes in your own church fellowship? What damage are they doing? Do you find traces of them in yourself?

B. GOOD RELATIONSHIPS (vv. 5-11, 17-18).
These are impossible where there are bad attitudes. Once they are righted we can cultivate qualities which improve relationships.

1. Frankness (vv. 5-7).

The Hebrew of verse 5 will bear translating into rhyming verse:

Better is reproof revealed than love concealed.

Frankness is not the whole of *love* but is an essential part. True *love* is costly, for to *rebuke* our *friend* is to *wound* him (**v. 6**), which we may not enjoy and he won't like. But if he is wrong then to *kiss* where we should kill is to put ourselves among his *enemies*. They are good at covering their evil intentions with blandishments, but to *trust* them is fatal. So this is a word to both parties in a friendship. He who sees the fault should not be afraid to tell the other (Lev. 19:17, 2 Sam. 12:7, Matt. 18:15), and he who is *rebuked* should receive it as a mark of *love*, in fact the *love* God himself shows us (Job 5:17f, Rev. 3:19).

Verse 7 here could be a veiled rebuke to one so used to affection and praise he can't take criticism. Previous remarks about *honey* have been analogies of higher things (16:24, 24:13, 25:16, 27). The idea here is that too much *sweet* food can sicken you and you will *loathe* it (literally 'trample on the honeycomb'). The Israelites and their manna are an example (Num. 11:6). Someone accustomed to basking in compliments ceases to appreciate and enjoy them, yet is hypersensitive to criticism, even from a friend. One so surfeited with rich food he complains about it should think of one who knows what it means to be *hungry* and to whom pig's food would be luxury (Luke 15:6f). So the over-praised should think about one who has no friends and to whom even a *bitter* word would be welcome as a sign that someone was at least interested in him.

2. Tolerance (v. 8).

With due respect to Henry and Bridges, who indeed say true things about people who forsake their homes, leave their callings and neglect their families, this almost certainly refers to banishment. The *bird* leaves its *nest* because it is frightened away, and 'the women of Moab' were compared to 'fluttering (frightened) birds' when they were driven to 'the fords of Arnon' by invaders (Isa. 16:2). David saw himself as a *bird* when driven from the land by Saul (Ps. 11:1). Originally this proverb may have been to discourage driving people from the community through disputes, debts, offences or bullying by rich oppressors. Such are as restless and vulnerable as frightened birds. To us it comes as a call to tolerate each other. Whatever disputes or differences may arise we have no right to drive others away. Church discipline has its place but there are principles governing it and these leave no room for personal dislikes. Paul told the Christians in Rome not to allow their differences over Jewish ceremonies to break Christian fellowship; they should learn to 'bear with the failings of the weak' and 'accept one another' (Rom. 15:1-7).

3. Encouragement (vv. 9, 17).

In a hot climate lacking washing facilities, *perfume and incense* in a house counteracted the bad odour of unwashed clothes and sweaty feet to *bring joy to the heart* via the sense of smell. Line 2 is difficult in the Hebrew and a different reading has been adopted by RSV, GNB, NEB which make it contrast with the *pleasantness* and *joy* of *perfume*. However, it is almost certainly a comparison, although clumsily constructed. The meaning is that *friendship* is *pleasant* when it gives words of *counsel* from the heart (*earnest* is literally 'from the soul'). It thus balances verses 5-6: true *friendship* gives both rebukes and encouragements.

Another aspect of mutual encouragement is brought out in **verse 17** by an entirely different comparison – with the *sharpening* of an *iron* tool or weapon. The clash of the *iron* file on the *iron* implement enables the latter to function more efficiently. So in friendship we need not only the sweetness of comforting words but sometimes the clash of opinions and insights. *Friends* don't always have to agree, but they can always discuss. This discussion may have the effect of *sharpening* their convictions, or it may rub off their roughness or bluntness, so that they temper their wilder ideas or soften their more abrasive mannerisms.

4. Constancy (v. 10).

Verses 5, 6, 9 and 17 should have said enough to persuade us to hang on to our *friends*. Their counsel is encouraging, their conversation invigorating and even their rebukes edifying. But such is the capriciousness of human nature we need it spelling out, particularly in the case of old family *friends* (*the friend of your father*). These being of an older generation may be less exciting than our new young friends, but they have proved themselves, and *when disaster strikes* it is they who can be relied on. If Rehoboam heard this from his father's mouth he soon forgot it (1 Kings 12). But those who sustain these friendships have someone to go to, especially if their relatives (*brother*) should be *far away*, that is, distant or estranged. Joseph and David are examples of this, as is Jesus, who when absent and alienated from his *brothers*, found a welcome in the house of Lazarus.

5. Consideration (vv. 11, 18).

(a) *For parents (v. 11).*
The principle underlying this exhortation has been stated several times – that the happiness and reputation of parents is bound up with the character and behaviour of their children (10:1, 15:20, 23:15f, 24f). But for the first time it is put in the form of an appeal to the child (*my son*). As with preaching, merely to state principles is not enough; people have to be moved to embrace them by appeals. This is what the parent or teacher is doing here with the child or pupil. Nor does he rely on emotion but gives grounds for his appeal, as good preaching does, in order to persuade. These are: (i) the parents' own happiness (line 1), for how can a child brought into the world and cared for be impervious to the feelings of the parent? (ii) the parents' reputation (line 2). In Israel the continuance of God's covenant promise to bless and defend the nation depended on parents training their children to be as faithful to God as they themselves had been. A foolish, immoral or godless child would open the parent to the charge of betraying the nation. Although we are not in the same covenant, it is still true that much in society depends on the upbringing of children. Well-disciplined children won't be unteachable, criminals and dropouts. Then our institutions will function with less wastage and corruption and more efficiency and honesty. Even the health services

will be in less demand! The principle can be applied to the education of Christians as children of God (2 John 4).

(b) *For masters (v. 18).* The appeal to the worker to show consideration for his *master* is in the lower key form of a promise. For the consequences of faithful service or otherwise were not so far-reaching as those of parenting. So the appeal here is made to personal profit – the *honour* perhaps of promotion (22:29) or even commendation (Matt. 25:21f). The analogy is with nurturing a *fig tree,* which was a staple product of Judea, but which required several years careful *tending* if it was to *give fruit.* The kind of service that is *honoured* is not the minimum attention to duty but that which is caring and personal, as the word *looks after* intimates: he is interested in his *master's* welfare and feelings. Although slavery or servitude as a form of employment has almost ceased, we are servants of Christ (Rom. 1:1) and of each other (Gal. 5:13).

Question
How can we cultivate good relationships (see Phil. 2:1-8)?

C. Cautions (vv. 12-16).
Wise living is not only a matter of what we think and do when we have the initiative, but how we react to those events and persons we can't control. So we need a few warning signs.

1. Against incautiousness (v. 12).
This repeats 22:3 but in a different context. What better way to begin a list of cautions than with a warning against incautiousness! To avoid an approaching *danger* we need a sense of *danger*; not the overcautious nervousness which inhibits all activity, but weighing up the consequences of a course of action, knowing whether what we do or allow may make us *suffer.* This is the foresight *the prudent* learn in contrast to *the simple.*

2. Against suretyship (v.13).
We have had this warning five times already, including the identical 20:16, but in this context it is an example of how failure to foresee the dangerous consequences of an action can

lead to suffering. *Putting up security* can be for a neighbour or, as here, for a *stranger* or 'foreigner' (rather than *wayward woman*). There can be no greater risk than covering for one we don't know, who may be a con-man taking advantage of our ignorance of him. The resulting suffering is sure and severe – utter destitution. *The garment* is the very last thing an ancient oriental would part with, for it was not only his clothing by day but his bedclothes at night. If *the garment* went, it meant everything else had already gone. We are not expected to be soft touches; generosity is to be blended with prudence.

3. Against flattery (v. 14).
Here is one over-exuberant in his praise: he rises *early in the morning* to be the first to greet you, and *loudly* pours *blessings* on you, perhaps because you have shown him some kindness or had some good fortune or success. Such a one is likely to have an ulterior motive: he wants more favours from you, a share in your good fortune or some benefit from your success. His *blessing* is thus a *curse*, for he will make himself a nuisance until you give in to him. So the advice is: don't be flattered by excessive gratitude or congratulations or you will regret it.

4. Against nagging (vv. 15-16).
Previous warnings against the termagant woman have all pointed out the impossibility of living with her (21:9, 19); once she has been compared to *dripping* water (19:13). These comparisons are developed here. The *dripping* is that of a rainstorm which you can't escape, for if you go indoors it is beating on your roof or walls. *Wind* and *oil* are mentioned to show the impossibility of *restraining her*: you can't hold back *wind or grasp oil*. This confirms the view of 21:9, 19 that separation is the only solution. This is no doubt why this case is brought up again here: as a warning against hoping for a cure which will avoid separation, and driving yourself mad in the process, or perhaps against marrying someone before you know them thoroughly!

Try translating these ancient cautions into practical warnings you would place before young people today.

D. COUNSELS (vv. 19-27).

Having closed the wrong roads he now opens the right ones, which if we take we shall make progress in wisdom.

1. Search your heart (v. 19).

The Hebrew lacks any verbs and can only be made sense of by supplying one like *reflect* or 'reveal', which is what *water* does when looked into. Line 2 is not only verbless but ambiguous: is this one *man* or two? Does it mean that the way to know yourself is to look into your *heart*, your thoughts and feelings? Or that in another person you see a *reflection* of yourself – one equally made in the divine image, equally fallen and, if another Christian, equally redeemed? Is the *water* my own *heart* or is it another *man*? The latter certainly follows verses 9 and 17 helpfully, but the use of *heart* seems to favour the former. I can see myself in another's appearance, words, beliefs, experiences, weaknesses, etc., but I can't see into his *heart* and know what he truly feels and thinks as I can my own. This I must do if I am to grow in wisdom.

2. Control your desires (v. 20).

Continuing the thought of verse 19, what do we find when we search our hearts? Restlessness, craving and dissatisfaction. *The eyes of a man* are the first and main way of contact with the world he lives in. What we see we want, so *the eyes* represent covetousness and possessiveness. They also represent the search for knowledge and therefore stand for inquisitiveness and curiosity. The comparison with *Sheol and Abaddon* show we are not totally to despise or repress the use of the *eyes*. We were given them by God to admire his works, to enjoy and possess them; we were given the eyes of the mind to enquire, and acquire knowledge. The comparison speaks of insatiability – *never satisfied*. Death (*Sheol*) claims all and Hell (*Abaddon*) all it can. There is no quota, they never say, 'Enough' (30:16). It is this excess against which we are to guard for it is the spirit of the world (1 John 2:16) which is not 'of the Father' but born in hell.

3. Listen to others (v. 21).

Another ambiguous statement, line 2 reads literally, 'By the mouth of his praise' and can therefore mean *a man is tested* either:

(a) by whom and what he *praises*, for our opinions and tastes say a great deal about us;

(b) by public opinion rather than his opinion of himself, for others are better judges of our character and ability than we ourselves, cf. verses 1-2;

(c) by the way he responds to the *praises* he receives: do they puff him up or make him feel unworthy and pass on the *praises* to God? The second is the one most favoured by interpreters. We need to submit ourselves to public scrutiny and not be 'wise in our own eyes'. Reputation even has a place in qualifications for the ministry (1 Tim. 3:7). However, it is not an infallible test, for people can be mistaken or misjudge out of prejudice.

4. Seek God's grace (v. 22).

This verse shows the limitations of discipline and corporal punishment. In the case of a child they are usually effective (22:15), but the child is called 'simple' rather than *a fool*. *The fool* is one who has not responded to the education and discipline of his childhood, so that *folly* has become ingrained in him. With the right tools and much strength you can separate the *grain* from the husk, but to separate a *fool* from his *folly* requires more – a special work of God's grace (denied to Pharaoh but granted to Manasseh). We learn that God's judgments are insufficient to bring about repentance and faith – his grace is also necessary.

5. Do your work (vv. 23-27).

The counsels conclude on a practical note. What is the use of building up your character and soul if your body starves? This passage is addressed to the cattle farmer, although it can equally apply to other types of farming, and to the ways we earn our keep today. The basic call (**v. 23**) is to constant inspection of (*know*) and *attention* to that from which you gain your livelihood, in this case animals, which cannot look after themselves. Don't think you can neglect them because you have built up some savings (**v. 24**), for these won't last for ever and are not self-propagating. Even the king can't guarantee his position and riches (*crown*), so how much less the peasant!

On the other hand, the grass that feeds your flocks costs you nothing and replaces itself (**v. 25**). You cut it for *hay* and it immediately starts growing again and your flock can continue feeding on it. Meanwhile you can be gathering in more from the mountain slopes and store it as fodder for the winter. It may be hard continual toil but it pays (**vv. 26-27**). The *lambs* yield wool and the *goats milk*, which provides *clothing* and food for you and your household, and the surplus can be sold to buy another *field* enabling you to increase still further.

Application.

1. Apply the above principles to your or some other modern occupation.

2. Apply them to Jesus' words to Peter about **his** flock (John 21:15-17), then see how Peter passed this on to the shepherds of the flocks he had formed (1 Pet. 5:2).

25

Righteousness – Personal and Public
Proverbs 28

Since Wisdom is 'the fear of the Lord', and the Lord is 'the Righteous One', the wise will make righteousness their chief aim both in their personal lives and their public affairs.

A. Personal Righteousness.
Most verses concern the individual, in whom righteousness begins.

1. Righteousness is the basis of confidence (vv. 1, 4, 17).
One of the first and chief marks of *the righteous* is confidence (*bold*), freedom from fear (**v. 1**). Some fears are imaginary and due to bad conscience. A *wicked man* who has committed a crime imagines he is being *pursued* by an avenger or policeman. **Verse 17** gives us a fuller description: he flees from the scene of his crime, but even if he evades arrest, trial, imprisonment and execution, he can't escape the *torment* of his conscience. This will last *till death*, making his life a living *death*, like Cain's (Gen. 4:12-14). His unsocial act makes him a social outcast – *no one* will *support him*; everyone's hand will be against him.

One who, however guilty, has 'confessed and renounced his sins' (v. 13), will have a conscience free from *torment*. Facing an offended God yet 'finding mercy' makes him feel he has nothing to fear from man. This confidence and *lion*-like *boldness* is nowhere more clearly exhibited than in the way he reacts to *the wicked* (**v. 4**). However well he knows them, however closely he is related to them, he will not commend or encourage them (*praise*). This would be tantamount to *forsaking the law* himself, for the *law* condemns *wickedness*. But he will go further than refraining from outright approval, he will actively *resist* them. For this is *the law's* function (Gal. 4:23f). Those who are on *the law's* side will do all they can, both by their conduct, words and actions to expose and oppose sin. In these days of post-modernism and moral relativism *righteous* people of this calibre are much needed.

Read of Daniel, more of a *lion* than a *lion* itself (Dan. 5:22-28, 6:10f)!

2. Righteousness forms good financial principles.

(a) *Righteousness is superior to riches (***v. 6***).*
Few would agree that *a poor man* in any circumstances is *better* than *a rich man*, for the prevailing ethos is that a society's economy rates higher than its morality. Many think *a poor man* justified in using dishonest means to escape poverty. He may even be treated leniently by the courts, but his conscience will not approve, and which is better in the end – to escape poverty and social ostracism, or to be able to live with yourself and be blameless before God? As for the *rich man*, while it is not a sin to be *rich*, the saying suggests that in this case it has been achieved by *perverse ways. Perverse* is literally 'double', suggesting he appears honest and charitable but is actually devious and selfish. Is he really *better* than the honest pauper?

(b) *All dubious methods are rejected (***vv. 8, 21, 22***).*
The righteous person avoids not only dishonesty but anything not straightforward.

(i) *Lending on interest (v. 8).* The laws against lending to a fellow-Israelite on interest (Lev. 25:36) were frequently honoured more in the breach than the observance. Here they are doubly broken, for *exorbitant interest* is two words 'interest and increase', the former being a deduction from the loan, which still had to be paid in full, and the latter an additional charge payable on repayment of the principal. If the authorities would not enforce the law God would. He would see that *wealth* amassed in this way would fall into the hands of one (the lender's heir?) who would use it, not to lend on interest, but for charitable purposes. Possibly in Israel this happened rapidly enough to be discernible. In our dispensation providence operates more slowly, possibly through the tax system! Internationally it is even slower, yet it can happen that a nation which has exploited others becomes poor whereas the poor one it has exploited grows rich. This is the hope of the Third World!

Consider. Do you agree that Israel's law on interest still applies to Christians lending to the needy, but not to finance companies?

(ii) *Partiality* (**v. 21**). Here is another shady financial practice: *showing partiality* for a price. A person has to be in a position of power to attract a bribe, such as a judge or witness in a lawsuit who can swing the case either way. But *partiality* and bribery are *not good* (18:5, 24:23); in fact they are *wrong* (Lev. 19:15). Nor is it any mitigation to plead the reward was trifling – *a piece of bread*, or that your life depended on it, for surely only a starving man would 'pervert justice' for a mere crust. In God's book, sins are not graduated – all 'sin is lawlessness' (1 John 3:4).

(iii) *Miserliness* (**v. 22**). Money acquired diligently and honestly can be unrighteous, where it is done to satisfy a *stingy* nature, literally 'an evil eye', as in 23:6. This describes the covetous heart which won't give or share and even grudges what it spends on itself. So it is already poor even while the money bags are growing. For surely *riches* are about living well and enjoying the luxuries of life. To have money but not spend it is to live in *poverty*. Also money is more vulnerable than real estate – easy to steal or lose value through inflation. Those who think they are *rich* because of the amount of cash they have are *unaware that poverty awaits them*.

Consider the spiritual meaning Jesus added to miserliness in Matthew 6:19-21, Luke 16:19-26.

(c) *Riches do not give security* (**v. 11**).

One danger of being rich is that it breeds a false security (18:11). Another is conceit, for it is easy to conclude that success proves cleverness or even the favour of God. The wisdom of the righteous man, however, does not lie in knowing how to make money, but in discerning the uncertainty of riches and not trusting them (Matt. 6:19, 1 Tim. 6:17). He is grateful for what God has given or made him in his gracious providence. He is trustful and content. This wisdom is available to all, including *the poor man* who *sees through* the conceited *rich man* and doesn't envy him.

(d) *Money is to be worked for* (**vv. 19-20**).

Verse 19 is almost a straight repeat of 12:11, but with a difference which more powerfully dramatises the differing results of diligence and idleness. Only rsv brings out the repetition of 'plenty' in both lines: 'plenty of food ... plenty of *poverty*'. What stinging irony is here! The two words are virtual opposites but juxtaposed they not only state a fact but highlight the utter destitution of the time-waster, whose larder, table and stomach are full of emptiness. Diligent work therefore has a moral aspect to it and idleness is a form of sin. When man fell his work was cursed (Gen. 3:17-19), but a merciful God has mitigated it by the promise of *abundant food* to those who, instead of unrealistically *chasing fantasies* and pursuing what might have been, accept reality and make the best of it (see also 27:23-27).

One who works diligently and honestly at his calling is *a faithful man* (**v. 20**), for he provides for his family, is charitable to the poor and pays his dues to God. He is respected and well-liked and enjoys God's favour. But one more concerned about ends than means, riches than righteousness, is vulnerable to temptation to dishonesty (1 Tim. 6:9f). In the ancient farming world profit was small and slow to come in, so that one who became suddenly *rich* was open to suspicion. Even today the first thing the police do in investigating a suspect in a robbery case is to see if his bank balance has received a sudden boost. In any case, God sees his heart is covetous, which to him is a sin like theft (Exo. 20:17) and will not *go unpunished*.

(e) *Righteousness includes generosity* (**v. 27**).

Everyone's ultimate ambition is to avoid want. Human reason says, Save, invest, only let your money out of your hand if you can recover it with interest. God's wisdom says, *Give* it to the *poor*. They can't repay with interest, they can't repay at all – not in cash, but they can in gratitude, prayer, friendship and moral support. Moreover *the poor* are God's own special concern and he will see you aren't the loser. You only lose if you *close* your *eyes* to them, pretend they don't exist or that you haven't noticed them. Such are always hated by *the poor*, whose *curses* may be heard by God, and whatever happens between now and then, will be put into effect when Christ returns (Matt. 25:41-45). It is not those who ignore the appeal of *the poor* who *lack nothing*, but those who have the Lord for their shepherd (Ps. 23:1).

Review these financial principles and examine your own use of money in the light of them to see whether it qualifies to be called 'righteous'.

3. Righteousness means respect for parents (vv. 7, 24).

(a) *Obedience to their teaching* (**v. 7**).

This book sets out to make the young and simple mature and wise (*discerning*): 1:1-4. This task was placed in the hands of parents who stood in the place of God, since their instruction is called *law* (TORAH, 1:8). The first lesson was 'Choose your companions carefully' (1:10-19), frequently repeated (e.g. 23:19-22). Here is a warning about what happens if he chooses badly – he *disgraces* the family name. In Israel this was far worse than, say, the son of a noble English family who, in spite of all his advantages falls into bad company, gets into trouble and runs up debts. For in Israel the continuance of God's covenant with the nation depended on the rising generation following their parents' teaching. It is only parallelled by the *disgrace* felt by a Christian couple who, after years of loving godly upbringing, see their children choosing the wrong friends or even spouses.

(b) *Respect for their property* (**v. 24**).

If charity begins at home so does righteousness. Duty to parents comes second only to that to God. This explains why the lesser sin of *robbery* is equated with that of murder (*destroys*). The greater the obligation the greater the sin. For the *robbery* here is clearly not violent, since he says '*It's not wrong.*' Perhaps he has helped himself to their money or goods, or wasted his allowance, or run up debts, or claimed his inheritance before it is due (Luke 15:12), or failed to provide for his parents in later life (1 Tim. 5:8). He could justify all this on the grounds that 'family money' is his by right and therefore it is impossible to steal from parents. God says otherwise: it is not only easier than stealing from anyone else but more serious.

4. Righteousness governs the devotional life (vv. 9, 13, 14).

(a) *Prayer* (**v. 9**).

It would seem to state the obvious to connect the devotional life with righteousness. Yet nothing was or is more common than to separate them. All in Israel heard *the law* recited, both at home and in the synagogue or Temple. To listen is one thing, to hear another (Mark 4:9). 'Hearing' means assent and obedience. To *turn a deaf ear* is to refuse these responses. Yet even those too proud to receive *the law* find the time comes when they are in such a plight that they pray to God to rescue them. Now it is God's turn to refuse and with the same deliberate rejection with which his *law* was refused, for *detestable* (literally 'abomination') is a strong term. The classic case is Saul and the Amalekites' sheep (1 Sam. 15), but the Bible is full of these warnings, indicating what a common condition this is. How many there are who refuse to hear preaching or read the Bible, yet expect God to help them when a desperate situation drives them to *prayer*!

(b) *Repentance* (**v. 13**).

This is probably the nearest PROVERBS comes to the Gospel itself and it stands alone, because the book concentrates on practicalities. However, in such an extended treatment of personal righteousness, it can scarcely be omitted. Yet the theme of *prosperity* is not lost sight of. Since this comes from the blessing of God, we must not love what God hates – *sins*. The tendency to *conceal sin* shows the division in human personality. *Sin* is *concealed* because it is cherished yet at the same time loathed as shameful. The only way out of this conflict is to face it openly before God (and if necessary others) and *renounce* it. Then God covers it – under the Law with a blood sacrifice and under the Gospel with the blood and righteousness of Christ (1 John 1:8f).

(c) *Consistency* (**v. 14**).
The position reached in verse 13 must be sustained, for repentance is not a 'one-off' action but a constant attitude of mind. Since the Hebrew lacks *the Lord* and the word *fears* is not the normal word for *fear of the Lord*, but a stronger one meaning intense dread, this probably refers to the *fear* of falling back into the state of verse 13a, or, as line 2 puts it, of *hardness* of *heart*. The stress is on *always*, that is, maintaining the position reached in verse 13b. For since that led to 'mercy', so this will assure God's *blessing* and his preservation from *trouble*.

Question
How far do you find your daily life harmonizes with your private devotions?

5. Righteousness acts responsibly towards others (vv. 10, 23).

(a) *It does not mislead* (**v. 10**).
Here we are warned against becoming so set on *evil* that we are not content with the company of our fellow-sinners but want to bring *the upright* down with us. This is the spirit of the Evil One who first brought down righteous Adam and Eve and even tried to lure the Son of God *along an evil path*. Small wonder he tries it with Christ's followers, for this gives him a taste of the victory which eluded him with Jesus (Rev. 12:13-17). *The upright*, however, have a triple insurance policy against enticers: they fail to bring *the upright down*; they themselves *fall into their own trap*; and they see *the upright* not

only escape but attain their inheritance. This principle of exact retribution, with its use of the illustration from *trapping*, is prominent in the Old Testament and underlies the reasoning of Job's friends. However, it has to be viewed in the long term, especially in the Gospel age, where the believer's life follows the pattern of Christ's, who *received a good inheritance* through apparent defeat. However, warnings against enticement are severe (Matt. 18:6).

(b) *It is frank* (**v. 23**).

Frankness in relationships received an airing in 27:5f and what was said there is taken a stage further here. There it was the teacher or author in the name of God who commended the practice, but we are not told how the friend received the wounding words. *In the end* implies he doesn't take it *favourably* at first. He prefers the smoothness of the *flattering tongue* (the word used of the seductive woman of 2:16, 7:5). Perhaps he feels hurt ('wounds' 27:6) and is offended. Later he realizes that what the *flatterer* said was untrue and leading him into trouble; then he remembers the *rebukes*, which are clearly right, which puts the one who made them into a better light. Nathan who charged David with his sin (2 Sam. 12:7) later took his side in the anointing of Solomon (1 Kings 1:32-40), and Peter, rebuked before the Galatian churches by Paul (Gal. 2:11), later commended him as a 'dear brother' who 'wrote with the wisdom that God gave him' (2 Pet. 3:15).

Question

Assuming you don't mislead in the drastic way of v. 10, are you ever guilty of it by a failure to be frank?

6. Righteousness is consistent in its conduct (v. 18).

Why is the one *whose walk is blameless* 'better' (v. 6) than the other? How is he 'blessed' (v. 14)? He has a security not promised to the others. Indeed, the only promise made to him *whose ways are perverse* is *sudden* and certain ruin. This has been a familiar theme in the book (see comments on 10:9, 25, 11:3-6, which also discuss the difference between old and new covenant security). Although to some extent a repetition, this verse has a logical place in a section on personal righteousness and is particularly appropriate after verse 17. Committing sin is committing suicide and failing to follow conscience is the sure road to disaster.

7. Righteousness lives by trust (vv. 25-26).

(a) *It avoids quarrels (***v. 25***).*
There are many ways of starting a quarrel: hatred (10:12), pride (13:10), craft (14:17), bad temper (15:18), mockery (22:10) and here *greed*. The selfish person is bound to find himself in a conflict of interest with others, especially other selfish people. This makes his acquisitiveness counterproductive, for all his assets go on financing the dispute. It is better to *trust in the Lord*, who has promised to supply our need, though not our *greed* (Matt. 6:19-34). Such may not *prosper* to the degree the *greedy man* aspires to, but their contentment makes them feel *prosperous* (13:4).

(b) *It enjoys safety (***v. 26***).*
Since living by faith in God leads to a life of peace and contentment (v. 25), it is the wisest way to live. It is the way not only of prosperity but *safety* – from those pitfalls into which we fall if we *trust in ourself*. For while, as God's images, we have much going for us, we are confined to the limits of our knowledge and ability. Worse, if we *trust in ourself* we place ourselves in the hands of what is corrupt and may mislead us (Jer. 17:9). We are therefore advised not to 'lean on our own understanding' (3:5). But merely to destroy self-confidence is equally unsafe, for while it may keep us from mistakes of our own making, it won't prevent things happening to us. But *the Lord* can and therefore to *trust* him is to *walk in wisdom*.

Question
What further 'safety' is promised to those who have a New Testament trust in Christ (see 2 Timothy 3:15)?

B. PUBLIC RIGHTEOUSNESS.
As seen in 14:34 the word 'righteousness' can be used of a nation as well as an individual. Fundamental to this national

righteousness is the way the nation is governed. Certain aspects of righteous government are referred to here.

1. Justice (vv. 5, 12, 28).

This is the basic principle of all government. Governments can't do everything but they are expected to use their good offices to see fair play (see 8:15f). Unhappily the fall of the human race from its original righteousness means that human government often falls far below this standard. There are those *men* so evil they do not even *understand* the necessity or nature of *justice* (**v. 5**). The word *evil* is emphatic and refers not just to a nonbeliever but to those who have risen to power with *evil* ambitions, which they fulfil with *evil* methods. Happily only a minority of governments are like that; most have some conception of *justice* and want to administer it. While only *those who seek the Lord understand it fully*, because their God is the God of *justice*, the 'common grace' of God normally sees that nations are governed reasonably if not perfectly justly.

The effects of government by just men on the one hand and *evil men* on the other are seen in **verses 12** and **28**. When *the righteous* are in power (*triumph*) people are happy, *there is great elation*. There is order in society, people are not oppressed, criminals are brought to book. However, in a fallen world it can happen that even in a well-run state *the wicked rise to power*. Fear, even terror, comes on the whole nation; people are afraid to speak, write, do anything or go anywhere – *men go into hiding*. Such is the police state, by which alone an evil regime can sustain itself. But in the goodness of God this doesn't last for ever; something happens – death, assassination, revolution or just evolution. The result is that the *wicked* rulers *perish, the righteous* come out of *hiding* and resume the reins of government.

2. Order (v. 2).

The *rebellious*ness of which line 1 speaks is not rebellion against king or government but against God, the word used having the sense of 'apostasy'. It is Solomon's warning to Israel to be loyal to God's rule for the sake of national unity. The warning was prophetic, for after his death ten tribes broke away and set up their own gods. This northern kingdom had *many* *rulers,* some of whom were replaced quickly by assassins and usurpers, whereas the southern kingdom retained David's dynasty until their apostasy put them under a foreign yoke. It is impossible to decide whether the *man of understanding* is the king, his chief counsellor or the common *man.* The principle is the same: true *order* and stability in a nation come not from its police but from the *understanding* of both government and people that 'righteousness exalts a nation but sin is a disgrace to any people' (14:34).

3. Freedom (vv. 3, 15-16).
The NIV reading of **verse 3** is based on an emendation of MT which reads literally 'a poor man' (see mg). This might refer to 'a poor man' who usurps power (cf. v. 2, Eccles. 10:16) and makes up for his previous poverty by *oppression* in order to enrich himself. This makes the poor even poorer and is compared to *driving rain* which instead of fattening *the crops* destroys them. By contrast the reign of a good *ruler* is like a gentle rain that refreshes the earth and brings prosperity (Ps. 72:5-7). Such was Solomon's reign which was thus a foreshadowing of Christ's. A government which is just will not terrorize people but give them freedom.

Another illustration of the tyrant is used in **verse 15**: he is *like a roaring lion or a charging bear.* He does not behave like a rational human being but an animal governed solely by appetite. Because he has taken all the power and resources *the people* are left in a *helpless* state. He well qualifies for the description of a *tyrannical ruler* who *lacks judgment* (**v. 16**). He not only misjudges his own responsibility but the people he is oppressing. It is implied in line 2 that they are not *so helpless* as they seemed. They resent his fattening himself at their expense. So he doesn't enjoy his *ill-gotten gain* for long. Oppressed people tend to rise up and take away the *life* of a *tyrannical ruler* long before his expected end.

Question
To what extent do you think these principles are fulfilled by our governments? Can you find examples in the world of where they are seriously infringed?

26

Justice
(Proverbs 29)

There are more explicit references to *Justice* here than in any other chapter, and where the word itself is not used, the idea can be perceived without putting too much strain on the text.

A. DIVINE JUSTICE.
Here are examples of the justice God shows to various kinds of people; the first four are positive and the last two negative.

1. To obstinate sinners (v. 1).
There is a sense in which the teaching of this verse underlies the whole chapter, as it sets down two aspects of God's justice.

(a) *That he gives fair warning.* He *rebukes* through parents, preachers and even State officials, and these warnings are echoed by the conscience. But he doesn't enforce complicity, he wants repentance and obedience to be freely given, otherwise the words *remains stiff-necked* would be meaningless.

(b) *That he acts decisively.* Persistent and deliberate wickedness upsets the balance of justice in a society. To restore this may require *sudden* and irreversible destruction, which sounds like capital punishment or at least the utter end of a way of life. Thus it typifies God's final judgment, which according to Jesus is 'everlasting' (Matt. 25:46, Mark 9:48).

2. To habitual sinners (v. 6).
This helps explain the obstinacy of verse 1. Why do some go lemming-like on their way, knowing it will lead to destruction?

Because they are *snared by* their *own sin*. They think they are acting freely and doing what they want. In fact they are doing what sin wants them to do, for it has conquered their will. They may appear and feel happy, then realize with horror they are weak and at the mercy of their habit. *A righteous one* is *glad* because he is not in this predicament. There are grounds for translating *can sing* as 'runs', which affords a good contrast between the two. A *righteous one* may fall but he is not *snared*, and gets up and goes on his way singing. So justice is not only reserved for the end, we reap what we sow in this life (Gal. 6:7f).

3. To the proud (v. 23).
God's ways with the proud are a favourite theme of Solomon's, cf. 11:2, 16:18, 18:12. Perhaps he had to keep reminding himself not to let his power and wealth go to his head. He certainly needed to warn his sons, who inherited without cost what he had obtained through humble prayer (1 Kings 3:7-9) and hard work. Here we see this principle against the background of justice. *Pride* is not so much exulting in one's achievements or possessions, as claiming to be the sole architect of them, taking credit which should go to God. Similarly a *lowly spirit* is not false modesty but acknowledging that whatever we are, do or obtain is through the goodness of God. Justice lies in God restoring the equilibrium by putting those who *honour* him above those who withhold that *honour*.

4. To the untrusting (v. 25).
Fear in itself is natural and frequently justified. Who can be blamed for fleeing in *fear* from a man waving a gun? Here, however it contrasts with *trust in the Lord*, part of 'the fear of the Lord' that constitutes wisdom, and describing a whole approach to life. The choice is between a life governed by what others think and do, and one based on what God is and has promised. The first is a life of bondage, a *snare*, for what pleases one will anger another. In the case of a believer it is fatal, as we see from Peter whose *fear of man* (or girl!) made him deny Christ (Matt. 26:69-74), and even after receiving the Spirit it caused him to deny the gospel (Gal. 2:12)! *Trust in the Lord* releases from this

snare, for it makes obedience to God the dominant motive and thus guarantees his personal protection (*safe*), cf. 18:10, 30:5.

5. To the wronged (v. 26).

How can a wronged person obtain *justice*? He will *seek an audience with* the *ruler* of his country or one of his representatives, who after all are appointed for this purpose (8:15, 16:10, Rom. 13:3f). *Rulers*, however, are human: their knowledge is limited, their discernment imperfect and their motives can be selfish. There is no guarantee that *justice* will be forthcoming from that quarter (Ps. 146:3f). But there is a higher court of appeal that never fails, although vindication may not be immediate and may even be delayed until the last day (Job 19:25).

6. To all (v. 13).

We are apt to dwell on the differences between people: sex, age, race, colour, culture, knowledge, ability, status, etc. Nowhere are we more conscious of these than in finance, and nowhere do the deprived feel the injustice more. The *oppressor* here is either the tyrant who increases his substance by laying crippling taxes on the people and making them *poor*, or the moneylender who charges exorbitant rates of interest and makes the *poor* poorer. Yet 'the Lord God made them all' (cf. 22:2). The things which differentiate us depend on the thing we have in common: life, for *sight to the eyes* is a Hebrew expression for life – 'the light of life' (Ps. 49:19; Isa. 53:11, NIV). When Jesus was counselling us to 'love our enemies' he appealed to what we have in common with them – the sun and rain by which life is sustained (Matt. 5:45).

For prayer. Pray that the assurance that God governs the world with justice will help your understanding of the other themes of this chapter and of life generally. Ask him for the wisdom not to expect from others what he alone can give. Read Psalm 146.

B. POLITICAL JUSTICE.

These verses are similar to those in chapter 28 under 'Public Righteousness'. Governments exist to uphold justice; these verses depict life where justice is maintained and where it breaks down.

1. Where Justice is maintained.

(a) *There is happiness (v. 2, cf. 11:10, 28:12, 28).*
This does not only refer to government, for *thrive* = 'increase'; *the righteous* majority set the tone of society. Public opinion is more powerful than strong government. Acceptability and unacceptability have more influence than law and punishment. We take more notice of what our neighbours think and do than of what the law says. A society in which good, right and just things are 'done' and the opposite 'not done' is a happy society. People trust and help each other. But *when the wicked rule* the roost, this trust and helpfulness break down and *the people groan.*

(b) *There is stability (vv. 4, 14).*
In **verse 4** the government is clearly in view, for whereas 'righteousness' is the duty of all, the administration of *justice* is in the hands of the authorities. This principle is to be applied not only to crime and punishment but to finance. The temptation to those in power is to abuse it to their own enrichment. This can be done by *bribes* (NIV): passing laws favourable to one section of the community in return for cash; or making judgments in court in favour of those who can pay for them. Others connect the expression (= 'man of offerings') with taxation. While taxes are essential to any government (Rom. 13:6f), they can be levied in such a way as to favour that section of the community most able to upset the ship of state at the expense of unfairly burdening *the poor* (**v. 14**) who are least capable of putting pressure on the government. This policy, however, is counter-productive and likely to *tear down* the fabric of state, for it causes unrest among the people and provokes the intervention of God, the Defender of *the poor* (22:22f, 23:10f). Justice for all is the way to *the stability* of a *country* and the *security* of the *throne.*

(c) *There is social concern* (**v. 7**).

This applies first to the judiciary. *Righteous* governors and judges conduct cases according to the rightness of the cause not the ability of the parties to defend them or remunerate the judges. Part of political *justice* is to see that *the poor* are not falsely condemned because of their weakness, which in our country includes the availability of legal aid. But the verse can be taken more widely of society in general. RSV translates 'the rights of the poor' (cf. 31:8), which includes his right to a reasonable standard of living. Sinai laid on Israel the responsibility of assisting *the poor*, thus making it a matter of social *justice* as well as human compassion. This makes *the wicked* not merely heartless but unjust, lacking in right principles.

Question

What do you think about 'human rights'? How far do our responsibilities to others extend? What is the answer to Genesis 4:9b?

2. Where Justice breaks down.

(a) *There is instability* (**v. 8**).

The *mockers* are probably the corrupt leaders, as in Isaiah 28:14f: 'You scoffers who rule this people in Jerusalem'. They *mock* at justice, law, consultation and agreement, and govern arbitrarily. This destabilizes the community and *stirs up the city*, that is, 'inflames' the people, who break up into factions. It takes *wise men* to reconcile these and restore order, and they need to be in authority to do so. In Isaiah 28:16f it is God who sweeps away the *mockers* and replaces them with just governors, whom he calls 'a foundation stone', for only justice can give stability.

(b) *There is deception* (**v. 12**).

Truth is essential to justice, which can only be administered where the true facts are accepted. Those in authority have to investigate and assess the information they receive (20:8), especially where it involves accusations against others. Where the authorities accept the lies they are fed, a spirit of deception permeates society and its *officials become wicked*. Saul listened to the slanderous accusations brought against David, and his counsellors were *wicked* (1 Sam. 22:8ff, Ps. 52:2-4). Ahab wanted his *officials* to proclaim lies against Naboth and had no difficulty in finding corrupt ones to do it (1 Kings 21:11-13). Nothing damages justice more than lying, which destroys trust (Eph. 4:25).

(c) *There is corruption (v. 16)*.

This is a further stage down the ladder. It is the opposite situation to verse 2 – *the wicked* are now the opinion-makers, so *sin thrives* and corruption sets in. Like sheep, people follow each other and if sin is in fashion they will have no conscience about it. If everyone else does it, it can't be bad. Why should I be different and miss the fun? Where this is the spirit of the age, life becomes very difficult for *the righteous*. The temptation to join in is powerful and the cost of separation high. All they can do is hold on until the tide turns, and turn it will: 28:12, 28 and 29:2 confirm this, and the psalms are full of it (Pss. 37:34-36, 58:10, 91:8, 92:9-11, 112:8). This was what kept Habakkuk going when the rule of the wicked in Judah was only replaced by that of the Chaldeans (Hab. 2:2-4, 12-14). This is what sustains the church during her long warfare with Satan and his host (Rev. 11:15).

(d) *There is anarchy (v. 18)*.

Here is the final stage in the breakdown of justice – *the people cast off restraint*, or 'go wild', as when Aaron was left in charge of Israel and failed to prevent their idolatrous orgy (Exod. 32:25). The absence of *revelation* which permits this situation to arise refers to the lack of prophetic preaching (see 1 Sam. 3:1). The prophets expounded *the law* to *the people*, applied it to their lives and called on them to repent of their departure from it. Ideally they worked with the King whose main duty was to uphold *the law*. But when the Kings themselves flouted it they silenced the prophets (Hosea 9:7f) and *the people* got away with anything. When the King withdrew the prophets, God withdrew his *blessing* (Hosea 4:6), and only restored it when *the people* returned to *the law*. Although we are not in that system, governments are still appointed by God to keep *people* in order. Christians and their preachers can cooperate with them in this by proclaiming and living the moral law and preaching the gospel.

Question
Where do you think our country is on this scale of breakdown at the present time? Does this spur you to pray more for it and to be more determined we should be 'salt in the earth' (Matt. 5:13) and thus prevent further degeneration?

C. DOMESTIC JUSTICE.
Justice like charity begins at home with the way members of a household treat each other.

1. Children (vv. 15, 17).
Justice as part of *wisdom* can be learned from an early age; specifying the *mother* may indicate this refers to young children, who were in her charge. It begins with instruction (1:8), which makes the simple wise (1:2-4), but due to indwelling sin the instruction is not always understood or the *child* may reject it and go his own way. Then *correction* is needed – first by word, reasoning and encouraging, and where this fails, by *the rod*, by some form of punishment. (See on 13:24 and 22:15 for discussion on corporal punishment). All this amounts to discipline (**v. 17**).

Although this form of education sounds hard work it pays in the long term: *he will give you peace*. Sometimes *peace* has to be won through war. In the case of children their tendency to rebelliousness, disobedience and mischief have to be opposed and defeated to establish a right and good relationship. You cannot *delight* in a disobedient wayward *child*; he will make you feel ashamed, especially if the *disgrace* becomes public. At the time you may feel the easiest way to *peace* is to give way to him; chastisement risks forfeiting his love. But *a child left to himself* is *left* to the dominance of a sinful nature, a wayward will, a wicked world and an evil devil. He needs parental protection from these. In the long term this is best for everyone including the *child*. Our society is littered with the casualties of the policy of leaving children to themselves. This is more unjust than punishment.

2. Youth (v. 3).

The child is now mature enough to be called *a man*, to choose his friends and be in danger from *prostitutes*. We have been told several times how the parents' happiness is bound up with their children's behaviour (10:1, 23:15f, 24f, 27:11), and one of the earliest lessons was in how to escape *prostitutes* (2:16-19, ch. 5, 6:20–7:27). This was partly why they sought to instil in him the *love of wisdom*. Here the principle of justice is brought into the equation. *Prostitutes* are costly, well beyond the means of the young, who can only afford them with financial help from their parents. But a *father* does not work all his life for his son to *squander his wealth* on them. The son in Jesus' parable appealed to justice when he demanded his inheritance, but quickly forgot it when he *squandered it on prostitutes* (Luke 15:12 and 30). Children have a right to financial help from their parents (2 Cor. 12:14) but not to waste it.

3. Servants (vv. 19, 21).

In the days when many people kept *servants* it was part of Wisdom to advise on how to treat them justly. **Verse 19** appears to have the bad *servant* in view, one who needs to be *corrected* because he is not doing what he should. So obstinate is he that however clear your instructions he won't do as you tell him (*respond*). Something more is needed, although the verse doesn't tell us what. Do you beat him? Do you dismiss him?

Verse 21 refers to the good *servant*. Wisdom warns against the danger of overindulging him. A *servant* however good is still a *servant* and shouldn't be treated like, or better than, a member of the family. What the consequence is cannot be said dogmatically, for the meaning of the last word in the Hebrew sentence (*grief*) is unknown. Most interpreters take it to mean 'he will become his son/heir/successor in the end'. Since there are three other warnings of this eventuality (17:2, 19:10, 30:22), this is the most likely meaning. A *pampered servant* will forget he is a *servant*, take advantage of his master's favour and end up usurping the rightful heir. Tenderness will have melted justice.

Question
This being fairly irrelevant in today's world, what principles can we deduce about work relationships in our culture?

D. PERSONAL JUSTICE.
Justice is not only about what officials do but about the way we treat each other. Here are some of the unjust ways.

1. Flattery (v. 5).
As seen in 26:28, *flattery* is a form of lying. It not only uses inaccurate words but has a dishonest motive. It may be done to put our *neighbour* under an obligation to us, or where done out of malice, to put him off his guard so that he blunders into trouble. This may be *the net* the *flatterer is spreading*. Perhaps he is envious of his *neighbour*, who is a threat to his popularity or even his business. Instead of attacking him outright he uses a subtler approach, so that when he ruins himself the *flatterer* is not implicated. Such is the way of Satan with believers who can't be toppled by direct attacks: he bolsters their pride and soon they fall (16:18). We learn nothing about justice from a *flatterer*.

2. Controversy (v. 9).
Don't expect justice when dealing with *a fool*! Whether it is a mere argument (as some see this) or a *court* case (as NIV takes it), you won't get the matter handled 'in a contemplative fashion' – *there is no peace*. For the *fool* by definition cannot think or behave reasonably; he is all emotion. Either he takes the matter too seriously and *rages*, or refuses to take it seriously and *scoffs*, tries to laugh it off. What a good reason for seeking to be *wise*!

3. Hatred (vv. 10, 27).
Nothing sums up the world-view of PROVERBS better than **verse 27**, and it is significant that Solomon's collection should end with it. There are only two kinds of people and two ways

of life according to the wisdom of PROVERBS: *righteous* and
wicked, those who are saved from the consequences of the Fall,
and those who are left to them. The former are God's 'delight'
and the latter his detestation (11:20). This reaction of God's is
reproduced in the relationship between the two kinds, who
detest each other. This too is a consequence of the Fall, on
account of which God put enmity between Satan's offspring
and the woman's (Gen. 3:15). The woman's offspring is strictly
Christ, who would crush the head of the serpent, but it includes
those in Christ, those who prior to his advent believed the
promise of him and those who after his coming believe that
God raised him from the dead for their justification (Rom. 4).

The Old Testament records many instances of this mutual
hatred, even among the people of Israel. This includes
examples of **verse 10**, where hatred reached the point of
seeking to *kill* them and shed their *blood*. It culminated in
the murder of Christ himself who warned his disciples they
would be treated similarly (John 15:18f, 16:1-3). This shows
where the *hatred* of *the righteous* differs from that of *the wicked*.
The latter are basically in enmity against God (Rom. 8:7) and
detest the righteous because they see God's image in them. *The
righteous detest the wicked* because they see in them sins which
God hates, which crucified Christ and from which they have
been delivered. So they don't *seek* to *kill the wicked*, but to
encourage them to loathe sin, turn from it, become friends of
God and of those who love him. What could be more just?

4. Anger (vv. 11, 22).

Nothing is further from justice than *anger*, which is totally
irrational. It **can** be righteous since it is found in God (Ps. 95:10,
Rom. 1:18) and in Jesus (Mark 3:5). But for fallen creatures it is
difficult to 'be angry and not sin' by refusing to be pacified or
reconciled and letting it rankle (Eph. 4:26). When this happens
it *stirs up dissension* (**v. 22**), it provokes an angry reaction and
this in turn leads to *many other sins*: bad language, insults, blows
and even murder. The *fool* never thinks of the consequences of
anger and is governed by emotion, so that he *gives full vent to
his anger* (**v. 11**). The *wise man*, realizing that getting cross about
a situation only makes it worse, *keeps himself under control*. The

literal words are interesting: 'quiets it in the background'. It paints a picture of one taking a fractious baby out of the room to soothe it! When we feel temper rising let's take it to somewhere quiet and give it a cool drink! Above all, let's think of God who although never unjustly angry, is 'slow' to come to the boil (Ps. 103:8) and soon goes off it (Ps. 30:5).

5. Thoughtless talk (v. 20).
In 26:12 we were told *there is more hope for a fool* than for one 'wise in his own eyes'. This is what really makes the person in view here *speak in haste*. He is so sure he is right that he states his case without consideration or consultation, regardless that there may be those present who know far more and better than he does. The self-opinionated person is one stage worse than a *fool*. The *fool* has no clear thoughts or firm convictions and is at least open to persuasion. The other has made up his mind and committed himself to it. Pride makes him defend his position and refuse all other views. Wise men such as 'Ecclesiastes' (Eccles. 5:2) and James (1:19) advise us to think well before we speak and be economical with our words.

6. Perjury (v. 24).
Here is justice at its most rigorous. *The accomplice of a thief* may think himself less guilty than the gang leader, for he didn't invent the plot, played only a small part and received but a fraction of the proceeds. In fact he is worse off, for when called as a witness he *can't testify* against the *thief* without implicating himself, and for fear of this lies on *oath*. Now he has two crimes to answer for, not only to the judge but to God (Lev. 5:1, 1 Tim. 1:9f). He can blame no one but himself, he *is his own enemy*, for he willingly consented to join the plot. Again we are taken back to the young person's first lesson (1:11-19).

Consider how common are the above six faults, even among Christians. Yet how seriously do we take them? Do we not often 'justify' what are basically sins against justice and therefore against a just God? Is this consistent with our belief that we are 'justified by faith' in the one who suffered through these faults in order to save us from them? Can we commit them if we keep him in our thoughts?

Three Appendices
(Proverbs 30–31)

27

First Appendix: The Sayings of Agur
(Proverbs 30)

The Proverbs of Solomon being complete, there follow three Appendices, of which the first is attributed to *Agur, son of Jakeh* (**v. 1**), one of a number of wise men contemporary either with Solomon himself or Hezekiah (cf. 22:17). It may be we can locate him if HAMASSAH means, not *oracle*, but 'of Massah', a clan of Ishmael which occupied North Arabia (Gen. 25:14-16). If so, it would make Lemuel his King (31:1). However, it is a kind of *oracle* or prophecy in the sense of an inspired utterance. *Agur's sayings* are thus of a different kind from Solomon's.

Another question is where *the sayings* begin. For, as NIV mg indicates, *Ithiel and Ucal* may not be Agur's pupils or scribes but his opening words. The confession 'I am weary, O God ... and faint' certainly connects well with verses 2-3 and is adopted by most modern translators and commentators. Agur's style is neither the continuous discourse of the Prologue (chs. 1-9) nor the strictly proverbial style of Solomon, but something in between. The collection centres around two themes: Man and God, and Man and Nature.

A. MAN AND GOD (vv. 2-17).

1. Man's ignorance of God confessed (vv. 2-3).
If wisdom begins with 'the fear of the Lord', or as it is here *the knowledge of the Holy One* (cf. 9:10), then that *knowledge* begins

with self-knowledge. The greatest teachers of divinity start by facing the fact that they know nothing of God, e.g. Jer. 1:6, 1 Cor. 8:2. This man feels he even lacks the *knowledge* that human reason can give: *I do not have a man's understanding*; he is subhuman – *the most ignorant of men* is literally 'more brutish than any man', as if he were an animal without the slightest vestige of God's image in him. While the language might sound exaggerated it is universally true, under the Gospel as well as the Law, that left to ourselves we are *ignorant of the Holy One*. For while we can acquire theoretical *knowledge* from books, sermons and lectures, we cannot know him personally in the sense of feeling he accepts, loves and delights in us (1 Cor. 2:6-16). This *knowledge* comes with the gift of eternal life (John 17:3), which begins when we are convicted of being in a state of unbelief (John 16:8f), as Agur was here.

2. Man's ignorance of God confirmed (v. 4).

The confession of ignorance (vv. 2f) is confirmed in this imaginary confrontation with 'the Holy One' whom he doesn't know (or with one speaking in his name). It may be taken in two ways:

(a) *What is* the *name* of someone who can claim the knowledge that Agur lacks? In other words, 'Agur, you're not exceptionally ignorant; everyone is in the same boat, for man only experiences the **works** of God (lines 2-4), not the one who performs them. To obtain this knowledge would require a journey to *heaven* from where these works are performed, and a return to *earth* with the information. Who can claim that? Not a real person, one with a human *name* and a *son* to prove he is human.' Or,

(b) *What is* the *name* of the One who has done all this (and more)? By *name* is meant not just a title but some knowledge of his nature. This is 'hidden' or 'secret' (Judg. 13:18) until God reveals it (Matt. 11:27). *The name of his son* even on this view doesn't necessarily refer to Christ who was not seen as 'Son of God' by the Jews, in spite of Psalm 2:7. It simply means a companion or agent, or even a personification of Wisdom, as in 8:22ff.

It is difficult to choose between the two interpretations, but each of them confirms that man is naturally ignorant of God.

Further study. Compare the dialogue between God and Job (Job 38–42, except that God's questions come before Job's confession).

3. How God reveals himself to ignorant man (vv. 5-6).

To those who have stared their own ignorance in the face, God's self-revelation is salvation itself, a *shield* and *refuge*. For they are not looking for information and answers but for God himself. Their ignorance of him exposes them not so much to the taunts of intellectuals as to the ravages of sin and the evil forces of the supernatural world. When *the word of God* comes to them it is God himself not a system of thought. It is therefore in him they *take refuge*. If God has spoken, what he has said is (a) *flawless*, it doesn't need checking for errors, as Modernists have done with Scripture; (b) *sufficient* (**v. 6**) and needs no supplementing, as the Jews did with the old covenant revelation, and Rome and others have done with the Gospel. Those who do either eventually turn out to be *liars*.

4. Praying to God in the face of death (vv. 7-9).

Is this the same man who deplored his ignorance, lack of wisdom and knowledge of God (vv. 2-3)? He certainly knew something of how to pray, for his prayer is remarkably similar to two of the three petitions in the second part of the Lord's Prayer: 'Give us today our daily bread ... And lead us not into temptation' (Matt. 6:11, 13). Interestingly he brings out the connection between them, but first notice his earnestness in **verse 7**. He knows exactly what to ask, for although he could produce a list as long as any of us, two things stand out above all. This clarity comes from his certainty of death, when he will have to answer to God for his sins, and that thought is intolerable. So he prays:

(a) *against the temptation to speak falsely* (**v. 8a**).
Falsehood is a particular kind of lying, being the word used in the Third Commandment (Exod. 20:7) 'misuse' or 'take in vain' the name of the Lord, that is, use it as an incantation in magic, in an oath that is broken or blasphemously. *Lies* are those *falsehoods* uttered in ordinary conversation (Exod. 20:16). Both are culpable before God.

(b) *for sufficient money or goods for his needs* (**vv. 8b-9**).

Daily is literally 'my portion', that which God sees as enough for me. More would be *riches* and less *poverty*. His motivation is that of a man whose eye is on death and judgment, who is therefore aware of the moral and spiritual dangers of both *poverty* and *riches*: *riches* produce complacency and self-sufficiency which take away dependence on and gratitude to God; *poverty* (in the sense of utter destitution) creates a temptation to *steal* (6:30f) which for one professing godliness is *dishonouring* to God. So the connection is that to have *daily bread* is in itself a defence against temptation.

Question
What does the thought of death move you to pray for above all else?

5. God favours the disadvantaged (v. 10).
The scenario behind this is probably making a false or at least exaggerated accusation against *a servant to his master*. The *servant* has no witnesses to appeal to and can offer no defence. It is his word against yours and if you are the *master's* equal he will take your word before that of a mere *servant*. However, God is witness and if you are lying he will hold you guilty (Exod. 20:16) and this will become evident at the last judgment if not before.

Application. Since we don't keep *servants* now, consider the following possibilities: speaking ill of someone we have at a disadvantage; judging our fellow-Christians ('God's servants', Rom. 14:4); a rebuke to Satan for falsely bringing a charge against those God has chosen and justified (Rom. 8:33).

6. Four types of behaviour God disapproves (vv. 11-14, 17).
This chapter is notable for numbers: two prayers (vv. 7-9) are followed by four types of people whose example is not to be followed by the student of Wisdom. *There are those* is literally 'a generation', that is, a class of people who set the tone for others (cf. Matt. 3:7, Acts 2:40). Even Israel had these, so how much more likely are we to find them in our mixed society.

(a) *Unfilial (***vv. 11, 17***).*
As charity begins at home so does sin, which first shows itself in attitude to parents, who become the target of the vile passions of this 'generation' – despising and disobeying them (v. 17) and even *cursing* (v. 11). Line 2 suggests failing to *bless* them is equivalent to *cursing*, for it means not only being ungrateful and unloving but failing to do their duty, especially of caring for them in later life (1 Tim. 5:4, 8). Since character and attitude are expressed by *the eye*, it is appropriate that it is the object of the punishment. The Old Testament demanded the death penalty for disobedient children (Lev. 20:9), to which is here added the exposure of the unburied corpse to the birds of prey (cf. 2 Sam. 21:10). This is no doubt symbolic language for shame and disgrace since this is what their behaviour brought on their parents.

(b) *Self-righteous (***v. 12***).*
This is a different class altogether. The first didn't try to hide themselves but rather gloried in their contemptuous behaviour; these are utterly blind to themselves. They think they are good people: perhaps they've been *cleansed* by religious ceremonies; or they do good works; or they refrain from crime and gross immorality. This was true of the Pharisees, of whom Jesus said they 'clean the outside of the cup and dish but inside are full of greed and wickedness' (Luke 11:39f). There is even a type of **Christian** who holds the right doctrines, has undergone the prescribed forms of church membership, observes the Lord's Day and attends the services of the church, but in his heart has an unloving and censorious attitude towards Christians who are less particular than himself, and to outsiders who have not been the objects of God's grace as he has. Doesn't that attitude qualify to be called *filth*?

(c) *Arrogant (***v. 13***).*
These are often the same as the self-righteous (v. 12). Because they are 'pure in their own eyes' they see others as inferior to them. The expressions 'lofty ... lifted up eyes' (Hebrew) bring out that they look down on everyone else, hence the use of the word *disdain* by NIV. This is perfectly illustrated by the

Pharisee and tax collector (Luke 18:9-14). The former 'looked down on everyone else', especially on the tax collector, but the latter 'would not even look up to heaven'. *Eyes* are expressive (cf. v. 17); the appropriate attitude for sinners is looking down in shame before God until he invites us to lift them up and look on him who bore our shame (Zech. 12:10). Those who reach this point then look up to their friends in esteem and love (Phil. 2:3f).

(d) *Cruel* (**v. 14**).
It may be that these four 'generations' are not separate types but four stages in the life-cycle of one type. In childhood or youth they turn against their parents (v. 11), but have no shame about this or anything else (v. 12); rather they look down on the obedient and humble as contemptible (v. 13), and eventually become so hard that they exploit these *poor* and *needy* ones to increase their own wealth (cf. 22:16). The strong language is metaphorical but meaningful. The prouder and stronger animals live off the weaker and more timid, for they have sharper *teeth*. These people are like them for without scruple or pity they seize their property, produce or even persons to make themselves rich.

Application. Would you apply verse 14 to such as loan sharks, property tycoons and dictators of one-party states? How did they become like that? Did something go wrong in their childhood? Does this make you pray more earnestly for the upbringing of the rising generation?

7. The condition underlying this behaviour (vv. 15-16).
These verses show why some people become like those of verse 14 – because human nature without God is insatiable. It is like a *leech* which lives on the blood of what it clings to. Its two suckers, one at each end, are its *two daughters* whose names (rather than cries) are *Give! give!* because they never stop sucking blood. It is also like *the grave* in the sense that there seems no limit to the number of the dead, since we are all destined for it. It is also like *the barren womb* which nothing will satisfy if it can't bear children (Gen. 30:1). It is also like

land which sees little rain – it soaks it up and is still dry. It is also like *fire* which will burn as long as there is fuel. These are of course hyperboles: *leeches* can only take so much blood without bursting; the number of dead will end when the world does; the *barren* woman's longing for children will fade with age; *land* can flood and *fire* eventually goes out. But the soul without God will always want more and never say, 'I've enough money, land, etc' (27:20, Eccles. 6:7). Such eventually become victims of other insatiable creatures, which may be why **verse 17** follows this passage and not v. 11, where we have commented on it.

B. Man and Nature (vv. 18-31).

1. Its wonder and mystery (vv. 18-20).
It is not only the being of God that is beyond unaided human reason (vv. 2-4) but the ways of nature. Yet it is the difficulty in *understanding* them that makes them *amazing*. Once we can explain something it loses its wonder. How can we explain how a large bird like an *eagle* can stay up in the sky and move in any direction? **We** can't do it. Or how a *snake* can move across a *rock* without feet or hands? Or how a *ship* can find its way across *the high seas* with no roads or landmarks to follow? Or what attracts *a man* and *a maid* to each other? No doubt increased knowledge of aeronautics, zoology, navigation and biology throw light on these subjects, but they don't sufficiently explain them to take the wonder out of them. Once we lose the sense of mystery we have lost more than our knowledge has gained for us.

By contrast **(v. 20)** *the way of an adulteress* is not to be admired but deplored. So *this is* does not refer backwards but forwards, perhaps as an answer to the questions, 'How does she get away with it, square it with her conscience, reconcile it with godliness?' The answer is she treats it as 'all in the day's work' – just as a meal, when it is over, is forgotten as soon as the *mouth* is *wiped*. If we don't call enjoying a meal *wrong*, why should this be? What harm does it do anyone? Here is another fact of fallen human nature to add to those already seen – its deceitfulness. This links up with the next passage.

2. Its disorders (vv. 21-23).

The examples he chooses of what makes *the earth tremble* and *under* which it can't *bear up* do not seem to justify the strong language of **verse 21**. In fact they seem an anticlimax. Realistically, however, each of us judges the world from what is happening in our small corner of it. It doesn't help if the rest of *the earth* doesn't suffer as we do – to us that is *the earth*. This may be why these examples are chosen – they could happen to anyone.

(a) *The political sphere* (**v. 22a**). We have already come up against the upstart ruler (see on 19:10, 28:3). He may only rule a small territory but those *under* him (this word is repeated at the beginning of each phrase) will suffer through his arrogance and brutal tyranny, and feel their world is turned upside down, however free others may be.

(b) *The social sphere* (**v. 22b**). This is not about gluttony but the sudden rise to prosperity of one who hasn't made it in the world. Perhaps he inherits a fortune or wins the lottery. His wealth gives him access to a new social class, and the airs and graces he adopts, especially to those who formerly despised him, make him insufferable. The world of that social circle is turned on its head.

(c) *The marriage sphere* (**v. 23a**). Here is a woman her acquaintances see as 'on the shelf' because she lacks beauty, grace, intelligence, accomplishment or anything which would attract the *love* of a husband. Suddenly she finds one and the pleasure she gets from making her friends eat their words is unbearable.

(d) *The domestic sphere* (**v. 23b**). The *displacement* here probably means inheritance. The old lady (*her mistress*) has outlived her relatives (or fallen out with them!) and leaves her estate to her *maidservant*. Now she who has penny-pinched her life long enjoys an embarrassment of riches and lets everyone know, especially anyone whose expectations from the will of the deceased were disappointed. As for the other servants in the household, who now have one of their number over them, their world is topsy-turvy.

Question
Do you think this reflects an outdated social system quite irrelevant to us, or is there such a thing as 'a station in life' for which each of us is fitted and in which we should remain?

3. Its wisdom (vv. 24-28).
Solomon occasionally appealed to the animal kingdom to drive home the lessons of Wisdom (1:17, 6:5-8), but never reached the heights Agur does here. He selects some of the weakest, most insignificant and vulnerable creatures to show how they overcome their limitations and are thus lessons to us in wisdom, for they succeed where many of us fail.

Ants (**v. 25**) sense when *summer* comes and take their opportunity to *store up their food*. How often has Solomon rebuked the slothful for sleeping at harvest when they should be working (20:4, 13)!

Conies (**v. 26**) are rock-badgers, much smaller than the British badger and about the size of a field mouse. They seem to realize their vulnerability and find strong protection by *making their home in the crags*. Part of Wisdom is to realize our weakness in the face of the evil powers of this world and make the Lord our 'strong tower' (18:10) as the *conies* do with the *crags*.

Locusts (**v. 27**) are a lesson in co-operation, organization and discipline. They do little damage alone or if a swarm moves haphazardly, so they form an army, *advance together in ranks* and wreak devastation (Joel 1:4-7, 2:8). Nor are they forced into this, for they *have no king*; their co-operative instinct is sufficient, and is a rebuke to our inability to agree and work together, our continual falling out (13:10, 17:14, 26:17-21) and our failure to manage without strong leadership (Judg. 21:25).

A *lizard* (**v. 28**) is easy to *catch with the hand* – if you can get near enough! But it knows its climbing skill and can scale the highest walls, even those built around *kings' palaces*, which are far beyond the reach of most of us. Wisdom doesn't cave in before obstacles and enemies, but overcomes them (28:1).

Think of a few creatures more familiar in this country (cats, dogs, cows, etc.) and make up your own proverbs about what they teach us.

4. Its movement (vv. 29-31).

This passage is generally found puzzling. Indeed it might almost be a conundrum – what have these in common: *a lion, a cock, a he-goat* and *a king*? Answer: they all walk in the same way, *striding* in *stately fashion*. Why? because they are leaders among their own kind: the *lion* in the animal kingdom, *who retreats before nothing* (no other animal); the *cock* in the farmyard; the *he-goat* in the herd and the *king* at the head of *his army* (or as some have it, 'over his people' who look up to him). These show their superiority even in the way they walk.

Questions
1. What is 'the Christian's walk'? See, for example, Colossians 2:6f, but you will need a KJV Concordance to study this word since NIV tends to translate it 'live', which is what it means although it destroys the force of the metaphor.
2. In what sense should our 'walk' or 'way of life' reflect the *stride* of the four beautiful movers of these verses?

Concluding Application (vv. 32-33).

The observation of verses 29-31 must not be misapplied; it isn't encouraging us to imitate the outward bearing of those four creatures, strut through the world like cocks or roar like lions. This would be to *exalt ourselves,* always the mark of *the fool* (26:12). An ambitious spirit expresses itself in making *plans* – not necessarily to do *evil,* for the word is neutral, but *planning* how to gain admiration.

So if you have got the wrong message from verses 29-31 then stop before it's too late and *clap your hand over your mouth,* don't give utterance to your boastful thoughts. Not only because it is sinful pride but because it is provocative, it will *stir up anger* and this will *produce strife.* Most translators, in the interests of style, have obscured the repetition of the word 'squeeze' or 'press', used in all three lines of **verse 33**. There is also a play on *nose,* for the word *anger* is its 'dual' form – 'nostrils'. A conceited attitude is like poking your fingers into someone's nostrils and squeezing! He won't like it! He may be wrong to be provoked to anger (1 Cor. 13:5), but if your behaviour is the cause, you are partly responsible.

28

Second Appendix:
The Sayings of King Lemuel
(Proverbs 31:1-9)

This second appendix contains some *sayings* recorded by *Lemuel, King* 'of Massah' (**v. 1** mg. cf. 30:1). It is reasonable to suppose that two collections of *sayings* from the North Arabian territory of Massah, one by a wise man, the other by a King, should be included along with others (22:17). The *sayings* recorded here are attributed to the Queen *mother*, who may, following the death of her husband, have occupied the position of Regent while *Lemuel* was under age. The brevity of this passage may indicate it was an extract from a larger collection, or that these *sayings* were chosen because they accord with the teaching of PROVERBS. For if we don't have 'Wine, women and song' here, we have the first two, which feature so much in PROVERBS.

1. Warning against women (vv. 2-3).
The Hebrew of **verse 2** shows the passionate concern of Lemuel's mother for the success of his reign in the thrice repeated 'What' (*O* in NIV). You can see the tears in her eyes and hear the sob in her voice. Her knowledge of the past and her experience as a King's consort have taught her that the greatest threats to the stability of the throne lie, not in ambitious rivals, factions in the state or hostile neighbours, but within the King himself – the temptations to which he is exposed. So the 'what?' may have the sense of 'what are you

doing spending your time in these carnal pursuits?' To shame him she reminds him of her love for him as the mother who bore and nursed him and of her *vows* dedicating him to God to be his servant in the State.

The first danger (**v. 3**) comes from *women*. She is not forbidding marriage, in fact encouraging it provided it is monogamous, for it has always been the extra wives or concubines that have sapped the *strength* of *kings* – the days and nights of passion rendering them unfit for their duties and thus bringing about their *ruin*. Samson, David and Solomon are all examples of great men whose reigns ended disastrously through this very temptation.

2. Warning against wine (vv. 4-7).

Another danger to which *kings* and *rulers* are exposed is drunkenness (**v. 4**). Their office involves social drinking at receptions, parties and banquets, which may give them a taste for strong drink. 'Let them not' (as some translate *It is not*) indulge this to the extent of developing a *craving* for it. For (**v. 5**) it will have a similar effect to sexual promiscuity by unfitting them for their duties. For it affects the mind in two ways: it dulls the memory, so that he may *forget what the law decrees*, which is fatal for the whole State since he is there to administer the law; also it clouds the judgment, so that he will make wrong adjudications and when *the oppressed* come to him to vindicate their cause, he will brush them aside and thus *deprive them of their rights*.

This is not to say that wine is evil in itself – it has its uses as well as abuses: in moderation it is refreshing (Ps. 104:15) and even medicinal (1 Tim. 5:23). Here however it seems to be recommended to those who, far from having useful functions, are quite worthless, and all they can gain is something to 'drown their sorrows'. It is difficult to see this as a serious piece of advice. Surely those who are *perishing* (dying?) should be *given* medicine, those in *anguish* comfort and counsel and those in *poverty* and *misery* (destitution) food and other basic needs? If they are treated with *wine* and *beer*, what happens when the effect wears off? *Give* them more and make them alcoholics? No, we must take verses 6-7 as an ironic confirmation of verses 4-5: the king has responsibilities and the means to discharge them; he is not like those of verses 6-7 whom *wine* can't harm because they have fallen as low as possible. He is best without too much of it.

3. Encouragement to reign justly (vv. 8-9).
Now we see more of why the king should avoid overindulgence, developing the thought of verse 5. This gives a very idealized view of kingship, for it seems to go beyond the normal duty of appointing just judges and supervising them (Deut. 16:18-20). The king is bidden to become a kind of defence counsel himself, to *speak up*, that is, act as advocate. For whom?

First, for those unable to *speak for*, that is, defend, *themselves*. They may have been too poor to hire a lawyer, too ignorant to conduct their own defence or too afraid to oppose their accuser.

Second, for those condemned to death, which seems to be the meaning of the phrase NIV renders *all who are destitute*, but which is literally 'sons of those passing away'. This may mean dying of *destitution*, but could equally mean those facing a capital charge from which they could not defend *themselves*.

Third, those who, because they were *poor and needy*, were particularly vulnerable to the oppression of the rich and unscrupulous. Though they had nothing else they still had *rights*, to be *judged fairly* if nothing else.

A king wasting his wealth, time and energy in wine and women would be ignorant of and insensitive to such people, and even if he became involved would not have the alertness of mind to conduct the case skilfully. Whether the king really was to do this or it simply means that he should so organize things that everyone had a fair trial, is debatable. But it is such an exalted view of kings that it stands alongside those prophecies of the reign of Messiah which crop up in the Old Testament, such as Psalm 72:1-4 – 'He will defend the afflicted' (cf. Isa. 11:4, 32:1f).

Application. See yourself as one condemned by and defenceless before Satan. What does your Advocate do (Rom. 8:33f)? Who defended him when he was unjustly charged (Isa. 53:7, Mark 14:61)?

29

Third Appendix:
The Wife of Noble Character

(Proverbs 31:10-31)

That the whole book should end in this way is a surprise and a puzzle. Why should the woman have the last word? It is clearly a deliberate choice on the part of the final editor to round off the whole collection thus, but why? Many answers have been given, of which the following are the strongest contestants.

1. It continues the advice given to King Lemuel by his mother (vv. 1-9). Having warned him against loose women (v. 3) she now describes the sort of woman with whom she would like him to settle down. This would balance the impossible duty given him in verses 8-9 to act as advocate for one unable to defend himself. The standard demanded of the *noble wife* (v. 10) is equally unattainable. If v. 8f were hinting at the ideal King, the Messiah, is this a picture of his bride, the church (cf. Eph. 5:25-33)? A tempting theory but LXX separates 31:1-9 from 10-31 by five chapters, and LXX antedates any existing Hebrew documents of PROVERBS by centuries!

2. It is marriage guidance for all, to be put alongside all the other advice given to the young to make them wise. 'It shows what wives the women should make and the men should choose' (Henry). The theme briefly touched on in 12:4, 14:1, 18:22, 19:14 is here developed fully. It is however an impossible ideal, one to be striven for rather than expected. This is implied in, *who can find?* and corresponds to what is

said of men in 20:6: 'A faithful man who can find?' However, verse 29 somewhat qualifies this view, though perhaps the apostles' pattern is more attainable (1 Tim. 2:9f, 1 Pet. 3:1-7).

3. It continues in the cynical vein of those earlier sayings about women who are impossible to live with: 11:22, 19:13, 21:9, 19, 25:24, 27:15. To say *who can find a wife of noble character* is to say, 'It would be a miracle if there were such a person and an even greater one if I managed to find her!' However, it is unlikely that a book of wisdom would end on such a negative note.

4. Another cynical explanation is that it is a male view of womanhood. It is what men would like their wives to be rather than how they see themselves and their role. But this makes it difficult to see the passage as the word of God.

5. It is to show that the home and family are foundational to life, since these qualities should be common to us all. But because domestic life is common doesn't mean it is common-place; in fact it can be the best, happiest and most beautiful aspect of life. Since its success depends most on the woman she is singled out as the chief character, although other members of the family have their place. Domesticity is thus a large part of Wisdom.

6. It affords a summary of the whole life-style of the wise. The many qualities and activities which feature here are all commended throughout the book as worthy aims. They are not to be seen as for special people but for the homely. Wisdom is most at home when it is at home! The woman verges on being the personification of Wisdom, of whom so much was said in the Prologue (4:5-9, 9:1-6) which may come from the same hand as the Epilogue. This would explain the idealization of the *wife*, since Wisdom is perfect, and also why she is compared with rubies (cf. 3:15, 8:11, 20:15).

The qualities which are described from verse 11 are arranged in 'acrostic' form, that is, each of the 22 verses begins with a different letter of the Hebrew alphabet, in order. Thus **verse 10** begins with the word 'ESHETH ('woman' or wife). The breathing represented by ' is ALEPH, the first letter in the Hebrew alphabet, the nearest to our A although it is neither vowel nor consonant. Now follow the characteristics of the *noble wife*.

1. Reliable and trustworthy (v. 11).

This verse begins with *BATACH*, 'trust'. This acrostic form not only made it easier to memorize in an age without printing, but also put a stress on the leading idea in the sentence, which makes this verse about *confidence*. The *husband* who is responsible for providing for the household may have many worries. If he can entrust the housekeeping to his wife his mind will be at rest and he will be able to concentrate better on his own work.

2. Supportive and loyal (v. 12).

This verse shows how *she* has gained the confidence of her husband – through her positive attitude to marriage. Her aim is to *bring him good, not harm*, hence the opening word *GAMAL* (the third letter of the Hebrew alphabet is GIMEL similar to our G) which means to perform or accomplish. It describes what she sees as the purpose of *the days of her life* as a married woman: to support her husband in his chosen calling. This may sound strange in these liberated days when partners often follow separate careers, but it has been proved to keep couples together for a life-time, as the word *all* here implies.

3. Efficient and energetic (v. 13).

The first word is *DARASH*, meaning carefully seeking and choosing (*selects*). Making clothes for the household from *wool* and *flax*, or linen, was common practice, for apart from the great and rich, clothes would all be home-made. What is 'noble' here is not just making the clothes but *selecting* good material (which might have needed spinning first, v. 19), plus the enjoyment she derived from doing it (*eager*). Although older daughters and servants may have helped, she both supervised and participated. Industriousness is encouraged under the Gospel as well as the law (1 Tim. 2:9f, 5:10f, Titus 2:5).

4. Considerate and painstaking (v. 14)

The opening word *HAY-THAH* begins with the fifth letter and means *she is*. Normally the personal pronoun is omitted which shows that it is emphasized here: it is the 'noble wife' herself who does or at least organizes the shopping. She is as careful in selecting a balanced and varied menu as she is in choosing her material (v. 13), for she wants her family to eat what is both nutritious and enjoyable. This may involve the inconvenience of travel. But since the *merchant ships* take the trouble to *bring food from afar* why shouldn't the mother? Also, she may be able to buy food more cheaply or in bulk further away.

5. Unselfish and disciplined (v. 15).
Food has not only to be purchased for the larder but prepared for the table. Whoever does this has to be at work far in advance of those who will eat it; in the case of breakfast this is before they are up. So the emphasis here falls on her early rising: *she gets up while it is still dark.* The sixth letter of the Hebrew alphabet is one to which our W is the nearest equivalent and is most frequently used for the conjunction 'and' or 'also' (not translated here by NIV, but see KJV, etc.). It indicates she takes trouble not only over the shopping (v. 14) but 'also' the cooking. She is even ahead of the *servant girls,* who need breakfast if they are to work efficiently. How few mistresses would see the advantage of freeing them from the chore of making their own breakfast so that they can give themselves to their other tasks?

6. Business-like and cautious (v. 16).
Having fed the household early she is free to improve the family fortunes. The opening word ZAM-MAH means examine, weigh up: *she considers* what the most profitable enterprise would be – land. Clearly her husband works in the town, possibly in government (v. 23), or he would be doing this. But what sort of land? *A field* fit for cultivation. So her thinking now is devoted to finding a *field* suitable for *planting a vineyard.* While researching this she also *considers* what funds are available not only for the purchase but the cultivation of the *field.* This means calculating her *earnings,* that is, the profits from the sale of some of the garments made (vs.13, 19, 24). A rare wife indeed!

7. Fit and strong (v. 17).
She does not confine herself to the administrative side of business and is not above manual work. The first word

CHAGARAH, beginning with the eighth letter (a guttural CH sound) means literally 'she girds herself' (NKJV), a metaphorical expression like our 'roll up the sleeves'. In order to tackle the job *vigorously* she needs to be physically fit. Her generally disciplined life and regular manual work make her *arms strong* for this demanding task.

8. Efficient and successful (v. 18).

Unlike others her duties are not over at sunset, for to *see that her trading is profitable* she must supervise the sale of the vineyard's produce. The opening word TACH-MAH is literally 'she tastes', meaning she personally ensures the profitability of the enterprise. This may involve her working into the evening at her correspondence and accounts. However, to say *her lamp does not go out at night* doesn't mean she never went to bed! Darkness began at about 6 p.m. which would leave several hours working by artificial light before bedtime. A wise person doesn't burn the candle at both ends (v. 15)!

9. Skilful and diligent (v. 19).

Before wool can be made into clothes (vv. 13, 24) it has to be spun. This is skillful work, done entirely *by hand* in those days, for the spinning wheel was still a long way off. So the stress falls on *her hands*, the word with which the sentence begins, whose initial letter corresponds to our Y. The terms translated *distaff* and *spindle* are unique and it is impossible to visualize exactly how the work was done. Presumably one *hand* held the *distaff* which spun the wool (possibly with the use of a weight) while the *fingers* of the other held the *spindle*, on to which the thread was wound. A difficult time-consuming job and she was 'noble' indeed to tackle it along with her other duties.

10. Generous and charitable (v. 20).

NIV doesn't bring out that the same two words for *hands* are used here as in verse 19, but in reverse order: the one that is second in verse 19 here begins the sentence – KAPPACH. The *hands* she used for spinning wool *she extends to the poor and needy*. She thinks not only of her own profit but others' poverty, and 'is as intent on giving as on getting' (Henry).

Here is the first indication that she was not only 'a noble wife' but a good child of God who expects the better-off to help the worse-off, both under the law (19:17, 22:9, Deut. 15:11) and the Gospel (Mark 14:7, Heb.13:16).

11. Practical and prepared (v. 21).

The sentence begins with LO, 'not', since in Hebrew the negative precedes the verb. It highlights the fact that 'a noble wife' thinks not only of prosperity but of possible adversity – she is practical. *Snow* is infrequent in the Middle East but not unknown, so she takes no chances but prepares for it by seeing her family and servants have warm as well as cool clothing. The *scarlet* cloth was expensive, being dyed as well as woven. Perhaps the bright colour had a psychological effect, being a startling contrast to the normal white clothing for hot weather. What a clever and thoughtful woman.

12. Tasteful and dignified (v. 22).

The opening word is MAR-BAD, *coverings*, but the question is whether they were for the *bed* (NIV), the walls (NKJV), the floors (RV) or the body (KJV)! The Hebrew simply says 'for herself', but *she is clothed* in line 2 makes clothing the most likely meaning. The material, which she made up herself, was imported, the *fine linen* from Egypt and the *purple* from Phoenicia. Does she turn out after all to be a worldly woman, breaking the rules of modesty in dress (1 Tim. 2:9f, 1 Pet. 3:3f)? Wasn't it 'the rich man who was dressed in *purple* and *fine linen*' (Luke 16:19)? However, dress needn't imply luxury and show, but can reflect position in society. She was wife to an elder of the city (v. 23) and had to command respect. It is those who try to ape the great, and especially neglect the inward graces and cover this with gorgeous apparel who are in view in 1 Peter 3:3. Verse 25 shows she had these.

13. Devoted and submissive (v. 23).

The verse begins with NODACH, 'known' which has the sense of *respected*, well-known, of good reputation. But it is *her husband* to whom this applies, for he has a *seat among the elders of the land* or district. Since throughout PROVERBS prosperity and success are the reward of Wisdom, he is clearly one of the wisest. But this is due in part to the character and ability of his wife. Although she herself is not prominent in local affairs, which were conducted *at the city gate*, she shares his reputation through her union with him. This explains her dress (v. 22).

14. Observant and opportunist (v. 24).
The *SADIN*, the *linen garment*, was probably a summer dress, for which she also made a *sash*, thus having a complete outfit for sale. The materials used for this were local and therefore plentiful, and having her own workers she could produce it cheaply and sell it to *merchants*, possibly in exchange for the more exotic winter clothes (v. 21). A woman who saw and took her opportunities.

15. Strong and secure (v. 25).
The sixteenth letter of the Hebrew alphabet is another guttural similar to the eighth and begins the word *CHOZ*, *strength*, which stands at the beginning of the sentence. One who has so much going for her as this wife can easily trust her position and possessions. **Her** security, however, lay in her *strength* of character, which gave her *dignity* or self-respect, qualities able to bear up should circumstances change *in the days to come*. She *can laugh at* these, not because she thought her fortunes would never change, like the Rich Fool (Luke 12:19), but because she was positive-minded.

16. Discreet and wise (v. 26).
The verse begins with *PIYAH*, 'her mouth', so for the first time we are told of what *she speaks*. Her conversation is characterised by two things: *wisdom* and love. We have heard enough to believe this was a wise woman, taking her place alongside such as Abigail (1 Sam. 25:24-31) and Priscilla (Acts 18:26). As the wife of a senator she would need to speak discreetly and be able to give sound advice to any who applied to her. But she did better than that, for the phrase *faithful instruction* brings together two of the greatest words in the Old Testament: TORAH, the teaching of God (cf. 1:8), and HESED, which describes the spirit of kindness and faithful

love with which God made his covenant with Israel. This was what she passed on, in and out of her home.

17. Aware and involved (v. 27).

The verse begins with *TSOPHIYAH*, so that *watches over* is the idea emphasised. Although a woman she is a true leader of those under her, whether children, servants or outside workers. She doesn't merely give orders and leave them to it, but sees how they are managing. She is in touch with what is happening, but still attends to her own work, so is far from *idle*. Long before Paul wrote, 'If a man will not work he shall not eat' (2 Thess. 3:10), she was practising it. If she did not do her share of the work of the house and estate she would feel she had no right to enjoy its profits (*bread*).

18. Appreciated and commended (vv. 28-31).

The passage ends by showing how others respond to her. **Verse 28** begins with *QAMO, arise,* which conjures up a picture of a standing ovation, an expression of the appreciation which comes from four directions.

(a) *Her children (v. 28a).* This must have made her happier than all the wealth, prosperity and success which had come her way. It is one thing to gain children's respect by force and another when they do it spontaneously. It makes all the work done for them worthwhile.

(b) *Her husband (vv. 28b-29).* He was hers before the children came, and from the time of their marriage it had been her aim to serve him personally and in his calling. How well she did this the preceding verses show, but it doesn't necessarily follow that *her husband* will appreciate her. Many wives do their best only to be met with churlishness or worse. So sincere is the gratitude of this one that his words are quoted (**v. 29**). This begins with *RABBOTH, many,* saying she is not alone in the qualities she displays and the work she does, but others too *do noble things.* This is the same word as in v. 10, so that we now see that, although rare such *women* are not unknown. To her husband she *surpasses them all* and he should know, for he has seen her at close quarters for a long time and would be aware of her faults as well as her virtues. Praise from him is praise indeed.

(c) *God himself* (**v. 30**). The verse begins with SHEQER, *deceptive*, and ends with *praised*, bringing out the sharp contrast between external and internal. There is nothing wrong with *charm* of manner or *beauty* of face and form in themselves. They are better than hardness and ugliness! But outward *charm* can cover a foolish character (see on 11:22) and physical *beauty* is too *fleeting* to build a life and its relationships on. We who 'look on the outward appearance' may be deceived by them, but 'the Lord looks on the heart' and sees our attitude to him. One based on *fear*, that is knowledge, trust and love, is *praised* by him (1 Pet. 3:4f). Moreover, since 'the fear of the LORD is the beginning of wisdom' (1:7), it is the source of all the qualities and activities attributed to the 'noble wife'. So if we ask, 'How can anyone attain to this standard?' the answer is through faith in the grace of God.

(d) *Her fellow-citizens* (**v. 31**). The passage and book end with the twenty-second and last letter of the Hebrew alphabet which begins the word *T-NU*, *give*. This is what the writer thinks is due to her. *The reward she has earned* is that her fellow-citizens should recognize her by proclaiming and *praising her works* where people gather – *at the city gate*. If this acrostic poem were publicly known, what encouragement it would be to others!

Although we have followed the verses as they stand in order to keep to the alphabetical order, another approach is to arrange them under themes, e.g. her approach to marriage (vv. 11-12, 23); her domesticity (vv. 13-15, 19, 21, 27); her business acumen (vv. 16, 24); her charity (v. 20); her care of herself (vv. 17, 22); her character (vv. 25-26); her acclaim (vv. 28-31).

Question
After working through this passage, which of the approaches listed under verse 10 do you now feel best fits?

Books alluded to.

Charles Bridges: *Exposition of Proverbs*
Franz Delitzsch: *Biblical Commentary on the Proverbs of Solomon*
Matthew Henry: *Exposition of the Old & New Testaments*
Derek Kidner: *Proverbs (Tyndale Series) Wisdom to live by*
David Thomas: *Commentary on Proverbs*
R.N. Whybray: *Proverbs* (New Century Bible)

Subject Index

Scripture Index

Christian Focus Publications
publishes books for all ages

Our mission statement –

STAYING FAITHFUL
In dependence upon God we seek to help make His infallible
Word, the Bible, relevant. Our aim is to ensure that the Lord
Jesus Christ is presented as the only hope to obtain forgive-
ness of sin, live a useful life and look forward to heaven with
Him.

REACHING OUT
Christ's last command requires us to reach out to our world
with His gospel. We seek to help fulfill that by publishing
books that point people towards Jesus and help them develop
a Christ-like maturity. We aim to equip all levels of readers for
life, work, ministry and mission.

Books in our adult range are published in three imprints.
Christian Focus contains popular works including biogra-
phies, commentaries, basic doctrine and Christian living.
Our children's books are also published in this imprint.
Mentor focuses on books written at a level suitable for Bible
College and seminary students, pastors, and other serious
readers. The imprint includes commentaries, doctrinal
studies, examination of current issues and church history.
Christian Heritage contains classic writings from the past.

Christian Focus Publications, Ltd
Geanies House, Fearn, Ross-shire,
IV20 1TW, Scotland, United Kingdom
info@christianfocus.com

For details of our titles visit us on our website
www.christianfocus.com